Rick Steves'
MONA Winks

Compliments of

aCIS™

The Ultimate Field Trip

Rick Steves'
MONA Winks

Self-Guided Tours of Europe's Top Museums

Fourth Edition

Rick Steves and Gene Openshaw

John Muir Publications
Santa Fe, New Mexico

Other JMP books by Rick Steves
  Asia Through the Back Door (with Bob Effertz)
  Europe 101: History & Art for the Traveler (with Gene Openshaw)
  Rick Steves' Postcards from Europe
  Rick Steves' Europe Through the Back Door
  Rick Steves' Best of Europe
  Rick Steves' France, Belgium & the Netherlands (with Steve Smith)
  Rick Steves' Germany, Austria & Switzerland
  Rick Steves' Great Britain & Ireland
  Rick Steves' Italy
  Rick Steves' Russia & the Baltics (with Ian Watson)
  Rick Steves' Scandinavia
  Rick Steves' Spain & Portugal
  Rick Steves' London
  Rick Steves' Paris
  Rick Steves' Phrase Books: French, Italian, German,
    Spanish and Portuguese, and French/Italian/German

Thanks to:
Dave Hoerlein, Steve Smith, Risa Laib, Rich Sorensen, and Dave Fox for
research help, Shirley Openshaw for maternal support, and Anne Steves for
athletic support.

John Muir Publications, P.O. Box 613, Santa Fe, NM 87504

Fourth edition. Third printing May 2000.
Printed in the United States of America

Library of Congress Cataloging-in-Publication Data
Steves, Rick, 1955-
  Mona winks : self-guided tours of Europe's top museums / Rick
  Steves & Gene Openshaw—4th ed.
    p.   cm.
  Includes index.
  ISBN 1-56261-421-5
  1. Art museums—Europe—Guidebooks. I. Openshaw, Gene.
II. Title.
N1010.S7 1998
708.94—dc21   98-22198
                                                                CIP

Europe Through the Back Door Editor: Risa Laib
Editors: Krista Lyons-Gould, Dianna Delling
Production: Mladen Baudrand, Nikki Rooker
Interior Design: Linda Braun
Mona Lisa Cover Art: Peter Aschwanden
Maps: David C. Hoerlein
Photography: Rick Steves and others
Printer: Publishers Press

Distributed to the book trade by
Publishers Group West
Berkeley, California

To
all the artists
whose works hang
in no museums—
and
to those
who appreciate them.

Contents

Introduction

Even at its best, museum-going is hard work. This book attempts to tame Europe's "required" museums, making them meaningful, fun, fast, and painless. Here are some tips on how to use this book to get the most out of your museum visits.

BEFOREHAND

Do Some Background Reading
The more you know, the more you'll appreciate the art. Before your trip, take a class or read a book on art.

Rip Up This Book
Before your trip, rip out, staple-bind, and pack just the individual chapters you'll use. (If this really bugs you, send all the pieces and $5.00 to Europe Through the Back Door, 120 4th Avenue North, Edmonds, WA 98020, and we'll send you a new copy. Really.)

Skim Chapters
Skim the chapter the night before you visit the museum. Get a feel for the kind of art and artists you'll see.

Check the Introductory Material
This is included on the first page of each chapter. It shows the museum hours, cost, availability of information, and so forth. Avoid tactical problems by planning ahead.

IN THE MUSEUM

Get Oriented
Use the overview map and paragraph to understand the general layout of the museum, how the art is arranged, and the basic tour route.

Use the Maps and Written Directions
All featured art appears on the room maps. Maps are usually oriented so you enter from the bottom (look for the "start" arrow). Written directions reinforce the maps.

Keep the Big Picture
As you enter each room, get the general feel. Scan for the common characteristics of the art. Next, study the specific example mentioned in the text. Then browse, trying out what you've learned.

Use the Index
Use the index to find supplemental information on artists and styles.

Partners, Take Turns Acting As Guide
It's easier if one looks while the other reads.

WATCH FOR CHANGES

Museums Change
Paintings can be on tour, on loan, out sick, or shifted at the whim of the curator. Even museum walls are often moved. To adapt:

(1) Pick up any available free floor plans as you enter.

(2) Let the museum information person glance at this book's maps to confirm locations of paintings.

(3) If you can't find a particular painting, ask any museum worker where it is. Just point to the photograph in this book and ask, "Where?" (*"Dove?" "Où est?" "¿Dónde?"*)

Museum Hours Change
Museums change their entrance hours, especially in Italy and off-season. Confirm by telephone or at the city tourist office upon arrival.

GENERAL MUSEUM POLICIES

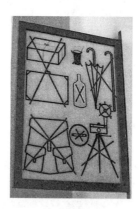

Last Entry
Many museums have "last entry" 30 to 60 minutes before closing. Guards usher people out before the official closing time.

Photography
Cameras are normally allowed, but no flashes or tripods (without special permission). Flashes damage oil paintings and distract others in the room. Video cameras are usually allowed. Even without a flash, a hand-held camera with ASA 400 film and an F-2 aperture will take a fine picture. Otherwise, buy slides or cards at the museum bookstore.

Bag Checks

For security reasons, museums often require that you check even small bags. Every museum has a free cloak and check room at the entrance. They're very safe. Check everything (except *Mona Winks*) and enjoy the museum. Or, to avoid checking your bag, try carrying it like a purse throughout your museum visit. (What scares officials is not just the backpack itself but the possibility of your bumping into priceless art with your backpack on your back.)

Toilets

WCs are free and better and cleaner than the European average.

Food

Museum-going stokes appetites. Most museums have cafeterias with reasonable prices and decent food. Check the information at the beginning of each chapter for evaluations and recommendations.

Museum Bookstores

These have cards, prints, posters, slides, and guidebooks. Thumb through a museum's biggest guidebook (or scan its index) to be sure you haven't overlooked something that is of particular interest to you.

NO APOLOGIES

This book drives art snobs nuts. Its gross generalizations, sketchy dates, oversimplifications, and shoot-from-the-hip opinions will likely tweeze art highbrows. *Rick Steves' Mona Winks* isn't an art history text; it's a quick taste of Europe's fascinating but difficult museums. Use it as an introduction—not the final word.

Note

From this point on, "we" (your co-authors) will shed our respective egos and become "I." Enjoy.

A victim of the Louvre

Art History
Five Millennia in Six Pages

Egypt: 3000–1000 B.C.

Tombs and mummies preserved corpses and possessions for the afterlife. Statues of pharaohs were political propaganda. Stiff, unrealistic, standing-at-attention statues and paintings seem built for eternity. Little change in 2,000 years.

You'll find examples in:
- British Museum (statues, mummies, Rosetta Stone)
- Vatican Museum
- Louvre

Greece: 700 B.C.–A.D. 1

Foundation of our "Western" civilization—science, democracy, art, and the faith that the universe is orderly and rational.

(1) Archaic (700–500 B.C.): In a time of wars the creative Greek spirit was beginning to show itself. Stiff statues reflect their search for stability and order amid chaos. Keen interest in but no mastery of the human body.
- "Kouros" statues (in Louvre and British Museum)

(2) Golden Age (500–325 B.C.): Athens rules a coalition of city-states in the days of Socrates, Pericles, Plato, and Aristotle. The Greek gods were portrayed as idealized human beings. Statues look natural, but their balanced poses show the order found in Nature. Nothing in extreme.

- *Apollo Belvedere* (Vatican Museum, see photo)
- Elgin Marbles from the Parthenon (British Museum)
- *Vénus de Milo* (Louvre)
- *Venus de' Medici* (Uffizi)

(3) Hellenism (325 B.C.–A.D. 1): Alexander the Great conquers Greece and spreads Greek culture around the Mediterranean. A time of individualism producing restless statues of people in motion—struggling against other people, animals, and themselves. Everything in extreme.

- *Laocoön* (Vatican Museum, see photo)
- *Winged Victory* (Louvre)

Rome: 500 B.C.–A.D. 500

The Romans conquered Greek lands and absorbed their culture and gods. The result: Greek style, with a "bigger is better" attitude. Romans

were engineers, not artists; but they built unprecedented grand structures using the arch and concrete, then decorated with Greek columns and statues. Realistic portrait busts of the emperors reminded subjects who was in charge.

- Colosseum, Forum, and Pantheon (Rome)
- Greek-style statues (Vatican Museum, Louvre, British Museum)
- Portrait busts (Vatican Museum and Louvre)

Byzantine: A.D. 300–1450

The Eastern half of the Roman Empire, centered in Constantinople (Istanbul), lived on after Rome fell. Byzantium preserved the classical arts and learning through the Dark Ages. These ideas reentered Europe via Venice.

- St. Mark's Church— mosaics, domes, and treasures (Venice)
- Icon-style gold-leafed paintings (many museums)

Medieval Europe: 500–1400

Rome falls, plunging Europe into "dark" centuries of poverty, war, famine, and hand-me-down leotards. The church is people's refuge, and Heaven is their hope. Art serves the church—Bible scenes, crucifixes, saints, and Madonnas (Mary, the mother of Jesus) decorate churches and inspire the illiterate masses. Gothic architects used the pointed arch to build tall, spired churches with walls of stained glass.

Art is symbolic, not realistic. Saints float in a golden, heavenly realm, far removed from life on earth. Humans are scrawny sinners living in a flat, two-dimensional world.

- Altarpieces in many museums and churches
- Notre Dame and Ste-Chapelle
- Illuminated manuscripts (British Museum)

Italian Renaissance: 1400–1600

The "rebirth" of the arts and learning of ancient Greece and Rome—democracy, science, and humanism. In architecture, it meant balanced structures using Greek columns and Roman domes and arches. In sculpture, 3-D realism of glorified human beings (like Greek nudes). In painting, capturing the 3-D world on a 2-D canvas using mathematical laws of perspective. Artists saw God in the orderliness of Nature and the beauty of the human body. Art is no longer tied to the church. Art for art's sake is OK.

(1) Florence (1400–1520): Birthplace of the Renaissance. Revived Greek-style sculpture and Roman-style architecture. Pioneered three-dimensional painting, placing statue-like people in spacious settings.

- Michelangelo's *David* (Florence's Accademia)
- Botticelli's *Birth of Venus* (Uffizi, see photo)
- Brunelleschi's dome (Florence)
- Donatello sculpture (Bargello)
- Leonardo da Vinci, Giotto, Raphael (Uffizi and other museums)

(2) High (or Roman) Renaissance (1500–1550): Grand rebuilding of the city of Rome by energetic, secular-minded Renaissance popes.

- Sistine Chapel, Michelangelo (Vatican Museum, see photo)
- The dome of St. Peter's Church, by Michelangelo (Rome)
- Raphael (Vatican Museum)

(3) Venetian Renaissance (1500–1600): Big, colorful, sensual paintings celebrate the Venetian good life, funded by trade with the East. Whereas Florentine painters drew their figures with heavy outlines, Venetians "built" figures out of patches of color.

- Titian (see photo), Veronese, Tintoretto (many museums)
- Best museums: Venice's Accademia, Madrid's Prado
- Doge's Palace (Venice)

Northern Protestant Art: 1500–1700

Bought by middle-class merchants, not popes and kings. Everyday things painted on small canvases in a simple, realistic, unemotional style. Loving attention to detail. Portraits, landscapes, still lifes, and wacky slice-of-life scenes.

- Rembrandt (many museums)
- Vermeer (see photo, Rijksmuseum)
- Durer (National Gallery, Uffizi)
- Bosch (Prado)
- Best museums: Rijksmuseum, Prado

Baroque: 1600–1700

The style of divine-right kings (Louis XIV) and the Counter-Reformation Catholic Church to overpower the common man. Big, colorful, ornamented, though based on Renaissance balance. Exaggerated beauty and violence. Greek gods, angels, nudes, and pudgy, winged babies.

- Palace of Versailles
- St. Peter's
- Rubens (many museums, see photo)

Rococo: 1700–1800

Baroque's frilly little sister. Smaller, lighter, even more ornamented; pastel colors, rosy cheeks, and pudgier winged babies. In architecture,

the oval replaces the circle as the basic pattern. Aristocratic tastes were growing more refined and more out of touch with the everyday world.

- Versailles' interior decoration
- Boucher (see photo), Watteau and Fragonard (Louvre)

Neoclassical: 1750–1850

With the French Revolution, Rococo became politically incorrect. Neoclassical is yet another rebirth of the Greek and Roman world. Simpler and more austere than Renaissance and Baroque versions of the classical style. The art of democracy and the "Age of Reason."

- J. L. David (Louvre)
- Ingres (Louvre and Orsay, see photo)
- Parts of Versailles

Romanticism: 1800–1850

Reaction against the overly rational neoclassical and Industrial Age. Return to Nature and Man's primitive roots. Dramatic, colorful art

expresses the most intense inner emotions. Both individuals and nations struggle to be free.

- Goya (Prado, see photo)
- Delacroix (Louvre)
- Blake and Turner (Tate)

Impressionism and Post-Impressionism: 1850–1900

Capturing quick "impressions" of everyday scenes (landscapes, cafés) with a fast and messy style. Thick brush strokes of bright colors laid side-by-side on the canvas blend at a distance, leaving the impression of shimmering light.

- Monet, Manet, Degas, and Renoir (see photo, Orsay)
- Van Gogh (Van Gogh Museum, Orsay)
- Gauguin, Cézanne, Rodin (Orsay)
- Best museums: Paris' Orsay, London's Tate and National Galleries

Modern Art: 20th Century

In our no-holds-barred modern world, the artist's task is to show life in a fresh, new way. There are two basic strains of modern art: Artists

continue to paint real things, but distort them to give us a new perspective (Surrealism, Expressionism, Pop Art). Artists use the building blocks of painting—color and line—to create new and interesting patterns that hint at the non-visual aspects of the world (Abstract art, Abstract Expressionism). Most modern art mixes the two strains.

But what does it *mean*? Modern art offers an alternative to our normal, orderly, programmed McLives. It's a wild, chaotic jungle that you'll have to explore and tame on your own. *Grrr.*

- Picasso (Cubism and many other styles)
- Dali (Surrealism)
- Mondrian (Abstract)
- Warhol (Pop Art)
- Pollock (Abstract Expressionism)
- Chagall (mix of various styles)
- Museums: London's Tate, and Venice's Peggy Guggenheim

Additional Information

If you'd like to read an entire book on art, history, and culture, let me humbly recommend *Europe 101: History and Art for the Traveler*, by my two favorite authors, Rick Steves and Gene Openshaw. While *Mona Winks* is your on-the-spot museum manual, *Europe 101* has the necessary background information. Written in the same fun and practical style, with many of the very same jokes, *Europe 101* brings Europe's churches, palaces, and statues to life.

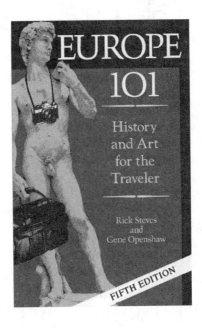

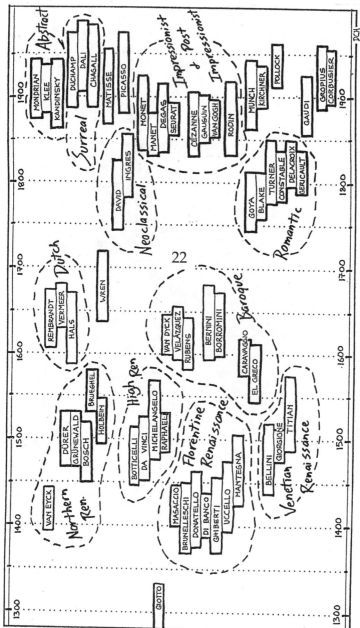

Artist Timeline: 1300—1985

Artists & Dates

Bernini (pron: bayr-NEE-nee), 1598–1680 — Baroque grandeur.

Blake, William, 1757–1827 — mystical visions.

Bosch, Hieronymous (pron: bosh), 1450–1516 — crowded, bizarre scenes.

Botticelli, Sandro (pron: bah-tih-CHELL-ee), 1445–1510 — delicate Renaissance beauty.

Braque, Georges (pron: brock), 1882–1963 — Cubist pioneer.

Brunelleschi, Filippo (pron: broon-uh-LESS-key), 1377–1446 — first great Renaissance architect.

Bruegel, Pieter (pron: BROY-gull), ca. 1525–1569 — Netherlands, peasant scenes.

Caravaggio (pron: car-rah-VAH-jee-oh), 1573–1610 — shocking ultra-realism.

Cézanne, Paul (pron: say-ZAH), 1839–1906 — bridged Impressionism and Cubism.

Chagall, Marc (pron: sha-GALL), 1887–1985 — fiddlers on roofs, magical realism.

Dali, Salvador (pron: DAH-lee), 1904–1989 — father of Surrealism.

Da Vinci, Leonardo (pron: dah VINCH-ee), 1452–1519 — a well-rounded Renaissance genius who also painted.

Degas, Edgar (pron: day-GAH), 1834–1917 — Impressionist snapshots, dancers.

Donatello, (pron: doh-na-TELL-oh), ca. 1386–1466 — early Renaissance sculptor.

Dürer, Albrecht (pron: DEWR-er), 1471–1528 — Renaissance symmetry with German detail; "the Leonardo of the north."

El Greco (pron: el GREK-oh), 1541–1614 — spiritual scenes, elongated bodies.

Fra Angelico (pron: frah an-JELL-i-co), 1387–1455 — Renaissance techniques, medieval piety.

Gauguin, Paul (pron: go-GAN), 1848–1903 — Primitivism, native scenes, bright colors.

Giorgione (pron: jor-JONE-ee), 1477–1510 — Venetian Renaissance, mysterious beauty.

Giotto (pron: ZHOTT-oh), 1266–1337 — proto-Renaissance painter (3-D) in medieval times.

Goya, Francisco (pron: GOY-ah), 1746–1828 — three stages: frilly court painter, political rebel, dark stage.

Hals, Frans (pron: halls), 1581–1666 — snapshot portraits of Dutch merchants.

Ingres, Jean Auguste Dominique (pron: ANG-gruh), 1780–1867 — Neoclassical.

Manet, Edouard (pron: man-NAY), 1823–1883 — forerunner of Impressionist rebels.

Mantegna, Andrea (pron: mahn-TAYN-ya), 1431–1506 — Renaissance 3-D and "sculptural" painting.

Matisse, Henri (pron: mah-TEES), 1869–1954 — decorative "wallpaper," bright colors.

Michelangelo (pron: mee-kell-AN-jell-oh), 1475–1564 — earth's greatest sculptor and one of its greatest painters.

Mondrian, Piet (pron: manh-dree-ahn), 1872–1944 — abstract, geometrical canvases.

Monet, Claude (pron: moh-NAY), 1840–1926 — father of Impressionism.

Picasso, Pablo (pron: pee-KAHSS-oh), 1881–1973 — master of many modern styles, especially Cubism.

Pollock, Jackson (pron: PAHL-luck), 1912–1956 — wild drips of paint.

Raphael (pron: roff-eye-ELL), 1483–1520 — epitome of the Renaissance—balance, realism, beauty.

Rembrandt (pron: REM-brant), 1606–1669 — greatest Dutch painter, brown canvases, dramatic lighting.

Renoir, Auguste (pron: ren-WAH), 1841–1919 — Impressionist style, idealized beauty, pastels.

Rodin, Auguste (pron: roh-DAN), 1840–1917 — classical statues with rough "Impressionist" finish.

Rubens, Peter Paul (pron: REW-buns), 1577–1640 — Baroque, fleshy women, violent scenes.

Steen, Jan (pron: steen), 1626–1679 — slice-of-life everyday Dutch scenes.

Tiepolo, Giovanni Battista (pron: tee-EPP-o-lo), 1696–1770 — 3-D illusions on ceilings.

Tintoretto (pron: tin-toh-RETT-oh), 1518–1594 — Venetian Renaissance plus drama.

Titian (pron: TEESH-un), 1485–1576 — greatest Venetian Renaissance painter.

Turner, Joseph Mallord William, 1775–1851 — messy "proto-Impressionist" scenes of nature.

Uccello, Paolo (pron: oo-CHELL-oh), 1396–1475 — early 3-D experiments.

Van Eyck, Jan (pron: van IKE), 1390–1441 — northern detail.

Van Gogh, Vincent (pron: van GO, or, more correctly, van GOCK), 1853–1890 — Impressionist style plus emotion.

Velázquez, Diego (pron: vel-LAHSS-kes), 1599–1660 — objective Spanish court portraits.

Vermeer, Jan (pron: vayr-MEER), 1632–1675 — quiet Dutch art, highlighting everyday details.

Veronese, Paolo (pron: vayr-oh-NAY-zee), 1528–1588 — huge, colorful scenes with Venetian Renaissance backgrounds.

LONDON

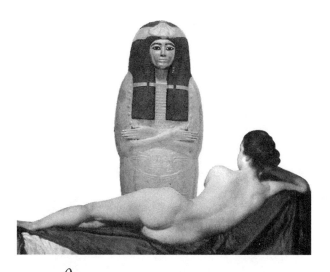

$\mathcal{I}$n the 19th century, the British flag flew over one-fourth of the world. And England collected art as fast as it collected colonies. In London you'll see much of the world's greatest art, from ancient Egypt, Greece, and Rome (the British Museum), through Medieval and Renaissance painting (National Gallery) and on up through the 20th century (Tate Gallery). Read the manuscripts that shaped our age (British Library) and stroll through historic Westminster in the company of Big Ben.

1 British Museum

The British Museum is *the* chronicle of Western civilization. It's the only place I know where you can follow the rise and fall of three great civilizations in a few hours with a coffee break in the middle. And, while the sun never set on the British Empire, it will on you, so on this tour, we'll see just the most exciting two hours.

Use your head.
Read *Mona* first.

BRITISH MUSEUM

Hours: Monday–Saturday 10:00–17:00, Sunday 14:30–18:00; closed on Good Friday; the first Monday in May; December 24, 25, and 26; January 1.

Cost: Free but £2 donation requested.

Tour length: Two hours

Getting there: Tube to Tottenham Court Road, Russell Square, or Holborn, and a four-block walk. Bus 7, 8, 10, 19, 22b, 24, 25, 29, 38, 55, 68, 73, 91, 98, 134, or 188. Taxis are reasonable if you buddy up.

Information: Main lobby information booth (English spoken) serves a free museum plan. The monthly events flyer lists free tours and lectures given most lunch times. Guided 1.5-hour tours for £6 are offered daily; call museum for times (tel. 0171/636-1555, recorded information tel. 0171/580-1788, Web site: www.british-museum.ac.uk. Rainy days and Sundays always get me down, because they're most crowded.

Cloakroom: Check your bags—anything left lying around that looks like a bomb will be treated as one. If the line is long and not moving, the cloakroom may be full.

Photography: Photos are allowed, flash OK, no tripod.

Cuisine art: Cheap and decent museum café and restaurant. The more comfortable and less crowded restaurant has a good salad bar and free water.

There are lots of fast, cheap, and colorful cafés, pubs, and markets along Great Russell Street. Covent Garden is nearby. Marx picnicked on the benches near the entrance.

Starring: Rosetta Stone, Egyptian mummies, Assyrian lions, Elgin Marbles. Note: The British Library (Magna Carta, manuscripts, etc.), which used to be a part of the British Museum, has moved nearly a mile north, near St. Pancras station.

ORIENTATION — THE NEW BRITISH MUSEUM

Expect construction until the year 2000, when the museum opens its new "Great Court" entrance hall with the round Reading Room in the center. Until then, you may have a five-minute detour to get to the start of the ancient collections.

● *Our tour starts at the southern entrance (Great Russell Street), on the ground floor. If you entered from the north side (Montague Place), you may be routed upstairs in order to traverse the building.*

Once you reach the southern lobby, pass through the bookshop. At the end, turn right and look down the long Egyptian Gallery. Introduce your-

BRITISH MUSEUM—OVERVIEW

self to the two huge statues of winged lions with bearded human heads on your left. We'll rendezvous here after our hikes through Egypt, Assyria, and Greece.

We'll see artifacts from the rise and decline of three great ancient civilizations—Egypt, Assyria, and Greece. History is a modern invention. Three hundred years ago people didn't care about crumbling statues and dusty columns. Nowadays, we value a look at past civilizations, knowing that "Those who don't learn from history are condemned to repeat it."

EGYPT (3000 B.C.–A.D. 1)

Egypt was one of the world's first "civilizations," that is, a group of people with a government, religion, art, and written language. The Egypt we think of—pyramids, mummies, pharaohs, and guys who walk funny—lasted from 3000–1000 B.C. with hardly any change in the government, religion, or arts. Imagine two millennia of Eisenhower.

● *Enter the Egyptian Gallery (Room 25), walking between the two black statues of pharaohs on their thrones. On your left you'll see a crowd of people surrounding a big black rock with writing on it.*

EGYPT

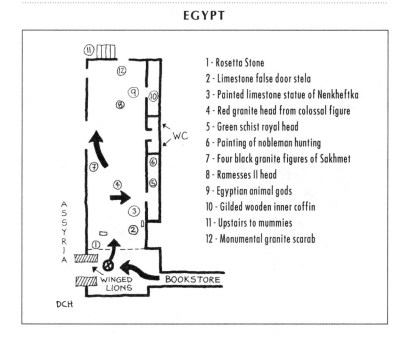

1 - Rosetta Stone
2 - Limestone false door stela
3 - Painted limestone statue of Nenkheftka
4 - Red granite head from colossal figure
5 - Green schist royal head
6 - Painting of nobleman hunting
7 - Four black granite figures of Sakhmet
8 - Ramesses II head
9 - Egyptian animal gods
10 - Gilded wooden inner coffin
11 - Upstairs to mummies
12 - Monumental granite scarab

ASSYRIA

WC

WINGED LIONS   BOOKSTORE

DCH

The Rosetta Stone (196 B.C)

When this rock was unearthed in the Egyptian desert in 1799, it caused a sensation in Europe. Picture a pack of scientists (I think of the apes in that scene from *2001: A Space Odyssey*) screeching with amazement, dancing around it, and poking curiously with their fingers. This black slab caused a quantum leap in the evolution of history. Finally, Egyptian writing could be decoded.

The writing in the upper part of the stone is known as hieroglyphics. For a thousand years, no one knew how to read this mysterious ancient language. Did, say, a picture of a bird mean "bird"? Or was it a sound, forming part of a larger word, like "burden"? As it turned out, hieroglyphics were a complex combination of the two.

The Rosetta Stone allowed them to break the code. It contains a single inscription repeated in three languages. The bottom third is plain old Greek (find your favorite frat or sorority), while the middle is more modern Egyptian. By comparing the two known languages with the one they didn't know, they figured it out.

The breakthrough came from the large oval in the sixth line from the top. They found out that the bird symbol represented the sound "a", part of the name Cleop-"a"-tr-"a". Simple.

● *Move on, passing between two lion statues. On the wall to your right you'll find …*

Limestone False Door from the Tomb of Bateti (c. 2400 B.C.)

In ancient Egypt, you *could* take it with you. They believed that after you died, your soul lived on, enjoying its earthly possessions. This small statue represents the soul of a dead man.

It decorated his tomb, which contained all that he'd need in the next life: his mummified body, a resume of his accomplishments on earth, and his possessions—sometimes including his servants who might be buried alive with their master. The great pyramids, besides being UFO psychic power stations, were also elaborate tombs for the rich and powerful. But most tombs were small rectangular rooms of brick or stone.

"False doors" like this were slapped on the outside of the tomb. The soul of the deceased, like the statue, could come and go through the "door" as he pleased—grave robbers couldn't. The deceased's relatives placed food outside the door to nourish such spirits who woke up in the middle of eternity with the munchies.

● *Just a few steps farther down the gallery, in a glass case on the right, you'll find the ...*

Painted Limestone Statue of Nenkheftka (2400 B.C.)

After a snack the soul might wander through the nether lands (somewhere north of Belgium) searching for paradise, meeting strange beings and weird situations. If things got too hairy, the soul could always find temporary refuge in statues like this one. It was helpful to have as many statues of yourself as possible to scatter around the earth, in case your soul needed a safe resting place.

This statue, like most Egyptian art, is not terribly lifelike—the figure is stiff, hands at the sides, left leg forward, mask-like face, stylized anatomy, and an out-of-date skirt.

And talk about uptight—he's got a column down his back! But it does have all the essential features, like the simplified human figures on international traffic signs. To a soul caught in the fast lane of astral travel, this symbolic statue would be easier to spot than a detailed one.

THE ANCIENT WORLD

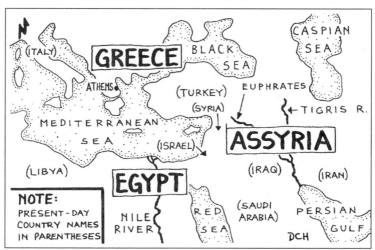

You'll see the same rigid features in almost all the statues in the gallery.

● *Head past two tall columns which give a sense of the grandeur of the Egyptian temples. About 30 yards farther down the gallery, you'll find a huge head with a broken-bowling-pin hat.*

Red Granite Head from a Colossal Figure of a King

Art also served as propaganda for the pharaohs, kings who called themselves gods on earth. Put this head on top of an enormous body (which still stands in Egypt) and you have the intimidating image of an omnipotent ruler who demands servile obedience. Next to the head is, appropriately, the pharaoh's powerful fist—the long arm of the law.

The crown is also symbolic. It's actually two crowns in one. The pointed upper half is the royal cap of Upper Egypt. This rests on the flat fez-like crown symbolizing Lower Egypt. A pharaoh wearing both crowns together is bragging that he rules a united Egypt.

● *Enter Room 25a, to the right. In a glass case you'll find ...*

Green Schist Royal Head (c. 1490 B.C.)

This pharaoh has several symbols of authority—the familiar pointed crown of Upper Egypt, a cobra-headed "hat pin" on the forehead, and a stylized "chin strap" beard. These symbols tell us clearly he's a powerful pharaoh, but which one?

Scholars aren't even sure if he's a he. Is it bearded King Tuthmosis III ... or the smooth-skinned Queen Hatshepsut, one of phour phemale pharaohs who actually did wear ceremonial "beards" as symbols of royal power?

● *Ponder the mystery of this AC/DC monarch, then turn to the painting at the end of the room.*

Painting of a Nobleman Hunting in the Marshes (1425 B.C.)

This nobleman walks like Egyptian statues look—stiff. We see his torso from the front and everything else—arms, legs, face—in profile, creating the funny walk that has become an Egyptian cliché. (Like an early version of Cubism, we see various perspectives at once.)

But the stiffness is softened by a human-ness. It's a family scene, a snapshot of loved ones from a happy time to be remembered for all eternity. The nobleman, taking a break from his courtly duties, is hunting. He's standing in a reed boat, gliding through the marshes. His arm is raised, ready to bean a bird with a snake-like hunting stick. On the right, his wife looks on, while his daughter crouches between his legs, a symbol of fatherly protection.

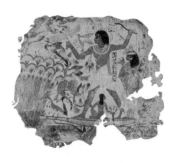

Though this two-dimensional hunter looks as if he were just run over by a pyramid, the painting is actually quite realistic. The birds above and fish below are painted like encyclopedia entries. The first "paper" came from papyrus plants like the bush on the left. The only truly unrealistic element is the house cat (thigh-high, in front of the man), acting as a retriever—just possibly the only cat in history that ever did anything useful.

● *In the main gallery, cross over to find four black lion-headed statues.*

Four Black Granite Figures of the Goddess Sakhmet (1400 B.C.)

This goddess was a good one to have on your side. She looks pretty sedate here, but this lion-headed woman could spring into a fierce crouch when crossed. Gods were often seen as part animal, admired for being stronger, swifter, or more fierce than puny Homo sapiens.

The gods ruled the Egyptian cosmos like a big banana republic (or the American Congress). To get a favor, Egyptians bribed their gods with offerings of food, animals, or money, or by erecting statues like these to them.

Notice the ankh that Sakhmet is holding. This key-shaped cross was the hieroglyph meaning "life," and was a symbol of eternal life. Later, it was adopted as a Christian symbol because of its cross shape and religious overtones.

● *Catch the happy couple nearby, seated hand in hand waiting for the Eternity Express. Then continue to the big glass case in the middle with leftovers from an ancient Egyptian arts-and-crafts fair. Respect that bronze cat with the nose ring. Cats were the sacred cows of Egypt. You could be put to death for harming one. Walk on to the big eight-foot granite head and torso further down.*

Upper Half of Colossal Statue of Ramesses II of Granite (1270 B.C.)

When Moses told the king of Egypt, "Let my people go!" this was the stone-faced look he got. Ramesses II (reigned c. 1290–1223 B.C.) was likely in power when Moses led the Israelites out of captivity in Egypt to their homeland in Israel. According to the Bible, Moses, a former Egyptian prince himself, appealed to the pharaoh to let them go peacefully. When the pharaoh refused, Moses cursed the land with a series of plagues. Finally, the Israelites just bolted with the help of their God, Yahweh, who drowned the Egyptian armies in the Red Sea. Egyptian records don't exactly corroborate the tale, but this Ramesses here looks enough like Yul Brynner in *The Ten Commandments* to make me a believer.

This statue, made from two different colors of granite, is a fragment from a temple in Thebes. Ramesses was a great builder of temples, palaces, tombs, and statues of himself. There are probably more statues of him in the world than there are cheezy fake *Davids*. He was so concerned about achieving immortality that he even chiseled his own name on other people's statues. Very rude.

Imagine, for a second, what the archaeologists saw when they came upon this—a colossal head and torso separated from the enormous legs, toppled into the sand, all that remained of the works of a once-great pharaoh. Kings, megalomaniacs, and workaholics, take note.

● *Say, "Ooh, heavy," and climb the ramp behind Ramesses, looking for animals.*

Various Egyptian Gods as Animals

Before technology made humans alpha animals on earth, it was easier to appreciate our fellow creatures. The Egyptians saw the superiority of animals and worshiped them as incarnations of the gods. The lioness was stronger, so she portrayed (as we saw earlier) the fierce goddess Sekhmet.

The clever baboon is Thote, the god of wisdom, and Horus has a falcon's head. The standing hippo is Theoris, protectress of childbirth. See her stylized breasts and pregnant belly supported by ankhs, the symbol of life. The god Amun, a powerful ram, protects a puny pharaoh under his powerful head.

● *Continuing up the ramp into Room 25b, you'll come face to face with a golden coffin.*

Gilded Wooden Inner Coffin of the Chantress of Amen-Re Henutmehit (1290 B.C.)

Look into the eyes of the deceased, a well-known singer, painted on the coffin. The Egyptians tried to cheat death by preserving their corpses. In the next life, the spirit was homeless without its body. They'd mummify the body, place it in a wooden coffin like this one and, often, put that coffin inside a larger stone one. The result is that we now have Egyptian bodies that are as well-preserved as Dick Clark.

The coffin is decorated with scenes of the deceased praising the gods, as well as magical spells to protect the body from evil and to act as crib notes for the confused soul in the nether world.

● *You can't call Egypt a wrap until you visit the mummies upstairs. If you*

can handle four flights of stairs (if not, cut straight to the next section from here), head on down to the end of the gallery past the giant stone scarab (beetle) and up the stairs lined with Roman mosaics, then left into Rooms 59 and 60. Snap a death mask photo of your partner framed by an open coffin, then step into the action ... Room 60.

Mummies

To mummify a body, disembowel it, fill the body cavities with pitch or other substances, and dry the body with natron, a natural form of sodium carbonate (and, I believe, the active ingredient in Twinkies). Then carefully bandage it head to toe with fine linen strips. Place in a coffin, wait 2,000 years, and, voilà! Or just dump the corpse in the desert and let the hot, dry Egyptian sand do the work—you'll get the same results.

The mummies in the glass cases here are from the time of the Roman occupation. The X-ray photos on the cases tell us more about these people. On the walls, murals showing the Egyptian burial rites as outlined in *The Book of the Dead*. In Roman times Egyptians painted a fine portrait in wax on the wrapping. And don't miss the animal mummies.

● *Linger here, but remember that eternity is about the amount of time it takes to see this entire museum. Head back down the stairs to the huge stone beetle in the center of the room at the end of the gallery . . .*

Monumental Granite Scarab (200 B.C.)

This species of beetle would burrow into the ground then reappear—like dying and rebirth—a symbol of resurrection.

Like the scarab, Egyptian culture was buried, first by Greece, then by Rome. Knowledge of the ancient writing died, condemning the culture to obscurity. But since the discovery of the Rosetta Stone, Egyptology is booming, and Egypt has come back to life.

● *Backtrack to the Rosetta Stone. Meet you on a bench in the shadow of those bearded Assyrian human-headed lions.*

ASSYRIA (1000–600 B.C.)

Assyria was the lion, the king of beasts of early civilizations. From its base in northern Mesopotamia (northern Iraq), it conquered and dominated the Middle East—from Israel to Iran—for more than three centuries. The Assyrians were a nation of warriors—hardy, disciplined, and often cruel conquistadors—whose livelihood depended on booty and slash-and-burn expansion.

Two Winged Lions with Human Heads (c. 870 B.C.)

These lions stood guard at key points in Assyrian palaces to intimidate enemies and defeated peoples. With lion body, eagle wings, and human head, these magical beasts—and therefore the Assyrian people—had the strength of a lion, the speed of an eagle, the brain of a man, and the beard of Z.Z. Top. They protected the palace from evil spirits and scared the heck out of foreign ambassadors and left-wing newspaper reporters.

(What has five legs and flies? Take a close look. These quintrupeds appear complete from both the front and the side.)

On the stone between the bearded lions' loins, you can see one of

ASSYRIA

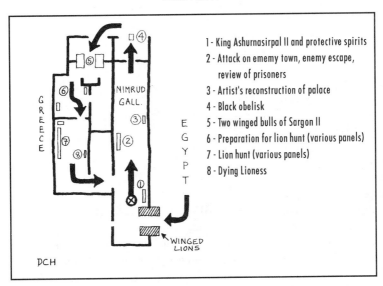

1 - King Ashurnasirpal II and protective spirits
2 - Attack on ememy town, enemy escape, review of prisoners
3 - Artist's reconstruction of palace
4 - Black obelisk
5 - Two winged bulls of Sargon II
6 - Preparation for lion hunt (various panels)
7 - Lion hunt (various panels)
8 - Dying Lioness

civilization's most impressive achievements—writing. This wedge-shaped ("cuneiform") script is the world's first written language, invented five thousand years ago by the Sumerians and passed down to their less-civilized descendants, the Assyrians.

● *Walk between the lions, glance at the large reconstructed wooden gates from an Assyrian palace, and turn right into the narrow red gallery lined with brown relief panels.*

Nimrud Gallery (ninth C. B.C.)

This gallery is a mini-version of the main hall of Ashurnasirpal II's palace. It was decorated with these pleasant sand-colored gypsum relief panels (which were, however, originally painted, as you'll see illustrated halfway down the hall).

That's Ashurnasirpal himself in the first panel on your right, with braided beard and fez-like crown, flanked by his supernatural hawk-headed henchman. The bulging muscles tell us that Ashurnasirpal was a conqueror's conqueror who enjoyed his reputation as a savage, merciless warrior who tortured and humiliated the vanquished. The following panels chronicle his bloody career.

● *Walk 15 yards farther. On your left find an upper panel labeled ...*

Attack on an Enemy Town

Many "nations" conquered by the Assyrians consisted of little more than a single walled city. Here, the Assyrians lay siege with the aid of a movable tower that gives them protection as they advance to the city walls. The king is shooting arrows from high atop that battering-ram "tank."

● *Next, to the right, you'll find ...*

Enemy Escape

This may represent enemies fleeing the Assyrians by swimming across the Euphrates, but it's more likely the Assyrians themselves with a unique amphibious assault technique. The soldiers inflate animal skins to keep them afloat as they sneak downstream to an enemy city.

● *Below, you'll see ...*

Review of Prisoners

The Assyrian economy depended on booty. Here a conquered nation is paraded before the Assyrian king. Above their heads the sculptor shows the rich spoils of war—elephant tusks, metal cauldrons, etc.

● *Notice the painted reconstruction on the opposite wall, then find the black obelisk.*

Black Obelisk of Shalmaneser III (c. 840 B.C.)

The Assyrians demanded annual tribute from the conquered lands. The obelisk shows people bringing tribute to Shalmaneser from all corners of the empire. The second band from the top shows the tribute from Israel. Parts of Israel were under Assyrian domination from the ninth century B.C. on. Old Testament prophets like Elijah and Elisha constantly warned their people of the corrupting influence of the Assyrian gods.

Also check out the parade of exotic animals on the third band, especially the missing-link monkeys.

● *Exit the gallery at the far end and hang a U-turn left into Room 16. More winged beasts.*

Two Winged Bulls from the Khorsabad Palace of Sargon II (c. 710 B.C.)

These 16-ton bulls guarded the palace of Sargon II. And speaking of large amounts of bull, "Sargon" wasn't his real name. It's obvious to savvy historians that Sargon must have been an insecure usurper to the throne, since the name meant "true king."

● *Sneak past these bulls, veering right into the small Room 17 where horses are being readied for the big hunt.*

Royal Lion Hunts

Lion hunting was Assyria's sport of kings. On the right wall, we see horses being readied for the hunt. On the left wall, hunting dogs. And next to them are beautiful lions. They rest peacefully in their idyllic garden, unaware that they will shortly be roused, stampeded, and slaughtered.

Lions lived in Mesopotamia up until modern times, and it had long been the duty of kings to keep the lion population down to protect farmers and herdsmen. This duty soon became sport as the kings of men proved their power by taking on the king of beasts. They actually bred lions to stage hunts. As we'll see, these "hunts" were as sporting as shooting fish in a barrel. Later Assyrian kings had grown soft and decadent, hardly the raging warriors of Ashurnasirpal's time.

● *Enter the larger lion-hunt room. Reading the panels like a comic strip, start in the right corner and gallop counterclockwise.*

The Lion-Hunt Room (c. 650 B.C.)

They're releasing the lions from their cages. Above, soldiers on horseback herd them into an enclosed arena. The king has them cornered. Let the slaughter begin. The chariot carries old King Ashurbanipal himself. The last of Assyria's great kings, he's ruled now for 50 years. He shoots ahead while spearmen hold off lions attacking from the rear.

● *At about the middle of the long wall . . .*

The fleeing lions, shot through with arrows and weighed down with fatigue, begin to fall, tragically. The lead lion carries on valiantly even while vomiting blood.

This, perhaps the low point of Assyrian cruelty, is the high point of their artistic achievement. It's a curious coincidence that civilizations often produce their greatest art in their declining years. Hmm.

Dying Lioness

● *On the wall opposite the vomiting lion . . .*

A dying lioness roars in pain and frustration, trying to run, but her body is too heavy. Her muscular hind legs, once the source of her power, are now paralyzed, a burden dragging her down.

Did the sculptor sense the coming death of his own civilization?

Like these brave, fierce lions, Assyria's once-great warrior nation was slain. Shortly after Ashurbanipal's death, Assyria was conquered, sacked, and looted by an ascendent Babylon. The mood of tragedy, of dignity, of proud struggle in a hopeless cause makes this *Dying Lioness* simply one of the most beautiful of all human creations.

● *Return to the winged lions (where we started) by exiting the lion-hunt room at the far end, soon connecting with familiar territory. Take a break.*

To reach the Greek section, enter the doorway opposite the bookstore (Room 1), walking past early Greek Barbie and Ken dolls from the Cycladic period (2500 B.C.). Just before the café, restaurant, and WCs, turn right, passing through Rooms 3 and 4 to the long Room 5. Relax on a bench and read, surrounded by vases and statues.

GREECE (600 B.C.–A.D. 1)

The history of ancient Greece could be subtitled "making order out of chaos." While Assyria was dominating the Middle Eastern world, "Greece" was floundering in darkness—a gaggle of warring tribes roaming the Greek peninsula. But by around 700 B.C. these tribes began settling down, experimenting with democracy, forming self-governing city-states and making ties with other city-states. Scarcely two centuries later, they would be a united community and the center of the civilized world.

During its "Golden Age" (500–430 B.C.), Greece set the tone for all of Western civilization to follow. Modern democracy, theater, literature, mathematics, philosophy, science, art, and architecture, as we know them, were all virtually invented by a single generation of Greeks in a small city of maybe 80,000 citizens.

● *On the wall in Room 5, find …*

Map of Greek World (500–30 B.C.)

Athens was the most powerful of the city-states and the center of the Greek world. Golden Age Greece was never really a full-fledged empire, but more a common feeling of unity among Greek-speaking peoples on the peninsula.

A century after the Golden Age, Greek culture spread still farther as the Macedonian Alexander the Great conquered the Mediterranean

EARLY GREECE

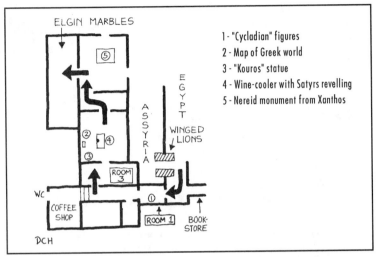

1 - "Cycladian" figures
2 - Map of Greek world
3 - "Kouros" statue
4 - Wine-cooler with Satyrs revelling
5 - Nereid monument from Xanthos

world and beyond. By 300 B.C., the "Greek" world stretched from Italy to India to Egypt (including most of what used to be the Assyrian Empire). Two hundred years later this Greek-speaking "Hellenistic Empire" was conquered by the Romans.

● *There's a nude male to the left of the map.*

Boy (Kouros) (490 B.C.)

The Greeks saw the human body as a perfect example of the divine orderliness of the universe. For the Greeks, even the gods themselves had human forms. The ideal man was a balance of opposites, the "Golden Mean." In a statue, that meant finding the right balance between motion and stillness, between realistic human anatomy (with human flaws) and the perfection of a Greek god. This Boy is still a bit uptight, stiff as the rock he's carved from. But—as we'll see—in just a few short decades, the Greeks would cut loose and create realistic statues that seemed to move like real humans.

● *Look in the glass case by the map, filled with decorated vases. One in the center is marked …*

Red-figured Psykter (Wine Cooler) with Satyrs Revelling (490 B.C.)

This clay wine cooler, designed to float in a bowl of cooling water, is decorated with satyrs holding a "symposium," or drinking party. These half-man/half-animal creatures (notice their tails) had a reputation for lewd behavior, reminding the balanced and moderate Greeks of their rude roots.

The revelling figures painted on this jar are more realistic, more three-dimensional, and suggest more natural movements than even the literally three-dimensional but quite stiff Kouros statue. The Greeks are beginning to conquer the natural world in art. The art, like life, is more in balance. And speaking of "balance," if that's a Greek sobriety test, revel on.

● *Carry on into Room 7 and sit facing the Greek temple at the far end.*

Nereid Monument from Xanthos (c. 400 B.C.)

Greek temples (like this reconstruction of a temple-shaped tomb) housed a statue of a god or goddess. Unlike Christian churches, which serve as meeting places, Greek temples kept worshipers gathered outside, so the most impressive part of the temple was its exterior. Temples were rectangular, surrounded by rows of columns, topped by a slanted roof.

The triangle-shaped roof, filled in with sculpture (reliefs or statues), is called the "pediment." The crossbeams supporting the roof are called "metopes" (pron: MET-o-pees). Look through the columns to the building itself. Above the doorway is another set of relief panels running around the building (under the "eaves") called the "frieze."

Next, we'll see pediment, frieze, and metope decorations from Greece's greatest temple.

● *Leave the British Museum. Take the Tube to Heathrow and fly to Athens. In the center of the old city, on top of the high, flat hill known as the Acropolis, you'll find ...*

The Parthenon

The Parthenon—the temple dedicated to Athena, goddess of wisdom and the patroness of Athens—was the crowning glory of an enormous urban renewal plan during Greece's Golden Age. After Athens was ruined in a war with Persia, the city, under the bold leadership of Pericles, constructed the greatest building of its day. The Parthenon was a model of balance, simplicity, and harmonious elegance, the

symbol of the Golden Age. Phidias, the greatest Greek sculptor, decorated the exterior with statues and relief panels.

While the building itself remains in Athens, many of its best sculptures are here—the so-called Elgin Marbles, named for the shrewd British ambassador who acquired them in the early 1800s. Though the Greek government complains about losing its marbles, the Brits feel they rescued and preserved the sculptures.

● *Enter through the glass doors labeled "Sculptures of the Parthenon."*

THE ELGIN MARBLES (450 B.C.)

The marble panels you see lining the walls of this large hall are part of the frieze that originally ran around the exterior of the Parthenon. The statues at either end of the hall once filled the Parthenon's triangular-shaped pediments. Near the pediment sculptures, we'll also find the relief panels known as metopes. Let's start with the frieze.

The Frieze

These 56 relief panels show Athenian's "Fourth of July" parade, celebrating the birth of their city. On this day, citizens marched up the Acropolis to symbolically present a new robe to the 40-foot gold and ivory statue of Athena housed in the Parthenon.

● *Start at the panels to your right (#134) and work counterclockwise.*

Men on horseback, chariots, musicians, animals for sacrifice, and young maidens with offerings are all part of the grand parade, all heading in the same direction. Prance on.

Notice the muscles and veins in the horses' legs (#128) and the intricate folds in the cloaks and dresses (#115). Some panels (#103) have holes drilled in them, where gleaming bronze reins were fitted to heighten the festive look. Despite the bustle of figures posed every which way, the frieze has one unifying element—all the heads are at the same level, creating a single ribbon around the Parthenon.

● *Cross to the opposite wall.*

ELGIN MARBLES

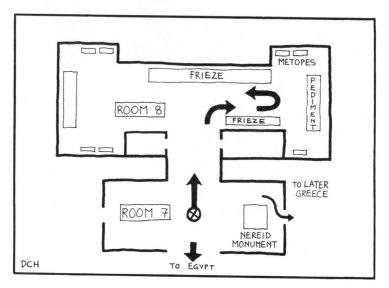

A three-horse chariot (#59) cut out of only two inches of marble is more lifelike and three-dimensional than anything the Egyptians achieved in a free-standing statue.

The procession culminates (#35) in the presentation of the robe to Athena. A man and a child fold the robe for the goddess while the rest of the gods look on. There's Zeus and Hera (#29), the king and queen of the gods, seated, enjoying the fashion show and wondering what length hemlines will be this year.

● *Head for the set of pediment sculptures at the right end of the hall.*

The Pediment Sculptures
These statues are nestled nicely in the triangular pediment above the columns at the Parthenon's east entrance. The missing statues at the peak of the triangle once showed the birth of Athena. Zeus had his head split open, allowing Athena, the goddess of wisdom, to rise from his brain fully grown and fully armed.

The other gods at this Olympian banquet slowly become aware of the amazing event. The first to notice is the one closest to them, Hebe, the cup-bearer of the gods (tallest surviving fragment). Frightened, she runs to tell the others, her dress whipping behind her. A startled Demeter (just left of Hebe) turns toward Hebe.

The only one that hasn't lost his head is laid-back Dionysus (the cool guy on the far left). He raises another glass of wine. Over on the right, Aphrodite, goddess of love, leans back luxuriously into the lap of her mother, too busy posing to even notice the hubbub. A horse screams, "These people are nuts—let me out of here!"

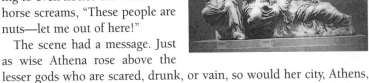

The scene had a message. Just as wise Athena rose above the lesser gods who are scared, drunk, or vain, so would her city, Athens, rise above her lesser rivals.

This is amazing workmanship. Compare Dionysus, with his natural, relaxed, reclining pose, to all those stiff Egyptian statues standing eternally at attention. The realism of the muscles is an improvement even over the Kouros we saw, sculpted only 50 years earlier.

Appreciate the folds of the clothes on the female figures (on the right half), especially Aphrodite's clinging, rumpled robe. Some sculptors would build a model of their figure first, put real clothes on it, and study how the cloth hung down before actually sculpting in marble. Others found inspiration at the *taverna* on wet T-shirt night.

Even without their heads, these statues with their detailed anatomy and expressive poses speak volumes.

Wander behind. The statues originally sat 40 feet above the ground. The backs of the statues—which were never intended to be seen—are almost as detailed as the fronts. That's quality control ...

● *The metopes are the panels on the walls to either side. Start with "South Metope XXXI" on the right wall, center.*

The Metopes

In #XXXI, a Centaur grabs a man by the throat while the man pulls his hair. The human Lapiths have invited some Centaurs—wild half-man/half-horse creatures—to a wedding feast. All goes well until the brutish Centaurs, the original party animals, get too drunk and try to carry off the Lapith women. A battle ensues.

The Greeks prided themselves on creating order out of chaos. Within just a few generations, they went from nomadic barbarism to the pinnacle of early Western civilization. These metopes tell the story of this struggle between the forces of civilization (Lapiths) and barbarism (Centaurs).

In #XXVIII (opposite wall, center), the Centaurs start to get the upper hand as one rears triumphant over a fallen man. The lion skin draped over the Centaur's arm roars a taunt at the prone man. The humans lose face.

In #XXVII (to the left), the humans finally rally and drive off the brutish Centaurs. A Centaur, wounded in the back, tries to run, but the man grabs him by the neck and raises his right hand (missing) to deliver the final blow. Notice how the Lapith's cloak drapes a rough-textured background that highlights the smooth skin of this graceful, ideal man. The Centaurs have been defeated. Civilization has triumphed over barbarism, order over chaos, and rational man over his half-animal alter-ego.

Centaurs slain around the world. *Dateline 500 B.C.—Greece, China, India: Man no longer considers himself an animal. Bold new ideas are exploding simultaneously around the world. Socrates, Confucius, Buddha, and others are independently discovering a non-material, unseen order in nature and in man. They say man has a rational mind or soul. He's separate from nature and different from the other animals.*

Why are the Elgin Marbles so treasured? The British of the 19th century saw themselves as the new "civilized" race subduing "barbarians" in their far-flung Empire. Maybe these rocks made them stop and wonder—will our great civilization also turn to rubble?

2 British Library

The British Empire built its greatest monuments out of paper. It's in literature that England has made her lasting contribution to history and the arts. The British Library houses millions of books and thousands of manuscripts. We'll concentrate on a handful of documents—literary and historical—that changed the course of history. Start with the top 10 (described in this tour), then stray according to your interests.

Hours: Monday–Saturday 9:30–18:00, Sunday 11:00–17:00.

Cost: Free

Tour Length: One hour

Getting there: Tube to King's Cross/St. Pancras Station. Leaving the station, turn right and walk a block to 96 Euston Road.

Information: Tours are offered usually Monday, Wednesday, Friday, and Sunday at 15:00, Saturday at 10:30 and 15:00, (one hour, £3, for schedule and to reserve, call 0171/412-7332 or see www.bl.uk; Library tel. 0171/412-7000).

Cloakroom: Free

Photography: No photos (or smoking, or chewing gum).

Cuisine art: Café and restaurant within library.

Starring: Magna Carta, Bibles, Shakespeare, and the Beatles.

ORIENTATION

The new British Library (moved from the British Museum to its new location near King's Cross station and opened in mid-1998) is the national archives of Britain. With the deepest basement in London and 180 miles of shelving, it has over 12 million books. Entering its courtyard you'll see a huge statue. It depicts the poet William Blake's vision of Isaac Newton bending forward to plot—with a pair of dividers—the immensity of the universe. This statue, symbolizing the union of nature and science, poetry and art, expresses the library's purpose: to preserve the record of man's endless search for truth.

Stepping inside you'll see the information desk. Cloakroom, WC, and café are to the right. The tiny but exciting area you'll tour is to the left under a sign marked "Exhibitions."

The priceless literary and historical treasures of the collection are in this one carefully designed and lit room. The adjoining "Turning the Pages" computer room is in the back. Down a few steps you'll find the history of printing "workshop" and the Pierson Gallery (with its recommended History of Children's Lit exhibit).

1. Maps

Navigate the wall of historic maps from left to right. One shows Britain in 1250. Another is the Christian world of 1260 with

WALKING TOUR STOPS

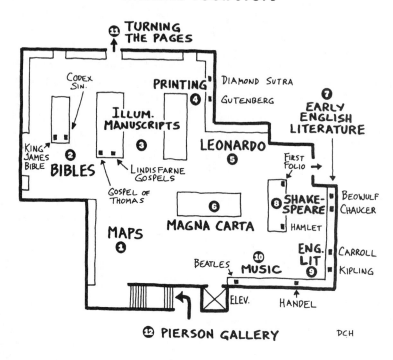

1. Maps
2. Bibles
3. Lindisfarne Gospels and Illuminated Manuscripts
4. Printing
5. Leonardo
6. Magna Carta
7. Early English Literature
8. Shakespeare
9. English Literature
10. Music
11. Turning the Pages computer room
12. Pierson Galleries, historical children's books

Jerusalem in the middle and Jesus on top. A 1490 map shows the best map Columbus could get. And then a 1506 map shows the first depiction of America ... as part of Asia. By 1562 the eastern coast of North America was fairly accurate. And you could plan your next trip with Mercator's 1570 map of Europe.

2. *Bibles*

My favorite excuse for not learning a foreign language is: If English was good enough for Jesus Christ, it's good enough for me! I don't know what that has to do with anything, but obviously Jesus didn't speak English—nor did Moses or Isaiah or Paul or any other Bible authors or characters. As a result, our present-day English Bible is not directly from the mouth and pen of these religious figures, but the fitful product of centuries of evolution and translation.

The Bible is not a single book; it's an anthology of books by many authors from different historical periods writing in different languages (usually Hebrew or Greek). So there are three things that editors must consider in compiling the most accurate Bible: (1) deciding which books actually belong; (2) finding the oldest and most accurate version of each book; and (3) translating it accurately.

Codex Sinaiticus (c. A.D. 350)

The oldest complete Bible in existence (along with one in the Vatican), this is one of the first attempts to collect various books together into one authoritative anthology. It's in Greek, the language in which most of the New Testament was written. The Old Testament portions are Greek translations from the original Hebrew. This particular Bible, and the nearby *Codex Alexandrus* (A.D. 425), contain some books not included in most modern English Bibles. (Even today Catholic Bibles contain books not found in Protestant Bibles.)

Fragment of an Unknown Gospel and The Gospel of Thomas

Here are pieces—scraps of papyrus—of two such books that didn't make it into our modern Bible. The "unknown" Gospel (an account of the life of Jesus of Nazareth) is as old a Christian manuscript as any in existence. Remember, the Gospels weren't written down for a full generation after Jesus died, and the oldest surviving manuscripts are from later than that. So why isn't this early version of Jesus' life part of our Bible right up there with Matthew, Mark, Luke, and John? Possibly because some early Bible editors didn't like the story it told about Jesus not found in the four accepted Gospels.

The "Gospel of Thomas" gives an even more radical picture of Jesus. This Jesus preaches enlightenment by mystical knowledge: "The kingdom is inside you ... " Jesus seems to be warning people against looking to gurus for the answers, a Christian version of "If you meet the Buddha on the road, kill him." This fragment dates from A.D. 150, more than a century after Jesus' death, but that's probably not the only reason why it's not in our Bible (after all, the Gospel of John is generally dated at A.D. 100). Rather, the message, which threatened established church leaders, may have been too scary to include in the Bible—whether Jesus said it or not.

The Authorized Version, or King James Bible (1611)

Jesus spoke Aramaic, a form of Hebrew. His words were written down in Greek. Greek manuscripts were translated into Latin, the language of medieval monks and scholars. By 1400 there was still no English version of the Bible, though only a small percentage of the population understood Latin. A few brave reformers risked death to make translations into English and print them with Gütenberg's new invention. Within two centuries English translations were both legal and popular.

The King James version (done during his reign) has been the most popular English translation. Fifty scholars worked for four years, borrowing heavily from previous translations, to produce the work. Its impact on the English language was enormous, making Elizabethan English something of the standard, even after all those *thees* and *thous* fell out of fashion in everyday speech.

In our century, many new translations are both more accurate (based on better scholarship and original manuscripts) and more readable, using modern speech patterns.

3. Lindisfarne Gospels (A.D. 698) and Illuminated Manuscripts

Throughout the Middle Ages, Bibles had to be reproduced by hand. This was a painstaking process usually done by monks for a rich patron. This beautifully illustrated (illuminated) collection of the four Gospels is the most magnificent of medieval British monk-u-scripts. The text is in Latin, the language of scholars ever since the Roman empire, but the elaborate decoration mixes Irish, classical, and even Byzantine forms.

These Gospels are a reminder that Christianity almost didn't make it in Europe. After the Fall of Rome (which had established Christianity as the official religion), much of Europe reverted to its pagan ways. This was the time of Beowulf, when people worshipped woodland spirits, smurfs, and terrible Teutonic gods. It took dedicated Irish missionaries 500 years to re-establish the faith on the Continent. Lindisfarne, an obscure monastery of Irish monks on an island off the east coast of England, was one of the few beacons of light after the Fall of Rome, tending the embers of civilization through the long night of the Dark Ages. (You can virtually flip through the Lindisfarne Gospels in the adjacent "Turning the Pages" computer room.)

Browse through more illuminated manuscripts (in the cases behind the Lindisfarne Gospels). This is some of the finest art from what we call the "Dark Ages." The little intimate details offer a fascinating and rare slice-of-life look at that age.

4. *Printing*

Diamond Sutra—a scroll from 868—is the earliest dated printed document. Printing was common in Asia from the mid-eighth century—700 years before Gütenberg "invented" the printing press in Europe. In texts like the Buddhist *Diamond Sutra*, carved blocks with Chinese characters were dipped into paint or ink to print. Notice also the fine wood block illustration. This was discovered in China in 1907.

The Gütenberg Bible (c. 1455)

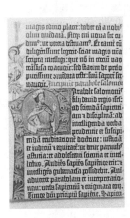

It looks like just another monk-made Latin manuscript, but it's the first book printed in Europe. Printing is one of the most revolutionary inventions in history. Johann Gütenberg (c. 1397–1468), a German goldsmith, devised a convenient way to reproduce written materials quickly, neatly, and cheaply by printing with movable type. You scratch each letter onto a separate metal block, then arrange them into words, ink them up and press them onto paper. When one job was done you could reuse the same letters for a new one.

This simple idea had immediate and revolutionary consequences. Knowledge became cheap and accessible to a wide audience, not just the rich. Books became the mass media of Europe, linking people by a common set of ideas. And, like a drug, this increased knowledge only created demand for still more.

Suddenly the Bible was available for anyone to read. Church authorities, more interested in protecting than spreading the word of God, passed laws prohibiting the printing of Bibles. As the Church feared, when people read the Bible, they formed their own opinions of God's message, which was often different from the version spoon-fed to them by priests. In the resulting Reformation, Protestants broke away from the Catholic Church, confident they could read the Bible without a priest's help.

5. Leonardo da Vinci's Notebook

Pages from Leonardo's notebook here show his genius for invention, powerful curiosity, and famous backward and inside out handwriting.

6. Magna Carta

How did Britain, a tiny island with a few million people, come to rule a quarter of the world? Not by force but by law. The Magna Carta was the basis for England's constitutional system of government.

In the year 1215, England's barons rose in revolt against the slimy King John. After losing London, John was forced to negotiate. The barons presented him with a list of demands. John, whose rule was worthless without the support of the barons, had no choice but to fix his seal to it.

This was a turning point in the history of government. Kings had ruled by God-given authority. They were above the laws of men, acting however and whenever they pleased. Now for the first time there were limits—in writing—on how a king could treat his subjects. More generally, it established the idea of "due process"—that is, the government can't infringe on people's freedom without a legitimate legal reason. This small step became the basis for all constitutional governments, including yours.

A few days after John agreed to this original document, it was rewritten in legal form, and some 35 copies of this final version of the "Great Charter" were distributed around the kingdom (with two displayed here). You'll also see letters from the Pope supporting John and annulling Magna Carta. The Pope knew what a radical principle the Magna Carta represented—the questioning of church-ordained authorities by the common rabble.

So what did this radical piece of paper actually say? Not much by today's standards. (Read the translated bit in the center case.) The specific demands had to do with things like inheritance taxes, the king's duties to widows and orphans, and so on. It wasn't the specific articles that were important, but the simple fact that the king had to abide by them as law.

Around the corner there are many more historical documents in the Library letters by Queen Elizabeth I, Isaac Newton, Wellington, Ghandi, and so on. But for now, let's trace the evolution of …

7. Early English Literature
Four out of every five English words have been borrowed from other languages. The English language, like English culture (and London today), is a mix derived from foreign invaders. Some of the historic ingredients that make this cultural stew are:

(1) The original Celtic tribesmen; (2) Romans (A.D. 1–500); (3) The Germanic tribes called Angles and Saxons (making English a Germanic language and naming the island Angle-land—England); (4) Vikings from Denmark (A.D. 800); and finally, (5) the French-speaking Normans under William the Conqueror, who reigned from 1066 to 1087.

Beowulf (c. 1000)
This Anglo-Saxon epic poem written in Old English, the early version of our language, almost makes the hieroglyphics on the Rosetta Stone look easy. The manuscript here is from A.D. 1000, although the poem itself dates to about 750. This is the only existing medieval manuscript of this first English literary masterpiece.

In the story, the young hero Beowulf (pron: BAY-uh-wolf) defeats two half-human monsters threatening the kingdom. *Beowulf* symbolized England's emergence from Dark Age chaos and barbarism.

Canterbury Tales (c. 1410)
Six hundred years later, England was Christian but it was hardly the pious, predictable, Sunday-school world we might imagine. Geoffrey Chaucer's bawdy collection of stories, told by pilgrims on their way to Canterbury, gives us the full range of life's experiences—happy, sad, silly, sexy, and pious. (Late in life, Chaucer wrote an apology for those works of his that tend toward sin.)

While most serious literature of the time was written in scholarly Latin, *The Canterbury Tales* was written in Middle English, the language that developed when the French invasion (1066) added a Norman twist to Old English.

8. Shakespeare
William Shakespeare (1564–1616) is the greatest author in any language. Period. He expanded and helped define modern English. In one fell swoop, he made the language of everyday people as important

as Latin. In the process, he gave us phrases like "one fell swoop" that we quote without knowing its Shakespeare.

Perhaps as important was his insight into humanity. With his stock of great characters—Hamlet, Othello, Macbeth, Falstaff, Romeo and Juliet, Lear—he probed the psychology of human beings 300 years before Freud. Even today, his characters strike a familiar chord.

Shakespeare as a Collaborator
Shakespeare co-wrote a play titled *The Booke of Sir Thomas More*. Some scholars have wondered if maybe Shakespeare had help on other plays as well. After all, they reasoned, how could a journeyman actor, with little education, have written so many masterpieces? Modern scholars, though, unanimously agree that Shakespeare did indeed write the plays ascribed to him.

The Good and Bad Quarto of *Hamlet*
Shakespeare wrote his plays to be performed, not read. He published a few, but as his reputation grew, unauthorized bootleg versions also began to circulate. Some of these were written out by actors, trying (with faulty memories) to recreate a play they'd been in years before. Here are two different versions of *Hamlet*: "good" and "bad."

The Shakespeare First Folio

It wasn't until seven years after his death that this complete-works collection of his plays came out (1623). The editors were friends and fellow actors.

The engraving of Shakespeare on the title page is one of only two likenesses done during his lifetime. Is this what he really looked like? No one knows. The best answer comes from his friend, poet Ben Jonson, in the introduction on the facing page. "Reader, look not on his picture, but his book."

9. Other Greats in English Literature
The rest of the "Beowulf/Chaucer wall" is a greatest hits sampling of British literature featuring the writing of Wordsworth, Blake, Dickens, and James Joyce. Especially interesting may be:

Coleridge *Xanadu*, an Earthly Paradise from *Kubla Khan*
One day Samuel Taylor Coleridge took opium. He fell asleep while reading about the fantastic palace of the Mongol emperor, Kubla Khan.

During his three-hour drug-induced sleep, he composed in his head a poem of from two- to three-hundred lines. When he woke up, he grabbed a pen and paper and instantly and eagerly wrote down the lines that are here preserved. But just then, a visitor on business knocked at the door and kept Coleridge busy for an hour. When Coleridge finally kicked him out, he discovered that he'd forgotten the rest! The poem *Kubla Khan* is only a fragment, but it's still one of literature's masterpieces.

Coleridge (aided by his Muse-in-the-medicine-cabinet) was one of the Romantic poets. Check out his fellow Romantics—Keats, Shelley, and Wordsworth—nearby.

Dickens
In 1400, no one but the select few could read. By 1850 in England, almost everyone could and did. Charles Dickens (1812–1870) gave them their first taste of literature. His books were serialized in periodicals and avidly read by the increasingly-educated masses. The story is told of American fans gathering in mobs at the docks waiting with "Who shot J.R?" enthusiasm for the ship from England with the latest news of their favorite character.

Dickens also helped raise social concern for the underprivileged—of whom England had more than her share. When Dickens was 12 years old, his father was thrown into debtor's prison, and young Charles was put to work to support the family. The ordeal of poverty scarred him for life and gave him experiences he'd draw on later for books like *Oliver Twist* and *David Copperfield*.

Lewis Carroll The Original *Alice in Wonderland*
I don't know if Lewis Carroll ever dipped into Coleridge's medicine jar or not, but his series of children's books makes *Kubla Khan* read like the phone book. Carroll was a stammerer, which made him uncomfortable around everyone but children. For them he created a fantasy world where grown-up rules and logic were turned upside-down.

10. *Music*
The Beatles
Future generations will have to judge whether this musical quartet ranks with artists like Dickens and Keats, but no one can deny the

group's historical significance. The Beatles burst onto the scene in the early 1960s to unheard-of popularity. With their long hair and loud music, they brought counterculture and revolutionary ideas to the middle class, affecting the values of a whole generation.

Here are photos of John Lennon, Paul McCartney, and George Harrison before their fame (the fourth Beatle was Ringo Starr).

Most interesting are the manuscripts of song lyrics written by Lennon and McCartney, the two guiding lights of the group. "I Wanna Hold Your Hand" was the song that launched them to super-stardom. John's song, "Help," was the quickly written title song for one of the Beatle's movies. "Yesterday," by Paul, was recorded with guitar and voice backed by a string quartet—a touch of sophistication by producer George Martin. Also glance at the rambling, depressed, cynical, but humorous letter by John on the left. Is that a self-portrait at the bottom?

Music Manuscripts

Kind of an anti-climax after the Fab Four, I know, but here are man-uscripts by Handel, Mozart, Beethoven, Schubert, and so on.

11. *Turning the Pages—Virtual Reality Room*

For a chance to virtually flip though the pages of a few of the most precious books in the collection, drop by the "Turning the Pages" room. Grab a computer and let your fingers do the walking.

12. *Pierson Gallery and Printing Workshop*

As you leave, browse through the Pierson Gallery for a chance to trace the story of writing, the evolution of printing and book-making, and a great exhibit on the history of children's books. "W is for the woman, who not overly nice, made very short work ... of the three blind mice."

The British Library's Restaurant and Café, while nothing special from an eating point of view, has a wall of 65,000 old books given to the people by King George IV in 1823. This 50-foot-tall mother of all bookshelves is pretty high-tech behind glass, movable, and with movable lifts.

3 National Gallery

The National Gallery lets you tour Europe's art without ever crossing the Channel. With so many exciting artists and styles, it's a fine overture to art if you're just starting a European trip, and a pleasant reprise if you're just finishing. Anytime, the "National Gal" is a welcome 90-minute interlude from the bustle of London sightseeing.

NATIONAL GALLERY

Hours: Monday–Saturday 10:00–18:00, Sunday 12:00–18:00, Wednesday until 20:00. Closed on Good Friday; December 24, 25, 26; and January 1. May be open later one evening a week in summer.

Cost: Free

Tour length: 90 minutes

Getting there: It's central as can be, overlooking Trafalgar Square, a 15-minute walk from Big Ben, 10 minutes from Piccadilly. Tube: Charing Cross or Leicester Square. Bus: 3, 6, 9, 11, 12, 13, 15, 23, 24, 29, 53, 88, 91, 94, 109.

Information: Information desk with a free and handy floor plan brochure in lobby. Excellent CD soundguide (£3) lets you dial up info on any painting in the museum. The latest events schedule and a listing of free lunch lectures is in the free National Gallery News flyer. Free one-hour general overview tours are offered most weekdays at 11:30 and 14:30 and Saturdays at 14:00 and 15:30. Tel. 0171/839-3321, recorded information 0171/747-2885.

Cloakroom: Free cloakrooms at each entrance welcome your coat and umbrella but probably not your bag. You can take in a bag.

Photography: Strictly forbidden.

Cuisine art: The Brasserie (first floor, Sainsbury Wing) is classy with reasonable prices and a petite menu. The Café (near the end of your *Mona* tour, just before the Impressionists) is a bustling, inexpensive, self-service cafeteria with realistic salads, Rubens sandwiches, and Gauguin juices. A block away, there's a good cafeteria in the crypt of St. Martin-in-the-Fields church (facing Trafalgar Square). For pub grub, walk a block toward Big Ben and dip into the Clarence.

Starring: You name it—Leonardo, Van Eyck, Raphael, Titian, Caravaggio, Rembrandt, Rubens, Velázquez, Monet, Renoir, and van Gogh.

ORIENTATION — PHYSICAL AND MENTAL

● *Two entrances face Trafalgar Square. Enter through what looks like a smaller separate building 50 yards to the left of the main entrance as you face it. Pick up a current map (free). Climb the stairs. At the top, turn left and grab a seat in Room 51 facing Leonardo's Virgin of the Rocks.*

The National Gallery offers a quick overview of European art history. We'll stay on one floor, and after a brief preview of Leonardo, we'll work chronologically through medieval holiness, Renaissance real-

NATIONAL GALLERY—OVERVIEW

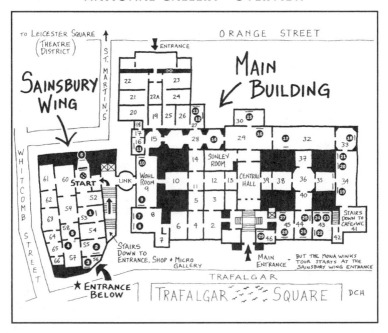

ism, Dutch detail, Baroque excess, British restraint, and the colorful French Impressionism that leads to the modern world. Cruise like an eagle with wide eyes for the big picture, seeing how each style progresses into the next.

THE ITALIAN RENAISSANCE (1400–1550)

Leonardo da Vinci — *The Virgin of the Rocks*
Mary, the mother of Jesus, plays with her son and little Johnny the Baptist (with cross, at left) while John's mother looks on. Leonardo brings this holy scene right down to earth. But looking closer we see that Leonardo has deliberately posed them into a pyramid shape, with Mary's head at the peak, creating an oasis of maternal stability and serenity amid the hard rock of the earth. Leonardo, who was illegitimate, may have sought after the young mother he never knew, in his art. Freud thought so.

NATIONAL GALLERY

Medieval and Early Renaissance
1. Wilton Diptych
2. UCCELLO—Battle of San Romano
3. VAN EYCK—Arnolfini Marriage
4. CRIVELLI—Annunciation With St. Emidius
5. BOTTICELLI—Venus and Mars

High Renaissance
6. LEONARDO DA VINCI—Virgin and Child (painting and cartoon)
7. MICHELANGELO—Entombment
8. RAPHAEL—Pope Julius II

Venetian Renaissance
9 TINTORETTO—Origin of the Milky Way
10. TITIAN—Bacchus and Ariadne

Northern Protestant Art
11.VERMEER—Young Woman Standing at a Virginal
12. REMBRANDT—Self-Portrait
13. REMBRANDT—Belshazzar's Feast

Baroque and Rococo
14. RUBENS—The Judgment of Paris
15.VAN DYCK—Charles I on Horseback

16. VELÁZQUEZ—The Rokeby Venus
17. CARAVAGGIO—Supper at Emmaus
18. BOUCHER—Pan and Syrinx

British
19. CONSTABLE—The Hay Wain
20. TURNER—The Fighting Téméraire
21. TURNER—Rain, Steam, Speed

Impressionism and Beyond
22. MONET—Gare St. Lazare
23. MANET—The Waitress (*La Servante de Bocks*)
24. DEGAS— Miss La La at the Cirque Fernando
25. RENOIR—The Umbrellas
26. SEURAT—Bathers at Asnieres
27. VAN GOGH—Sunflowers
28. CÉZANNE—Bathers
29. MONET—Water Lilies

The Renaissance—or "rebirth" of the culture of ancient Greece and Rome—was a cultural boom that changed people's thinking about every aspect of life. In politics, it meant democracy. In religion, a move away from church dominance and toward the assertion of man (humanism) and a more personal faith. Science and secular learning were revived after centuries of superstition and ignorance. In architecture, it was a return to the balanced columns and domes of Greece and Rome.

In painting, the Renaissance meant realism. Artists rediscovered the beauty of nature and the human body. With pictures of beautiful people in harmonious surroundings, they expressed the optimism and confidence of this new age.

● *We'll circle back around to Leonardo in a couple hundred years. But first, turn your back on the Renaissance and cruise through the medieval world in Rooms 52, 53, and 54.*

Medieval and Early Renaissance (1260–1510)

Shiny-gold paintings of saints, angels, Madonnas, and crucifixions. One thing is very clear: Middle Ages art was religious, dominated by the church. The illiterate faithful could meditate on an altarpiece and visualize heaven.

Medieval heaven was different from medieval earth. The holy wore gold plates on their heads. Faces were serene and generic. People posed stiffly, facing directly out or to the side, never in-between. Saints are recognized by symbols they carry (a key, a sword, a book), rather than human features. They floated in an ethereal nowhere of gold leaf. In other words, medieval artists had no need to master the techniques of portraying the "real" world of rocks, trees, and distinguished noses, because their world was … otherworldly.

● *One of the finest medieval altarpieces is in a glass case in Room 53.*

The Wilton Diptych — anonymous (c. 1395)

In this two-panelled altarpiece, a glimmer of human realism peeks through the gold leaf. The kings on the left have distinct, down-to-earth faces as they adore Mary and the baby on the right. And the back side shows—not a saint, not a god, not a symbol—but a real-life deer lying down in the grass of this earth.

Still, the anonymous artist is struggling with reality. Look at the left
panel—John the Baptist is holding a
"lamb of God" that looks more like a
chihuahua. Nice try. In the right
panel, the angels with their flame-
like wings and cloned faces bunch
together single file across the back

rather than receding realistically into the distance. Mary's exquisite
fingers hold an anatomically impossible little foot. The figures are flat,
scrawny, and sinless with cartoon features—far from flesh-and-blood
human beings.

● *Walking straight into Room 55, you'll leave this gold leaf peace and
you'll find ...*

Uccello — *Battle of San Romano* (c. 1450)

This colorful battle scene
shows the victory of Florence
over Siena—and the battle for
literal realism on the canvas. It
is an early Renaissance attempt
at a realistic, non-religious,
three-dimensional scene.

Uccello challenges his ability by posing the horses and soldiers at
every conceivable angle. The background of farmyards, receding
hedges, and tiny soldiers creates a 3-D illusion of distance. In the foreground, Uccello actually constructs a 3-D grid out of fallen lances,
then places the horses and warriors within it. Still, Uccello hasn't
quite worked out the bugs—the figures in the distance are far too big,
and the fallen soldier on the left isn't much bigger than the fallen
shield on the right.

● *In Room 56, you'll find ...*

Van Eyck — *The Arnolfini Marriage* (1434)

Called by some "The Shotgun Wedding," this painting of a simple
ceremony (set in Bruges, Belgium) is a masterpiece of down-to-earth
details. Van Eyck has built us a medieval dollhouse, then invites
us to linger over the finely crafted details. Feel the texture of the
fabrics, count the terrier's hairs, trace the shadows generated by
the window. In fact, each object is painted at an ideal angle, with
the details you'd see if you were only a foot away. So the strings

of beads hanging on the back wall are as crystal-clear as the bracelets on the bride.

And to top it off, look into the round mirror on the far wall—the whole scene is reflected backwards in miniature, showing the loving couple and two mysterious visitors. Is it the concerned parents? The minister? Van Eyck himself at his easel? Or has the artist painted you, the home viewer, into the scene?

In medieval times (this was painted only a generation after *The Wilton Diptych*) everyone could read the hidden meaning of certain symbols—the chandelier with its one lit candle (love), the fruit on the windowsill (fertility), the whisk broom (the bride's domestic responsibilities), and the terrier (Fido—fidelity).

By the way, she may not be pregnant. The fashion of the day was to wear a pillow to look pregnant in hopes you'd soon get that way. At least, that's what they told their parents.

The surface detail is extraordinary, but the painting lacks true Renaissance depth. The tiny room looks unnaturally narrow, cramped, and claustrophobic, making us wonder: where will the mother-in-law sleep?

● *Continue into Room 57.*

Crivelli — *The Annunciation with Saint Emidius*

Mary, in green, is visited by the dove of the Holy Ghost who beams down from the distant heavens in a shaft of light.

Like Van Eyck's wedding, this is a brilliant collection of realistic details. Notice the hanging rug, the peacock, the architectural minutiae that lead you way way back, then, bam, you've got a giant pickle in your face.

It's detail combined with Italian spaciousness. The floor tiles and building bricks recede into the distance. We're sucked right in, accelerating through the alleyway, under the arch and off into space. The Holy Ghost spans the entire distance, connecting heavenly background with earthly foreground. Crivelli creates an Escher-esque labyrinth of rooms and walkways that we want to walk through, around, and into, or is that just a male thing?

Renaissance Italians were interested in—some would say obsessed with—portraying 3-D space. Perhaps they focused their burning spiratal passion away from heaven, and toward the physical world. With so much restless energy, they needed lots of elbow room. Space, the final frontier.

● *In Room 58 ...*

Botticelli — ### *Venus and Mars*

Mars takes a break from war, succumbing to the delights of Love (Venus), while impish satyrs play innocently

with the discarded tools of death. In the early spring of the Renaissance, there was an optimistic mood in the air, the feeling that enlightened man could solve all problems, narrowing the gap between mortals and the Greek gods. Artists felt free to use the pagan Greek gods as symbols of human traits, virtues, and vices. Venus has sapped man's medieval stiffness and welcomed him roundly out of the darkness and into the Renaissance.

● *Now return through Room 59 to the Leonardo in Room 51, where we started.*

The High Renaissance (1500)

With the "Big Three" of the High Renaissance—Leonardo, Michelangelo, and Raphael—painters had finally conquered realism. But these three Florentine artists weren't content to just copy nature, cranking out photographs-on-canvas. Like Renaissance architects (which they also were), they carefully composed their figures on the canvas, "building" them into geometrical patterns that reflected the balance and order they saw in nature.

● *Enter the small dark cave behind the* Rocks.

Leonardo da Vinci — ### *Virgin and Child with St. John the Baptist* ### *and St. Anne*

At first glance this chalk drawing, or cartoon, looks like a simple snapshot of two loving moms and two playful kids. The two children play—oblivious to the violent deaths they'll both suffer—beneath their mothers' Mona Lisa smiles.

But follow the eyes: shadowy-eyed Anne turns toward Mary who looks tenderly down to Jesus who blesses John who gazes back dreamily. As your eyes follow theirs, you're led back to the literal and psychological center of the composition—Jesus. Without resorting to heavy-handed medieval symbolism, Leonardo drives home a theological concept in a natural, human way. Leonardo the perfectionist rarely finished paintings. This sketch gives us an inside peek at his genius.

● *Enter the large Room 9. We'll return to these big, colorful canvases, but first, turn right into Room 8.*

Michelangelo — *Entombment* (unfinished)

Michelangelo, the greatest sculptor ever, proves it here in this "painted sculpture" of the crucified Jesus being carried to the tomb. The figures are almost like chiseled statues of Greek gods, especially the musclehead in red rippling beneath his clothes. Christ's naked body, shocking to the medieval church, was completely acceptable in the Renaissance world where classical nudes were admired as an expression of the divine.

In true Renaissance style, balance and symmetry reign. Christ is the center of the composition, flanked by two equally-leaning people who support his body with strips of cloth. They in turn are flanked by two more.

Where Leonardo gave us expressive faces, Michelangelo lets the bodies do the talking. The two supporters strain to hold up Christ's body, and in their tension we, too, feel the great weight and tragedy of their dead god. Michelangelo expresses the divine through the human form.

Raphael — *Pope Julius II* (1511)

The new worldliness of the Renaissance even reached the church. Pope Julius II, who was more a swaggering conquistador than a pious pope, set out to rebuild Rome in Renaissance style (including hiring Michelangelo to paint the Vatican's Sistine Chapel).

Raphael has captured this complex man with perfect realism and psychological insight. On the one hand the pope is an imposing pyramid of power, with fancy rings boasting of wealth and success. But at the same time he's a bent and broken man, his throne backed into a corner, with an expression that seems to say, "Is this all there is?"

In fact, the great era of Florence and Rome was coming to an end. With Raphael's death in 1520, the Renaissance shifted to Venice.

● *Return to the long Room 9.*

Venetian Renaissance (1510–1600)

Big change. The canvases are bigger, the colors brighter. Madonnas and saints are being replaced by goddesses and heroes. And there are nudes—not Michelangelo's lumps of noble, knotted muscle, but smooth-skinned, sexy, golden centerfolds.

Venice got wealthy by trading with the luxurious and exotic East. Its happy-go-lucky art style shows a taste for the finer things in life. But despite all the flashiness and fleshiness, Venetian art still keeps a sense of Renaissance balance.

Titian — *Bacchus and Ariadne* (1523)

In this Greek myth, Bacchus, the god of wine, comes leaping into the picture, his red cape blowing behind him, to cheer up Ariadne (far left), who has been jilted by her lover. Bacchus' motley entourage rattles cymbals, bangs on tambourines, and literally shakes a leg.

Man and animal mingle in this pre-Christian orgy, with leopards, a snake, a dog, and the severed head and leg of an ass ready for the barbecue. Man and animal also literally "mix" in the satyrs—part man, part goat. The fat, sleepy guy in the background has had too much.

Titian uses a pyramid composition to balance an otherwise unbalanced scene. Follow Ariadne's gaze up to the peak of Bacchus' flowing cape, then down along the snake handler's spine to the lower right corner. In addition he "balances" the picture with harmonious colors—most everyone is dressed/undressed in greens and golds that blend into the landscape, while the two main figures stand out with loud splotches of red.

Tintoretto — *The Origin of the Milky Way*

In another classical myth, the god Jupiter places his illegitimate son, baby Hercules, at his wife's breast. Juno says, "Wait a minute. That's not my baby!" Her milk spills upwards, becoming the Milky Way, and down becoming lilies.

Tintoretto places us right up in the clouds, among the gods who swirl around at every angle. An "X" composition unites it all—Juno slants one way while Jupiter slants the other. The result is more dramatic and complex than the stable pyramids of Leonardo and Raphael. Also, notice how Jupiter appears to be flying almost right at us. Such shocking 3-D effects hint at the Baroque art we'll see later.

● *Exit Room 9 at the far end, turning left into the small Room 16 for Dutch art.*

NORTHERN PROTESTANT ART (1600–1700)

We switch from CinemaScope to a nine-inch TV—smaller canvases, subdued colors, everyday scenes, and not even a bare shoulder.

Money shapes art. While Italy had wealthy aristocrats and the powerful Catholic Church to purchase art, the North's patrons were middle-class, hardworking, Protestant merchants. They wanted simple, cheap, no-nonsense pictures to decorate their homes and offices. Greek gods and Virgin Marys were out, hometown folks and hometown places were in—portraits, landscapes, still lifes, and slice-of-life scenes. Painted with great attention to detail, this is art meant not to wow or preach at you, but to be enjoyed and lingered over. Sightsee.

Vermeer — *A Young Woman Standing at a Virginal*

Here we have a simple interior of a Dutch home with a prim virgin playing a "virginal." We've surprised her and she pauses to look up at us. Contrast this quiet scene with, say, Titian's bombastic, orgiastic Bacchus and Ariadne.

The Dutch took (and still take) great pride in the orderliness of their small homes. Vermeer, by framing off such a small world to look

at—from the blue chair in the foreground to the wall in back—forces us to appreciate the tiniest details, the beauty of everyday things. We can meditate on the shawl, the tiles lining the floor, the subtle shades of the white wall and, most of all, the pale diffused light that soaks in from the window. The painting of a nude cupid on the back wall only strengthens this virgin's purity.

● *Stroll down the long Room 28, turning left into Room 27.*

Rembrandt — *Belshazzar's Feast*

The wicked king has been feasting with God's sacred dinnerware when the meal is interrupted. Belshazzar turns to see the finger of God, burning an ominous message into the wall that Belshazzar's number is up. As he turns, he knocks over a goblet of wine. We see the jewels and riches of his decadent life.

Rembrandt captures the scene at the most ironic moment. Belshazzar is about to be ruined. We know it, his guests know it, and judging by the look on his face, he's coming to the same conclusion.

Rembrandt's flair for the dramatic is accentuated by the strong contrast between light and dark. Most of his canvases are a rich, dark brown, with a few crucial details highlighted by a bright light.

Rembrandt — *Self-Portrait Aged 63*

Rembrandt throws the light of truth on ... himself. This craggy self-portrait was done the year he died. Contrast it with one done three decades earlier (hanging nearby). Rembrandt, the greatest Dutch painter, started out as the successful, wealthy young genius of the art world. But he refused to crank out commercial works. Rembrandt painted things that he believed in but no one would invest in—family members, down-to-earth Bible scenes, and self-portraits like these.

Here, Rembrandt surveys the wreckage of his independent life. He was bankrupt, his mistress had just died, and he had also buried several of his children. We see a disillusioned, well-worn, but proud old genius.

● *Return to the long Room 28.*

BAROQUE (1600–1700)

Rubens

This room is full of big, colorful, emotional works by Peter Paul Rubens and others from Catholic Flanders (Belgium). While Protestant and democratic Europe painted simple scenes, Catholic and aristocratic countries turned to the style called "Baroque." Baroque art took what was flashy in Venetian art and made it flashier, gaudy and made it gaudier, dramatic and made it shocking.

Rubens painted anything that would raise your pulse—battles, miracles, hunts and, especially, fleshy women with dimples on all four cheeks. *The Judgment of Paris*, for instance, is little more than an excuse for a study of the female nude, showing front, back, and profile all on one canvas.

● *Exit Room 28 at the far end. To the left, in Room 30, you'll see the large canvas of …*

Van Dyck — *Charles I on Horseback*

Kings and bishops used the grandiose Baroque style to impress the masses with their power. This portrait of England's Catholic, French-educated, divine-right king portrays him as genteel and refined, yet very much in command. Charles is placed on a huge horse to accentuate his power. The horse's small head makes sure that little Charles isn't dwarfed.

Charles ruled firmly as a Catholic king in a Protestant country until England's Civil War (1648), when Charles' genteel head was separated from his refined body by Cromwell and company.

Van Dyck's portrait style set the tone for all the stuffy, boring portraits of British aristocrats who wished to be portrayed as sophisticated gentlemen—whether they were or not.

● *For the complete opposite of a stuffy portrait bust, back-pedal into Room 29 for ...*

Velázquez — The Rokeby Venus

Though horny Spanish kings bought Titian-esque centerfolds by the gross, this work by the king's personal court painter is the first (and, for over a century, the only) Spanish nude. Like a Venetian model, she's posed diagonally across the canvas with flaring red, white, and grey fabrics to highlight her white skin and inflame our passion. About the only concession to Spanish modesty is the false reflection in the mirror—if it really showed what the angle should show, Velázquez would have needed two mirrors ... and a new job.

● *Turning your left cheek to hers, tango into Room 32.*

Michelangelo Merisi de Caravaggio — The Supper at Emmaus

After Jesus was crucified, he rose from the dead and appeared without warning to some of his followers. Jesus just wants a quiet meal, but the man in green, suddenly realizing who he's eating with, is about to jump out of his chair in shock. To the right, a man spreads his hands in amazement, bridging the distance between Christ and us by sticking his hand in our face.

Baroque took reality and exaggerated it. Most artists amplified the prettiness, but Caravaggio exaggerated the grittiness. He shocked the public by using real, ugly, unhaloed people in Bible scenes. Caravaggio's paintings look like a wet dog smells. Reality.

We've come a long way since the first medieval altarpieces that wrapped holy people in a golden foil. From the torn shirts, to the five o'clock shadows, to the uneven part in Jesus' hair, we are witnessing a very human miracle.

● *Leave the Caravaggio room under the sign reading "East Wing, painting from 1700–1900," into Room 33.*

FRENCH ROCOCO (1700–1800)

As Europe's political and economic center shifted from Italy to France, Louis XIV's court at Versailles became its cultural hub. Every aristocrat spoke French, dressed French, and bought French paintings. The Rococo art of Louis' successors was as frilly, sensual, and suggestive as the decadent French court at Versailles. We see their rosy-cheeked portraits and their fantasies: lords and ladies at play in classical gardens, where mortals and gods cavort together.

● *One of the finest examples is the tiny ...*

Boucher — *Pan and Syrinx* (1739)

Rococo art is like a Rubens that got shrunk in the wash—smaller, lighter pastel colors, frillier, and more delicate than the Baroque style. Same dimples, though.

● *Enter Room 34.*

BRITISH (1800–1850)

Constable — *The Hay Wain*

The more reserved British were more comfortable cavorting with nature rather than with the lofty gods. Come-as-you-are poets like Wordsworth found the same ecstasy just being outside. This was the original "back to nature" era.

Constable spent hours in the out-of-doors, capturing the simple majesty of billowing clouds, billowing trees, and everyday human activities. Even British portraits (by Thomas Gainsborough and others) placed refined lords and ladies amid idealized greenery.

This simple style—believe it or not—was considered shocking in its day. The rough, thick paint and crude country settings scandalized art lovers used to the high-falutin', prettified sheen of Baroque and Rococo.

● *Take a hike and enjoy the peaceful English country garden ambience of this room.*

Turner — *The Fighting Téméraire*

Constable's landscape was about to be paved over by the Industrial Revolution. Soon, machines began to replace humans, factories belched smoke over Constable's hay cart, and cloud gazers had to punch the clock. Romantics tried to resist it, lauding the forces of nature and natural human emotions in the face of technological "progress." But, alas, here a modern steamboat symbolically drags a famous but obsolete sailing battleship off into the sunset to be destroyed.

Turner — *Rain, Steam and Speed*

A train emerges from the depths of fog, rushing across a bridge toward us. The red-orange glow of the engine's furnace burns like embers of a fire. (Turner was fascinated by how light penetrates haze.) Through the blur of paints, the outline of a bridge is visible, while in

the center, shadowy figures (spirits?) head down to the river.

Turner's messy, colorful style gives us our first glimpse into the modern art world—he influenced the Impressionists. Turner takes an ordinary scene (like Constable), captures the play of light with messy paints (like Impressionists), and charges it with mystery (like wow).

● *London's Tate Gallery (see the next chapter) has an enormous collection of Turner's work. For now, enter Room 41, past some interesting Pre-Raphaelite paintings (more in the Tate, as well). Fake left, then turn right, past the door leading downstairs to the café and WC, into Room 43. The Impressionist paintings are scattered through Rooms 43–46.*

IMPRESSIONISM AND BEYOND (1850–1910)

For 500 years, a great artist was someone who could paint the real world with perfect accuracy. Then along came the camera and, click, the artist was replaced by a machine. But unemployed artists refused to go the way of the *Fighting Téméraire*.

They couldn't match the camera for painstaking detail, but they could match it—even beat it—in capturing the fleeting moment, the candid pose, the play of light and shadow, the quick impression a scene makes on you. A new breed of artists burst out of the stuffy confines of the studio. They set up their canvases in the open air or carried their notebooks into a crowded café, dashing off quick sketches in order to catch a momentary … impression.

● *Start with the misty Monet train station. (For more information on the following artists, see the chapter on the Orsay Museum.)*

Monet — *Gare St. Lazare* (1877)

Claude Monet, the father of Impressionism, was more interested in the play of light off his subject than the subject itself. Here, the sun filters through the glass roof of the train station and is refiltered through the clouds of steam.

Renoir — *The Umbrellas* (1880s)

View this from about 15 feet away. It's a nice scene of many-colored umbrellas. Now move in close. The "scene" breaks up into almost random patches of bright colors. The "gray" dress of the woman in the foreground is actually built from blotches of lavender, blue, green, yellow, and orange. Up close it looks like a mess, but when you back up to a proper distance, *voilà!* It shimmers. This kind of rough, coarse brushwork (where you can actually see the brushstroke) is one of the telltale signs of Impressionism.

Degas — *Miss La La at the Cirque Fernando* (1879)

Degas, the master of the candid snapshot, enjoyed catching everyday scenes at odd angles.

Manet — *The Waitress (Corner of a Café-Concert)*

Imagine how mundane (and therefore shocking) Manet's quick "impression" of this café must have been to a public that was raised on Greek gods, luscious nudes, and glowing Madonnas.

● *Into Room 44, the biggest canvas, on your left, is …*

Seurat — *Bathers at Asnieres* (1883)

Seurat took the Impressionist color technique to its logical extreme. These figures are "built," dot by dot, like newspaper photos, using small points of different colors. Only at a distance do they blend together to make a hat, a patch of "green" grass, or a bather.

Van Gogh — *Sunflowers* (1888)

In military terms, van Gogh was the point-man of his culture. He went ahead of his cohorts, explored the unknown, and caught a bullet young. He added an emotional element to the Impressionist style, seeming to infuse his love of life even into inanimate objects. These sunflowers, painted with van Gogh's characteristic swirling brushstrokes, seem to shimmer and writhe in either agony or ecstasy—depending on your own mood.

Van Gogh painted these during his stay in southern France, a frenzied time when he himself hovered between bliss and madness. Within two years of painting this, he shot himself.

In his day van Gogh was a penniless nobody, selling only one painting in his whole career. Nowadays, a *Sunflowers* with Vincent's signature on the vase (this is one of a half dozen versions he did) sells for $40 million (that's a salary of about $5,000 a day for 70 years), and it's not even his highest-priced painting. Hmm.

Cézanne — *Bathers (Les Grandes Baigneuses)*

These "bathers" are arranged in strict triangles à la Leonardo—the five nudes on the left form one triangle, the seated nude on the right forms another, and even the background trees and clouds are triangular patterns of paint.

Cézanne uses the Impressionist technique of building a figure with dabs of paint (though his "dabs" are larger-sized "cube" shapes) to make more solid, three-dimensional, geometrical figures in the style of the Renaissance. In the process, his cube shapes helped inspire a radical new art style—"Cube"-ism—bringing us into the 20th century.

Monet — *Water Lilies* (1916)

We've traveled from medieval spirituality to Renaissance realism to Baroque elegance and Impressionist colors. Before you spill out into the 21st-century hubbub of busy London, relax for a second in Monet's garden at Giverny near Paris. Monet planned an artificial garden, rechanneled a stream, built a bridge, and planted these water lilies—a living work of art, a small section of order and calm in a hectic world.

4 Tate Gallery

The Tate is the world's best collection of British art. This is people's art, with realistic paintings rooted in the people, landscape, and stories of the British Isles.

TATE GALLERY

Hours: Daily 10:00–18:00, closed on December 24, 25, 26.

Cost: Free

Tour length: One hour

Getting there: Subway to Pimlico or bus 88 or 77A, or 10-minute walk along Thames from Big Ben.

Information: Free current map at information desk. Free tours (normally 11:00—British, Noon—Impressionism, 14:00—Turner, 15:00—20th century). Tel. 0171/887-8000, recorded information 0171/887-8008, e-mail: information@tate.org.uk. Great bookshop.

Cloakroom: Free

Photography: Without a flash is permitted.

Cuisine art: Coffee shop (affordable gourmet buffet line) and restaurant (expensive, but delightful atmosphere).

Starring: Hogarth, Gainsborough, Reynolds, Blake, Constable, Pre-Raphaelites, and Turner.

TATE GALLERY—OVERVIEW

ORIEN-TATE — Warning: gallery in motion.

Expect changes. The Tate is shedding its wacky modern collection (to be housed in a new museum—opening in May 2000—across the Thames from St. Paul's) and focusing on what it does best: British art. Until the Tate settles down after the Millennium, a painting-by-painting tour is impossible. In this chapter, we'll keep the big picture, seeing the essence of each artist and style, then let the Tate surprise us with its ever-changing wardrobe of paintings.

Orient yourself from the rotunda near the entrance, facing the long central sculpture gallery. The traditional British collection—the core of what we'll see—is in the left half of the museum. The 20th century is to the right. The Turner collection in the Clore Gallery is also to the right.

If you're interested in the Tate's modern art, the Modern Art chapter at the end of this book will be helpful.

● *From the rotunda, walk down the central gallery, turn left, and find Room 1.*

EARLY BRITISH ART (1500–1800)

British artists painted people, horses, countrysides, and scenes from daily life, all done realistically and without the artist passing judgment. (Substance over style.) What you won't see here is the kind of religious art so popular elsewhere. The largely Protestant English abhorred the "graven images" of Catholic saints and the Virgin Mary. Many were even destroyed during the 16th-century Reformation. They preferred landscapes of the quaint English countryside and flesh-and-blood English folk.

Portrait of Lord and Lady Whoevertheyare

These stuffy portraits of a beef-fed society try to make uncultured people look delicate and refined. English country houses often had a long hall built specially to hang family portraits. You could stroll along and see your noble forebears looking down their noses at you. Britain's upper crust in the 1600s had little interest in art other than as a record of themselves along with their possessions—their wives, children, clothes, and guns.

You'll see plenty more portraits in the Tate, right up to modern times. Each era had its own style, some stern and dignified, some more relaxed and elegant.

Stubbs — Various Pictures of Horses

In the 1700s, as British art came into its own, painters started doing more than just portraits. Stubbs was the Michelangelo of horses, studying their anatomy and painting them with incredible detail and realism. Normally, he'd paint the horses first on a blank canvas, then fill in the background landscape around them.

William Hogarth (1697–1764)

Hogarth loved the theatre. "My picture is my stage," he said, "and my men and women my players." The curtain goes up and we see one scene that tells a whole story, often satirizing English high society. Hogarth often painted series based on popular novels of the time.

THE BRITISH COLLECTION

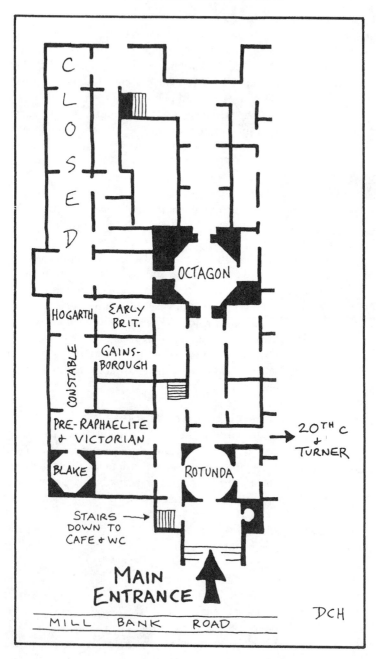

DCH

William Hogarth revelled in the darker side of "merry olde England." An 18th-century Charles Dickens, Hogarth's best paintings were slices of real England. Not content to paint just pretty portraits, he chose models from real life and put them into real-life scenes.

A born Londoner, Hogarth loved every gritty aspect of the big city. You could find him in seedy pubs and brothels, at the half-price ticket booth in Leicester Square, at prizefights, cockfights, duels, and public executions—sketchpad in hand. With biting satire, he exposed the hypocrisy of the upper class ... and exposed the upper classes to the hidden poverty of society's underbelly.

Thomas Gainsborough (1727–1788)

Portraits were still the bread and butter for painters, and Thomas Gainsborough was one of the best. His specialty was showcasing the elegant, educated women of his generation. The results were always natural and never stuffy. The cheeks get rosier, the poses more relaxed, the colors brighter and more pastel, showing the influence of the refined French culture of the court at Versailles. His models' clear, Ivory-soap complexions stand out from the swirling greenery of the background.

Reynolds and the "Grand Style" (1750–1800)

Real life wasn't worthy to be painted. So said Britain's Royal Academy. People, places, and things had to be gussied up with Greek columns, symbolism, and great historic moments, ideally from classical Greece.

By combining history and portraits, they could turn Lord Milquetoast into a heroic Greek patriot, or Lady Bagbody into the *Vénus de Milo*. Combining the Grand Style with landscapes, you got Versailles-type settings of classical monuments amid landscaped greenery.

Sir Joshua Reynolds, the pillar of England's art establishment, stood for all that was noble, upright, tasteful, rational, brave, clean, reverent, and boring. According to Reynolds, art was meant to elevate viewers, appealing to their rational nature and filling them with noble sentiment.

Since so much of the art we'll see from here on was painted in the looming shadow of Reynolds, and since his technique and morals are flawless, let's dedicate a minute's silence to his painting. 59, 58 ... I'll be in the next room.

Constable's Landscapes (1776–1837)

While the Royal Academy thought Nature needed make-up, Constable thought she was just fine. He painted the English landscape just as it is, realistically, and without idealizing it.

Constable's style became more "Impressionistic" near the end of his life—messier brushwork. He often painted full-scale "sketches" of works he'd perfect later (such as the Salisbury cathedral).

It's rare to find a Constable (or any British) landscape that doesn't have the mark of man in it—a cottage, hay cart, country lane, or tiny worker in the field. For him, the English countryside and its people were one.

Cloudy skies are one of Constable's trademarks. Appreciate the effort involved in sketching ever-changing cloud patterns for hours on end. His subtle genius wasn't fully recognized in his lifetime, and he was forced to paint portraits for his keep. The neglect caused him to tell a friend: "Can it therefore be wondered at that I paint continual storms?"

Other Landscapes

Compare Constable's unpretentious landscapes with others you'll find scattered throughout the Tate. Some artists mixed landscapes with intense human emotion to produce huge, colorful canvases of tumultuous storms, burning sunsets, towering clouds, crashing waves, all dwarfing puny humans and their endeavors. Others made supernatural, religious fantasy-scapes. Artists in the "Romantic" style saw the most intense human emotions reflected in the drama and mystery in Nature. God is found within Nature, and Nature is charged with the grandeur and power of God.

The Industrial Revolution (1800–1900)

Think of England at mid-century. New-fangled inventions were everywhere. Railroads laced the land. You could fall asleep in Edinburgh and wake up in London, a trip that used to take days or weeks. But along with technology came factories coating towns with soot, urban poverty, regimentation, and clock-punching. Machines replaced honest laborers, and once-noble Man was viewed as a naked ape.

Strangely, you'll see little of the modern world in paintings of the time—except in reaction to it. Many artists rebelled against "progress" and the modern world. They looked back to ancient Greece as a happier, more enlightened time (Neoclassicism of Reynolds). Or to the Middle Ages (Pre-Raphaelites). Or they escaped the dirty cities to commune with nature (Romantics). Or found a new spirituality in intense human emotions (dramatic scenes from history or literature). Or they left our world altogether (which brings us to …).

William Blake

At the age of four, Blake saw the face of God. A few years later, he ran across a flock of angels swinging in a tree. Twenty years later he was living in a rundown London flat with an illiterate wife, scratching out a thin existence as an engraver. But even in this squalor, ignored by all but a few fellow artists, he still had his heavenly visions, and he described them in poems and paintings.

One of the original space cowboys, Blake was also a unique painter who is often classed with the "Romantics" because he painted in a fit of ecstatic inspiration rather than by studied technique. He painted angels, archangels, thrones, and dominions rather than the dull material world. While Britain was conquering the world with guns and nature with machines, and while his fellow Londoners were growing rich, fat, and self-important, Blake turned his gaze inward, painting the glorious visions of the soul.

Blake's work hangs in a darkened room to protect the watercolors. Enter his mysterious world and let your pupils dilate opium-wide.

His pen and watercolor sketches glow with an unearthly aura. In visions of heaven and hell, his figures have superhero musculature. The colors are almost translucent.

Blake saw the material world as bad, trapping the divine spark inside each of our bodies and keeping us from true communion with God. Blake's prints illustrate his views on the ultimate weakness of material, scientific man. Despite their Greek-god anatomy, his men look noble but tragically lost.

A famous poet as well as painter, Blake summed up his distrust of the material world in a poem addressed to "The God of this World," that is, Satan:

Though thou art worshipped by the names divine
Of Jesus and Jehovah, thou art still
The son of morn in weary night's decline,
The lost traveler's dream under the hill.

Pre-Raphaelites (1850–1880)— Millais, Rossetti, Waterhouse, Burne-Jones, etc.

You'll see medieval damsels in dresses and knights in tights, legendary lovers from poetry, and even a very human Virgin Mary as a delicate young woman. The women wear flowing dresses, with long wavy hair and delicate, elongated, curving bodies. Beautiful.

You won't find Pre-Raphaelites selling flowers at the airport, but this "Brotherhood" of young British artists had a cult-like intensity. (You may see the initials P.R.B.—Pre-Raphaelite Brotherhood—by the artist's signature in some paintings.) After generations of the pompous Grand Style art, the Pre-Raphaelites finally said enough's enough.

They returned to a style "Pre-Raphael." Their art was intended to be "medieval" in its simple style, in the melancholy mood, and often in subject matter. "Truth to Nature" was their slogan. Like the Impressionists who followed, they donned their scarves, barged out of the stuffy studio, and set up outdoors, painting trees, streams, and people as they really were. Despite the Pre-Raphaelite claim to paint life just as it is, this is so beautiful it hurts. Be prepared to suffer, unless your heart is made of stone.

This is art from the cult of femininity, worshipping Woman's haunting beauty, compassion, and depth of soul. (Proto-feminism or retro-chauvinism?) The artists' wives and lovers were their models and muses, and the art echoed their love lives. The people are surrounded by nature at its most beautiful, with every detail painted crystal-clear. Even without the people, there is a mood of melancholy.

The Pre-Raphaelites hated gushy sentimentality and overacting. Their subjects—even in the face of great tragedy, high passions, and moral dilemmas—barely raise an eyebrow. Outwardly, they're reflective, accepting their fate. But subtle gestures and sinuous posture speak volumes. These volumes were footnoted by small objects with symbolic importance placed around them: red flowers denoting passion, lilies for purity, pets for fidelity, and so on.

The colors—greens, blues, and reds—are bright and clear, with everything evenly lit so we see every detail. To get the luminous color, they painted a thin layer of bright paint over a pure white undercoat, which subtly "shines" through. These canvases radiate a pure spirituality, like stained glass windows.

Victorian (1837–1901)

Middle-class Brits loved to see Norman Rockwell–style scenes from everyday life. The style has Pre-Raphaelite realism, but is too sentimental for Pre-Raphaelite tastes.

We see families and ordinary people eating, working, and relaxing. Some works tug at the heartstrings, with scenes of parting couples, the grief of death, or the joy of families reuniting. Dramatic scenes from popular literature get the heart beating. There's the occasional touching look at the plight of the honest poor, reminiscent of Dickens. And many paintings warn us to be good little boys and girls, by showing the consequences of a life of sin.

Stand for a while and enjoy the exquisite realism and human emotions of these Victorian works ... real people painted realistically. Get your fill, because beloved Queen Victoria is about to check out, the modern world is coming, and with it, new art to express modern attitudes.

● *To help ease the transition ...*

J. M. W. Turner (1775–1851)

The Tate has the world's best collection of Turners. Walking through his life's work, you can trace his progression from a painter of realistic historical scenes, through his wandering years, to "Impressionist" paintings of color-and-light patterns.

● *The Turner Collection is in the Clore Gallery, the wing jutting out to the right of the Tate. The main entrance is outside, but you can also enter through Room 18, on the other side of the rotunda.*

THE TURNER COLLECTON

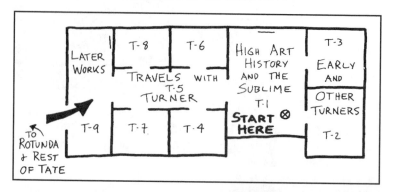

Start in the large square Room T1, marked "High Art, History, and the Sublime." From these early paintings, the collection runs roughly chronologically as you work your way through to Room T9.

Room T1 — High Art, History, and the Sublime

Trained in the Reynolds school of grandiose epics, Turner painted the obligatory big canvases of great moments in history—the Battle of

Waterloo, Hannibal in the Alps, Destruction of Sodom, the Lost Traveler's Checks, Jason and the Argonauts, and various ship-wrecks. Not content to crank them out in the traditional staid manner, he sets them in expansive land-scapes. Nature's stormy mood mirrors the human events, but is so grandiose it dwarfs them.

Room T2

See his self-portrait as a young man and read details of his life.

Room T3 — Travels with Turner

Turner's true love was Nature. And he was a born hobo. Oblivious to the wealth and fame that his early paintings gave him, he set out traveling—mostly on foot—throughout England and the Continent, with a rucksack full of sketchpads and painting gear.

He found the "Sublime" not in the studio or in church, but in the overwhelming power of Nature. The landscapes throb with life and motion.

● *Walk up the hallway (T5) back towards the Tate, popping into the four rooms along the way.*

Room T5 — Italy: Landscape and Antiquity

With *Mona Winks* in hand, Turner visited the great museums of Italy, drawing inspiration from the Renaissance masters. He painted the classical monuments and Renaissance architecture. He copied masterpieces, learned, assimilated, and fused a great variety of styles—a true pan-European vision.

Room T7 — "Venice"

I know what color the *palazzo* is. But what color is it at sunset? Or after filtering through the watery haze that hangs over Venice? Can I paint the glowing haze itself? Maybe if I combine two different colors, and smudge the paint on …

Venice titilated Turner's lust for reflected light. This room contains both finished works and unfinished sketches … uh, which is which?

Room T8 — Marine and Coastal Subjects

Seascapes were his specialty, with waves, clouds, mist, and sky churning and mixing together, all driven by the same forces.

Turner used oils like many painters use watercolors. First he'd lay down a background (a "wash") of large patches of color, then add a few dabs of paint to suggest a figure. The final product lacked photographic clarity but showed the power and constant change in the forces of nature. He was perhaps the most prolific painter ever, with some 2,000 finished paintings and 20,000 sketches and watercolors.

Room T9 — "Later Works"

The older he got, the messier both he and his paintings became. He was wealthy, but died in a rundown dive where he'd set up house with a prostitute. Yet the colors here are brighter and the subjects less pessimistic than in the dark brooding early canvases. His last works—whether landscape, religious, or classical scene—are a blur and swirl of colors in motion, lit by the sun or a lamp burning through the mist.

They're "modern," in that the subject is less important than the style. You'll have to read the title to "get" it.

You could argue that an Englishman helped invent Impressionism, a generation before Monet and ilk boxed the artistic ears of Paris in the 1880s. Turner's messy use of paint to portray reflected light "chunneled" its way to France to inspire the Impressionists.

● *Back in the Tate, on the right side of the rotunda, you'll find works from the 20th century.*

THE MODERN COLLECTION

People who refuse to see modern art must be the same ones who hunch up and squint against the rain. First, it won't kill you. Second, if you'd relax, you might find you enjoy it—at least in small doses. Fortunately, the Tate collection is a light summer shower of art, a little taste of everything, giving a quick overview of the major trends of the past century, arranged pretty much chronologically. (See the chapter on Modern Art for an overview.) Or is it raining too hard in here? Enough Tate? Great. It's late.

5 Westminster Abbey

Westminster Abbey is the greatest church in the English-speaking world. England's kings and queens have been crowned and buried here since 1066. The history of Westminster Abbey and of England are almost the same. A thousand years of English history—3000 tombs, the remains of 29 kings and queens, and hundreds of memorials—lie within its walls and under its stone slabs.

Hours: Monday 9:30–16:45, Tuesday–Friday 9:00–16:45, Saturday 9:00–14:45, additional hours on Wednesday 18:00–19:45, last entry 60 minutes before closing.

Cost: £5, half-price Wednesday evenings. Praying is free; use separate marked entrance.

Tour length: 90 minutes

Getting there: Tube to Westminster.

Information: Up to six guided 90-minute tours are offered daily (£3, tel. 0171/222-7110 for times) and £2 Walkman tours are offered until 15:00 on weekdays and until 13:00 on Saturday. Evensong is on Monday, Tuesday, Thursday, and Friday at 17:00; Saturday and Sunday at 15:00. An organ recital is held at 17:45 on Sunday. Confirm these times at tel. 0171/222-5152.

Photography: Prohibited, except on Wednesday evening.

Starring: Edwards, Elizabeths, Henrys, Annes, Richards, Marys, and the Poets' Corner.

ORIENTATION

You'll have no choice but to follow the steady flow of tourists in through the north transept, wandering among tombstones, circling behind the altar, into "Poets' Corner" in the south transept, detouring through the cloisters and finally back out through the west end of the nave. It's all one way and the crowds can be a real crush. If you have an hour and an interest in English kings and characters, rent the headphones or follow one of the vergers on a live guided tour. They are great. If you prefer to float through at your own tempo, here are the Abbey's top 10 stops:

● *Walk straight in, pick up the map flier which locates the most illustrious tombs and belly up to the barricade in the center.*

1. North Transept

Look down the long, narrow center aisle of the church. It's lined with the praying hands of the Gothic arches, glowing with light from the stained glass. It's clear that this is more than a museum. With saints

WESTMINSTER ABBEY

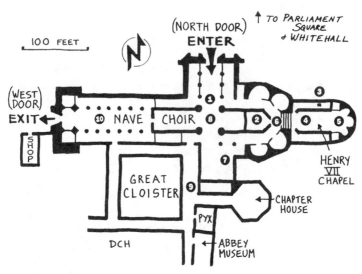

- **1** NORTH TRANSEPT
- **2** TOMB OF EDWARD CONFESSOR
- **3** TOMB OF ELIZABETH
- **4** CHAPEL OF HENRY VII
- **5** ROYAL AIR FORCE CHAPEL
- **6** CORONATION CHAIR
- **7** POETS' CORNER
- **8** CORONATION SPOT
- **9** CLOISTER + MUSEUM
- **10** NAVE

in stained glass, heroes in carved stone, and the bodies of England's greatest under the floorstones, Westminster Abbey is the religious heart of England.

The tomb of the church's founder, King Edward the Confessor, is at the high altar. He felt God wanted him to go to St. Peter's Basilica at the Vatican. But—with Normans thinking conquest—it was too dangerous for him to leave England. Instead, he built this grand church and dedicated it to St. Peter.

The first Abbey was finished just in time to bury Edward (1065) and to crown his foreign rival, William the Conqueror (1066). People prayed on Edward's tomb and after getting fine results, Edward was canonized—the only English king ever to be sainted.

For the next 250 years the Abbey was built and remodeled to become essentially the church you see today, not withstanding an extensive resurfacing in the 19th century. Thankfully, later architects, ignoring building trends of their generation, honored the vision of the original planner and the building was completed in one relatively harmonious style. The nave is the tallest in England. The chandeliers (including 16 given to the Abbey by the Guinness family), each 10 feet tall, look small in comparison.

The north transept (through which you entered) is nicknamed "statesmen's corner" and specializes in famous prime ministers. The musicians are to the right.

● *Now, turn left and follow the crowd. Walk under Robert Peel, the prime minister whose policemen were nicknamed "bobbies" and stroll a few yards into the land of dead kings and queens. Stop at the blocked wooden staircase on your right.*

2. Tomb of Edward the Confessor
The most holy part of the church is above you (where the wooden staircase leads, behind the canopied medieval coffins). Step back to look over the tomb of Henry III (with its lower gold mosaic stones picked clean by thieving hands) and you can see a bit of the black and green coffin of Edward the Confessor. This elevated, central tomb is surrounded by the tombs of eight kings and queens.

● *Continue to the top of the large staircase; detour left into the private burial chapel of Elizabeth I.*

3. Tomb of Queen Elizabeth I
Although there's only one effigy on the tomb (Elizabeth's), there are two queens buried beneath it, each daughters of Henry VIII (by different mothers). Mary—meek, pious, sickly, and Catholic—enforced Catholicism during her reign by burning "heretics" at the stake. Elizabeth—strong, clever, "virginal" and Protestant—steered England on an Anglican course. Her long reign was one of the greatest in English history: a time when England ruled the seas and Shakespeare explored human emotions. The effigy, taken from Elizabeth's death mask, is considered very accurate. Now these two half-sisters who disliked each other in life lie side-by-side for eternity, with a prayer for Christians of all persuasions to live peacefully together.

● *Go with the flow, continuing into the ornate room behind the main altar. Take a seat in …*

4. The Chapel of King Henry VII
The light from the stained glass windows and the colorful banners overhead give the room the festive air of a medieval tournament. The prestigious Knights of Bath meet here, under the magnificent ceiling studded with gold pendants. Unless you're going to Cambridge's

King's College Chapel, this ceiling is the finest English Perpendicular Gothic and fan vaulting you'll see. The brilliant stone ceiling was built in 1509 at the end of the Gothic period.

The knights sit in the wooden stalls with churches on their heads, capped by their own insignia. When the queen worships here, she sits in the corner chair under the carved wooden throne.

Behind the fine painting of a madonna and child is an iron cage housing tombs of the old warrior Henry VII of Lancaster and his wife, Elizabeth of York. Their love and marriage finally settled the "War of the Roses" between the two clans. The combined red-and-white rose symbol decorates the ironwork. Henry VII was the first Tudor king. (Later Tudors included Henry VIII and Elizabeth I.) This exuberant chapel heralds a new optimistic post-war era in English history.

● *Walk past Henry and Elizabeth to the far end of the church. Stand at the bannister in front of the bright modern set of stained glass windows.*

5. *The Royal Air Force Chapel*
Saints in robes and halos mingle with pilots in bomber jackets and parachutes in this tribute to World War II flyers who earned their angel wings in the Battle of Britain. These were the fighters about whom Churchill said, "Never has so much been owed by so many to so few."

The Abbey survived the blitz virtually unscathed. As a memorial, a tiny bit of bomb-damage—the little glassed-over hole in the wall—is left below the windows in the lower lefthand corner. The book of remembrances lists each of the casualties of the Battle of Britain.

Hey. Look down at the floor. You're standing on the grave of Oliver Cromwell, leader of the rebel forces in England's Civil War. Or rather, Cromwell was buried here from 1658 to 1661. Then his corpse was exhumed, hanged, drawn, quartered, and decapitated, with the head displayed on a stake as a warning to future king-killers.

● *Circulate back through the Chapel of Henry VII, pass the side chapel with the tomb of Mary Queen of Scots. Step out of the flow at the top of the stairs to stand before the old chair. Immediately behind the chair is the tomb of Henry VII. Behind that, again, is the tomb of the church's founder, Edward the Confessor.*

6. *The Coronation Chair*
The gold-painted wooden chair waits here—with its back to the high altar—for the next coronation. For every English coronation since 1296, it's been moved to its spot before the high altar to receive the royal buttocks. The chair's legs rest on lions, England's symbol.

● *Continue through the golden gates, out of the royal chapels. Turn left into the south transept. You're in "Poets' Corner."*

7. Poets' Corner

England's greatest contribution to art is not painting, sculpture, or music. It's the written word. Here lie buried the masters of (arguably) the world's most complex and expressive language. (Note that while many writers are honored with plaques and monuments, relatively few are actually buried here.)

Geoffrey Chaucer, 1340–1400, (buried eye-level in the wall under the blue windows) is considered the father of English literature. He was buried here first. Later, Poets' Corner was built around his tomb. His *Canterbury Tales* told of earthy people speaking everyday English. The plaques on the floor are memorials to England's literary greats.

Although Shakespeare is not buried here, a fine statue of this greatest of English writers stands at the end of the transept, overlooking the others. High on the wall opposite Shakespeare, with another death mask–accurate face, is George Frederick Handel (most famous for composing the Messiah). His tomb is on the floor next to Charles Dickens (whose serialized novels brought "literature" to the masses). You'll also find tombs of Samuel Johnson (wrote first English dictionary), Alfred Lord Tennyson (conscience of the Victorian age), and the great English actor Lawrence Olivier. (Olivier disdained the "Method" style of living intense emotions in order to portray them. When his co-star stayed up all night in order to appear haggard for a scene, Olivier said, "My dear boy, why don't you simply try acting?")

● *Walk to the center of the Abbey in front of the high altar. Stand directly under the central spire.*

8. The Coronation Spot

The area between the choir (with the elaborately carved wooden chairs) and the altar is bigger than normal because this is the site where kings and queens are crowned.

Here is where every English coronation since 1066 has taken place. The nobles, in robes and powdered wigs, look on from the choir area. The archbishop stands at the high altar (the table with the candlesticks). The coronation chair is placed in the center of the church, directly below the cross on the ceiling, which is high in the middle of the central tower. Surrounding the whole area are temporary bleachers for V.I.P.'s, creating a "theatre" for this unique spectacle. During Queen Elizabeth's 1953 coronation, seating was created for 7,000 with bleachers going halfway up the rose windows of each transept.

Imagine the day, sometime soon when Prince William becomes king. Long silver trumpets hung with banners will be raised and sound a fanfare, as the monarch-to-be enters the church from the main entrance and parades slowly down the center of the nave, through the choir and up the steps to the altar. After a church service, he'll be seated in the chair, facing the nobles. A royal scepter and orb will be placed in his hands, and—dut, dutta dah—the archbishop lowers the crown of St. Edward the Confessor onto the royal head. Finally, King William will stand up, descend the steps and be presented to the people for their approval. The people will cry, "God save the king!"

● *Before leaving, pause in the center and remember that royalty are also given funerals here. Princess Diana's coffin lay here before the funeral service attended by 2,000. She was then buried on her family estate. Exit the church at the south door, leading to …*

9. The Cloisters and Museum

The church is known as the "Abbey" because it was the headquarters of Benedictine monks—until Henry VIII kicked them out in 1540. The buildings that adjoin the church housed the monks. Cloistered courtyards gave them a place to meditate on God's creation.

Look back at the church through the cloisters. Notice the "flying buttresses," the stone bridges that push in on the church walls, allowing Gothic architects to build so high.

If you're into all this history, pay £1 extra for three more rooms: the Chapter House (where monks had daily meetings, today fine architecture with faded but well-described medieval art), the tiny Pyx Chamber (with an exhibit about the King's treasury), and the Abbey museum (formerly the monks' lounge with a cozy fire and snacks, now a small museum with fascinating exhibits on royal coronations, funerals, and abbey history). Consider the shop, cafeteria, and WC before continuing back into the church for the last stop.

10. Nave

On the floor near the west entrance of the Abbey is the flower-lined Grave of the Unknown Warrior, one ordinary WW I soldier buried in soil from France with lettering made from melted down weapons from that war. Hanging on a column next to it is the United States Congressional Medal of Honor presented to England's WW I dead by General Pershing in 1921. Closer to the door is a memorial to Winston Churchill.

Look back down the nave of the Abbey, filled with the remains of the people who made Britain great. Now step back outside into a city filled with the same kind of people.

6 Westminster Walk

Walk the street that connects the religious and political center of England with the gathering place of today's London. Start halfway across Westminster Bridge first looking upstream (Parliament) and then downstream.

1. Westminster Bridge: View of Big Ben and Parliament

Ding dong ding dong. Dong ding ding dong. Yes indeed, you are in London. Big Ben is actually "Not the clock, not the tower, but the bell that tolls the hour," but since the 14-ton bell is not visible, everyone just calls the whole tower Big Ben. Although Ben (named for a fat bureaucrat) is scarcely older than my great-grandmother, it has quickly become the city's symbol. The tower is 320-feet high with 23-foot clock-faces. The 14-foot minute-hands sweep the length of your body every five minutes.

Big Ben is the north tower of a long building stretching along the Thames. This is the Houses of Parliament.

Britain is ruled from this building. For centuries, it was the home of kings and queens. Then, as democracy was foisted on tyrants, a parliament of nobles was allowed to meet in some of the rooms. Soon, commoners were elected to office, the neighborhood was shot, and royalty moved down the road to Buckingham Palace. The current building, though it looks medieval, was built in the 1800's after a fire gutted old Westminster Palace.

Today, the House of Commons, which is more powerful than the Queen and Prime Minister combined, meets in the north half of the building. The rubber-stamp House of Lords grumbles and snoozes in the southern end of this 1,000-room complex.

2. Westminster Bridge: City View

Until 1750 only London Bridge crossed the Thames. Then a bridge was built here. Downstream and on the other side of the river stands the huge former city hall (GLC or Greater London Council building). In a monumental conflict with conservative Prime Minister Margaret Thatcher, the liberal city government was basically shut down. The GLC building, while now a hotel complex, still seems to snarl across the river at the home of the national government.

(Margaret Thatcher made a huge impact on London life. Until her administration, the standard litmus test to see if someone was insane was to ask "Who's the prime minister?" But in the time of "The Iron Lady," even the certifiably nuts knew who was at the helm.)

WESTMINSTER WALK

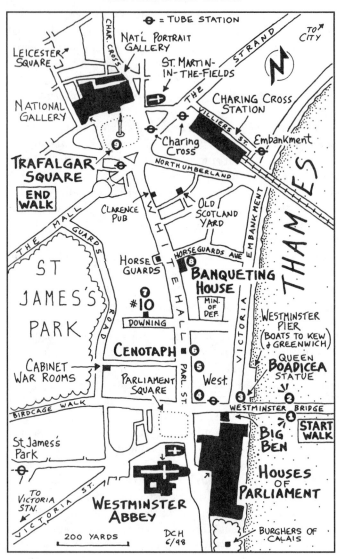

1 - Westminster Bridge:
   Parliament view
2 - Westminster Bridge: city view
3 - Queen Boadicea statue
4 - Parliament Square and
   Westminster Abbey
5 - Walking Whitehall
6 - Cenotaph
7 - #10 Downing St. Ministry
   of Defense
8 - Banqueting House
9 - Trafalgar Square

The GLC building marks the start of London's vibrant new gentrified arts and cultural zone. A pleasant riverside jogging path leads downhill from here past several miles of trendy new restaurants, theaters, and museums including the new Tate Gallery of Modern Art (open in 2000) and the new Globe Theater.

Toward Big Ben, notice the Westminster Pier (boats departing here for Tower of London, Greenwich, and Kew, fine free public WC). Beyond the pier are little green copper lion heads with rings for tying up boats. Before the construction of the Thames Barrier (the world's largest movable flood barrier, downstream near Greenwich), floods were a reoccurring London problem. The police measured the river by these lions. "When the lions drink, the city's at risk."

London's history is tied to the Thames, the highway that links the interior of England with the North Sea. Early in the morning of September 3, 1803, William Wordsworth stood where you're standing and described what he saw:

"This city now doth like a garment wear

The beauty of the morning; silent, bare,

Ships, towers, domes, theaters, and temples lie

Open unto the fields, and to the sky;

All bright and glittering in the smokeless air."

● *Walk to the edge of the bridge to the black statue of a lady on a chariot.*

3. *Boadicea, Queen of the Iceni*
Riding in her two-horse chariot, daughters by her side, this Celtic Xena leads her people against Roman invaders. Julius Caesar had been the first Roman to cross the Channel, but even he was weirded out by the island's strange inhabitants who worshipped trees, sacrificed virgins, and went to war painted blue. Later Romans subdued and civilized them, building roads and making this spot on the Thames— "Londinium"—into a major urban center.

But Boadicea refused to be Romanized. In 60 A.D., after Roman soldiers raped her daughters, she rallied her people, liberated London, and massacred 70,000 Romans. But the brief revolt was snuffed out, and she and her family took poison rather than surrender.

● *There's a civilized public toilet down the stairs, behind Boadicea. Now cross the street and walk under Big Ben to the busy intersection. You should be standing kitty-corner across from a big black statue of Winston Churchill.*

4. *Parliament Square*
The Houses of Parliament and the two big towers of Westminster Abbey are the heart of the medieval city of Westminster. Like Buda

and Pest, London is two cities which grew into one. The City of London (formerly Londinium) was the place to live. But Edward the Confessor decided to build the Abbey here, outside the city walls, in Westminster. And to oversee its construction, he moved his court here and built the Palace of Whitehall at Westminster ... or Westminster Palace. Here in Westminster, the abbey came first, then the palace. And when the king needed to sort out a problem with his subjects, he provided them with a place where their representatives could meet with the king. Gradually this evolved into the parliament buildings which to this day are in what's called the "Palace of Westminster."

The cute little church, which snuggles under the Abbey "like a baby lamb under a ewe," is St. Margaret's Church. Since 1480 this has been the place for a high society wedding.

Parliament Square, the small park between Westminster Abbey and Big Ben, is filled with statues of famous Brits. The statue of Winston Churchill—the man who saved Britain from Hitler—is shown wearing the military coat he wore as he stepped victoriously onto the beaches at Normandy after D-Day. According to tour guides, the statue has a current of electricity running through it to honor Churchill's wish that if a statue is made of him, his head shouldn't be soiled by pigeons.

In 1868, the world's first traffic light was installed on this corner. And speaking of lights, the little yellow lamp atop the concrete post marking the street corner closest to Parliament says "taxi". When a member of parliament needs a taxi, this blinks to hail one.

● *Turn right and walk away from parliament, down Parliament Street which becomes Whitehall. For the rest of this walk you'll be walking along the edge of what was a sprawling palace complex called Whitehall—and a street by that name.*

5. Walking Along Whitehall

Today, Whitehall is the most important street in Britain, lined with the ministries of finance, treasury, and so on. As you walk notice the security measures. For example, iron grates seal off the concrete ditches between the buildings and sidewalks for protection against explosives. Notice also the ornamental arrow-head tops of the iron fences. Originally these were colorfully painted. When Prince Albert died in 1861, Queen Victoria ordered them all painted black. Probably the world's most determined mourner, when her beloved Albert died ("the only one who called her Vickie") she wore black for the standard two-and-a-half year period of mourning for a Victorian widow—and added an extra 38 years.

● *Continue toward the tall square concrete monument in the middle of the road. On your right is a colorful pub, the Red Lion. Across the street, a 225-meter detour down King Charles Street leads to the Cabinet War Rooms, the underground 20-room bunker which was the nerve center for Britain's campaign against Hitler.*

6. Cenotaph

The big white stone monument in the middle of Parliament Street honors those who died in two events that most shaped modern Britain—World Wars I and II. The monumental devastation of these wars helped turn a colonial superpower into a cultural colony of an American superpower.

The actual "cenotaph" is the tomb-shaped slab that sits atop the obelisk. You'll notice no religious symbols on this memorial. It honors the dead from all corners of Britain's empire and from many creeds.

It's hard for an American to understand the impact of the Great War on Europe. It's said that if all the WW I dead from the British Empire were to march four abreast past the Cenotaph, the sad parade would last for seven days.

● *Continue up Parliament Street. Just past the Cenotaph, look across Whitehall at Downing Street, blocked off by an iron security gate.*

7. #10 Downing Street and the Ministry of Defense

Britain's version of the White House is where the Prime Minister and his family live at #10—a hundred yards down the blocked-off street on the right. It looks modest, but the entryway does open up into fairly impressive digs. There's not much to see here unless a V.I.P. happens to drive up. Then the bobbies check credentials, the gates open, the traffic barrier midway down the street drops into its batcave, the car drives in, and then ... the bobbies go back to joking with the tourists again.

The huge bleak building across Whitehall from Downing Street is the Ministry of Defense. This place looks like a Ministry of Defense should. When the building was being built, in the 1930s, they discovered and restored Henry VIII's wine cellar. English soldiers and politicians have drunk together here for 500 years ... that's continuity.

One more security note: the drapes of the MOD are too long for good reason. They come with lead weights on the bottom. If a bomb blew out the windows, the drapes would billow in and contain the flying glass.

In front of the MOD are statues of illustrious defenders of Britain.

"Monty" is Field Marshal Montgomery, the great British general of WW II fame. Monty beat the Nazis in North Africa (defeating "the Desert Fox" at El Alamein). Along with Churchill, Monty breathed confidence back into a demoralized British army, persuading them they could ultimately beat Hitler. Nearby, the statue of Walter Raleigh marks the spot where he was presented to Queen Elizabeth. Nothing marks the spot—a few hundred yards back towards Big Ben—where he was beheaded a few years later. He's buried in St. Margaret's Church.

You may be enjoying the shade of London's plane trees. They do well in the polluted London: roots which work well in clay, waxy leaves which self-clean in the rain, and bark that sheds so the pollution doesn't get into its vascular system.

● *At the equestrian statue you're flanked by the Welsh and Scottish offices. At the next corner you find the Banqueting House. From here you'll cross the street to get close to the horse guards.*

8. Banqueting House

The Banqueting House is just about all that remains of what was once the biggest palace in Europe, stretching from here to the current Halls of Parliament. Henry VIII, Elizabeth I, Charles I, and others lived here. The Banqueting House was the only part of the palace to survive a great fire in 1698.

At 110 feet wide by 55 feet tall by 55 feet deep, the Banqueting House is a perfect double cube. London's first Renaissance building must have been a wild contrast to the higgledy-piggledy sprawl of the Whitehall Palace complex of which it was just one segment.

On January 27, 1649, a man dressed in black appeared at one of the Banqueting House's first floor windows and looked out at a huge crowd that surrounded the building. He stepped out of the window and onto a wooden platform. It was King Charles I. He gave a short speech to the crowd, framed by the magnificent backdrop of the Banqueting House. His final word was, "Remember." Then he knelt and laid his neck on a block as another man in black approached. It was the executioner—who cut off the king's head.

With a plop, the concept of divine monarchy in Britain died. But there would still be kings after Cromwell. In fact, the royalty was soon restored and Charles' son, Charles II, got his revenge here in the Banqueting House by living well. His elaborate parties under the chandeliers of the Banqueting House celebrated the restoration of the monarchy. But from now on, every king would know that he rules by the grace of parliament.

Charles I is remembered today with a statue at one end of Whitehall (in Trafalgar Square, at the base of the tall column), while his killer, Oliver Cromwell, is given equal time with a statue at the other—at the Houses of Parliament.

● *Cross the street for a close look at the horse guards. Continue up Whitehall dipping into the guarded entry court of the next big building with the too-long Ionic columns. These are the offices of the Old Admiralty, headquarters of the British navy. Ponder the scheming that must have gone on behind these walls as the British navy built the greatest empire the earth has ever seen. Across the street behind the old Clarence Pub stood the original Scotland Yard, headquarters of London's crack police force in the days of Sherlock Holmes. Finally, Whitehall opens up into the grand, noisy, traffic filled …*

9. Trafalgar Square

London's "Times' Square" bustles around the monumental column with Admiral Horatio Nelson standing 170 feet high in the crow's nest. Nelson saved England at a time as dark as World War II. In 1805, Napoleon (the Hitler of his day) was poised on the other side of the Channel, preparing to invade England. Meanwhile, a thousand miles away, the one-armed, one-eyed, daring—sometimes reckless—Lord Nelson attacked the French fleet off the coast of Spain at Trafalgar. The French were routed, Britannia ruled the waves, and the once-invincible French army would be slowly worn down and defeated at Waterloo.

Nelson—while victorious—was shot by a sniper in the battle. He died gasping, "Thank God, I have done my duty."

Surrounding the column are four huggable lions—cast from melted down enemy cannons—dying to have their photo taken with you. The artist had never seen a lion before so he used his dog as a model. The legs look like doggie paws. At least his kitten might have had them crossed like felines do.

In front of the column (nearer you) stands the statue of Charles I. Directly behind Charles is a pavement stone marking the center of London.

In medieval times, Westminster was the seat of government but the city action was downstream in London. When people from "the City" and the government needed to meet halfway, it was here. Today, Trafalgar is the center of modern London.

Trafalgar Square feels cohesive because of a bannister which cuts from building to building right around the square. Follow it counter-clockwise from the South Africa house on the right, along St. Martin-in-the-Field church, across the National Gallery, and finally along the Canada house on the left. Harmony.

St. Martin-in-the-Fields was built in 1722. Many Americans feel at home with this church because its style—a church spire atop a classical building—inspired many town churches in New England.

You may see me at the top of Trafalgar Square on December 31, 1999, gazing down Whitehall, waiting for Big Ben to ring me into the future.

PARIS

The Louvre

Orsay Museum

Versailles

Historic Paris Walk

*P*aris, the city of light, has been a beacon to cultured souls for centuries. It represents the finest and most beautiful products of our civilization—cuisine, fashion, literature, art, and escargot forks. It's a city fit for ultimates, from *Vénus de Milo* and *Mona Lisa* to Louis XIV and Napoleon. Gazing at the wonders of this city, even presidents and dictators become mere tourists.

7 The Louvre

Paris walks you through history in two world-class museums—the Louvre (ancient world to 1850) and the Orsay (1850 to 1914, including Impressionism). Start your art-yssey at the Louvre. The Louvre's collection—more than 300,000 works of art—is a full inventory of Western civilization. To cover the entire collection in one visit is in-Seine. We'll enjoy just three of the Louvre's specialties—Greek sculpture, Italian painting, and French painting.

MUSÉE DU LOUVRE

Hours: Wednesday–Monday 9:00–18:00, closed Tuesday, all wings open Wednesday until 21:45, Richelieu wing (only) open until 21:45 on Monday evening. Galleries start closing 30 minutes early. Closed January 1, Easter, May 1, November 1, and Christmas Day. Crowds are worst on Sunday, Monday, Wednesday, and in the morning. Save money and avoid crowds by visiting in the afternoon.

Cost: 45 F, 26 F after 15:00 and on Sunday, those under 18 enter free. Tickets good all day. Re-entry allowed.

Paris Museum Card: All major sightseeing admissions (including Versailles) are covered by a card sold at museums, TI's, and Métro stations (1 day—80 F, 3 days—160 F, 5 days—240 F). Summer lines can be an hour or two long. With this card, you zip straight through.

Tour length: Two hours

Getting there: The Métro stop "Palais Royale Musée de Louvre" is closer to the new entrance than the stop called "Louvre Rivoli." The line into the pyramid—for security checks only, not admission—can be very long. There's a line-skipping, underground shortcut directly from the Métro stop. Signs to "Musée du Louvre" put you in a slick underground shopping mall that connects with the pyramid.

Information: Helpful English-speaking information booth in pyramid (free floor plan). Ninety-minute English tours leave nearly hourly. Tel 01 40 20 50 50, Web site: www.louvre.fr.

Cloakroom: Bags are not permitted. The coat check does not take bags. The bag check is separate from the coat check and may have a much shorter line.

Photography: Without a flash is allowed.

Cuisine art: Most services are clustered in the pyramid. Two cafeterias in the museum, a dozen easy eateries (take the escalator up) just off the underground inverted pyramid (visible from information booth and near Métro entrance), and plenty of cafés and snack bars on rue de Rivoli.

Starring: *Vénus de Milo*, *Winged Victory*, Leonardo, the French painters, Raphael, Titian.

Surviving the Louvre

The Louvre, the world's largest museum, fills three wings in this immense U-shaped palace. The north wing (Richelieu) houses French, Dutch, and Northern art. The east wing (Sully) houses the extensive French painting collection.

We'll concentrate on the south wing (Denon), which houses the Louvre's superstars: ancient Greek sculpture, Italian Renaissance painting, and French Neoclassical and Romantic painting.

Expect changes. The Louvre is in flux for several years as they shuffle the deck. If you can't find a particular painting, ask a guard. Point to the photo in your book and ask, *"Où est?"* (pron: oo ay).

● *From inside the big glass pyramid you'll see signs to the three wings. Head for the Denon wing.*

Escalate up several floors. At the top, go past four statues contemplating their … navels (?), up the final few steps, and get oriented. The pyramid is outside the window. To the right is a staircase capped by the Winged Victory (barely visible).

Now turn left into "salle 4," with Italian sculpture. At the far end, you'll see a large, twisting male nude looking like he's just waking up after a thousand-year nap.

THE LOUVRE—A BIRD'S-EYE VIEW

N

RIGHT BANK

METRO: PALAIS ROYALE
Ⓜ — MUSEE du LOUVRE

RUE DE RIVOLI

TUILERIES GARDENS

RICHELIEU

ARC DU CARROUSEL

AXIS VIEW

TUILERIES PALACE (DESTROYED 1852)

FRENCH + NORTHERN

PEDESTRIAN PASSAGEWAY

FRENCH

ENTRANCE ➡

Ⓜ METRO: LOUVRE RIVOLI

SULLY
COUR CARRÉE

DENON

ITALIAN + FRENCH

GREEK

WINGED VICTORY

CAFES
▫ ▫ ▫▫

QUAI DU LOUVRE

SEINE RIVER

QUAI VOLTAIRE

PONT ROYAL

PONT DU CARROUSEL

PONT DES ARTS (PEDESTRIAN)

DCH

← TO ORSAY MUSEUM (15 MIN WALK)

LEFT BANK

TO LATIN QUARTER → (10 MIN. WALK)

Michelangelo Buonarotti — *Slaves (L'Esclave Mourant and L'Esclave Rebelle)* (c. 1513)

These two statues by earth's greatest sculptor remind us that this museum spans both the ancient and modern worlds. Michelangelo, like his fellow Renaissance artists, learned from the Greeks. The perfect anatomy, twisting poses, and idealized faces look like they could have been done 2,000 years earlier. But these definitely have the personal touch of Michelangelo.

The so-called *Dying Slave* (also called the *Sleeping Slave*, who looks like he should be stretched out on a sofa) twists listlessly against his T-shirt-like bonds, revealing his smooth skin. Compare the polished detail of the rippling, bulging left arm with the sketchy details of the face and neck. With Michelangelo, the body does the talking. Since Michelangelo rarely finished a work enough to get to the polishing stage, he must have loved this one, probably the most sensual nude ever done by the master of the male body.

The *Rebellious Slave* fights against his bondage. His shoulders turn one way while his head and leg turn the other, straining to get free. He even seems to be trying to free himself from the rock he's made of. Michelangelo said that his purpose was to carve away the marble to reveal the figures God put inside. This Slave shows the agony of that process and the ecstasy of the result.

● *Now let's see the source of Michelangelo's inspiration—the classical world. Backtrack to the foot of the staircase with the* Winged Victory *on top. (Look for the* Borghese Gladiator *en route; see map and description below.) We'll climb these stairs later, but first go down them (to the left) and into a world of classical statues.*

GREEK STATUES (600 B.C.–A.D. 1)

Every generation defines beauty differently. For the Greeks, beauty was balance, combining opposites in just the right proportions. They thought that the human body—especially the female form—embodied the order they saw in the universe. In the Louvre, we'll see a series of "Venuses" throughout history. Their different poses and gestures tell us about the people who made them. We'll see how the idea of beauty (as balance) began in ancient Greece, how it evolved, and then how it resurfaced in the Renaissance 2,000 years later.

Pre-Classical Greece

These statues are noble but crude. A woman (*Core*) is essentially a column with breasts. A young, naked man (*Couros*) stands rigid like he's got a gun to his back—hands at sides, facing front, with sketchy muscles and a mask-like face. "Don't move."

The early Greeks who admired such statues found stability more attractive than movement. Like their legendary hero, Odysseus, the Greek people had spent generations wandering, warweary, and longing for the comforts of a secure home. The noble strength and sturdiness of these works looked beautiful.

GREEK STATUES

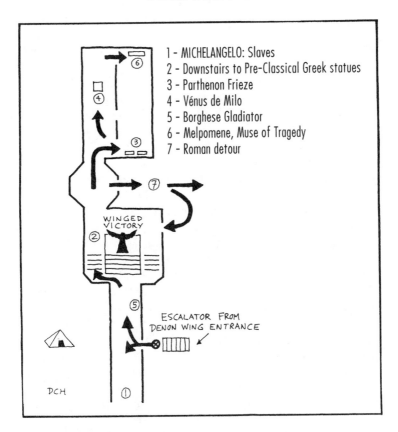

1 - MICHELANGELO: Slaves
2 - Downstairs to Pre-Classical Greek statues
3 - Parthenon Frieze
4 - Vénus de Milo
5 - Borghese Gladiator
6 - Melpomene, Muse of Tragedy
7 - Roman detour

● *Continue through the Greek section, where you'll find two relief sculptures from the Parthenon.*

Golden Age Greece

The great Greek cultural explosion that changed the course of history happened in a 50-year stretch (around 450 B.C.) in Athens, a city smaller than Muncie, Indiana. They dominated the ancient world through brain, not brawn, and the art shows their love of rationality and order.

In a sense, we're all Greek. Democracy, mathematics, theater, literature, and science were practically invented in ancient Greece. Most of the art that we'll see in the Louvre either came from Greece or was inspired by it.

Parthenon Frieze (Fragment de la Frise des Panathenees) (c. 440 b.c.)
These stone fragments once decorated the exterior of the greatest Athenian temple, the Parthenon. The right panel shows a half-man/half-horse creature sexually harassing a woman. It tells the story of how these rude Centaurs crashed a party of humans. But the Greeks fought back and threw the brutes out, just as Athens (metaphorically) conquered its barbarian neighbors and became civilized.

The other relief shows the sacred procession of young girls who marched up the hill every four years with an embroidered veil for the 40-foot statue of Athena—the goddess of wisdom. The maidens, carved in only a couple of inches of stone, are amazingly realistic and three-dimensional—more so than anything we saw in the Pre-Classical period. They glide along horizontally (their belts and shoulders all in a line), while the folds of their dresses drape down vertically. The man in the center is relaxed and realistic—notice the veins in his arm.

Greeks of the Golden Age valued the Golden Mean, that is, balance. The ideal person was well-rounded—an athlete and a bookworm, a lover and a philosopher, a Realtor who plays the piano, a warrior, and a poet. In art, the balance between stability and movement made beauty. The maidens' pleated dresses make them look as stable as fluted columns, but their arms and legs step out naturally—the human form is emerging from the stone.

● *Now seek the goddess of love. You'll find her floating above a sea of worshiping tourists. It's been said that, among the warlike Greeks, this was the first statue to unilaterally disarm.*

Vénus de Milo (Aphrodite) (c. 100 b.c.)

The *Vénus de Milo* (or goddess of love from the Greek island of Milos) created a sensation when it was discovered in 1820. Europe was already in the grip of a classical fad, and this statue seemed to sum up all that ancient Greece stood for. The Greeks pictured their gods in human form, telling us they had an optimistic view of the human race.

The *Vénus de Milo* is a harmonious balance of opposites. Venus is stable, resting her weight on one leg (called *contrapposto*, or "counter-pose"), yet her other leg is slightly raised, ready to take a step. This slight movement sets her whole body in motion, though she remains perfectly still.

Split Vénus down the middle (left and right) and see how the movement of one half balances the other. As she lifts her left leg, her right shoulder droops down. And as her knee points one way, her head turns the other. The twisting pose gives an S-curve to her body (especially noticeable from the back view) that the Greeks and succeeding generations found beautiful.

Other opposites balance as well, like the rough-cut texture of her dress (size 14) that sets off the smooth skin of her upper half. She's actually made from two different pieces of stone plugged together at the hips (the seam is visible). The face is realistic and anatomically accurate, but it's also idealized, a goddess, too generic, and too perfect. This isn't any particular woman but Everywoman—all the idealized features that the Greeks found beautiful.

What were her missing arms doing? Several archaeologists' theories are on a plaque nearby. Some say her right arm held her dress while her left arm was raised. Others say she was hugging a man statue or leaning on a column. I say she was picking her navel.

● *This statue is interesting and different from every angle. Remember the view from the back—we'll see it again later. Orbit Vénus. Make your re-entry to earth at the ...*

Borghese Gladiator (Guerrier Combattant, Dit Gladiateur Borghese)

We see a fighting gladiator at the peak of action. He blocks a blow with the shield that used to be attached to his left arm while his right hand, weighted with an early version of brass knuckles, prepares to deliver the counter-punch. His striding motion makes a diagonal line from his left foot up his leg, along the body, and out the extended arm. It's a dramatic, precariously balanced pose.

This is the motion and emotion of Greece's Hellenistic Age, the time after the culture of Athens was spread around the Mediterranean by Alexander the Great (c. 325 B.C.).

Golden Age Greeks might have considered this statue ugly. His ripling, knotted muscles are a far cry from the more restrained Parthenon sculptures and the soft-focus beauty of *Vénus*. And the statue's off-balance pose leaves you hanging, like an unfinished melody. But Hellenistic Greeks loved these cliff-hanging scenes of real-life humans struggling to make their mark. The artist himself made his mark, signing the work proudly on the tree trunk: "Agasias of Ephesus, son of Dositheos, did this."

Greece went from Pre-Classical stiffs to Golden Age balance (*Vénus*). Then Hellenistic art tipped the balance from stability to movement.

● *Before leaving Greece, wander among the Greek statues near the Vénus de Milo. Try to find even one that's not contrapposto. Before heading back upstairs, take a ...*

Roman Detour

The Romans were great conquerors, but bad artists. Fortunately for us, they had a huge appetite for Greek statues and made countless copies. They took the Greek style and wrote it in capital letters—like the huge statue of Melpomene, holding the frowning mask of tragic plays.

One area the Romans excelled in was realistic portrait busts, especially of their emperors, who were worshiped as gods on earth. Stroll among the Caesars and try to see the man behind the public persona—Augustus, the first emperor, and his wily wife, Livia; Nero ("Neron") who burned part of his own city; Hadrian (who popularized the beard), crazy Caligula, the stoic Marcus Aurelius, and Claudius of "I" fame.

The Roman rooms also contain sarcophagi and an impressive mosaic floor. Weary? Relax with the statues in the Etruscan Lounge.

● *Now ascend the staircase to the ...*

Winged Victory of Samothrace (Victoire de Samothrace)

This woman with wings, poised on the prow of a ship, once stood on a hilltop to commemorate a great naval victory. Her clothes are windblown and sea-sprayed, clinging to her body like the winner of a wet T-shirt contest. (Notice the detail in the folds of her dress around the navel, curving down to her hips.) Originally her right arm was stretched high celebrating the victory like a Super Bowl champion, waving a "we're-number-one" finger.

This is the *Vénus de Milo* gone Hellenistic—a balance of opposites that produces excitement, not grace. As Victory strides forward, the wind blows her and her wings back. Her feet are firmly on the ground, but her wings (and missing arms) stretch upward. She is a pillar of vertical strength while the clothes curve and whip around her. These opposing forces create a feeling of great energy making her the lightest two-ton piece of rock in captivity.

In the glass case nearby is *Victory's* open right hand, discovered in 1950, a century after the statue itself was unearthed. Also in the case is the statue's finger. When the French discovered this was in Turkey they negotiated with the Turkish government for rights to it. Considering all the other ancient treasures the French had looted from Turkey in the past, the Turks thought it only appropriate to give France the finger.

● *Enter the octagonal room to the left of the* Winged Victory *and bench yourself under a window. Look out towards the pyramid.*

FRENCH HISTORY

The Louvre as a Palace
The Louvre, a former palace, was built in stages over several centuries. On your right (the east wing) was the original medieval fortress. Next, another palace, the Tuileries, was built 500 yards to the west—in the open area past the pyramid and past the triumphal arch. Succeeding kings tried to connect these two palaces, each one adding another section onto the long, skinny north and south wings. Finally, in 1852 after three centuries of building, the two palaces were connected creating a rectangular Louvre. Soon after that, the Tuileries palace burned down during a riot, leaving the U-shaped Louvre we see today.

The glass pyramid was designed by the American architect I. M. Pei. Many Parisians hated the pyramid, like they used to hate another new and controversial structure 100 years ago—the Eiffel Tower.

The plaque above the doorway to the Apollo Gallery (Galerie d'Apollon) explains that France's Revolutionary National Assembly (the same people who brought you the guillotine) founded this museum in 1793. What could be more logical? You behead the king, inherit his palace and art collection, open the doors to the masses, and *voilà!* you've got Europe's first public museum. Major supporters of the museum are listed on the walls—notice all the Rothschilds.

● *Enter the Apollo Gallery (Galerie d'Apollon).*

The Apollo Gallery
The Gallery gives us a feel for the Louvre as the glorious home of the French kings (before Versailles). Imagine a chandelier-lit party in this room: drenched in stucco and gold leaf, with tapestries of leading

Frenchmen and paintings with mythological and symbolic themes.

In the glass case at the far end, you'll find the crown jewels. There's the jewel-studded crown of Louis XV; the 140-carat Regent Diamond worn by Louis XV, Louis XVI, and Napoleon; and the dragon-shaped 107-carat Côte de Bretagne Ruby. You'll also see the pearl and diamond earrings worn by Napoleon's wife, Josephine, and the golden crown of the pin-headed Empress Eugenie.

In another glass case is the cameo crown of that great champion of democracy, Napoleon—we'll see this crown in a painting later.

The inlaid tables made from marble and semi-precious stones and many other art objects show the wealth of France, Europe's #1 power for two centuries.

● *The Italian collection is on the other side of the* Winged Victory. *Cross to the other side, past her damaged digit, and pause at the two fresco paintings on the wall to the left.*

THE ITALIAN RENAISSANCE

A thousand years after Rome fell, plunging Europe into the Dark Ages, the Greek ideal of beauty was "reborn" in 15th-century Italy. This was the Renaissance, the cultural revival of ancient art.

In these two frescoes by the Italian Renaissance artist Botticelli, we see echoes of ancient Greece. The maidens, with their poses, clear sculptural lines, and idealized beauty, are virtual *Vénus de Milos* with clothes.

The key to Renaissance painting was realism, and for the Italians "realism" was spelled "3-D." Painters were inspired by the realism and balanced beauty of Greek sculpture.

● *The Italian collection—including* Mona Lisa—*is scattered throughout the next few rooms, in the long Grand Gallery, and in adjoining rooms. To see the paintings in chronological order may require a little extra shoe leather. When in doubt, show the photo to a guard and ask, "Où est?"*

Medieval and Early Renaissance Italian (1300–1500)

Painting a 3-D world on a 2-D surface is tough, and after a millennium of Dark Ages, artists were rusty. Living in a religious age, they mostly painted altarpieces full of saints, angels, Madonnas, and crucifixes floating in an ethereal gold-leaf heaven. Gradually, they brought these otherworldly scenes down to earth.

Painters like Giotto, Fra Angelico, and Uccello broke Renaissance ground by learning to paint realistic, 3-D humans. Then they placed them in a painted scene with a definite foreground, background, and middle ground to create the illusion of depth. Composition was simple, but symmetrically balanced in the Greek style—two angels to the left, two to the right, and so on. Art was a visual sermon, appreciated for its moral message not its beauty.

Mantegna — *St. Sebastian*

No, this isn't the patron saint of porcupines. He's a Christian martyr, though he looks more like a classical Greek statue. Notice the *contrapposto* stance and the Greek ruins scattered around. His executioners look like ignorant medieval brutes bewildered by this enlightened Renaissance Man. Italian artists were learning how to create human realism and earthly beauty on the canvas. Let the Renaissance begin.

● *The long Grand Gallery displays Italian Renaissance painting, some masterpieces, some not. Mona Lisa is in a room about halfway down on the right.*

The Grand Gallery

The Grand Gallery was built in the late 1500s to connect the old palace with the Tuileries palace. From the doorway look to the far end and consider this challenge: I hold the world's record for the Grand Gallery Heel-Toe-Fun-Walk-Tourist-Slalom—end to end in one minute 58 seconds, two injured. Time yourself—it's a good break, if a bit of a detour.

Along the way, notice some of these general features of Italian Renaissance painting: (1) *Religious*—There are lots of Madonnas, children, martyrs, and saints. (2) *Symmetrical*—The Madonnas are flanked by saints, two to the left, two to the right, and so on. (3) *Realistic*—Real-life human features are especially obvious in the occasional portrait. (4) *3-Dimensional*—Every scene gets a spacious setting with a distant horizon. (5) *Classical*—You'll see some Greek gods and classical

THE GRAND GALLERY—ITALIAN AND FRENCH BIGGIES

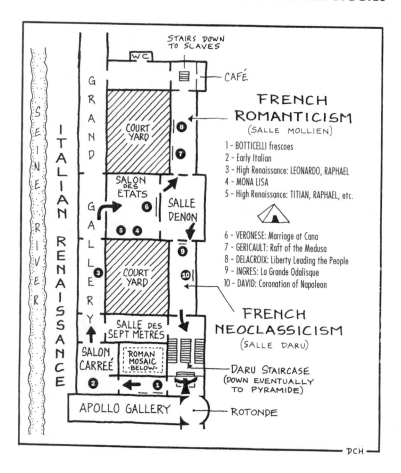

STAIRS DOWN
TO SLAVES

WC

CAFÉ

SEINE RIVER

ITALIAN RENAISSANCE

GRAND GALLERY

COURT YARD

SALON DES ETATS

COURT YARD

SALLE DES SEPT MÈTRES

SALON CARREÉ

ROMAN MOSAIC -BELOW-

APOLLO GALLERY

SALLE DENON

FRENCH ROMANTICISM
(SALLE MOLLIEN)

1 - BOTTICELLI frescoes
2 - Early Italian
3 - High Renaissance: LEONARDO, RAPHAEL
4 - MONA LISA
5 - High Renaissance: TITIAN, RAPHAEL, etc.

6 - VERONESE: Marriage at Cana
7 - GERICAULT: Raft of the Medusa
8 - DELACROIX: Liberty Leading the People
9 - INGRES: La Grande Odalisque
10 - DAVID: Coronation of Napoleon

FRENCH NEOCLASSICISM
(SALLE DARU)

DARU STAIRCASE
(DOWN EVENTUALLY TO PYRAMIDE)

ROTONDE

DCH

nudes, but even Christian saints pose like Greek statues, and Mary is a "Venus" whose face and gestures embody all that was good in the Christian world.

Before you reach *Mona*, look for other masterpieces by Leonardo, Raphael, and Titian (see below).

● *Have a seat again and prepare for the* Mona Lisa *mob scene. Best to read ahead here.*

Italian High Renaissance (1500–1600)

The two masters of Renaissance grace and balance were Raphael and Leonardo da Vinci.

Leonardo was the consummate Renaissance Man. Musician, sculptor, engineer, scientist, and sometimes painter, he combined knowledge from all areas to create beauty. If he were alive today he'd create a Unified Field theory in physics—and set it to music.

Leonardo was already an old man when Francois I invited him to France. He took a few paintings with him. One was a portrait of a Lisa del Giocondo, the wife of a wealthy Florentine merchant. When he arrived, Francois immediately fell in love with the painting, making it the centerpiece of the small collection of Italian masterpieces that would, in three centuries, become the Louvre Museum. He called it *La Gioconda*. We know it as a contraction of the Italian for "my lady Lisa"—*Mona Lisa*.

Advance warning: *Mona* may disappoint you. She's smaller than you'd expect, darker, engulfed in a huge room, and hidden behind a glaring pane of glass. So, you ask, "Why all the hubbub?" Let's take a closer look. Like any lover, you've got to take her for what she is, not what you'd like her to be.

● *Follow the crowds and the signs to* Mona Lisa *in the Salle des Etats.*

Leonardo da Vinci — *Mona Lisa*

The famous smile attracts you first. Leonardo used a hazy technique called *sfumato*, blurring the edges of Mona's mysterious smile. Try as you might, you can never quite see the corners of her mouth. Is she happy? Sad? Tender? Or is it a cynical supermodel's smirk? Every viewer reads it differently, projecting his own mood onto Lisa's enigmatic face. *Mona* is a Rorschach inkblot ... so how are you feeling?

Now look past the smile and the eyes that really do follow you (most portraits do) to some of the subtle Renaissance elements that make this work work. The body is surprisingly massive and statuelike, a perfectly balanced pyramid turned at three-quarters angle so that we can see its mass. Her arm is resting lightly on the chair's armrest almost on the level of the frame itself, like she's sitting in a window looking out at us. The folds of her sleeves and her gently folded hands are remarkably realistic and relaxed. The typical Leonardo landscape shows distance by getting hazier and hazier.

The overall mood is one of balance and serenity, but there's also an element of mystery. Her smile and long-distance beauty are subtle and elusive, tempting but always just out of reach like strands of a street-singer's melody drifting through the Métro tunnel. *Mona* doesn't knock your socks off, but she winks at the patient viewer.

● *The following masterpieces by Leonardo, Raphael, and Titian are either here in the* Mona Lisa *room (Salle des Etats) or back out in the Grand Gallery.*

Leonardo da Vinci — *Virgin, Child, and St. Anne (La Vierge, l'Enfant Jesus, et Sainte Anne)*

Three generations—grandmother, mother, and child—are arranged in a pyramid form with Anne's face as the peak and the lamb as the lower right corner. Within this balanced structure, Leonardo sets the figures in motion. Anne's legs are pointed to our left. (Is Anne Mona? Hmm.) Her daughter Mary, sitting on her lap, reaches to the right. Jesus looks at her playfully while turning away. The lamb pulls away from him. But even with all the twisting and turning, this is still a placid scene. It's balanced.

There's a psychological kidney-punch in this happy painting. Jesus, the picture of childish joy, is innocently playing with a lamb—the symbol of his inevitable sacrificial death.

The Louvre has the greatest collection of Leonardos in the world—all five of them. Don't miss the neighboring *Madonna of the Rocks* and his androgynous *John the Baptist.*

Raphael — *La Belle Jardinière*

Raphael (pron: roff-eye-ELL) perfected the style Leonardo pioneered. This Madonna, Child, and John the Baptist is also a balanced pyramid with hazy grace and beauty. Mary is a mountain of maternal tenderness (the title translates as "The Beautiful Kindergarten Teacher"), eyeing her son with a knowing look. Jesus looks up innocently, standing *contrapposto* like a chubby Greek statue.

With Raphael, the Greek ideal of beauty reborn in the Renaissance reached its peak. His work spawned so many imitators who cranked out sickly sweet generic Madonnas that we often take him for granted. Don't. This is the real thing.

While the *Jardinière* has an idealized beauty, Raphael could deliver photo-realism, too. See his portrait of black-hatted, clear-eyed *Balthazar Castiglione.*

Titian — *Pastoral Symphony (Le Concert Champêtre)*

Venus enters the Renaissance in this colorful work by Titian the Venetian (they rhyme). The nymph turning toward the well at left is like a Titian reconstruction of the *Vénus de Milo,* but what a difference! The Greek Venus was cold and virginal but these babes are hot, voluptuous, sensual.

The three seated figures form a pyramid, giving the scene a balanced, classical beauty, but this appeals more to the senses than to the mind. The golden glow of the skin, the ample flesh, and hazy outlines became the standard for centuries of female nudes. French painters, especially, learned from Titian's rich colors and sensual beauty.

● *The huge canvas at the far end of the Salle des Etats is ...*

Veronese — *Marriage at Cana*

Stand 10 steps away from this enormous canvas to where it just fills your field of vision, and suddenly ... you're in a party! Pull up a glass of wine. This is the Renaissance love of beautiful things gone hog-wild. Venetian artists like Veronese painted the good life of rich, happy-go-lucky Venetian merchants.

In a spacious setting of Renaissance architecture we see colorful lords and ladies decked out in their fanciest duds, feasting on a great spread of food and drink while the musicians fuel the fires of good fun. Servants prepare and serve the food, jesters play, and animals roam. In the upper left, a dog and his master look on. A sturdy linebacker in yellow pours wine out of a jug, while nearby a ferocious cat battles a lion.

Believe it or not, this is a religious work showing the wedding celebration where Jesus turned water into wine. And there's Jesus in the dead center of 130 frolicking figures wondering if maybe wine coolers might not have been a better choice. With true Renaissance optimism, Venetians pictured Christ as a party animal, someone who loved the created world as much as they did.

Now, let's hear it for the band! On bass—the bad cat with the funny hat—Titian the Venetian! And joining him on viola—Crazy Veronese!

● *Exit behind the* Marriage at Cana *into the Salle Denon. The grand Neoclassical room is to your right and the dramatic Romantic room is on your left. They feature the most exciting French canvases in the Louvre. In the Neoclassical room, kneel before the largest canvas in the Louvre.*

FRENCH PAINTING — NEOCLASSICAL (1780–1850)

J. L. David — *The Coronation of Napoleon*

France's last kings lived in a fantasy world, far out of touch with the hard lives of their subjects. The people revolted, and this decadent world was decapitated—along with the head of state, Louis XVI. Then, after a decade of floundering under an inefficient revolutionary government, France was united by a charismatic, brilliant, temperamental upstart general who kept his feet on the ground, his eyes on the horizon, and his hand in his coat—Napoleon Bonaparte.

Napoleon quickly conquered most of Europe, and insisted on being made emperor (not merely king) of this "New Rome." He staged an elaborate coronation ceremony in Paris. The painter David (pron: dah-VEED) recorded it for posterity.

We see Napoleon holding aloft the crown—the one we saw in the Apollo Gallery. He has just made his wife, Josephine, the empress, and she kneels at his feet. Seated behind Napoleon is the pope who journeyed from Rome to place the imperial crown on his head. But Napoleon felt that no one was worthy of the task. At the last moment, he shrugged the pope aside, grabbed the crown, held it up for all to see ... and crowned himself. The pope looks p.o.'d.

The radiant woman in the gallery in the background center wasn't actually there. Napoleon's mother couldn't make it to see her boy become the most powerful man in Europe, so he had her painted in anyway. (There's a key on the frame telling who's who in the picture.)

The traditional place of French coronations was the ultra-Gothic Notre Dame cathedral. But Napoleon wanted a setting that would reflect the glories of Greece and the grandeur of Rome. So interior decorators erected stage sets of Greek columns and Roman arches to give the cathedral the architectural political correctness you see in this painting. (The *Pietà* statue on the right edge of the painting is still in Notre Dame today.)

David was the new republic's official painter and propagandist in charge of costumes, flags, and so on for all public ceremonies and spectacles. His "Neoclassical" style influenced French fashion. Take a look at his portrait of *Madame Récamier* nearby, showing a modern Parisian woman in ancient garb and Pompeii hairstyle reclining on a Roman couch. Nearby paintings such as *The Death of Socrates* and the *Oath of the Horatii (Le Serment des Horaces)* are fine examples of Neo-classicism with Greek subjects, patriotic sentiment, and a clean, simple style.

Ingres — *La Grande Odalisque*

Take *Vénus de Milo*, turn her around, lay her down, and stick a hash pipe next to her and you have the *Grande Odalisque*. Okay, maybe you'd have to add a vertabra or two.

Using clean, polished, sculptural lines, Ingres (pron: ANG-gruh, with a soft "gruh") exaggerates the S-curve of a standing Greek nude. As in the *Vénus de Milo*, rough folds of cloth set off her smooth skin. The face too has a touch of *Vénus'* idealized features (or like Raphael's kindergarten teacher), taking nature and improving on it. Also, contrast the cool colors of this statue-like nude with Titian's golden girls.

The link with *Vénus de Milo* is even more apparent in Ingres' *La Baioneuse*, where he preserves Venus' backside for posterior—I mean, posterity.

● *Cross back through the Salle Denon and into the opposite room gushing with …*

ROMANTICISM (1800–1850)

Géricault —
The Raft of the Medusa (Le Radeau de la Méduse)

Not every artist was content to copy the simple, unemotional style of the Golden Age Greeks. Like the ancient Hellenists they wanted to express motion and emotion. In the artistic war between hearts and minds, the heart-style was known as Romanticism. It was the complete flip-side of Neoclassicism, though they both flourished in the early 1800s.

What better setting for an emotional work than a shipwreck? This painting was based on the actual sinking of the ship *Medusa* off the coast of Africa. The survivors barely did, floating in open seas on a raft, suffering hardship and hunger, even resorting to cannibalism—all the exotic elements for a painter determined to shock the public and arouse their emotions.

That painter was young Géricault (pron: zher-ee-KO). He'd honed his craft sketching dead bodies in the morgue and the twisted faces of lunatics in asylums. Here he paints a tangle of bodies and lunatics sprawled over each other. The scene writhes with agitated, ominous motion—the ripple of muscles, churning clouds, and choppy seas. On the right is a deathly-green corpse sprawled overboard. In the face of the man at left cradling a dead body, we see the despair of spending weeks stranded in the middle of nowhere.

But wait. There's a stir in the crowd. Someone has spotted something. The bodies rise up in a pyramid of hope culminating in a waving flag. They wave frantically trying to catch the attention of the tiny, tiny ship on the horizon, their last desperate hope ... which did finally save them. Géricault uses rippling movement and powerful colors to catch us up in the excitement. If art controls your heartbeat, this is a masterpiece.

Delacroix — *Liberty Leading the People (La Liberté Guidant le Peuple)*

France is the symbol of modern democracy. They weren't the first (America was), nor are they the best working example of it, but they've had to work harder to achieve it than any country. No sooner would they throw one king or dictator out than they'd get another. They're now working on their Fifth Republic.

In this painting, the year is 1830. The Parisians have taken to the streets once again to fight royalist oppressors. There's a hard-bitten proletarian with a sword (far left), an intellectual with a top hat and a sawed-off shotgun, and even a little boy brandishing pistols.

Leading them on through the smoke and over the dead and dying is the figure of Liberty, a strong woman waving the French flag. Does this symbol of victory look familiar? It's the *Winged Victory*, wingless and topless. (You may also recognize it from the 100-franc note.)

Liberty stirs our emotions. Delacroix (pron: dell-ah-KWAH) purposely uses only three major colors in the composition—the red, white, and blue of the French flag.

This symbol of freedom is a fitting end to a tour of the Louvre, the first museum ever opened to the common rabble of humanity. It's a reminder that the good things in life don't belong only to a small, wealthy part of society, but to everyone—even us common rabble. And liberty is worth the fight. The motto of France is *"Liberté, Egalité, Fraternité"*—liberty, equality, and the brotherhood of all people.

● *Finished? I am. Où est la sortie?*

MORE FRENCH? THE LOUVRE, PART DEUX

While you've seen the Louvre's greatest hits (as judged by postcards sold), the Louvre has the best collection of French paintings anywhere. And you've only seen a few of these.

French painting from the 14th through the 19th centuries is displayed in the Richelieu and Sully wings (second floor). It's laid out chronologically; just follow the room numbers. If you go, plan on an hour to see it all.

● *From the pyramid, enter the Richelieu wing. Past the ticket-taker, turn right and go up three escalators to the top. You're looking for* Jean le Bon *(a small portrait in a glass case).*

Early French Painting (1300–1650)

Jean II le Bon

In an age when religious paintings were the norm, this was a breakthrough—the first easel portrait of a French king ever. Saints, angels, and Madonnas were headed out, real people were coming in.

● *Follow the rooms in order, and you'll see French art unfold. I've selected about one painting per room.*

Avignon Pietà (Quarton-Pietà de Villeneuve-les-Avignon)

This simple, poignant scene of Mary grieving over her crucified son is not realistic or exactly "beautiful"—but you can't deny its emotional power. In fact, it's the unrealistic distortion of Jesus' body that makes it so forceful. His corpse, suffering rigor mortis, has snapped in two like a broken stick. The other figures melt in a sad arc around this rigid symbol of death.

Clouet — *Portrait of Francois I*

Thank this man for the Louvre's collection. He was the one who first bought great Italian art. He encouraged French painters and invited Leonardo da Vinci to visit France. He also fostered the Renaissance spirit of humanism.

École de Fontainebleau—*Diana the Huntress (Diane Chassereuse)*

This was a portrait of the king's mistress as the Greek goddess Diana, with her bow and hunting dog. Not only is the subject Greek-influenced, but so is the beauty. Renaissance artists gloried in the natural beauty of the human body as an expression of the divine.

École de Fontainebleu — *Gabrielle d'Estree et une de ses Soeurs*

Two sisters are taking a bath together, the one twisting the other's nipple. This may be idealized beauty to some, but to others it's just plain smut. Some interpret this painting as an indictment of the loose morals of the French Renaissance court. In contrast to the two sisters in the foreground is a more domestic scene in the back—the way things should be—a woman fully clothed and industriously sewing before a fire, oblivious to a man's open crotch.

Others say it's about an engaged woman (with ring), concerned about her fertility, being reassured by a friend. (Although every engaged woman I've reassured . . .)

● *Reach the Later French Painting by turning left into the Sully wing, Rooms 19–75.*

Later French Painting (1600–1850)

The French loved to paint beautiful things, nudes, scenes from Greek mythology, and historical events. Religious scenes are rare. I defy you to find even one crucifixion. This is colorful art designed to tickle the fancies of Louis XIV and his pleasure-seeking court at Versailles. As we move to the later Louises, it gets even frillier and prettier, as Renaissance turns to Baroque and Rococo.

Alongside these idealized paintings, you'll see grittier, more realistic ones. France had two worlds existing side by side—dreamy Versailles and the reality of the working poor.

Nicolas Poussin — Shepherds of Arcadia (Les Bergers d'Arcadie)

The shepherds here are idealized humans, like Greek gods. They live in the Greek Paradise where everything's perfect. The colors are bright and the atmosphere serene. However, they've stumbled upon a tomb and read the inscription and it worries them—there's Death even in Arcadia.

Claude de Lorrain (1600–1682) — Port de Mer au Soleil Couchant

In a typical Claude painting, the sun sets slowly on a harbor bordered by classical buildings. A boulevard of water stretches away from us, melting into an infinite sky. The tiny humans are dwarfed by both the majestic buildings and the sea and sky. A soft, proto-Impressionist haze warms the whole scene, showing the harmony of man and nature. Claude's painted fantasies became real in the landscaped gardens and canals at Versailles.

Georges de la Tour — *St. Joseph in the Carpenter's Shop (Saint Joseph Charpentier)*

In this human look at a religious scene, the boy Jesus has joined his father in the carpentry shop and holds a candle for him while he works. Realism has been conquered here—notice the glow of the candle through Jesus' hand.

Louis le Nain — *Peasant Family (Famille de Paysans)*

When Marie-Antoinette said to France's poor, "Let them eat cake," this was the look she got. While lords and ladies feasted and frolicked in the rich French court, the common people continued to live the hard life. Most artists painted glorified visions of Greek gods, but this dark, drab-colored "snapshot" shows the other side—the people whom Marie-Antoinette told to eat cake. The peasants look up from their activities, staring at us like we're rich kids who've just stumbled onto their turf.

Charles le Brun — *Chancellor Seguir (Le Chacelier Seguir)*

This portrait is a frilly contrast to Le Nain's peasant family. Here a court official rides under a parasol, accompanied by wimpy servants with ribbons on their shoes. French aristocrats were the first in Europe to develop a refined taste in clothes, manners, and art. Soon feudal lords in other countries followed the French lead, leaving their farms, scraping the cow pies off their boots, and learning "cultchah."

Rigaud — *Portrait of Louis XIV (1701)*

Louis called himself the Sun King, whose radiance warmed all of France. In his youth, he was strong, handsome, witty, charming, and a pretty good hoofer—note the legs. He made France a world power and the hub of culture by centralizing the government around himself

as a cult figure. Anything he did—eating, dressing, even making love—was like a ritual of state.

Here, he goes through one of those rituals, re-enacting his coronation. Rigaud shows all the trappings of power: the huge fleur-de-lis robe, the canopied throne, the crown and sceptre. But he also gives us a peek-a-boo glimpse of the human Louis underneath the royal robe. Louis is a bit older now, a bit weary. He poses for the obligatory photo-op. But the face that peers out from the elaborate wig and pompous surroundings doesn't put on any airs. It's an honest face that seems to say, "Hey, it's my job."

Jean Antoine Watteau (1684–1721) — *Embarkation for Cythera (Pelerinage a l'Ile de Cythere)*

Louis and his successors kept the nobility from meddling in government affairs by entertaining them at the playground of Versailles. Here lords and ladies frolic in a mythical landcape with antigravity babies. This painting was the first of many showing these *"fêtes galantes,"* where well-manicured aristocrats enjoy the delights of well-manicured nature.

Watteau's warm, almost phosphorescent colors also set a new artistic tone. Gone is the majestic Baroque grandeur of Louis XIV. Now French paintings become smaller, lighter, frillier, more intimate, more sensual.

Watteau — *Gilles*

A clown, looking ridiculous dressed in an oversized suit, must perform for the amusement of the rich. The crowd is jaded and indifferent. The look on his face says, "Why am I here?" This may be a portrait of Watteau himself.

Francois Boucher (1703–1770) — *The Forge of Vulcan (Les Forges de Vulcain)*

In the world at Versailles, Woman (like Venus in the painting) was to rule over and civilize brutish Man (Vulcan), teaching him the indoor arts. Men wore wigs, make-up, and pantyhose, while women dictated government policy. Society was changing fast, servants were challenging masters, and role-playing games were a part of the gay life.

Boucher chronicled the cult of the female body. Here, the man and woman complement each other, forming part of a stable pyramid. But there's more frill than form. Boucher's pastel pinks and blues must have been popular at Versailles baby showers.

Honore Fragonard (1732–1806) — *Women Bathing*

Guess who was teacher's pet in Boucher's class? Fragonard takes us to the pinnacle of French Rococo. Compare these puffy pastel goddesses with the clean lines of the *Vénus de Milo*, and you'll see how far we've come from the Greek ideal of beauty. This is sweet, cream-filled art that can only be taken, like French pastry, in small doses.

Hubert Robert — Various Scenes of Roman Ruins in France

These overgrown Roman ruins inspired Robert when he landscaped the gardens at Versailles with designer "ruins." The French were fascinated with earlier civilizations that had risen, dominated, and declined. They were becoming aware of their own cultural mortality.

19TH CENTURY — NEOCLASSICAL AND ROMANTIC

J. L. David (1748–1825) — Various Portraits of Citizens (Including Citizen Bonaparte)

When the Revolution exploded, Rococo became politically incorrect. The bourgeois middle class wielded power, simple dress became the fashion, and painters returned to clean and sober realism.

J. A. D. Ingres (1780–1867) —
Nudes and Portraits

The great defender of the Neoclassic tradition paints classical nudes. He also paints clothed Frenchmen with the clean lines and bulk of classical statues.

Eugene Delacroix (1797–1863) —
Portrait of Chopin

Here we see the great pianist/composer with his face half in shadow. Romantics explored the hidden world of human emotion. Chopin expressed the turmoil of his soul in flurries of notes, while Delacroix used messy patches of color. Though their mediums were different, this reminds us that the various arts held hands as they walked from Renaissance, through Baroque, Neoclassical, Romantic, and beyond.

8 Orsay Museum

The Musée d'Orsay (pron: mew-ZAY dor-SAY) houses French art of the 1800s, picking up where the Louvre leaves off. For us, that means Impressionism, the art of sun-dappled fields, bright colors, and crowded Parisian cafés. The Orsay houses the best general collection of Manet, Monet, Renoir, Degas, van Gogh, Cézanne, and Gauguin anywhere. If you like Impressionism, visit this museum. If you don't like Impressionism, visit this museum. I personally find it a more enjoyable and rewarding place than the Louvre. Sure, ya gotta see *Mona* and *Vénus de Milo*, but after you get your gottas out of the way, enjoy the Orsay.

MUSEE D'ORSAY

Hours: Tuesday, Wednesday, Friday, Saturday 10:00–18:00; Thursday 10:00–21:45; Sunday 9:00–18:00; closed Monday. June 20–September 20, the museum opens at 9:00. Last entrance 45 minutes before closing. Galleries start closing 30 minutes early. Note: The Orsay is very crowded on Tuesday, when the Louvre is closed.

Cost: 40 F; 30 F age 18–25 and over 60; free for those under 18. Tickets are good all day. Money exchange with decent rates is available. The Orsay is included in the Paris Museum Card (as are all the Paris entries in this book), a great time- and money-saver. See chapter 7, on the Louvre, for specifics.

Tour length: Two hours

Getting there: Walk from the Louvre across the Seine and 10 minutes downstream towards the Eiffel Tower. The RER-C train line zips you right to "Musée d'Orsay" (Métro tickets are good). Métro: "Solferino" is three blocks south of the Orsay.

Information: The booth near entrance gives free floor plans in English. English-language tours usually run daily except Sunday at 11:30. The

90-minute tours cost 38 F and are available on audiotape. Tel. 01 40 49 48 48.

Cuisine art: The elegant second-floor restaurant has a buffet salad bar. A simple fourth-floor café is sandwiched between the Impressionists.

Starring: Manet, Monet, Renoir, van Gogh, and Cézanne.

ORIENTATION — GARE D'ORSAY

● *Pick up the free English map at the info desk, buy your ticket, and check bags to the right. Belly up to the stone balustrade overlooking the main floor and orient yourself.*

Trains used to run right under our feet down the center of the gallery. This former train station barely escaped the wrecking ball in the 1970s when the French realized it'd be a great place to house their enormous collections of 19th-century art scattered throughout the city in smaller museums.

The main floor has early 19th-century art (as usual, Conservative on the right, Realism on the left). Upstairs (not visible from here) is the core of the collection—the Impressionist rooms. Finally, we'll end the tour with "the other Orsay" on the mezzanine level you see to the left. Clear as Seine water? *Bon.*

THE ORSAY'S 19TH "CENTURY" (1848–1914)

Einstein and Geronimo. Abraham Lincoln and Karl Marx. The train, the bicycle, the horse and buggy, the automobile, and the balloon. Freud and Dickens. Darwin's *Origin of Species* and the Church's *Immaculate Conception*. Louis Pasteur and Billy the Kid. V. I. Lenin and Ty Cobb.

The 19th century was a mix of old and new side by side. Europe was entering the modern Industrial Age with cities, factories, rapid transit, instant communication, and global networks. At the same time it clung to the past with traditional, rural—almost medieval—attitudes and morals.

According to the Orsay, the "19th century" began in 1848 with the socialist and democratic revolutions (Marx's *Communist Manifesto*). It ended in 1914 with the pull of an assassin's trigger, igniting War I and ushering in the modern world.

The museum shows art that is also both old and new, conservative

ORSAY GROUND FLOOR—OVERVIEW

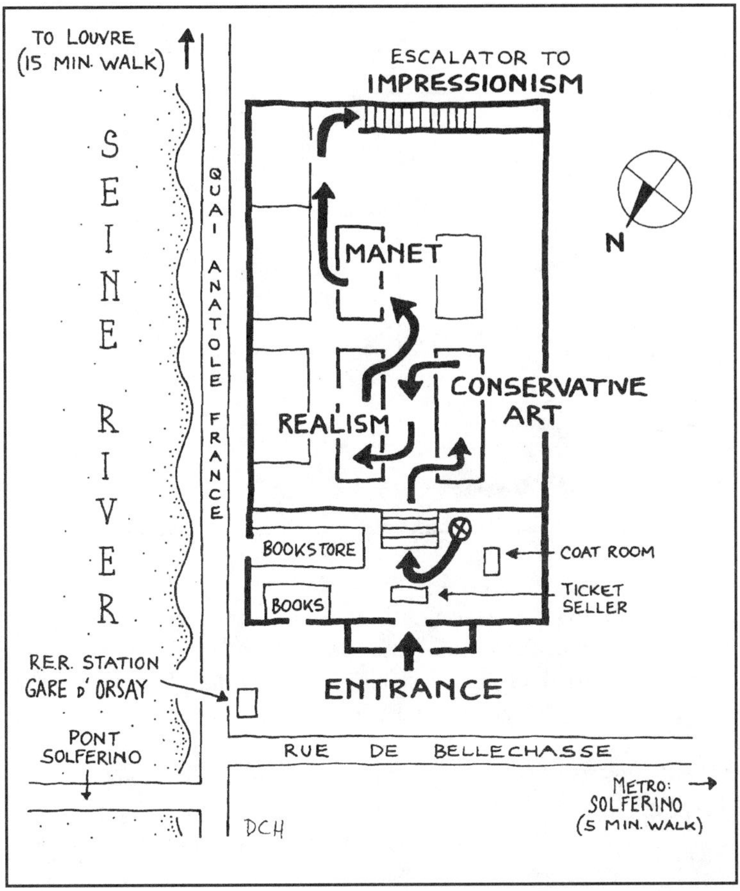

TO LOUVRE
(15 MIN. WALK)

ESCALATOR TO
IMPRESSIONISM

SEINE RIVER

QUAI ANATOLE FRANCE

N

MANET

REALISM

CONSERVATIVE
ART

BOOKSTORE

BOOKS

COAT ROOM

TICKET
SELLER

R.E.R. STATION
GARE D' ORSAY

ENTRANCE

PONT
SOLFERINO

RUE   DE   BELLECHASSE

METRO: →
SOLFERINO
(5 MIN. WALK)

DCH

and revolutionary. We'll start with the Conservatives and early rebels on the ground floor, then head upstairs to see how a few visionary young artists bucked the system and revolutionized the art world, paving the way for the 20th century.

● Walk down the steps to the main floor, a gallery filled with statues.

Conservative Art

No, this isn't ancient Greece. These statues are from the same century as the Theory of Relativity. It's the Conservative art of the French schools that was so popular throughout the 19th century. It was popular because it's beautiful. The balanced poses, perfect anatomy, and

CONSERVATIVE ART

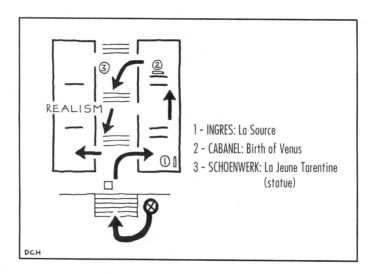

1 - INGRES: La Source
2 - CABANEL: Birth of Venus
3 - SCHOENWERK: La Jeune Tarentine
(statue)

sweet faces, the curving lines, the gleaming white stone—all this is very beautiful. (I'll be bad-mouthing it later, but for now appreciate the exquisite craftsmanship of this "perfect" art.)

● *Take your first right into the small Room 1 marked "Ingres." Look for a nude woman with a pitcher of water.*

Ingres — *The Source (La Source)*

Let's start where the Louvre left off. Ingres whose works help cap the Louvre collection, championed a Neoclassical style. *The Source* is virtually a Greek statue on canvas. Ingres worked on this over the course of 35 years and considered it his "image of perfection." Famous in its day, *The Source* influenced many artists whose classical statues and paintings are in the Orsay gallery.

In this and the next few rooms you'll see more of these visions of idealized beauty— nude women in languid poses, Greek myths, and so on. The "Romantics," like Delacroix, added bright colors, movement, and emotion to the classical coolness of Ingres.

● *Walk uphill (quickly, this is background stuff) to the last room, with a pastel green painting.*

Cabanel — *Birth of Venus (Naissance de Vénus)*

This goddess is a perfect fantasy, an orgasm of beauty. This is art of a pre-Freudian society, when sex was dirty and mysterious and had to be exalted into a more pure and divine form. The sex drive was channeled into an acute sense of beauty. French folk would literally swoon in ecstasy before these works of art.

Get a feel for the ideal beauty and refined emotion of these Greek-style works. You'll find a statue with a pose similar to Venus' back out in the gallery. Go ahead, swoon. If it feels good, enjoy it.

● *Now, take a mental cold shower, grab a bench in the main gallery of statues, and read on.*

Academy and Salon

Who liked this stuff? The art world was dominated by two conservative institutions: the Academy (the state art school) and the Salon, where works were exhibited to the buying public. If artists didn't conform to the artistic "Nielsen Ratings," they couldn't get training, make connections, or sell their work.

Now let's literally cross over to the "wrong side of the tracks" to the art of the early rebels.

● *Head back toward the entrance and turn right into Room 4 marked "Daumier" (opposite the Ingres room).*

Realism — Early Rebels

Daumier — Thirty-six Caricature Busts (Ventre Legislatif)

This is a liberal's look at the stuffy bourgeois establishment that controlled the Academy and the Salon. In these 36 bust-lets, Daumier, trained as a political cartoonist, captures with vicious precision the pomposity and self-righteousness of these self-appointed

REALISM—EARLY REBELS

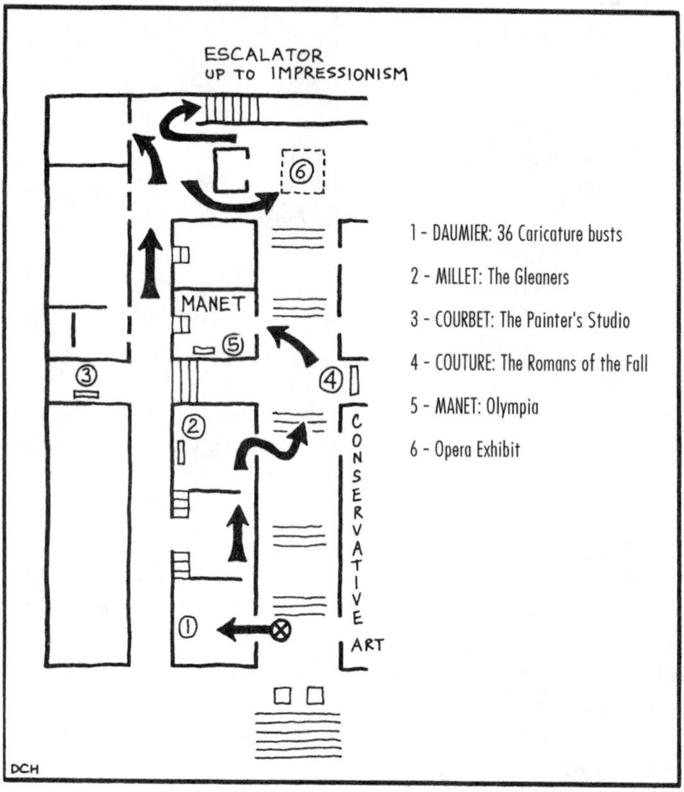

ESCALATOR
UP TO IMPRESSIONISM

MANET

CONSERVATIVE ART

1 – DAUMIER: 36 Caricature busts

2 – MILLET: The Gleaners

3 – COURBET: The Painter's Studio

4 – COUTURE: The Romans of the Fall

5 – MANET: Olympia

6 – Opera Exhibit

DCH

arbiters of taste. The labels next to the busts give the name of the person being caricatured, his title or job (most were members of the French parliament), and an insulting nickname (like "gross, fat, and satisfied" and Monsieur "Platehead"). Give a few nicknames yourself. Can you find Reagan, Clinton, Yeltsin, Thatcher, Gingrich?

These people hated what you're about to see. Their prudish faces tightened as their fantasy world was shattered by the Realists.

● *Go uphill four steps and through a few romantic and pastoral rooms to the final room, #6.*

Millet — *The Gleaners (Les Glaneuses)*

Millet (pron: mee-YAY) grew up on a humble farm. He didn't attend the Academy and hated the uppity Paris art scene. Instead of idealized

gods, goddesses, nymphs, and winged babies, he painted simple rural scenes. He was strongly affected by the Revolution of 1848 with its affirmation of the working class. Here he shows three gleaners, the poor women who pick up the meager leavings after a field has already been harvested by the wealthy. Millet captures the innate dignity of these stocky, tanned women who work quietly in a large field for their small reward.

This is "Realism" in two senses. It's painted "real"-istically, unlike the prettified pastels of Cabanel's *Birth of Venus*. And it's the "real" world—not the fantasy world of Greek myth, but the harsh life of the working poor.

● *Swoon briefly through the main gallery and hang a U-turn left, climbing the steps to a large alcove with two huge canvases. On the left ...*

Courbet — The Painter's Studio (L'Atelier du Peintre)

Also rejected by the so-called experts, Courbet (pron: coor-BAY) held his own one-man exhibit. He built a shed in the middle of Paris, defiantly hung his art out, and basically "mooned" the shocked public.

Here we see Courbet himself in his studio working diligently on a Realistic landscape, oblivious to the confusion around him. Looking on are a nude model—not a goddess but a real woman—and a little boy with an adoring look on his face. Perhaps it's Courbet himself as a child admiring the artist who sticks to his guns, whether it's popular or not.

● *Return to the main gallery. Back across the tracks, the huge canvas you see is ...*

Couture — The Romans of the Fall (Les Romains de la Décadence)

We see a society that's stuffed with too much luxury, too much classical beauty, too much pleasure, wasted, burned-out, and in decay. The old, backward-looking order was about to be slapped in the face.

● *Continue up the gallery, then left into Room 14 ("Manet, avant 1870"). Find the reclining nude.*

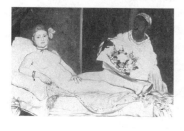

Manet — *Olympia*

"This brunette is thoroughly ugly. Her face is stupid, her skin cadaverous. All this clash of colors is stupefying." So wrote a critic when Edouard Manet's nude hung in the Salon. The public hated it, attacking Manet (pron: man-NAY) in print and literally attacking the canvas.

Think back on Cabanel's painting, *The Birth of Venus*—an idealized, pastel, Vaseline-on-the-lens beauty. Cabenel's nude was soft-core pornography, the kind you see selling lingerie and perfume. The public lapped it up (and Napoleon III purchased it).

Manet's nude doesn't gloss over anything. The pose is classic, used by Titian, Goya, and countless others. But the sharp outlines and harsh contrasting colors are new and shocking. Her hand is a clamp and her stare is shockingly defiant, with not a hint of the seductive, hey-sailor look of most nudes. This prostitute, ignoring the flowers sent by her last customer, looks out to us as if to say "next." Manet replaced soft-core porn with hard-core art.

Manet had an upper-class upbringing and some formal art training, and had been accepted by the Salon. He could have cranked out pretty nudes and been a successful painter. Instead he surrounded himself with a group of young artists experimenting with new techniques. With his reputation and strong personality, he was their master, though he learned equally from them. Let the Impressionist revolution begin.

● *Continue to the end of the gallery. Before taking the covered escalator up to the often-crowded Impressionist rooms, take a break and read ahead. Or you could visit the nearby ...*

Opera Exhibit

Float over to the Opera exhibit (near the escalator) where you can hover over a scale model section of the city. There's the 19th-century Garnier Opera House with its green roof in a diamond-shaped block in the center.

You'll also see a cross-section model of the Opera House. You'd enter from the right end, buy your ticket in the foyer, then move into the entrance hall with its grand staircase. At curtain-time, you'd find your seat in the auditorium, topped by a glorious painted ceiling. (The current ceiling is even more wonderful than the model, done by Marc Chagall.) Notice that the stage is as big as the seating area, with elaborate riggings to raise and lower scenery. Nearby, there are models of set designs from some famous productions. These days, Parisians enjoy their Verdi and Gounod mostly at a new opera house at Place Bastille.

IMPRESSIONISM

The camera threatened to make artists obsolete. A painter's original function was to record reality faithfully like a journalist. Now a machine could capture a better likeness faster than you could say Etch-a-Sketch.

But true art is more than just painting reality. It gives us reality from the artist's point of view, putting a personal stamp on the work. It records not only the scene—a camera can do that—but the artist's impressions of the scene. Impressions are often fleeting, so you have to work quickly.

The Impressionists rejected camera-like detail for a quick style more suited to capturing the passing moment. Feeling stifled by the rigid rules and stuffy atmosphere of the Academy, the Impressionists' motto was "out of the studio, into the open air." They grabbed their scarves and took excursions to the country, setting up their easels on riverbanks and hillsides or sketching in cafés and dance halls. Gods, goddesses, nymphs, and fantasy scenes were out, common people and rural landscapes were in.

The quick style and simple subjects were ridiculed and called childish by the "experts." Rejected by the Salon, the Impressionists staged their own exhibition in 1874. They brashly took their name from an insult thrown at them by a critic who laughed at one of Monet's "impressions" of a sunrise. For the next decade they exhibited their own work independently. The public, opposed at first, was slowly drawn in by the simplicity, the color, and the vibrancy of Impressionist art.

● *Ride the escalator to the top floor. Take your first left for a commanding view of the Orsay. Second left takes you between a bookshop and a giant "backwards" clock to the art.*

The Impressionist collection is scattered somewhat randomly through the next 10 or so rooms. Shadows dance and the displays mingle. You'll find nearly all of these paintings, but exactly where they're hung is a lot like their brushwork ... delightfully sloppy. (If you don't see a described painting, move on. It's either hung farther down or on holiday.) Now, let there be ...

Impressionism —
Manet, Degas, Monet, Renoir

Light! Color! Vibrations! You don't hang an Impressionist canvas—you tether it. Impressionism features: light colors, easygoing open-air scenes, spontaneity, broad brush strokes, and the play of light.

The Impressionists made their canvases shimmer by a simple but revolutionary technique. If you mix, say, red, yellow, and blue together you'll get brown, right? But Impressionists didn't bother to mix them. They'd slap a thick brushstroke of yellow down, then a stroke of green next to it, then red next to that. Up close all you see are the three messy strokes, but as you back up ... *voilà!* Brown! The colors blend in the eye at a distance. But while your eye is saying "bland brown" your subconscious is shouting, "Red! Yellow! Blue! Yes!"

There are no lines in Nature. Yet someone in the classical tradition (Ingres, for example) would draw an outline of his subject, then fill it in with color. But the Impressionists built a figure with dabs of paint ... a snowman of color.

Manet —
Luncheon on the Grass
(Le Déjeuner sur l'Herbe)

Manet really got a rise out of people with this one. Once again the public judged a painting on moral terms rather than artistic ones. What are these scantily clad women doing with these fully clothed men, they wondered? Or rather, what will they be doing after the last baguette is eaten?

A new revolutionary movement is budding: Impressionism. Notice the messy brushwork of the trees and leaves in the background, and the play of light on the pond in back and filtering through the trees onto the hazy woman stooping behind. And the strong contrasting colors (white skin, black clothes, green grass). And the fact that this is a true out-of-doors painting, not a studio production. The first shot had been fired.

Whistler —
Whistler's Mother (Portrait de la mére de l'Auteur)

Why so famous? I don't know either. It shouldn't be, of course, but it

is. Perhaps because it's by an American, and we see in his mother some of the monumental solidity of our own ancestral moms made tough by pioneering the American wilderness.

Or perhaps because it was so starkly different in its day. In a roomful of golden goddesses, it'd stand out like a fish in a tree. The experts hated it and didn't understand it. (If music is the fear of silence, is art the fear of reality?) The subtitle is "Arrangement in Grey and Black," and the whole point is the subtle variations on dark shades, but the critics kept waiting for it to come out in colorization.

Degas — *The Dance Class (La Classe de Danse)*

Edgar Degas (pron: day-GAH) was a rich kid from a family of bankers who got the best classical-style art training. Adoring Ingres' pure lines and cool colors, he painted in the Conservative style. His work was exhibited in the Salon. He gained success and a good reputation and then … he met the Impressionists.

Degas blends classical lines with Impressionist color and spontaneity. His dancers have outlines, and he's got them in a classic 3-D setting—with the floor lines slanting to the upper right.

So why is Degas an Impressionist? First off, he's captured a candid, fleeting moment, a momentary "impression"—look at the girl on the left scratching her back restlessly and the cuddly little bundle of dog in the foreground. Degas loved the unposed "snapshot" effect, catching his models off guard.

Clearly, Degas loved dance and the theater. (Catch his statue, *Tiny Dancer, 14 Years Old*, in the glass case.) The play of stage lights off his dancers, especially the halos of ballet skirts, is made to order for an Impressionist.

Finally, he's got that Impressionistic "fury" of the brush. In *The Dance Class*, look at the bright green bow on the girl with her back to us. Not only are the outlines sketchy, but see how he slopped green paint onto her dress and didn't even say, *"Excusez-moi."*

EARLY IMPRESSIONISM

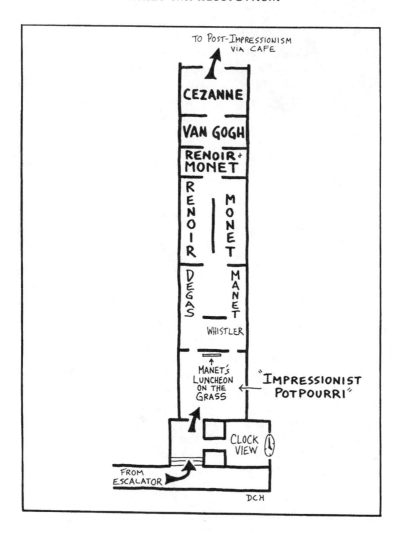

Degas — *The Glass of Absinthe (Au Café, dit L'Absinthe)*

Degas hung out with low-life Impressionists discussing art, love, and life in the cheap cafés and bars in Montmartre (the original Bohemia-ville). He painted Impressionistic snapshots of everyday people. Here a weary lady of the evening meets morning with a last lonely coffin-nail drink in the glaring light of a four-in-the-morning café.

Look across the room at some later works by Manet. The old dog was learning new tricks from his former disciples.

● *The next rooms feature works by two Impressionist masters at their peak, Monet and Renoir. You're looking at the quintessence of Impressionism.*

Monet — *Gare St. Lazare*

Claude Monet (pron: mo-NAY) is the father of Impressionism. He learned from Manet (a before o) but quickly went beyond even Manet's shocking slabs of colors. Monet fully explored the possibilities of open-air painting and lighter, brighter colors. He could even make this drab train station glow with reflected light. The sun diffuses through the skylight and mingles with the steam from the engine.

Stand a good six feet from the canvas and look at the tall building with the slanted Mansard roof behind the station. Looks fine? Now get close up. At six inches it's a confusing pile of color blobs. Light on!

Monet — *The Cathedral of Rouen* (series of five paintings)

Monet went to Rouen, rented a room across from the cathedral, set up his easel ... and waited. He wanted to catch "a series of differing impressions" of the cathedral façade at different times of day and year. He often had several canvases going at once. In all he did 30 canvases, and each is unique. These five are labeled: In the morning, in grey weather, morning sun, full view, full sunlight.

As Monet zeroes in on the play of the colors and the light, the physical subject—the cathedral—is dissolving. It has become only a rack upon which to hang the light and color. Later artists would boldly throw away the rack, leaving purely abstract modern art in its place.

Monet — Paintings from Monet's Garden at Giverny

One of Monet's favorite places to paint was the garden of his home in Giverny, west of Paris (and worth a visit if you like Monet more than you hate crowds). You'll find several different views of it along with the painter's self-portrait. The *Blue Water Lilies* is similar to the large and famous water-lily paintings you'll find in the nearby Orangerie Museum across the river at Place de la Concorde.

Renoir — *Dance at the Moulin de la Galette (Bal du Moulin de la Galette)*

On Sunday afternoons, working-class folk would dress up and head for the fields on Butte Montmartre (near the Sacré-Coeur church) to dance, drink, and eat little cakes (*galettes*) till dark. Renoir (pron: ren-WAH) liked to go there to paint the common Parisians living and loving in the afternoon sun. The sunlight filtering through the trees creates a kaleidoscope of colors, like a 19th-century mirrored ball throwing darts of light on the dancers.

This dappled light is the "impression" that Renoir came away with. He captures it with quick blobs of yellow. Look at the sun-dappled straw hat (right of center) and the glasses (lower right). Smell the powder on the ladies' faces. The painting glows with bright colors. Even the shadows on the ground, which should be grey or black, are colored a warm blue. As if having a good time were required, even the shadows are caught up in the mood, dancing. Like a photographer uses a slow shutter speed to show motion, Renoir paints a waltzing blur.

Renoir — *The City Dance/The Country Dance (La Danse à la Ville/La Danse à la Campagne)*

In contrast to Monet's haze of colors,

Renoir clung to the more traditional technique of drawing a clear outline, then filling it in.

This two-panel "series" by Renoir shows us his exquisite draftsmanship, sense of beauty, and smoother brushwork. Like Degas, Renoir had classical training and exhibited at the Salon.

Renoir's work is lighthearted with light colors, almost pastels. He seems to be searching for an ideal, the pure beauty we saw on the ground floor. In later years he used more and more red tones as if trying for even more warmth.

● *On the divider in the center of the room, you'll find ...*

Pissarro and Others

We've neglected many of the founders of the Impressionist style. Browse around and discover your own favorites. Pissarro is one of mine. He's more subtle and subdued than the flashy Monet and Renoir, but as someone said, "He did for the earth what Monet did for the water."

You may find the painting *Young Girl in the Garden (Jeune Fille en Jardin)* with a pastel style as pretty as Renoir's. It's by Mary Cassatt, an American who was attracted to the strong art magnet that was and still is Paris.

● *Take a break. Look at the Impressionist effect of the weather on the Paris skyline. Notice the skylight above you—these Impressionist rooms are appropriately lit by ever-changing natural light. Then carry on ...*

POST-IMPRESSIONISM

Take a word, put "-ism" on the end, and you've become an intellectual. Commune-ism, sex-ism, Cube-ism, computer-ism ... Post-Impressionism.

"Post-Impressionism" is an artificial and clumsy concept to describe those painters who used Impressionist techniques after Monet and Renoir. It might just as well be called something like "Pre-Modernism," because it bridged Impressionism with the 20th century ... or you could call it bridge-ism.

● *The Orsay's Post-Impressionist collection (we'll see van Gogh, Cézanne, Gauguin, Rousseau, Seurat, and Toulouse-Lautrec) flip-flops back and forth between here and the end of this gallery. Be prepared to skip around.*

Van Gogh

Impressionists have been accused of being lightweights. The colorful style lends itself to bright country scenes, gardens, sunlight on the

POST-IMPRESSIONISTS

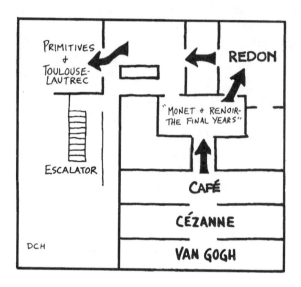

water, and happy crowds of simple people. It took a remarkable genius to add profound emotion to the Impressionist style.

Vincent van Gogh (pron: van-GO, or van-GOCK by the Dutch and the snooty) was the son of a Dutch minister. He too felt a religious calling, and he spread the gospel among the poorest of the poor—peasants and miners. When he turned to painting, he channeled this same spiritual intensity into his work. Like Michelangelo, Beethoven, Rembrandt, Wayne Newton, and a select handful of others, he put so much of himself into his work that art and life became one. In this room you'll see both van Gogh's painting style and his life unfold.

Van Gogh — *Peasant (Paysanne près de l'Atre)*

As a young man, van Gogh left his steady clerking job to work with poor working people in overcast Belgium and Holland. He painted these hardworking, dignified folks in a crude, dark style reflecting the oppressiveness of their lives ... and the loneliness of his own as he roamed northern Europe in search of a calling.

Van Gogh — *Self-portrait, Paris (Portraite de l'Artiste)* (1887)

Encouraged by his art-dealer brother, van Gogh moves to Paris, and *voilà!* The color! He meets Monet and hobnobs with Gauguin and Toulouse-Lautrec. He rents a room in Montmartre, learning the Impressionist style. (See how he builds a bristling brown beard using thick strokes of reds and greens side by side.)

At first he paints like the others but soon develops his own style. By using thick swirling brushstrokes he infuses life into even inanimate objects. Van Gogh's brushstrokes curve and thrash around like a garden hose pumped with wine.

Van Gogh — *Mid-day (La Méridienne),* based on a painting by Millet (1890)

The social life of Paris becomes too much for the solitary van Gogh. He moves to the south of France. At first in the glow of the bright spring sunshine, he has a period of incredible creativity and happiness, overwhelmed by the bright colors—an Impressionist's dream. Here again we see his love of the common people taking a glowing siesta in the noon sun.

Van Gogh — *Van Gogh's Room at Arles (La Chambre de Van Gogh à Arles)* (1889)

But being alone in a strange country begins to wear on him. The distorted perspective of this painting makes his tiny rented room look even more cramped. He invites his friend Gauguin to join him, but after two months together arguing passionately about art, nerves get raw. Van Gogh threatens Gauguin with a knife, driving him back to Paris. In crazed despair, van Gogh mutilates his own ear.

The people of Arles realize they have a madman on their hands, and convince van Gogh to seek help. He enters a mental hospital.

Van Gogh — *The Church at Auvers-sur-Oise (L'Église d'Auvers-sur-Oise)* (1890)

Van Gogh's paintings done in the peace of the mental hospital are more meditative—fewer bright landscapes, more closed-in scenes with deeper and almost surreal colors.

There's also a strong sense of mystery. What's behind this church? The sky is cobalt blue and the church's windows are also blue, like we're looking right through the church to an infinite sky. There's something mysterious lurking on the other side. You can't see it, but you feel its presence like the cold air from an approaching Métro train still hidden in the tunnel. There's a road that leads from us to the church, then splits to go behind. A choice must be made. Which way?

Van Gogh — *Self-portrait, St. Remy (Portrait de l'Artiste)* (1889)

Van Gogh wavered between happiness and madness. He despaired of ever being sane enough to continue painting.

This self-portrait shows a man engulfed in a confused but beautiful world. The background brushstrokes swirl and rave, setting in motion the waves of the jacket. He's caught in the current, out of control. But in the midst of this rippling sea of mystery floats a still, detached island of a face with probing, questioning, wise eyes.

Do his troubled eyes know that only a few months later he would take a pistol and put a bullet through his chest?

Cézanne

Cézanne's art brought Impressionism into the 20th century. There's less color here, less swirling brushwork, less passion. It's cleaner, chunkier, more intellectual. Cézanne (pron: say-ZAHN) can be difficult to appreciate after the warmth of Renoir, and he won't give you the fireworks of van Gogh. But he's worth the effort.

Cézanne — *Self-portrait (Portrait de l'Artiste)*

Cézanne was virtually unknown and unappreciated in his lifetime. He worked alone, lived alone, and died alone, ignored by all but a few

revolutionary young artists who understood his efforts.

And Cézanne couldn't draw. His brush was a blunt instrument. With it, he'd bludgeon reality into submission, drag it across a canvas, and leave it there to dry. But Cézanne, the mediocre painter, was a great innovator. His works are not perfected, finished products but revolutionary works-in-progress—gutter balls with wonderful spin. His work spoke for itself—which is good because, as you can see here, he had no mouth.

Cézanne — *Landscape (Rochers près des Grottes au dessus de Château-Noir)*

Cézanne used chunks of color as blocks to build three-dimensional forms. The rocky brown cliffs here consist of cubes of green, tan, and blue that blend at a distance to create a solid 3-D structure. It only makes sense from a distance. Try this: start at six inches and fade

CÉZANNE

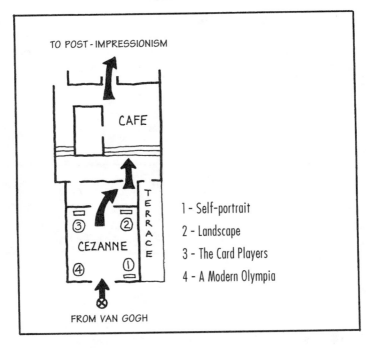

TO POST-IMPRESSIONISM

CAFE

TERRACE

CEZANNE

③   ②

④   ①

FROM VAN GOGH

1 - Self-portrait

2 - Landscape

3 - The Card Players

4 - A Modern Olympia

back. At some point the messy slabs become reality on the rocks.

Why is this revolutionary? Past artists created the illusion of 3-D with lines (like when we draw receding lines to turn a square into a cube). The Impressionists pioneered the technique of using blobs of color, not lines, to capture a subject. But most Impressionist art is flat and two-dimensional, a wall of color like Monet's Rouen Cathedral series. Cézanne went 3-D with chunks.

These chunks are like little "cubes." No coincidence that his experiments in reducing forms to their geometric basics influenced the … Cubists.

Cézanne — *The Card Players (Les Joueurs de Cartes)*

These aren't people. They're studies in color and pattern. The subject matter—two guys playing cards—is less important than the pleasingly balanced pattern they make on the canvas, two sloping forms framing a cylinder (a bottle) in the center. Later abstract artists would focus solely on the shapes and colors.

Again, notice how the figures are built with chunks of color. The jacket of the player at right consists of tans, greens, and browns. As one art scholar put it: "Cézanne confused intermingled forms and colors, achieving an extraordinarily luminous density in which lyricism is controlled by a rigorously constructed rhythm." Just what I said—chunks of color.

Cézanne — *A Modern Olympia (Une Moderne Olympia)*

Is this Cézanne himself paying homage to Manet? And dreaming up a new, more radical style of painting? We've come a long way since Manet's Olympia, which seems tame to us now.

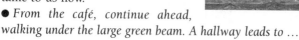

● *From the café, continue ahead, walking under the large green beam. A hallway leads to …*

Redon

Now flip out the lights and step into his mysterious world. If the Orsay's a zoo, this is the nocturnal house. Prowl around. This is wild stuff, intense—imagine Richard Nixon on mushrooms playing sax.

● *At cockcrow pass into the gallery lined with metal columns containing the Primitive art of Rousseau and Gauguin. Start in the first alcove to the left.*

Henri Rousseau — *War (Le Guerre ou La Chevauchée de la Discorde)*

Some artists, rejecting the harried, scientific, and rational world, remembered a time before "-isms" when works of art weren't scholarly "studies in form and color" but voodoo dolls full of mystery and magic power. They learned from the art of primitive tribes in Africa and the South Seas, trying to recreate a primal Garden of Eden of peace and wholeness. In doing so they created another ism: "Primitivism."

One such artist was Rousseau, a man who painted like a child. He was an amateur artist who palled around with all the great painters, but they never took his naive style of art seriously.

This looks like a child's drawing of a nightmare. The images are

PRIMITIVISM

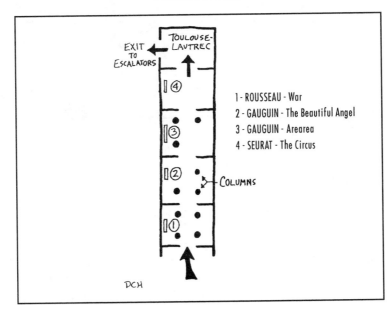

1 - ROUSSEAU - War
2 - GAUGUIN - The Beautiful Angel
3 - GAUGUIN - Arearea
4 - SEURAT - The Circus

primitive—flat and simple, with unreal colors—but the effect is both beautiful and terrifying. War in the form of a woman with a sword flies on horseback across the battlefield, leaving destruction in her wake—broken bare trees, burning clouds in the background, and heaps of corpses picked at by the birds.

Gauguin — *The Beautiful "Angel" (La Belle Angele)*

A woman in peasant dress, sits in a bubble like the halos in a medieval religious painting. Next to it is a pagan idol. This isn't a scene, but an ordered collage of images with symbolic overtones. It's left to us to make the connection.

Paul Gauguin (pron: go-GAN) learned the bright clashing colors from the Impressionists, but diverged from this path about the time van Gogh waved a knife in his face.

Gauguin simplifies. His figures are two-dimensional with thick dark outlines filled in with basic blocks of color. He turned his back on the entire Western tradition of realism begun in the Renaissance which tried to recreate the 3-D world on a 2-D canvas. Instead he returns to an age where figures become symbols.

Gauguin — *Arearea (Pleasantries) (Joyeusetes)*

Gauguin got the travel bug early in childhood and grew up wanting to be a sailor. He became a stockbroker instead. In his spare time he painted and was introduced to the Impressionist circle. At the age of 35, he got fed up with it all, quit his job, abandoned his wife and family and, took refuge in his art. He traveled to the South Seas in search of the exotic, finally settling on Tahiti.

In Tahiti, Gauguin found his Garden of Eden. He simplified his life to the routine of eating, sleeping, and painting. He simplified his painting still more to flat images with heavy black outlines filled in with bright, pure colors. He painted the native girls in their naked innocence (so different from Cabanel's seductive *Venus!*). But this simple style had a deep undercurrent of symbolic meaning.

Arearea shows native women and a dog. In the "distance" (there's no attempt at traditional 3-D here) a procession goes by with a large pagan idol. What's the connection between the idol and the foreground figures who are apparently unaware of it? Gauguin makes us dig deep down into our *medulla oblongata* to make a mystical connection between the beautiful women, the dog, and religion. In primitive societies, religion permeates life. Idols, dogs, and women are holy.

Seurat — *The Circus (Le Cirque)*

With "pointillism," Impressionism is brought to its logical conclusion—little dabs of different colors placed side by side to blend in the viewer's eye. Using only red, yellow, blue, and green points of paint, Seurat (pron: sur-RAH) creates a mosaic of colors that shimmers at a distance.

Toulouse-Lautrec — *The Clownesse Cha-U-Kao*

Henri de Toulouse-Lautrec was the black sheep of a noble family. At age 15 he broke both legs, which left him a cripple. Shunned by his family, a freak to society, he felt more at home in the underworld of other outcasts—prostitutes, drunks, thieves, dancers, and actors. He painted the nightlife low-life in the bars, cafés, dance halls, and brothels he frequented. Toulose-Lautrec died young of alcoholism.

This is one of his fellow freaks, a fat lady clown who made her living being laughed at. She slumps wearily after a performance, indifferent to the applause, and adjusts her dress to prepare for the curtain call.

Toulouse-Lautrec was a true "impression"-ist, catching his models in candid poses. He worked spontaneously, never correcting his mistakes, as you can see from the blotches on her dark skirt and the unintentional yellow sash hanging down. Can you see a bit of Degas here? In the subject matter, the snapshot pose, and the colors?

Toulouse-Lautrec — *Jane Avril Dancing*

Toulouse-Lautrec hung out at the Moulin Rouge dance hall in Montmartre. One of the most popular dancers was this slim, graceful, elegant, and melancholy woman who stood out above the rabble of the Moulin Rouge. Toulouse-Lautrec the artistocrat might have identified with her noble face—sad and weary of the nightlife, but stuck in it.

● *You've seen the essential Orsay and are permitted to cut out (the exit is straight below you). But there's an "Other Orsay" I think you'll find entertaining.*

To reach the mezzanine (niveau median)*, cross to the other side of the gallery and go down three flights. At the foot of the escalator, the mezzanine (which overlooks the main floor) is to your right. But first, go left to the palatial room of mirrors and chandeliers, marked "Salle des Fetes," or "Arts et Decors de la IIIème République" (Room 52).*

THE "OTHER" ORSAY

The beauty of the Orsay is that it combines all the art of the 1800s (1848–1914), both modern and classical, in one building. The classical art, so popular in its own day, has been maligned and forgotten in the 20th century. It's time for a reassessment. Is it as gaudy and god-awful as we've been led to believe? From our end-of-the-century perspective, let's take a look at the opulent, *fin de siècle* ("end of the century") French high society and its luxurious art.

The Grand Ballroom (Arts et Decors de la IIIème République)

This was one of France's most luxurious night spots when the Orsay hotel was here. You can easily imagine gowned debutantes and white-gloved dandies waltzing the night away to the music of a chamber orchestra. Notice:

(1) The interior decorating: Raspberry marble-ripple ice-cream columns, the pastel ceiling painting, gold work, mirrors, and leafy strands of chandeliers.

(2) The statue *Bacchante Couchée* sprawled in the middle of the room. Familiar pose? If not, you flunk this tour.

(3) The statue *Aurore*, with her canopy of hair, hide-and-seek face, and silver-dollar nipples.

(4) The large painting, *The Birth of Venus (La Naissance de Vénus)* by William Bouguereau. Van Gogh once said: "If I painted like Bouguereau, I could hope to make money. The public will never change—they love only sweet things."

(5) *Le Souvenir*, with the only see-through veil of marble I've ever seen through.

So here's the question—is this stuff beautiful or merely gaudy? Divine or decadent?

THE "OTHER" ORSAY—MEZZANINE

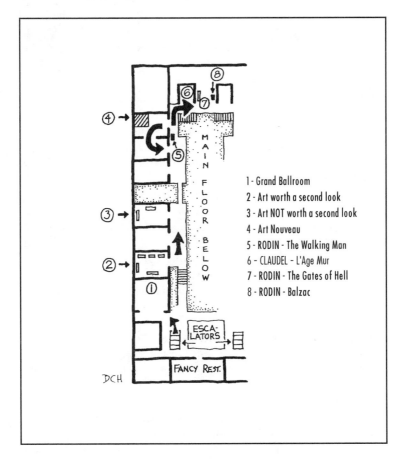

1 - Grand Ballroom
2 - Art worth a second look
3 - Art NOT worth a second look
4 - Art Nouveau
5 - RODIN - The Walking Man
6 - CLAUDEL - L'Age Mur
7 - RODIN - The Gates of Hell
8 - RODIN - Balzac

DCH

● *Return to the mezzanine overlooking the main gallery, turn left "vers Naturalisme et le Symbolisme." Head toward the far end. Enter the first room on the left (#55).*

Art Worth a Second Look

We've seen some great art, now let's see some not-so-great art—at least, that's what modern critics tell us. This is realistic art with a subconscious kick, art from a neurotic society before Freud articulated its demons.

● *Working clockwise, you'll see ...*

Cain

The world's first murderer is exiled with his family. Archaeologists had recently discovered a Neanderthal skull, so the artist shows them as a prehistoric hunter/gatherer tribe.

The Dream (Le Rêve)

Soldiers sleep, while visions of gattling-guns dance in their heads.

Payday (La Paye des Moissonneurs)

Peasants getting paid, painted by the man called "the grandson of Courbet and Millet." The subtitle of the work should be, "Is this all there is to life?"

The Excommunication of Robert Le Pieux

The bishops exit after performing the rite. The king and queen are stunned, the sceptre dropped. The ritual candle has been snuffed out, it falls, fuming, echoing through the huge hall ...

Again, is this art or only cheap theatrics?

● *Return to the mezzanine. Skip the next room, then left into Room 55 labeled "Symbolisme."*

Art Not Worth a Second Look

The Orsay's director said: "Certainly we have bad paintings. But we have only the greatest bad paintings." And here they are.

Serenity

An idyll in the woods. Three nymphs with harps waft off to the right. These people are stoned on something.

The School of Plato (L'École de Platon)

Subtitled, "The Athens YMCA." A Christ-like Plato surrounded by adoring, half-naked nubile youths gives new meaning to the term "Platonic relationship."

Will the pendulum shift so that one day art like *The School of Plato* becomes the new, radical avant-garde style?

● *Return to the mezzanine and continue to the far end. Enter the last room on the left (#65) and head for the far corner.*

ART NOUVEAU

The Industrial Age brought factories, row houses, machines, train stations, geometrical precision—and ugliness. At the turn of the century
some artists reacted against the unrelieved geometry of harsh, pragmat-
ic iron-and-steel, Eiffel-Tower art with a "new art"—Art Nouveau (pron:
art new-VO). Hmm. I think I had a driver's ed teacher by that name.

Charpentier — *Dining Room of Adrien Benard (Boiserie de la Salle à Mangé de la Propriété Benard)*

Like Nature, which also abhors a straight line,
Art Nouveau artists used the curves of flowers
and vines as their pattern. They were convinced
that "practical" didn't have to mean "ugly" as well.
They turned everyday household objects into art.

This wood-paneled dining room with its organic shapes is one of the finest examples of the Art
Nouveau style (called Jugendstil in Germanic
countries). Another is the curvy wrought-iron work of some of Paris'
early Métro entrances (some survive) built by the same man who commissioned this dining room for his home.

● *Browse through the Art Nouveau rooms to the left. You'll spill out back
onto the mezzanine. Grab a seat in front of the Rodin statue of a man
missing everything but his legs.*

Auguste Rodin

Rodin completes the tour—from classical sculpture to Impressionist
painting to an artist who brought them both together. Rodin combined classical solidity with Impressionist surfaces to become the
greatest sculptor since Michelangelo.

Rodin — *The Walking Man (L'Homme qui Marche)*

This muscular, forcefully striding man could be a
symbol of the Renaissance Man with his classical
power. But Rodin also learned a thing or two from
the comparatively lightweight Impressionist
painters. Get close and look at the statue's surface.
This rough "unfinished" look reflects light like
the rough Impressionist brushwork, making the
statue come alive, never quite at rest in the viewer's eye.

● *Near the far end of the mezzanine you'll see a small bronze couple (L'Age Mur) by Camille Claudel, a student of Rodin's.*

Claudel — *L'Age Mur*

Camille Claudel, Rodin's student and mistress, may have portrayed their doomed love affair here. A young girl desperately reaches out to an older man, who is led away reluctantly by an older woman. The center of the composition is the empty space left when their hands separate. In real life, Rodin refused to leave his wife, and Camille (see her head sticking up from a block of marble) ended up in an insane asylum.

Rodin — *The Gates of Hell (Porte de l'Enfer)*

Rodin worked for decades on these doors, and it contains some of his greatest hits, small statues that he later executed in full size. Find "The Thinker" squatting above the doorway, contemplating Man's fate. And in the lower left is the same kneeling man eating his children ("Ugolin") you'll see in full size nearby.

Rodin paid models to run, squat, leap, and spin around his studio however they wanted. When he saw an interesting pose he'd yell "freeze" (or "statue maker") and get out his sketch pad. Many of these snapshots found their way into these doors based on Dante's *Inferno*.

Rodin — *Balzac*

The great French novelist is given a heroic, monumental ugliness. Wrapped in a long cloak, he thrusts his head out at a defiant angle, showing the strong individualism and egoism of the 19th-century Romantic movement. Balzac is proud and snooty—but his body forms a question mark, and underneath the twisted features we can see a touch of personal pain and self-doubt. This is hardly camera-eye realism—Balzac wasn't that grotesque—but it captures a personality that strikes us even if we don't know the man.

From this perch, look over the main floor at all the classical statues between you and the big clock and realize how far we've come—not in years, but in style changes. Many of the statues below—beautiful, smooth, balanced, and idealized—were done at the same time as Rodin's powerful, haunting works. Rodin is a good place to end the tour. With a stable base of 19th-century stone, he launched art into the 20th century.

9 Versailles

If you've ever wondered why your American passport has French writing in it, you'll find the answer at Versailles (pron: vehr-SIGH). The powerful court of Louis XIV at Versailles set the standard of culture for all of Europe right up to modern times. Versailles was every king's dream palace, and today, if you're planning to visit just one palace in all of Europe, make it Versailles.

CHÂTEAU DE VERSAILLES

Hours: Tuesday–Sunday 9:00–18:30, October–April closes one hour early, closed all Mondays and some holidays. The fountains play marvelously each summer Sunday at 15:30.

Note: Sometimes there are big **crowd problems**. Summertime crowds can be horrendous, especially on Tuesday, Sunday, and daily around 10:00 and 13:00. It's less crowded early and late. Individuals join the longest line (door A1). Those with the Paris Museum Card (or who took the private guided tour) are allowed in through A2 without a wait. Remember, the crowds gave Marie-Antoinette a pain in the neck too, so relax and let them eat cake.

Cost: 45 F (discounted after 15:30 or all day Sunday—35 F); 35 F for those ages 18–25 and over 60; free for those under 18. The grounds are free, except for fountain-filled Sundays (every Sunday from May through October, 11:15–11:35 and 15:30–17:00, 25 F). The Paris Museum Card includes admission to Versailles (as well as to all Paris sights in this book). This can be a great time- and money-saver, especially at Versailles where two-hour lines are common and card holders have the no-wait A2 door. (For specifics on the Museum Card, see chapter 7.)

Tour length: Six hours round-trip from Paris (an hour each way in transit, two hours for the palace, two for the grounds).

Getting there: Take the RER-C train (30 minutes, 26 F round-trip) to "Versailles R.G." (not "Versailles C.H."). Trains, usually named "Vick," leave about five times an hour for the palace. Get off at Versailles Rive Gauche (the end of the line). RER-C trains leave from these RER/Métro stops: "Invalides" (Napoleon's Tomb, military museum, Rodin museum), "Champ de Mars" (Eiffel Tower), "Musée d'Orsay," "St Michel" (Notre Dame, Latin Quarter), and "Gare d' Austerlitz." Then walk 10 minutes to the palace. Your Eurailpass is good on the RER trains (show it to get a ticket for the turnstiles, keep this ticket to get out upon arrival). When returning, look through the windows past the turnstiles for the departure board. Any train leaving Versailles goes as far as downtown Paris (they're marked "all stations until Austerlitz").

Information: Information booths at several locations have specifics on English-language tours. General tours to the private apartments leave throughout the day. In addition to the base admission price to the palace (45 F), you'll pay 25 F at door C for a 60-minute guided tour, 37 F for a 90-minute tour, or 30 F for an audiotape. Tel. 01 30 84 76 18 or 01 30 84 74 00. WC and phones are near the general entrance.

Cuisine art: The cafeteria is near the general entrance. Restaurants line the street to right of equestrian statue. There's a handy McDonald's immediately across from the train station (WC without crowds).

Starring: Louis XIV and the Old Regime.

KINGS AND QUEENS AND GUILLOTINES

● *Read this on the train ride out there. Relax, the palace is the last stop.*

Come the Revolution, when they line us up and make us stick out our hands, will you have enough calluses to keep them from shooting you? A grim thought, but Versailles raises questions like that. It's the symbol of the Old Regime, a time when society was divided into rulers and rulees, when you were born to be rich or to be poor. To some it's the pinnacle of civilization, to others the sign of a civilization in decay. Either way it remains one of Europe's most impressive sights.

Versailles was the residence of the king and seat of France's government for a hundred years. Louis XIV (reigned 1643–1715) moved out of the Louvre in Paris, the previous royal residence, and built an elaborate palace in the forests and swamps of Versailles, 12 miles west. The reasons for the move were partly personal—Louis loved the out of doors and disliked the sniping environs of stuffy Paris—and partly politics.

Louis was creating the first modern, centralized state. At Versailles he consolidated Paris' scattered ministries so he could personally control policy. More important, he invited to Versailles all of France's nobles so he could control them. Living a life of almost enforced idleness, the "domesticated" aristocracy couldn't interfere with the way Louis ran things. With 18 million people united under one king (England had only 5.5 million), a booming economy, and a powerful military, France was Europe's #1 power.

Versailles was also the cultural heartbeat of Europe. Every king wanted a palace like Versailles. Everyone learned French. French taste in clothes, hairstyles, table manners, theater, music, art, and kissing spread across the Continent. That cultural dominance has continued to some extent right up to our century.

LOUIS XIV

At the center of all this was Europe's greatest king. He was a true Renaissance Man a century after the Renaissance—athletic, good looking, a musician, dancer, horseman, statesman, art lover, lover. For all his grandeur he was one of history's most polite and approachable kings, a good listener who could put even commoners at ease in his presence.

Louis called himself the Sun King, because he gave life and warmth to all that he touched. He was also thought of as Apollo, the Greek god of the sun. Versailles became the personal temple of this god on earth, decorated with statues and symbols of Apollo, the sun, and Louis himself.

Louis was a hands-on king who personally ran affairs of state. All decisions were made by him. Nobles, who in other countries were the center of power, became virtual slaves dependent on Louis' generosity. For 70 years he was the perfect embodiment of the absolute monarch. He summed it up best himself with his famous rhyme—"*L'état, c'est moi!*" ("The state, that's me!").

Only Two More Louises To Remember

Three kings lived in Versailles during its century of glory. Louis XIV built it and established French dominance. Louis XV, his great-grandson (Louis XIV reigned for 72 years), carried on the tradition and policies but without the Sun King's flair. During Louis XV's reign, France's power abroad was weakening and there were rumblings of rebellion from within.

France's monarchy was crumbling, and the time was ripe for a strong leader to re-establish the old feudal order. They didn't get one. Instead, they got Louis XVI, a shy, meek bookworm, the kind of guy who lost sleep over Revolutionary graffiti ... because it was misspelled. Louis XVI married a sweet girl from the Austrian royal family, Marie-Antoinette, and together they retreated into the idyllic gardens of Versailles while revolutionary fires smoldered.

They finally got their rude awakening in October 1789, when a mob of angry Parisians stormed the palace, trashed it, and kidnapped the Royal Family, taking them back to Paris. Four years later they lost their heads under the guillotine. The Old Regime was dead. No longer the center of Europe, Versailles became a museum.

ORIENTATION

This *Mona* tour covers the ceremonial center of the palace (the State Apartments) and the extensive grounds.

The only way to see the "King's Apartments"—the actual bedroom and private rooms—is to pay for a guided tour (Tour C). The advantages of Tour C are: (1) these rooms are more lavishly furnished than the ones we'll see; (2) you visit the Opera House, the single most stunning place in the whole complex; and (3) it gets you into the palace (where you can then take this self-guided tour) without standing in line quite so long.

The disadvantages: (1) it costs more; (2) it takes an hour and a half, sometimes with a boring guide; and (3) you see pretty much the same kinds of things covered in your *Mona* tour. If you do it, do it first to get into the palace quicker. For true Versailles-o-philes, two more guided tours feature the queen's apartments and the royal opera and chapel.

● *Leave the Versailles R.G. train station and turn right, following signs to "chateau." Walk about a hundred yards, turn left, and make the grand approach over Europe's biggest cobblestones up to the palace. Enter the iron-work gates and stop at the equestrian statue in the middle of the large court.*

Locate the entrances. The self-guided tour we'll take starts at door A, located on the right side of the courtyard—where the line is. The guided tour (door C) is ahead on the left, in an alleyway. Remember, those with a Museum Card can cro enter door A2. (If the lines are long, get in line now, but orient yourself from the statue.)

The central palace, the part we'll tour, forms a U around the courtyard in front of you. The right half (King's Wing) is separated from the left half (Queen's Wing) by the Hall of Mirrors ahead of you. Then two long wings shoot out to the right and left (north and south) of this U. In our Mona tour, we'll walk counterclockwise through the U-shaped part on the middle floor.

VERSAILLES

The Original Château

The part of the palace directly behind the horse in the statue, at the far end of the courtyard, is the original château. Louis XIV's dad used to come out to the forests of Versailles to escape the worries of king-ship. Here he built this small hunting lodge. His son spent the happi-est times of his boyhood at the lodge, hunting and riding. Louis XIV's three arched bedroom windows (beneath the clock) overlooked the courtyard. Naturally, it faced the rising sun. The palace and grounds are laid out on an east-west axis.

When he became king, Louis XIV spent more and more time here, away from the hubbub of Paris. He expanded the lodge, planted gar-dens, and entertained guests. The reputation spread about this "Enchanted Island," a kind of Disneyworld for dukes and duchesses. As visitors flocked here, Louis expanded around the original hunting chateau, attaching wings to create the present U-shape. Then, the long north and south wings were built. The total cost of the project has been guess-timated to be half of France's entire GNP for one year.

Think how busy this courtyard must have been 300 years ago. There were as many as 5,000 nobles here at any one time, each with an entourage. They'd buzz from games to parties to amorous rendezvous in sedan-chair taxis. Servants ran about delivering secret messages and roast legs of lamb. Horse-drawn carriages arrived at the fancy gate with their finely-dressed passengers, having driven up the broad boulevard that ran direct from Paris. (You can still see the horse stables lining the boulevard.) Incredible as it seems, both the grounds and most of the palace were public territory where even the lowliest peasant could come to gawk. Of course this meant that there were, then as now, hordes of tourists, pickpockets, and dark-skinned men selling wind-up children's toys.

● *Enter at Entrance A (or at A2, if you have a museum card) and buy your ticket. After showing your ticket, you first pass through the 21 rooms of the history museum, with paintings on the background of Versailles and its kings.*

Our tour starts upstairs, in the room that overlooks the lavish Royal Chapel. If you took the guided tour, you may spill out here, looking at the upper level of the Royal Chapel.

The State Apartments

Royal Chapel

In the vast pagan "temple" that is Versailles, built to glorify one man, Louis XIV—the Sun King and Apollo on earth—this Royal Chapel is a paltry tip of the hat to that "other" god, the Christian one. It's virtually the first, last, and only hint of Christianity you'll see in the entire complex. Versailles celebrates Man, not God, by raising Louis to almost godlike status, the personification of all good human qualities. In a way, Versailles is the last great flowering of Renaissance humanism and revival of the classical world.

Louis attended Mass here every morning. While he sat on the upper level, the lowly nobles below would turn their backs to the altar and look up—worshiping Louis worshiping God. Important religious ceremonies took place here, including the marriage of young Louis XVI to Marie-Antoinette.

● *Take a seat in the next room, a large room with a fireplace and a colorful painting on the ceiling.*

Hercules Drawing Room

Pleasure ruled at Versailles. The main suppers, balls, and official receptions were held in this room. Picture elegant party-goers in fine silks, wigs, rouge, and lipstick (and that's just the men) dancing to the strains of Mozart played by a string quartet.

On the wall opposite the fireplace is an appropriate painting, showing Christ in the middle of a Venetian party. The work by Veronese, a gift from the Republic of Venice, was one of Louis' favorites, so they decorated the room around it.

The ceiling painting of Hercules being crowned a god gives the room its name. Hercules (with his club) rides up to heaven on a chariot, where the king of the gods is ready to give him his daughter in marriage. Louis XIV built the room for his own daughter's wedding reception.

● *The following rooms are listed in order. The names of the rooms generally come from the paintings on the ceiling. From here on it's a one-way tour—getting lost is not allowed. Follow the crowds into the small green room with a goddess in pink on the ceiling.*

The King's Wing

Cornucopia Room

If the party in the Hercules Room got too intense, you could always step in here for some refreshments. Silver trays were loaded up with liqueurs, coffee, juice, chocolates, and on really special occasions, three-bean salad.

The ceiling painting shows the cornucopia of riches poured down on invited guests. Around the edges of the ceiling are painted versions of the king's actual dinnerware and treasures.

Louis himself might be here. He was a gracious host who enjoyed letting his hair down at night. If he took a liking to you, he might sneak you through those doors there (in the middle of the wall), into his own private study where he'd show off his collection of dishes, medals, jewels, or … the *Mona Lisa*, which hung on his wall.

Venus Room

Love ruled at Versailles. In this room, couples would cavort beneath a canopy of golden garlands (on the ceiling) sent down to earth by the goddess of love to ensnare mortals in love.

Notice how a painted garland goes "out" the bottom of the central painting, becomes a gilded wood garland held by a satyr, then back to a painting again—Baroque artists loved to mix their media to fool the eye. Another illusion is in the paintings at both ends of the room that extend this grand room into mythical courtyards.

Don't let the statue of a confident Louis as a Roman emperor fool you. He started out as a poor little rich kid with a chip on his shoulder. His father had died before he was old enough to rule, and during the regency period the French Parliament treated little Louis and his mother like trash. They were virtual prisoners, humiliated in their home (the Louvre), surviving on bland meals, hand-me-down leotards, and pointed shoes. Once he attained power and wealth, there was one topic you never discussed in Louis' presence—poverty. Maybe Versailles was his way of saying, "Living well is the best revenge."

Diana Room

This was the billiards room. Men played on a table that stood in the center of the room, while ladies sat surrounding them on Persian-carpet cushions.

The famous bust of Louis by Bernini (now in the center) shows a handsome, dashing, 27-year-old playboy-king. His gaze is steady amid his wind-blown cloak and hair. Young Louis loved life. He hunted by day (notice Diana the Huntress on the ceiling) and partied by night.

Games were actually an important part of Louis' political strategy known as "the domestication of the nobility." By distracting the nobles with the pleasures of courtly life, he was free to run the government his way. Billiards, dancing, and concerts were popular, but the biggest was gambling, usually a card game similar to "21." Louis lent money to the losers, making them even more indebted to him. The good life was an addiction, and Louis kept the medicine cabinet well-stocked.

Mars Room

Decorated with a military flair, this was the room for Louis' Swiss bodyguards. On the ceiling, there's Mars, the Greek god of war, in a chariot pulled by wolves. The bronze cupids in the corners are escalating from love arrows to heavier artillery. Notice the fat walls that hid thin servants who were to be at their master's constant call—but out of sight when not needed. Don't miss the view of the sculpted gardens out the window.

Mercury Room

Louis' life was a work of art, and Versailles was the display case. Everything he did was a public event designed to show his subjects how it should be done. This room served as Louis' official bedroom, where the Sun King would ritually rise each morning to warm his subjects.

The tapestry on the wall shows how this ceremony might have looked. From a canopied bed, Louis would rise, dress, and take a seat for morning prayer. Meanwhile, the nobles (on the left), stand behind a balustrade, in awe of his piety, nobility, and clean socks. When Louis went to bed at night, the nobles would fight over who got to hold the candle while he slipped into his royal jammies. Bedtime, wake-up, and meals were all public rituals.

The two chests that furnish the room, with their curved legs, gilding, and heavy animal feet, are done in the "Louis the XIVth" style. Later furniture found in other rooms is lighter, straighter, and less ornamented. The clock dates from Louis' time. When the cocks crowed at the top of the hour and the temple doors opened, guess who popped out?

Apollo Room

This was the grand throne room. Louis held court from a 10-foot silver-canopied throne on a raised platform placed in the center of the room. (Notice the four metal bolts in the ceiling that once supported the canopy.)

Everything in here reminds us that Louis was not just any ruler, but the Sun King who lights the whole world with his presence. The ceiling shows Apollo in his chariot, dragging the sun across the heavens every day. Notice the ceiling with its beautifully gilded frame and *Goldfinger* maidens.

In the corners are the four corners of the world, all, of course, warmed by the sun. Counterclockwise from above the exit door are (1) Europe, with a sword, (2) Asia, with a lion, (3) Africa, with an elephant, and (4) good old America, an Indian maiden with a crocodile.

The famous portrait by Rigaud over the fireplace gives a more human look at Louis. He's shown in a dancer's pose, displaying the legs that made him one of the all-time dancing fools of kingery. At night, they often held parties in this room, actually dancing around the throne.

Louis (who was 63 when this was painted) had more than 300 wigs like this one, changing them many times a day. This fashion first started when his hairline began to recede, then sprouted all over Europe, spreading even to the American colonies in the time of George Washington.

Louis may have been treated like a god, but he was not an overly arrogant man. His subjects adored him because he was a symbol of everything a man could be, the fullest expression of the Renaissance Man.

The War Room

Versailles was good propaganda. It showed the rest of the world how rich and powerful Louis was. One look at this eye-saturating view of the gardens sent visitors reeling.

But France's success also made other countries jealous and nervous. The semi-circles on the ceiling show Germany (with the double eagle), Holland (with its ships), and Spain (with a red flag and roaring lion) ganging up on Louis. Two guesses who won. Of course, these mere mortals were no match for the Sun King. The stucco relief on the wall shows Louis on horseback triumphing over his fallen enemies.

But Louis' greatest triumph may be the next room, the one that everybody wrote home about.

The Hall of Mirrors

No one had ever seen anything like this hall when it was opened. Mirrors were still a great luxury at the time, and the number and size of these monsters were astounding. The hall is almost 250 feet long. There are 17 arched mirrors matched by 17 windows with that breathtaking view of the gardens. Lining the hall are 24 gilded candelabra, eight busts of Roman emperors, and eight classical-style statues (seven of them ancient). The ceiling decoration chronicles Louis' military accomplishments, topped off by Louis himself in the central panel (with cupids playing cards at his divine feet) doing what he did best—triumphing.

This was where the grandest festivities were held for the most important ambassadors and guests. The throne could be moved from the Apollo Room and set up at the far end of the hall. Imagine this place filled with guests dressed in silks and powdered wigs, lit by the flames of thousands of candles. The mirrors are a ... reflection of an age when beautiful people loved to look at themselves. It was no longer a sin to be proud of good looks or fine clothes or to enjoy the good things in life, laughing, dancing, eating, drinking, flirting, and enjoying the view.

From the center of the hall, you can fully appreciate the epic scale of Versailles. The huge palace (by architect Le Brun), the fantasy interior (Le Vau), and the endless gardens (Le Notre) made Versailles le best.

In more recent times, the Hall of Mirrors is where the Treaty of Versailles was signed ending World War I (and, some say, starting WWII).

● *Enter the small Peace Room and grab a bench.*

The Peace Room

"Louis Quatorze was addicted to wars ..." but by the end of his life, he was tired of fighting. In this sequel to the War Room, peace is granted to Germany, Holland, and Spain as cupids play with the discarded cannons, armor, and swords.

The oval painting above the fireplace shows 19-year-old Louis bestowing an olive branch on Europe. Beside him is his wife, Marie-Therese, cradling their two-year-old twin daughters. If being a father at 17 seems a bit young, remember that Louis was married when he was ... four.

The Peace Room marks the beginning of the queen's half of the palace. On Sunday the queen held chamber music concerts here for family and friends.

● *Enter the first room of the Queen's wing, with its canopied bed.*

The Queen's Wing

The Queen's Bedchamber

This was the queen's official bedroom. Sometimes the queen actually slept here, and it was here that she would rendezvous with her husband. Two queens died here. This is where 19 princes were born. The chandelier is where two of them were conceived. Just kidding.

True, Louis was not the most faithful husband. There was no attempt to hide the fact that the Sun King warmed more than one bed, for he was above the rules of mere mortals. Adultery became acceptable—even fashionable—in court circles. The secret-looking doors on either side of the bed were for Louis' late-night liaisons—they lead straight to his rooms.

Some of Louis' mistresses became more famous and powerful than his rather quiet queen, but he was faithful to the show of marriage and had genuine affection for his wife. Their private apartments were connected, and Louis made a point of sleeping with the queen as often as possible, regardless of whose tiara he tickled earlier in the evening.

This room looks like it did in the days of the last queen, Marie-

Antoinette. That's her bust over the fireplace and the double-eagle of her native Austria in the corners. The big chest to the left of the bed held her jewels.

The queen's canopied bed is a reconstruction. The bed, chair, and wall coverings switched with the seasons. This was the cheery summer pattern.

Drawing Room of the Nobles

The queen's circle of friends met here, seated on the stools. Discussions ranged from politics to gossip, food to literature, fashion to philosophy. The Versailles kings considered themselves enlightened monarchs who promoted the arts and new ideas. Folks like Voltaire—a political radical—and the playwright Moliére participated in the Versailles court. Ironically, these discussions planted the seeds of liberal thought that would grow into the Revolution.

Queen's Antechamber

This is where the Royal Family dined publicly while servants and nobles fluttered around them, admiring their table manners and laughing at the king's jokes like courtly Paul Shaeffers. A typical dinner consisted of four different soups, two whole birds stuffed with truffles, mutton, ham slices, fruit, pastry, compotes, and preserves.

The portrait in the center is of luxury-loving, "Let-them-eat-cake" Marie-Antoinette, who became a symbol of decadence to the French peasants. The portrait at the far end is a P.R. attempt to soften her image, showing her with three of her nine children.

On the ceiling is a scene showing pilgrims bowing before Darius, with the world's shortest legs. (If you think that's a stretch, try looking for levity in the palace guidebook.)

Queen's Guard Room

On October 6, 1789, a mob of revolutionaries—appalled by their queen's taste in wallpaper—stormed the palace. They were fed up with the life of luxury led by the ruling class in the countryside while they were starving in the grimy streets of Paris.

The king and queen locked themselves in. Some of the Revolutionaries got access to this upper floor. They burst into this room, where Marie-Antoinette had taken refuge, then killed three of her bodyguards and dragged her and her husband off. (Some claim that, as they carried her away, she sang "Louis, Louis, oh-oh ... we gotta go now.")

The enraged peasants then proceeded to ransack the place, taking revenge for the years of poverty and oppression they'd suffered. Marie-Antoinette and Louis XVI were later taken to the Place de la Concorde in Paris, where they knelt under the guillotine and were made a foot shorter at the top.

Did the king and queen deserve it? Were the Revolutionaries destroying civilization or clearing the decks for a new and better one? Was Versailles progress or decadence?

Coronation Room

No sooner did they throw out a king than they got an emperor. The Revolution established democracy, but it was shaky in a country that wasn't used to it. In the midst of the confusion, the upstart general Napoleon Bonaparte took control and soon held dictatorial powers. This room captures the glory of the Napoleon years when he conquered most of Europe. In the huge canvas on the left-hand wall, we see him crowning himself emperor of a new, revived "Roman" Empire. (This is a lesser quality copy of a version hanging in the Louvre. For a full description of David's *The Coronation of Napoleon*, see chapter 7.)

Catch the portrait of a dashing, young, charismatic Napoleon by the window on the right. This shows him in 1796 when he was just a general in command of the Revolution's army in Italy. Compare this with the portrait next to it from 10 years later—looking less like a Revolutionary and more like a Louis. Above the young Napoleon is a portrait of Josephine, his wife and France's empress. In David's *Distribution of Eagles* (opposite the *Coronation*) the victorious general (in imperial garb) passes out emblems of victory to his loyal troops. In *The Battle of Aboukir* (opposite the window), Napoleon looks rather bored as he slashes through a tangle of dark-skinned warriors. His horse, though, has a look of "What are we doing in this mob?! Let's get out of here!"

Let's.

● *Pass through a couple of rooms to the exit staircase on your left. The long Battle Gallery ahead of you shows 130 yards of scenes from famous French battles arranged chronologically clockwise around the gallery. The exit staircase puts you outside on the left (south) side of the palace.*

The Gardens — Controlling Nature

Louis was a divine-right ruler. One way he proved it was by controlling nature like a god. These lavish grounds, so elaborately planned out, pruned, and decorated showed everyone that Louis was in total command.

● *Exiting the palace into the gardens, veer to the left toward the concrete railing about 75 yards away. You'll pass through flowers, cookie-cutter patterns of shrubs, and green cones. Stand at the railing overlooking the courtyard below and the Louis-made lake in the distance.*

The Orangerie

The warmth from the Sun King was so great that he could even grow orange trees in chilly France. Louis had a thousand of these and other exotic plants to amaze his visitors. In wintertime they were kept warm in the long greenhouses (beneath your feet) that surround the courtyard. On sunny days they were wheeled out in their silver planters and scattered around the grounds.

● *From the stone railing, turn about-face and walk back toward the palace, veering left toward the two large pools of water. Sit on the top stair and look away from the palace.*

View down the Royal Drive

This, to me, is the most impressive spot in all of Versailles. In one direction, the palace. Stretching out in the other, the endless grounds. Versailles was laid out along an eight-mile axis that included the grounds, the palace, and the town of Versailles itself, one of the first instances of urban planning since Roman times and a model for future capitals like Washington, D.C., and Brasilia.

Looking down the Royal Drive (also known as "the Green Carpet") you see the round Apollo fountain way in the distance. Just beyond that is the Grand Canal. The groves on either side of the Royal Drive were planted with trees from all over, laid out in an elaborate grid and dotted with statues and fountains. Of the original 1,500 fountains, 300 remain.

Looking back at the palace you can see the Hall of Mirrors—it's the middle story, with the arched windows.

● *Stroll down the steps to get a good look at the frogs and lizards that fill the round Latona Basin.*

The Latona Basin

The theme of Versailles is Apollo, the god of the sun, associated with Louis. This round fountain tells the story of the birth of Apollo and his sister Diana. On top of the fountain are Apollo and Diana as little kids with their mother, Latona (they're facing toward the Apollo fountain). Latona, an unwed mother, was insulted by the local peasants. She called on the king of the gods, Zeus (the children's father), to avenge the insult. Zeus swooped down and turned all the peasants into the frogs and lizards that ring the fountain.

● *As you walk down past the basin toward the Royal Drive, you'll pass by "ancient" statues done by 17th-century French sculptors. The Colonnade is hidden in the woods on the left-hand side of the Royal Drive about three-fourths of the way to the Apollo Basin.*

The Colonnade

Versailles had no prestigious ancient ruins so they built their own. This pre-fab Roman ruin is a 100-foot circle of 64 marble columns supporting arches. Beneath the arches are small bird-bath fountains. Nobles would picnic in the shade to the tunes of a string quartet, pretending they were the enlightened citizens of the ancient world.

The Apollo Basin

The fountains of Versailles were its most famous attraction, a marvel of both art and engineering. This one was the centerpiece, showing the Sun God—Louis—in his sunny chariot starting his journey across the sky. The horses are half-submerged, giving the impression, when the fountains play, of the sun rising out of the mists of dawn. Most of the fountains were only turned on when the king walked by, but this one played constantly for the benefit of those watching from the palace.

All the fountains are gravity-powered. They work on the same principle as when you block a hose with your finger to make it squirt. Underground streams, flowing from basins up at the palace, feed into smaller pipes at the fountains which shoot the water high into the air.

Looking back at the palace from here, realize that the distance you just walked is only a fraction of this vast complex of buildings, gardens, and waterways. Be glad you don't have to mow the lawn.

The Grand Canal

Why visit Venice when you can just build your own? In an era before virtual reality, this was the next-best thing to an actual trip. Couples in gondolas would pole along the waters accompanied by barges with orchestras playing "O Sole Mio." The canal is actually cross-shaped, this being the long arm, a mile from end to end. Of course, this too is a man-made body of water with no function other than to please.

The Trianon Area — Retreat from Reality

Versailles began as an escape from the pressures of kingship. In a short time, the palace was as busy as Paris ever was. Louis needed an escape from his escape and built a smaller palace out in the tulies. Later, his successors retreated still farther into the garden, building a fantasy world of simple pleasures from which to ignore the real world, crumbling all around them.

● *You can rent a bike or catch the tourist tram, but the walk is half the fun. It's about a 30-minute walk from here to the end of the tour, plus another 30 minutes to walk back to the palace. The Grand Trianon (pron: TREE-ah-non) is 10 minutes northwest of the Apollo Basin (the palace is due east).*

The Grand Trianon

This was the king's private residence away from the main palace. Louis usually spent a couple nights a week here, but the later Louises spent more and more time retreating.

The façade of this one-story building is a charming combination of pink, yellow, and white, a cheery contrast to the imposing Baroque façade of the main palace. Ahead you can see the gardens through the columns. The king's apartments were to the left of the columns.

The flower gardens were changed daily for the king's pleasure—so he'd have new color combinations to look at, but also to create interesting new "nasal cocktails."

Walk around the palace (to the right) if you'd like, for a view of the gardens and rear façade.

● *Facing the front do an about-face. The Summer House is not down the driveway, but about 200 yards away along the smaller pathway at about 10 o'clock.*

The Summer House of the French Garden

This small white building with four rooms fanning out from the center was one more step away from the modern world. Here the queen spent summer evenings with family and a few friends listening to music or playing parlor games. All avenues of *la douceur de vivre*— "the sweetness of living"—were explored. To the left are the buildings of the Menagerie where cows, goats, chickens, and ducks were bred.

● *Continue frolicking along the path until you run into ...*

The Petit Trianon

Louis XV developed an interest in botany. He wanted to spend more time near the French Gardens, but the Summer House just wasn't big enough. He built the Petit Trianon (the "small" Trianon), a masterpiece of Neoclassical architecture. This grey, cubical building has four distinct façades, each a perfect and harmonious combination of Greek-style columns, windows, and railings. Walk around it and find your favorite.

Louis XVI and his wife, Marie-Antoinette, made this their home base. Marie-Antoinette was a sweet girl from Vienna who never quite fit in with the fast, sophisticated crowd at Versailles. Here at the Petit Trianon she could get away and recreate the simple home life she remembered from her childhood. On the lawn outside she installed a merry-go-round.

● *Five minutes more will bring you to ...*

The Temple of Love

A circle of 12 marble Corinthian columns supporting a dome decorate a path where lovers would stroll. Underneath, there's a statue of Cupid making a bow (to shoot arrows of love) out of the club of Hercules. It's a delightful monument to a society whose rich could afford that ultimate luxury, romantic love. When the Revolution came, I bet they wished they'd kept the club.

● *And finally you'll reach ...*

Le Hameau — The Hamlet

Marie-Antoinette longed for the simple life of a peasant. Not the hard labor of real peasants—who sweated and starved around her—but the fairy-tale world of simple country pleasures. She built this complex of 12 buildings as her own private village.

This was an actual working farm with a dairy, a water-wheel mill, and domestic animals. The harvest was served at Marie's table. Marie didn't do much work herself, but she "supervised," dressed in a plain white muslin dress and a straw hat.

The Queen's House is the main building, actually two buildings connected by a wooden gallery. Like any typical peasant farmhouse it had a billiard room, library, elegant dining hall, and two living rooms.

Nearby was the small theater. Here Marie and her friends acted out plays far from the rude intrusions of the real world ...

● *The real world and the main palace are a 30-minute walk to the southeast. Along the way, stop at the Neptune Basin near the palace, an impressive mini-lake with fountains, and indulge your own favorite fantasy.*

10 Historic Paris Walk
Ile de la Cité, Notre Dame,
Ste-Chapelle, and in Between

Paris has been the capital of Europe for centuries. We'll start where it did, on the Île de la Cité, with forays onto both the Left and Right Banks on a walk that laces together the story of Paris: Roman, medieval, the Revolution, café society, the literary scene of the '20s, and into the modern world.

HOURS AND COSTS

Notre Dame: Daily 8:00–18:45, free, Sunday Mass at 8:00, 8:45, 10:00, 11:30, 12:30, and 18:30. Leaflet with church schedule at booth inside entrance. Ask about free English tours, normally Wednesday and Thursday at noon and Saturday at 14:30. Tower climb—400 steps and 30 F, expensive but worth it for the gargoyle's-eye view of the cathedral, Seine, and city, 9:00–17:00.

Notre Dame Archaeological Crypt: Daily 10:00–18:00, entry 100 meters in front of the cathedral, 50 F includes Notre Dame Tower.

Deportation Memorial: Weekdays 8:30–21:45, opens at 9:00 on weekends, shorter hours off-season, free.

Sainte-Chapelle: Daily 9:30–18:00, shorter hours off-season, 32 F.

Conciergerie: Daily 9:30–18:30, shorter hours off-season, 28 F.

Paris Museum Card: Each of these sights is covered on the card, which for many is a great time- and money-saver. (See chapter 7, on the Louvre, for details.)

NOTRE DAME

● *Start at the Notre Dame Cathedral on the island in the River Seine, the physical and historic bull's-eye of your Paris map. Closest Métro stops are Cité, Hotel de Ville, and St-Michel, each requiring a short walk. On the square in front of the cathedral, stand far enough back to take in the whole façade. Look at the circular window in the center.*

For centuries, the main figure in the Christian "pantheon" has been the goddess Mary, the mother of Jesus. Common people pray to her directly in times of trouble, for comfort and to ask her to convince God to be compassionate with them. The church is dedicated to "Our Lady" (Notre Dame), and there she is, cradling God, right in the heart

ÎLE DE LA CITÉ

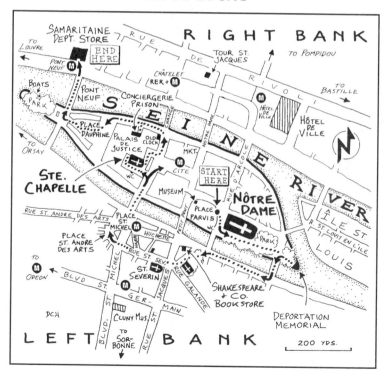

of the façade, surrounded by the halo of the rose window. Though the church is massive and imposing, it has always stood for the grace and compassion of Mary, the "mother of God."

The people of Paris broke ground in 1163. The cathedral was finished by their great-great-great-great-great-great grandchildren in 1345, a testament to the faith of these people. Look up the 200-foot bell towers and imagine a tiny medieval community mustering the money and energy to build this. Master masons supervised, but the people did much of the grunt work themselves for free—hauling the huge stones from distant quarries, digging a 30-foot-deep trench to lay the foundations, and treading like rats on a wheel designed to lift

NOTRE DAME FAÇADE

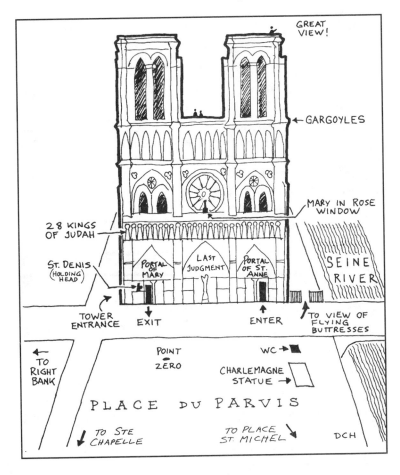

the stones up, one by one. This kind of backbreaking, arduous manual labor created the real hunchbacks of Notre Dame.

● *Walk this way toward the cathedral, and view it from the bronze plaque on the ground marked ...*

Point Zero

You're standing at the very "center" of France, from which all distances are measured. The "Cité" started here in the third century B.C. In 52 B.C., the Romans booted out the Parisii tribe, built their government palace at the end of the square behind you, and a Temple of Jupiter where the cathedral sits. Two thousand years of dirt and debris have raised the city's altitude. The archaeological crypt nearby offers a fascinating look at the remains of the earlier city and church below today's street level.

Still facing the church, on your right is a grand equestrian statue of Charlemagne ("Charles the Great"), whose reign marked the birth of modern Europe. Crowned in A.D. 800, he briefly united much of Europe during the Dark Ages. (Maybe more interesting than Chuck the Great are nearby restrooms—the cleanest you'll find in downtown Paris.)

Before renovation, 150 years ago, this square was much smaller, a characteristic medieval shambles facing a run-down church, surrounded by winding streets and countless medieval buildings. The huge church belltowers rose above this tangle of smaller buildings, inspiring Victor Hugo's story of a deaf, bell-ringing hunchback who could look down on all Paris.

● *Now turn your attention to the church façade. Look at the left doorway and, to the left of the door, find the statue with his head in his hands.*

Notre Dame Façade

When Christianity began making converts in Roman Paris, this Bishop of Paris was beheaded. But these early Christians were hard to keep down. St. Denis got up, tucked his head under his arm, headed north, paused at a fountain to wash it off, and continued until he found just the right place to meet his maker. The Parisians were convinced of this miracle, Christianity gained ground, and a church soon replaced the pagan temple.

By the way, Montmartre (the one hill overlooking Paris) is named for this martyr. Denis eventually died on the edge of town where the church of St. Denis was built (famous in history books as the first Gothic church, but not much to see today).

● *Now look above the central doorway, where you'll find scenes from the Last Judgment.*

Central Portal

It's the end of the world, and Christ sits on the throne of Judgment (just under the arches, holding his hands up). Below him, an angel and a demon weigh souls in the balance. The good people stand to the left, looking up to heaven. The naughty ones to the right are chained up and led off to ... a six-hour tour of the Louvre on a hot day. Notice the crazy sculpted demons to the right, at the base of the arch.

● *Above the arches is a row of 28 statues, known as ...*

The Kings of Judah

In the days of the French Revolution (1789–93), these Biblical kings were mistaken for the hated French kings, and Notre Dame represented the oppressive Catholic hierarchy. The citizens stormed the church, crying, "Off with their heads!" Plop, they lopped off the crowned heads of these kings with glee, creating a row of St. Denises, that wasn't repaired for decades.

But the story doesn't end there. A schoolteacher who lived nearby collected the heads and buried them in his backyard for safekeeping. There they slept until 1977, when they were accidentally unearthed. Today, you can stare into the eyes of the original kings in the Cluny Museum, a few blocks away.

● *Enter the church and find a spot to view the long, high central aisle.*

Notre Dame Interior

Remove your metaphorical hat and become a simple bareheaded peasant, entering the dim medieval light of the church. Take a minute to let your pupils dilate, to take in the subtle, mysterious light-show God beams through the stained glass windows. Follow the slender columns up to the praying-hands arches of the ceiling and contemplate the heavens. Let's say it's dedication day for this great stone wonder. The priest intones the words of the Mass that echo through the hall: *"Terribilis est locus iste"*—"This place is *terribilis*," meaning awe-inspiring, or even terrifying. It's a huge, dark earthly cavern lit with an unearthly light.

This is Gothic. Taller and filled with light, this was a major improvement over the earlier Romanesque style. Gothic architects needed only a few structural columns topped by pointed arches that crisscross the columns to support the weight of the roof. This let them build higher than ever, freeing up the walls for windows. The church is designed in the shape of a cross, with the altar where the cross-beams intersect.

● *Walk up to the main altar.*

The Altar

This marks the spot where Mass is said and the bread and wine of communion are prepared and distributed. In olden days, there were no chairs. The church can hold up to 10,000 faithful. Join the statue of Joan of Arc (Jeanne d'Arc, in the right transept) in gazing up to the rose-shaped window, the only one of the three with its original medieval glass.

This was the holy spot for Romans, Christians … and even atheists. When the Revolutionaries stormed the church, they gutted it and turned it into a "Temple for the Cult of Reason." A woman dressed up like the Statue of Liberty held court at the altar as a symbol of the divinity of Man. France today, while nominally Catholic, remains aloof from Vatican dogmatism. Instead of traditional wooden confessional booths, notice the open, glass-walled room where modern sinners seek counseling as much as forgiveness.

Just past the altar are the walls of the choir, where more intimate services can be held in this spacious building. The aisles are lined with chapels, each dedicated to a particular saint. The faithful can pause at their favorite, light a candle as an offering, and meditate in the cool light of the stained-glass. (The nearby Treasury, containing lavish robes and golden relic-holders, probably isn't worth the 15 francs entry fee.)

● *Amble around the ambulatory, spill back outside, and make a U-turn left. Walk along the side of the cathedral that faces the river.*

Notre Dame Side View

Along the side of the church, you'll notice the flying buttresses. These 50-foot stone "beams" that stick out of the church were the key to the complex architecture of Gothic. The pointed arches we saw inside caused the weight of the roof to push outward rather than downward. The "flying" buttresses support the roof by pushing back inward. Gothic architects were masters at playing

architectural forces against each other to build loftier and loftier churches.

Picture Quasimodo running around along the railed balcony at the base of the roof among the gargoyles. These grotesque beasts that stick out from pillars and buttresses represent souls caught between heaven and earth. They also function as rain spouts when there are no evil spirits to do battle with.

The neo-Gothic 90-meter spire is a product of the 1860 reconstruction of the dilapidated old church. Around its base are apostles and evangelists (the green men) as well as Viollet-le-Duc, the architect in charge of the work. Notice how the apostles look outward, blessing the city while the architect (at top) looks up the spire, marvelling at his fine work.

● *Behind Notre Dame, squeeze through the tourist buses, cross the street, and enter the iron gate into the park at the tip of the island.*

Deportation Memorial (Mémorial de la Déportation)

This memorial to the 200,000 French victims of the Nazi concentration camps draws you into their experience. As you descend the steps, the city around you disappears. Surrounded by walls, you have become a prisoner. Your only freedom is your view of the sky and the tiny glimpse of the river below.

Enter the dark, single-file chamber ahead. You'll see barred windows and the names of concentration camps. The circular plaque in the floor reads, "They descended into the mouth of the earth and they did not return."

A hallway stretches in front of you, lined with 200,000 lighted crystals, one for each French citizen who died. Flickering at the far end is the eternal flame of hope. The tomb of the unknown deportee lies at your feet. Above, the inscription reads, "Dedicated to the living memory of the 200,000 French Deportees sleeping in the night and the fog, exterminated in the Nazi concentration camps."

Above the exit as you leave is the message you'll find at all Nazi sights: "Forgive, but never forget."

Île St-Louis

Back on street level, look across the river to the Île St-Louis. If the Île de la Cité is a tug laden with the history of Paris, it's towing this classy little residential dinghy laden only with boutiques, characteristic restaurants, and famous sorbet shops. This island wasn't developed until much later (18th century). What was a swampy mess is now harmonious Parisian architecture.

● *From the tip of the Île de la Cité, cross the bridge to the Left Bank and turn right. Walk along the river, toward the front end of Notre Dame. Stairs detour down to the riverbank if you need a place to picnic. This side view of the church from across the river is one of Europe's great sights.*

LEFT BANK (RIVE GAUCHE)

The Left Bank of the Seine—"left" if you were floating downstream—still has many of the twisting lanes and narrow buildings of medieval times. The Right Bank is more modern and business-oriented, with wide boulevards and stressed Parisians in suits. Here along the river-bank, the "big business" is books, displayed in the green metal stalls on the parapet. These literary entrepreneurs pride themselves on their easygoing business style. With flexible hours and literally no overhead, they run their business as they have since medieval times.

● *When you reach the bridge (Pont au Double) that crosses over in front of Notre Dame, veer to the left, across the street to a small park (Square Viviani). Go through the park to the small rough-stone church of Saint-Julien-le-Pauvre.*

Medieval Paris (1000–1400)

This church dates from the 12th century, and the area around it keeps the same feel. A half-timbered house stands to the right of the entrance. Many buildings in medieval times were built like this, with a wooden frame filled in with a plaster of mud, straw, and dung. Back then, the humble "half-timbered" structure would have been hidden by a veneer of upscale stucco.

Looking along nearby Rue Galande, you'll see a few old houses built every which way. In medieval days, people were piled on top of each other, building at all angles, as they scrambled for this prime real estate near the main commercial artery of the day—the Seine. The smell of fish competed with the smell of neighbors in this knot of humanity.

These narrow streets would have been dirt (or mud). Originally the streets sloped from here down into the mucky Seine, until modern quays cleaned that up. Many Latin Quarter lanes were named for their businesses or crafts. The rue de la Bucherie (or "butcher street," just around the corner, in the direction of the river) was where butchers slaughtered livestock. The blood and guts drained into the Seine and out of town.

● *At #37 rue de la Bucherie is ...*

"Shakespeare and Company" Bookstore

Along with butchers and fishmongers, the Left Bank has been home to scholars, philosophers, and poets since medieval times. This funky bookstore—a reincarnation of the original shop from the 1920s—has picked up the literary torch. In the '20s, it was famous as a meeting place of Paris' literary expatriate elite. Ernest Hemingway, a struggling American writer, strangled and cooked pigeons in the park and borrowed books from here to survive. Fitzgerald, Joyce, and Pound also got their English fix here.

Today it does its best to carry on that literary tradition. Struggling writers are given free accommodations upstairs in tiny, book-lined rooms with views of Notre Dame. Downstairs, travelers enjoy the best selection of used English books in Paris. Pick up *Free Voice*, published for today's American expatriates, and say hi to George.

● *Return to St-Julien-le-Pauvre, then turn right (west) on Rue Galande, which immediately intersects with the busy Rue St. Jacques (also called Rue du Petit Pont). Way back in Roman times, this was the straight, wide, paved road that brought chariots racing in and out of the city. (Romaniacs can see remains from the third-century baths, along with a fine medieval collection, at the Cluny Museum, two blocks to the left.) Cross Rue St. Jacques to the small Gothic church of Saint-Severin.*

Saint-Severin

Don't ask me why, but it took a century longer to build this church than Notre Dame. This is Flamboyant, or "flame-like," Gothic, and you can see the short, prickly spires meant to make this building flicker in the eyes of the faithful. The church gives us a close-up look at gargoyles. This weird, winged species of flying mammal, now extinct, used to swoop down on unwary peasants, occasionally carrying off small children in their beaks. Today, they're most impressive in thunderstorms, when they vomit rain.

The Latin Quarter

While it may look more like the Tunisian Quarter today, this area is the Latin Quarter, named for the language you'd hear on these streets if you walked them in the Middle Ages. The University, one of the leading universities of medieval Europe, was (and still is) nearby.

A thousand years ago the "crude" or vernacular local languages were sophisticated enough to communicate basic human needs, but if you wanted to get philosophical, the language of choice was Latin. The educated elite of Dark Ages Europe was a class that transcended nations and borders. From Sicily to Sweden, they spoke and corresponded in Latin. The most Latin thing about this area now is the beat you may hear coming from some of the subterranean jazz clubs.

Along rue Saint-Severin you can still see the shadow of the medieval sewer system. (The street slopes into a central channel of bricks.) In the days before plumbing and toilets, when people still went to the river or neighborhood wells for their water, flushing meant throwing it out the window. Certain times of day were flushing times. Maids on the fourth floor would holler *"Garde de l'eau!"* ("Look out for the water!") and heave it into the streets, where it would eventually wash down into the Seine.

● *At #22 rue Saint-Severin, you'll find the skinniest house in Paris, two windows wide. Continue along rue Saint-Severin to …*

Boulevard St-Michel

Busy Boulevard St-Michel (or "Boul' Miche") is famous as the main artery for bohemian Paris, culminating a block away (to the left) where it intersects with Boulevard St-Germain. Although nowadays you're more likely to find pantyhose at 30 percent off, there are still many cafés, boutiques, and bohemian haunts nearby.

The Sorbonne—the University of Paris—is also close, if you want to make a detour. Turn left on Boulevard St-Michel and go two blocks. It's on the left, set back in a courtyard. For centuries, children of kings and nobles were sent here to become priests, though many returned as heretics, having studied radical new secular ideas as well. Paris still is a world center for new intellectual trends.

● *Cross Boulevard St-Michel. Just ahead is a tree-filled square lined with cafés and restaurants.*

Place Saint Andre des Arts

In Paris, most serious thinking goes on in cafés. For centuries, these have been social watering-holes, where you could buy a warm place to sit and stimulating conversation for the price of a cup of coffee.

Every great French writer—from Voltaire and Rousseau to Sartre and Derrida—had a favorite haunt.

Paris honors its writers. If you visit the Pantheon (a few blocks down Boulevard St-Michel and to the left), you will find great French writers buried in a setting usually reserved for warriors and politicians.

● *Adjoining this square on the river side is the triangular-shaped Place St-Michel, with a Metro stop and a statue of St. Michael killing a devil.*

Place St-Michel

You're standing at the traditional core of the Left Bank's artsy, liberal, hippie, bohemian district of poets, philosophers, and winos. You'll find international eateries, far-out bookshops, street singers, pale girls in black berets, jazz clubs, and—these days—tourists. Small cinemas show avante-garde films, almost always in the *version originale* (V.O.). For colorful wandering and café-sitting, afternoons and evenings are best. In the morning, it feels sleepy. The Latin Quarter stays up late and sleeps in.

In less commercial times, Place St-Michel was a gathering point for the city's malcontents and misfits. Here, in 1871, the citizens took the streets from the government troops, set up barricades "Les Miz"–style, and established the Paris Commune. In World War II, the locals rose up against their Nazi oppressors (read the plaques by the St. Michael fountain). And in the spring of 1968, a time of social upheaval all over the world, young students battled riot batons and tear gas, took over the square, and demanded change.

● *From Place St-Michel, look across the river and find the spire of Sainte-Chapelle church, with its weathervane angel. Cross the river on the Pont St-Michel and continue along Boulevard du Palais.*

On your left, you'll see the doorway to Sainte-Chapelle. But first, carry on another 30 meters and turn right at a wide pedestrian street, the rue de Lutece.

Cité "Metropolitain" Stop

Of the 141 original turn-of-the-century subway entrances, this is one of 17 survivors now preserved as a national art treasure. (New York's Museum of Modern Art even exhibits one.) The curvy, plant-like iron work is a textbook example of Art Nouveau, the style that rebelled against the Erector-set squareness of the Industrial Age.

The flower market on Place Louis Lepine is a pleasant detour. On

Sunday this square chirps with a busy bird market. And across the way is the Prefecture de Police, where Inspector Clouseau of *Pink Panther* fame used to work, and where the local resistance fighters took the first building from the Nazis, leading to the allied liberation of Paris a week later.

● *Pause here to admire the view. Sainte-Chapelle is a pearl in an ugly architectural oyster, part of a complex of buildings that includes the Palace of Justice (to the right of Sainte-Chapelle, behind the iron and bronze gates).*

Return to the entrance of Sainte-Chapelle. You'll need to pass through a metal-detector to get into Sainte-Chapelle. (It's best to leave your Uzi at the hotel.) Walk through the security scanner. Toilets are ahead, on the left. The line into the church may be long. (Museum cardholders can go directly in.) Enter the humble ground floor ...

SAINTE-CHAPELLE

Sainte-Chapelle, the triumph of Gothic church architecture, is a cathedral of glass like no other. It was speedily built from 1242 to 1248 for St. Louis IX (France's only canonized king), to house the supposed Crown of Thorns. Its architectural harmony is due to the fact that it was completed under the direction of one architect and in only six years—unheard of in Gothic times. Recall that Notre Dame took over 200.

The design clearly shows an Old Regime approach to worship. The basement was for staff and more common folks. Royal Christians worshiped upstairs. The paint job, a 19th-century restoration, helps you imagine how grand this small, painted, jewelled chapel was. (Imagine Notre Dame painted as this is ...)

● *Climb the spiral staircase to the "Haute Chapelle." Leave the rough stone of the earth, and ...*

The Stained Glass

Fiat lux. "Let there be light." Christianity, like many religions, intuitively recognized the sun as the source of life on earth. Light shining through stained glass was a symbol of God's grace shining down to earth,

SAINTE-CHAPELLE

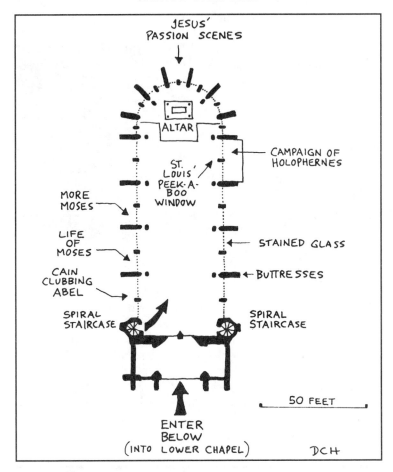

JESUS' PASSION SCENES

ALTAR

CAMPAIGN OF HOLOPHERNES

ST. LOUIS' PEEK-A-BOO WINDOW

MORE MOSES

LIFE OF MOSES

STAINED GLASS

CAIN CLUBBING ABEL

BUTTRESSES

SPIRAL STAIRCASE

SPIRAL STAIRCASE

50 FEET

ENTER BELOW (INTO LOWER CHAPEL)

DCH

and Gothic architects used their new technology to turn dark stone buildings into lanterns of light. For me, the glory of Gothic shines brighter here than in any other church.

There are 15 separate panels of stained glass, with over 1,100 different scenes, mostly from the Bible. In medieval times, scenes like these helped teach Bible stories to the illiterate. These cover the entire Christian history of the world, from the Creation in Genesis (first window on the left), to the coming of Christ (over the altar), to the end of the world (the rose window at the rear of the church). Each individual scene is interesting, and the whole effect is overwhelming.

Let's look at a single scene. Head toward the altar to the fourth big window on the right. Look at the bottom circle, second from the left. It's a battle scene (the campaign of Holophernes) showing three soldiers with swords slaughtering three men. The background is blue.

The men have different colored clothes—red, blue, green, mauve, and white. Notice some of the details. You can see the folds in the robes, the hair, and facial features, and look at the victim in the center—his head is splotched with blood!

Craftsmen made glass (which is, essentially, melted sand), coloring it by mixing in metals like cobalt (blue) or copper (green). Then they'd assemble pieces of different colored glass to make,

It takes 13 tourists to build a Gothic church: six columns, six buttresses, and one steeple.

say, the soldier in blue with a green shield (upper right). The pieces were held together by lead. Details like the folds in the robes (see the victim in white, lower left) came by either scratching on the glass, or by baking in imperfections. It was a painstaking process of finding just the right colors, fitting them together to make a scene … and then multiplying by 1,100.

Other scenes worth a look:

(1) Cain clubbing Abel (first window on the left, second row of circles, far right—Cain is in red).

(2) The life of Moses (second window, the bottom row of diamond panels). First panel shows baby Moses in a basket, placed by his sister in the squiggly brown river. Next, he's found by pharaoh's daughter. Then, he grows up. And finally, he's a man, a prince of Egypt on his royal throne.

(3) In the next window (third on left) you'll see various scenes of Moses. He's often given "horns" because of a medieval mistranslation of the Biblical description of his "aura" of holiness.

(4) Over the altar are scenes from Jesus' arrest and crucifixion. Stand at the stairs in

front and look over the altar, through the canopy, to find Jesus being whipped (left), Jesus in purple being crowned with thorns (right), Jesus in yellow carrying his cross (a little above), and finally, Jesus on the cross being speared by a soldier (above, left).

(Note: the sun lights up different windows at different times of day. Overcast days give the most even light. On bright sunny days, some sections are glorious while others look like a sheet of lead.)

If you can't read much into the individual windows, you're not alone. The medieval worshiper was a stained glass speed reader, and we're the illiterate ones. (For some tutoring, a little book with color photos is on sale downstairs with the postcards.)

The altar was raised up high (notice the staircase for the priest to the right to better display the relic around which this chapel was built—the Crown of Thorns. This was the crown put on Jesus when the Romans were torturing and humiliating him before his execution. King Louis was convinced he'd found the real McCoy and paid three times as much money for it as was spent on this entire chapel. Today, the supposed crown of thorns is kept in the Notre Dame Treasury and shown only on Good Friday.

Notice the little private viewing window in the wall to the right of the altar. Louis was both saintly and shy. He liked to be able to go to church without dealing with the rigors of public royal life. Here he could worship still dressed in his jammies.

Lay your camera on the ground and shoot the ceiling. Those pure and simple ribs growing out of the slender columns are the essence of Gothic structure.

Palais du Cité

Back outside, as you walk around the church exterior, look down and notice how much Paris has risen in the 800 years since Sainte-Chapelle was built. You're in a huge complex of

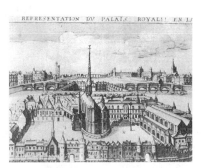

Paris' City Palace in 1650, with Ste-Chapelle, the Conciergerie, and Pont Neuf (then 30 years old) in the background.

buildings that has housed the local government since ancient Roman times. It was the site of the original Gothic palace of the early kings of France. The only surviving medieval parts are the Sainte-Chapelle church and the Conciergerie prison.

Most of the site is now covered by the giant Palais de Justice, home of France's supreme court, built in 1776. *"Liberté, Egalité, Fraternité"* over the doors is a reminder that this was also the headquarters of the Revolutionary government. Here they doled out justice, condemning many to torture in the Conciergerie prison downstairs, or to have their head removed St. Denis–style by *"Monsieur de Paris"*—the guillotine.

● *Now pass through the big iron gate to the noisy boulevard du Palais and turn left (toward the Right Bank).*

On the corner is the site of the oldest public clock (1334) in the city. While the present clock is Baroque, it somehow still manages to keep accurate time.

Turn left onto Quai d'Horloge and walk along the river. The round medieval tower just ahead marks the entrance to the Conciergerie. Even if you don't pay to see the Conciergerie, you can visit the courtyard and lobby. Step past the serious-looking guard into the courtyard.

Conciergerie

The Conciergerie, a former prison and place of torture, is a gloomy place. Kings used it to torture and execute failed assassins. The leaders of the Revolution put it to similar good use. The tower next to the entrance, called "the babbler," was named for the painful sounds that leaked from it.

Look at the stark printing above the doorways. This was a no nonsense Revolutionary time. Everything, including lettering, was subjected to the test of reason. No frills or we chop 'em off.

Marie-Antoinette was imprisoned here. During a busy eight-month period in the Revolution, she was one of 2,600 prisoners kept here on their way to the guillotine. The interior (requires ticket) with its huge vaulted and pillared rooms, echoes with history, but is pretty barren. You can see Marie-Antoinette's cell, with a collection of Marie-Antoinette mementoes. In another room, a list of those made "a foot shorter at the top" by the guillotine includes ex-King Louis XVI,

Charlotte Corday (who murdered Marat in his bathtub), and the chief Revolutionary who got a taste of his own medicine—Maximilien Robespierre.

● *Back outside, wink at the flak-vested guard (but no jokes about your Uzi), turn left, and continue your walk along the river. Across the river you can see the rooftop observatory of the Samaritaine department store, where we'll end this walk. At the first corner, veer left into a sleepy triangular square called "Place Dauphine."*

Place Dauphine

It's amazing to find such coziness in the heart of Paris. The French Supreme Court building looms behind like a giant marble gavel. Enjoy the village-Paris feeling in the park. You may see lawyers on their lunchbreak playing *boules.*

● *Walk through the park to the statue of Henry IV who, in 1607 inaugurated the Pont Neuf. If in need of a romantic little hideaway in the midst of this mega-city, take the steps down into the park on the tip of the island and dangle your legs over the prow of this concrete island.*

From the statue, turn right onto the old bridge. Walk to the little rest nook halfway across.

Pont Neuf

The Pont Neuf, or "new bridge," is now Paris' oldest. Its 12 arches span the widest part of the river. The fine view includes the park on the tip of the island (note Seine boats), the Orsay Museum, and the Louvre. These turrets were originally for vendors and street entertainers. In the days of Henry, who originated the promise of "a chicken in every pot," this would have been a lively scene.

● *Directly over the river, the first building you'll hit on the Right Bank is the venerable old department store Samaritaine. Go through the door, veer left, and catch the elevator to the ninth floor. Climb two sets of stairs to the panorama. (Don't confuse the terrace level with the higher, better panorama. Light meals are served on the terrace. Public WCs on fifth and ninth floors.)*

THE REST OF PARIS

From the circular little crow's nest of the building, ponder the greatest skyline in Europe. Retrace the walk you just made, starting with Notre Dame and Sainte-Chapelle. Then spin counterclockwise (or run down the stairs to hop on the Métro) and check out the rest of Paris:

The Pompidou Center, the wild and colorful rectangular tangle of pipes and tubes, is filled with art that makes this building's exterior look tame (closed for renovation until 2000).

Sacré-Coeur is a Neo-Romanesque church built on Montmartre as a "praise the Lord anyway" gesture after the French were humiliated by the Germans in the very short Franco-Prussian war in 1871. The Montmartre area is an atmospheric quarter after dark, its streets filled with strolling tourists avoiding strolling artists.

The **Palais du Louvre** is the largest building in Paris, largest palace in Europe, and largest museum in the Western world (covered somehow by only the third-largest chapter in this book).

Stretching away from the Louvre, the **Tuileries Gardens**, Place de la Concorde, and Champs-Élysées lead to the Arc de Triomphe. The gardens are Paris' "Central Park" filled with families at play, cellists in the shade, carousels, pony rides, and the ghost of Maurice Chevalier.

The gardens overlook the grand **Place de la Concorde**, marked by an ancient obelisk, where all of France seems to converge. It was "guillotine central" during the revolution and continues to be a place of much festivity.

Europe's grandest boulevard, the **Champs-Élysées**, runs uphill from the Place de la Concorde about a mile to the Arc de Triomphe. While pretty hamburgerized, and with rich-and-single aristocrats more rare than ever, the people-watching is still some of Europe's best.

Napoleon began constructing the magnificent **Arc de Triomphe** in 1806 to commemorate his victory at the Battle of Austerlitz. It was finished in 1836, just in time to be a part of the Emperor's funeral parade. Today it commemorates heroes of past wars. There's no triumphal arch bigger (50 meters high, 40 meters wide). And, with 12 converging boulevards, there's no traffic circle more thrilling to experience—either on foot or behind the wheel.

Paris, the capital of Europe, is built on an appropriately monumental plan with an axis that stretches from the Louvre, up the Champs-Élysées, past the Arc de

Triomphe, all the way to the modern arch among the skyscrapers at La Defense. (Find the faint shadow of this arch, just above the Arc de Triomphe.)

The **Orsay Museum**, the train-station-turned-art museum, is located just beyond the Louvre on the Left Bank. (See chapter 8.)

The body of Napoleon lies under the gilded dome. This is surounded by **Les Invalides**, the giant building designed to house his wounded troops. Today this building houses Europe's greatest military museum. The Rodin Museum is nearby.

The **Eiffel Tower** is a thousand-foot exclamation point celebrating the 100th anniversary of the French Revolution. Built in 1889 as a temporary engineering stunt, Paris decided to let it be a rare exception to a downtown building code that allows the skyline to be broken only by a few prestigious domes and spires.

The 52-story **Montparnasse Tower**—also known as "the Awful Tower"—looks like the box the Eiffel Tower came in. It's a city in itself with a work force of 5,000 and an altitude of 700 feet, reminding us that, while tourists look for hints of Louis and Napoleon, today's work-a-day Paris looks to the future.

AMSTERDAM

Rijksmuseum

Van Gogh Museum

*A*msterdam today looks much as it did in its Golden Age, the 1600s. It's a retired sea captain of a city, still in love with life, with a broad outlook and a salty story to tell. The canvases that hang in the Rijksmuseum and the Van Gogh Museum tell that story vividly.

11 Rijksmuseum

Holland: windmills, wooden shoes, tulips, cheese, and great artists. In its 17th-century glory days, tiny Holland was a world power—politically, economically, and culturally—with more great masters per kilometer than any other country.

At the Rijksmuseum (rhymes with "yikes"), Holland's Golden Age shines with the best collection around of Rembrandt, Vermeer, Hals, and Steen. And the art we'll see is a clog dance with Holland's past, from humble family meals to the Dutch Masters.

RIJKSMUSEUM

Note: while the Van Gogh Museum is being renovated from September 1, 1998, to April 23, 1999, some of his art will appear in the south wing of the Rijksmuseum.

Hours: Daily 10:00–17:00, closed only on January 1.

Cost: 15 guilders, discounts for those under 19 and over 65, tickets good all day.

Tour length: 90 minutes

Getting there: From the station, trams 2 and 5 stop at rear of building (to get to the front, backtrack to last intersection and go right a half block).

Information: Helpful info booth has free maps and a good "Tour of the Golden Age" brochure (1 guilder). Free 20-minute movies are sometimes shown in English. They are restful and informative but not necessary. Tel. 020/673-2121. Audio tours for 7.5 guilders offer two hours of art history with punch-in-the-painting-number directness.

Photography: Without a flash is permitted.

Cuisine art: The cafeteria is crowded and expensive, with no free water. Picnic-pleasant Vondelpark is four blocks away.

Starring: Rembrandt, Vermeer, Frans Hals, Jan Steen.

ORIENTATION

● *The Rijksmuseum straddles a road. It was built to show off Rembrandt's* Night Watch. *Entrances on either side of the road have cloak rooms. Check your bag (encouraged and free), and climb the stairs (or take the elevator). To get oriented, look down the long gallery to* The Night Watch.

Our tour is in about 10 rooms on this floor to the left of *The Night Watch.* (The right half of the museum is an impressive, but normally ignored, collection of Golden Age hutches and their contents.)

We'll concentrate on only four painters—Rembrandt, Frans Hals, Vermeer, and Jan Steen. All of them lived during Holland's "Golden Age"—the 1600s—when foreign trade made it one of Europe's richest lands. But first, a couple of quick stops to get a feel for Dutch art before its ship came in.

RIJKSMUSEUM—OVERVIEW

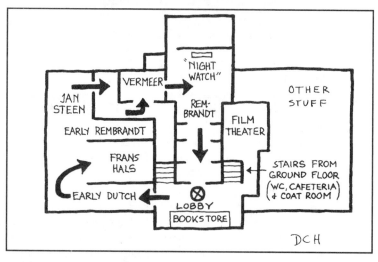

Dutch art is meant to be enjoyed, not studied. It's straightforward, meat-and-potatoes art for the common man. The Dutch love the beauty of everyday things painted realistically and with exquisite detail. So set your cerebral cortex on "Low" and let this art pass straight from the eyes to the heart with minimal detours.

● *Start in Room 201, located through the glass door (marked "Painting 15th–16th century") at the left end of the lobby. Start with the first painting on your right.*

DUTCH ART BEFORE THE GOLDEN AGE

STAIRS TO
GROUND FLOOR

TO
"NIGHT
WATCH"

TO ROOMS 208-9
FRANS HALS

ROOM
206

ROOM
201

MAIN
LOBBY

BOOKSTORE

205 | 204 | 203 | 202 | 201

③

②

①

④

1 - Eighteen Scenes from the Life of Christ
2 - The Tree of Jesse
3 - Feast of the Golden Calf
4 - Christ in the House of Mary and Martha

DCH

DUTCH ART BEFORE THE GOLDEN AGE (PRE-1600)

Gelderland School —
Eighteen Scenes from the Life of Christ (c. 1435)

In the days when 90 percent of Europe was illiterate, art was Sunday school. These first few rooms are filled with Bible scenes. This painting can be read "page by page," going left to right. "Page 1" is the Annunciation, where an angel tells Mary she'll give birth to Christ. "Page 2" is the birth, "page 3" is Jesus being circumcised, then the visit of the Three Wise Men, and so on through Jesus' arrest, execution, and resurrection. I like the next-to-last scene of Jesus ascending into heaven. Holy toes.

Attributed to Jan Mostaert —
The Tree of Jesse (c. 1520)

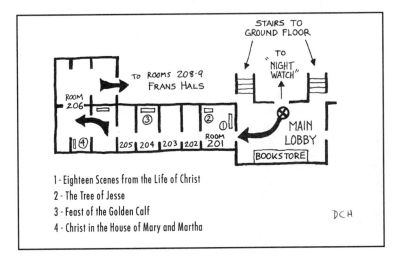

Here we see Jesus' family tree—literally. At the top is Mary with the baby Jesus. His ancestors are below—David (with the harp), Solomon (with the scepter), and others stacked like an early version of *Hollywood Squares*. Again, this is an instructional aid for illiterate masses. But notice the care the artist has taken with the little details, especially the beautiful faces, clothes, and scepters. The painting is packed with pretty things to please the eye.

● *Walk through the next two rooms of mostly religious scenes, stopping in Room 204 at a colorful three-panel work.*

Lucas Van Leyden — *The Feast of the Golden Calf* (c. 1530)

The Dutch love to fill a picture with people having a good time. Here, folks in colorful robes are exchanging good food, wine, and conversation in an outdoor setting. It's a pleasant scene to look at.

Or is it? What are those people in the background dancing around? A golden idol. And who are the two tiny, faint figures in the dark distance at the foot of a smoking mountain? It's Moses (with tablets of stone) and Aaron.

Their leader's been away, and the children of Israel play. Everyone's partying, but nobody's smiling. They're trying desperately to enjoy themselves in Sinai's Red Light District. Look at the couple making out in the right panel. She's kissing him, but he's thinking about what will happen when Moses gets back.

● *Now enter Room 206 and find a large, appetizing painting.*

Joachim Bueckelaer — *Christ in the House of Mary and Martha* (1566)

Here we see the Dutch painters' favorite subject. While Italians painted saints, angels, and Madonnas, the Dutch painted ... food. For the middle-class merchant, food was a religion, and he worshiped thrice daily. Notice the delicious realism—the skin of the martyred birds, the temptation of the melons, the artichokes in ecstasy. The sacred detail! You can practically count the hares' hairs.

But this too is a Bible scene. In the faint background someone is preaching. The title is *Christ in the House of Mary and Martha.* Compare the sketchy, sloppy work on Christ with the painstaking detail of the food. Dutch priorities.

● *Leave the medieval world through the glass door leading into the large Room 208–209 and take a seat.*

THE GOLDEN AGE (1600s)

Who bought this art? Look around the room and you'll see—ordinary middle-class people, merchants, and traders. Even in their Sunday best, you can see that these are hardworking, businesslike, friendly, simple people (with a penchant for ruffled lace collars).

Dutch fishermen sold their surplus catch in distant areas of Europe, importing goods from these far lands. In time, fishermen became traders, and by 1600, Holland's merchant fleets ruled the waves with colonies as far away as India, Indonesia, and America (New York was originally "New Amsterdam"). The Dutch slave trade—selling Africans to Americans—generated a lot of profit for luxuries like the art you're looking at.

Look around the room again. Is there even one crucifixion? One saint? One Madonna? Okay, maybe one. But this is people art, not church art. In most countries, Catholic bishops and rich kings supported the arts. But the Republic of the Netherlands, recently free of Spanish rule and Vatican domination, was independent, democratic, and largely Protestant, with no taste for saints and Madonnas.

Instead, Dutch burghers bought portraits of themselves, and pretty, unpreachy, unpretentious works for their homes. Even poor people bought smaller canvases by "no-name" artists designed to fit the budgets and lifestyles of this less-than-rich-and-famous crowd. We'll see examples of their four favorite subjects—still lifes (of food and everyday objects), landscapes, portraits (often of groups), and scenes from everyday life.

THE GOLDEN AGE

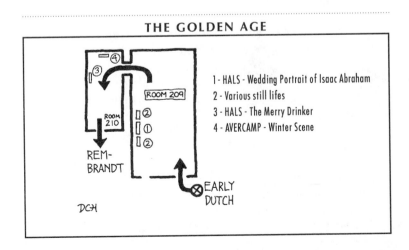

1 - HALS - Wedding Portrait of Isaac Abraham
2 - Various still lifes
3 - HALS - The Merry Drinker
4 - AVERCAMP - Winter Scene

Frans Hals — *Wedding Portrait of Isaac Abrahamsz Massa and Beatrix van der Laen* (1622)

In this wedding portrait of a chubby, pleasant merchant and his bride, Hals tells us the story of the Golden Age. This overseas trader was away from home for years at a time on business. So Hals makes a special effort to point out his patron's commitment to marriage. Isaac has his hand over his heart as a pledge of fidelity. Beatrix's wedding ring is prominently displayed, dead center between them (on her right-hand forefinger, Protestant style). The vine clinging to a tree is a symbol of man's support and woman's dependence. And in the distance at right, in the classical love garden, are other happy couples strolling arm in arm amid peacocks, a symbol of fertility.

Frans Hals (c. 1580–1666) was the premier Golden Age portrait painter. Merchants hired him like we'd hire a wedding photographer. With a few quick strokes (time was money for businessmen who couldn't sit for hours for a portrait), Hals captured not only the features but the personality. In the case of Isaac and Beatrix, Hals didn't need symbolism to tell us that these two are prepared for their long-distance relationship—they seem relaxed together, but they each look at us directly, with a strong, individual identity.

By the way, this painting is unusual for a wedding portrait. Normally, a man and wife were portrayed separately, like in the twin canvases nearby (also by Hals).

● *Nearby in this room, you'll find …*

Various Still Lifes (c. 1630)

The Dutch people love their homes, cultivating them like gardens till they're immaculate, decorative, and well-ordered. This same sense of pride is reflected in Dutch still lifes like these, where everyday objects are arranged in the most pleasant way possible. They showed expensive delicacies, like lemons from the south, or those most rare and exotic of spices of the time … salt and pepper.

Pick one. Get so close that the guard joins you. Linger over the little things: the pewterware, the seafood, the lemon peels, the rolls, and the glowing goblets that cast a warm reflection on the tablecloth.

You'd swear you can see yourself reflected in the pewter vessels. At least you can see the faint reflections of the food and even of the surrounding room. The closer you get the better it looks.

Before you leave, glance at the big bright canvas of Prometheus being chained to a rock (by Dirck van Baburen, 1623). It sticks out like an American tourist in Bermuda shorts. This is one of the few Greek myth paintings in the entire building, though whole museums in Italy are nothing but classical subjects and nudes.

● *Enter Room 210 …*

Frans Hals — *The Merry Drinker*

You're greeted by a jovial man in a black hat. Again, notice the details—the happy red face of the man offering us a glass of wine, the sparkle in his eyes, the lacy collar, the decorative belt buckle, and so on.

Now move in closer. All these meticulous details are accomplished with a few quick, thick, and messy brushstrokes. The beard is a tangle of brown worms, the belt buckle a yellow blur. His hand is a study in smudges. Even the expressive face is done with a few well-chosen patches of color. Unlike the still-life scenes, this canvas is meant to be viewed from a distance where the colors and brushstrokes blend together.

Hals was a "snapshot" portrait painter. Rather than posing his subject, making him stand for hours with "cheese" on his lips, Hals tried to catch him at a candid moment. He often painted common people, fishermen and barflies like this one. He had to work quickly to capture the serendipity of the moment.

Two centuries later the Impressionists learned from Hals' messy brushwork. In the Van Gogh Museum you'll see how van Gogh painted, say, a brown beard by using thick dabs of green, yellow, and red that blend at a distance to make brown.

Avercamp — *Winter Scene*

A song or a play is revealed to the audience at the writer's pace. But in a painting, we set the tempo, choosing where to look and how long to linger.

Exercise your right to loiter at this winter scene by Hendrick Avercamp. Avercamp, who was deaf and mute and unfamiliar with the structure of music or theater, would never want to force your attention in any direction. But I will. Can you find the couple making out in the hay-tower silo? Also, there's a "bad moon on the rise" in the broken-down outhouse at left, and another nearby. The whole scene is viewed from a height (the horizon line is high), making it seem as if the fun goes on forever. Just skate among these Dutch people—rich, poor, lovers hand in hand, kids, and moms—and appreciate the silent beauty and this intimate look at old Holland.

● *Around the partition, in Room 211, you'll find several Rembrandts. Find the tiny self-portrait.*

Rembrandt — Early Works

Rembrandt van Rijn (1606–1669) is the greatest Dutch painter. Whereas most painters specialized in one field—portraits, landscapes, still lifes—in order to make a living, Rembrandt excelled in them all.

Rembrandt — *Self-Portrait, Age 22*
Rembrandt was a precocious kid. His father insisted he be a lawyer. His mother hoped he'd be a preacher (see a portrait of her reading the Bible, nearby). Rembrandt combined the secular and religious worlds by becoming an artist, someone who can hint at the spiritual by showing us the beauty of the created world.

He moved to Amsterdam and entered the highly competitive art world. Amsterdam was a booming town and, like today, a hip and cosmopolitan city.

Here we see the young country boy about to launch himself into whatever life has to offer. But even at this young age, he is something of a mystery. Rembrandt portrays himself divided—half in light, half hidden by hair and shadows—looking out but wary of an uncertain future.

Rembrandt — *Portrait of Saskia* (1633)
It didn't take long for the big city to recognize Rembrandt's great talent. Everyone wanted their portrait done by the young master. He became wealthy and famous. He fell in love with and married the rich, beautiful, and cultured Saskia. By all accounts, the two were enormously happy,

REMBRANDT—EARLY WORKS

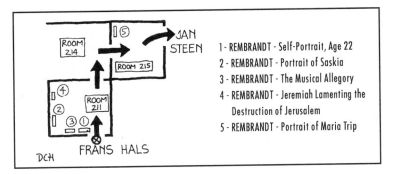

1 - REMBRANDT - Self-Portrait, Age 22

2 - REMBRANDT - Portrait of Saskia

3 - REMBRANDT - The Musical Allegory

4 - REMBRANDT - Jeremiah Lamenting the Destruction of Jerusalem

5 - REMBRANDT - Portrait of Maria Trip

entertaining friends, decorating their house with fine furniture, raising a family, and living the high life. In this wedding portrait (thought to be Saskia), her face literally glows. Barely 30 years old, Rembrandt was the most successful painter in Holland. He had it all.

Rembrandt — *Musical Allegory* (1626)

Rembrandt's paintings are, of course, even more sought after today. This rather crude, early work was lost for centuries, hidden unknown in some attic, discovered by accident and sold at auction for a small fortune. Painted when Rembrandt was 19, it's actually a portrait of his own family in funny costumes—his father (in turban), mother, grandmother, and himself standing in back.

By the way, of the 500 so-called Rembrandts in existence, 100 have been officially declared fakes by a panel of Dutch experts, with some 50 more under serious scrutiny.

Most of the fakes are not out-and-out forgeries, but works executed by his adoring students. In this room and elsewhere, you'll see real Rembrandts, paintings by others that look like his, portraits of Rembrandt by his students, and one or two "Rembrandts" that may soon be "audited" by the Internal Rembrandt Service. So be careful the next time you plunk down $4 million for a "Rembrandt."

Rembrandt — *Jeremiah Lamenting the Destruction of Jerusalem* (1630)

The Babylonians have sacked and burned Jerusalem. But what's important for Rembrandt isn't the pyrotechnics (in the murky background at left). That's for Spielberg and the big screen. Instead,

Rembrandt tells us the whole story of Israel's destruction in the face of the prophet who predicted the disaster. Jeremiah is deep in thought, confused, and despondent, trying to understand why this evil had to happen. Rembrandt turns his floodlight of truth on the prophet's face.

This is a far cry from Hals' *Wedding Portrait*. Rembrandt wasn't satisfied cranking out portraits of fat merchants in frilled bibs, no matter what they paid him. He wanted to experiment, trying new techniques and more probing subjects. Many of his paintings weren't commissioned and were never even intended for sale. His subjects could be brooding and melancholy, a bit "dark" for the public's taste. So was his technique.

You can recognize a Rembrandt canvas by his play of light and dark. Most of his paintings are a deep brown tone, with only a few bright spots glowing from the darkness. This allows Rembrandt to "highlight" the details he thinks are most important.

Light has a primal appeal to humans. (Dig deep into your DNA and remember the time when fire, a sacred thing, was not tamed. Light! In the middle of the night! This miracle separated us from our fellow animals.) Rembrandt strikes us at that instinctive level.

● *For more Rembrandts, pass through the next room (worth coming back to), into Room 215, and find the young and beautiful ...*

Rembrandt —
Portrait of Maria Trip (1639)

When he chose to, Rembrandt could dash off a commissioned portrait like nobody's business. The surface details are immaculate—the clothing, the pearls behind the veil, the subtle face and hands. But Rembrandt gives us not just a person but a personality. This debutante daughter of a wealthy citizen is shy and reserved, maybe a bit awkward in her new dress and adult role, but still self-assured.

Look at the rings around her eyes, a detail a lesser painter would have air-brushed out. Rembrandt takes this feature unique to her and uses it as a setting for her luminous, jewel-like eyes. Without being prettified, she's beautiful.

Compare this masterpiece to the lackluster portrait next to it. Rembrandt's breathes.

● *Continue on to the frolicking people scenes in Room 216.*

Jan Steen (1626–1679)

Not everyone could afford a Rembrandt, but even the poorer people wanted works for their own homes (the way some people today put a Sears landscape over the sofa). Jan Steen, the Norman Rockwell of his day, painted humorous scenes from the lives of the lower classes.

Jan Steen —
The Feast of St. Nicholas

It's Christmas time and the kids have been given their gifts. A little girl got a doll. The mother says, "Let me see it," but the girl turns away playfully.

Everyone is happy except …the boy who's crying. His Christmas present is only a rod in his shoe—like coal in your stocking, the gift for bad boys. His sister gloats and passes it around gleefully. The kids laugh at him. But wait, it turns out the family is just playing a trick. In the background, the grandmother is beckoning to him saying, "Look, I have your real present in here." Out of the limelight but smack in the middle sits the father providing ballast to this family scene.

Steen has frozen the moment, sliced off a piece, and laid it on a canvas. He's told a story with a past, present, and future. These are real people in a real scene.

JAN STEEN

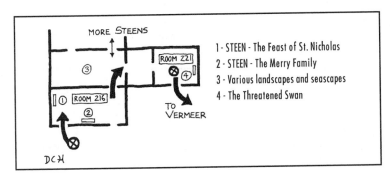

1 - STEEN - The Feast of St. Nicholas
2 - STEEN - The Merry Family
3 - Various landscapes and seascapes
4 - The Threatened Swan

Steen's fun art reminds us that museums aren't mausoleums.

● *If you're keen on Steen, you'll find more of his people-scapes in this room and in Room 219. Otherwise, browse through the next few rooms …*

Jan Steen — *The Merry Family* (1668)

This family is eating, drinking, and singing like there's no tomorrow. The broken eggshells and scattered cookware are symbols of waste and extravagance. The neglected proverb tacked to the fireplace reminds us that children will follow the footsteps of their parents. The father in this jolly scene is very drunk—ready to topple over—while in the foreground his mischievous daughter is feeding her brother wine straight from the flask. Mom and Grandma join the artist himself (playing the bagpipes) in a raucous singalong, but the child learning to smoke would rather follow dad's lead. Today, the Dutch describe such a family as a "Jan Steen household."

Various Landscapes, Seascapes and Church-scapes

The things that we think of as typically Dutch—windmills, flowers, wooden shoes—are products of the flat, wet Dutch countryside. The windmills used wind-power to pump water out of the soil, reclaiming land that was once part of the sea. To walk on the marshy farmland, you needed wooden shoes. The sandy soil wasn't the best for farming, but tulips (originally from Turkey) grew great.

The seascapes remind us that this great art was financed by wealth from a far-flung trading empire. And the meticulous paintings of church interiors tell us of the meticulous, hardworking nature of the country's people, who made good with little to start with. As the saying goes: "God made the Dutch; the Dutch made Holland."

● *End your quick Viewmaster-slide tour of Holland in the large Room 221, with a picture of a swan at the far end.*

Shhh ... Dutch Art

You can be sitting at home late one night and it's perfectly quiet. Not a sound, very peaceful. And then ... the refrigerator motor turns off ... and it's *really* quiet.

Dutch art is really quiet art. It silences our busy world so that every sound, every motion is noticed. You can hear sheep tearing off grass 50 yards away. Dutch art is still. It slows our fast-lane world so we notice the motion of birds. We notice how the cold night air makes

the stars sharp. We notice that the undersides of leaves and of cats are always a lighter shade than the tops. Dutch art stills the world so we can hear our own heartbeat and reflect upon that most noble muscle that without thinking gives us life.

To see how subtle Dutch art is, realize that the most exciting, dramatic, emotional, and extravagant Dutch painting in this whole museum is probably *The Threatened Swan* on the wall in front of you. Quite a contrast to the rape scenes and visions of heaven of Italian Baroque from the same time period.

Vermeer (1632–1675)

Jan Vermeer is the master of quiet and stillness. He creates a clear and silent pool that is a world in itself. The Rijksmuseum has the best collection of Vermeers in the world—all four of them. (There are only 30 in captivity.) But each is a small jewel worth lingering over.

● *The only thing quiet and still about the often-crowded Vermeer room (221A) is its paintings.*

Vermeer — *The Kitchen Maid*

Shhh … This painting is so calm, you can practically hear the milk pouring into the bowl.

Vermeer brings out the beauty in everyday things. The subject is ordinary, a kitchen maid, but you could look for hours at the tiny details and rich color tones. These are everyday objects, but we see them as though for the very first time, glowing in a diffused light: the crunchy crust, the hanging basket, even the nail in the wall with its tiny shadow. The maid is alive with radiant yellow, blue, and white. She is content, solid, and sturdy. Her full arms seem constructed by reflected light. Vermeer squares off a little world in itself (framed by the table in the foreground, the wall in back, the window to the left and the foot stool at right), then fills this space with objects for our perusal.

Vermeer — *The Little Street*

Vermeer lived his whole life in the quiet picturesque town of Delft. This is the view from his front door.

Here, the details actually aren't very detailed—the "cobblestone" street doesn't have a single individual stone in it. What Vermeer wants to show us is the beautiful interplay of colored rectangles on the buildings. Our eye moves back and forth from shutter to gable to window ... and then from front to back as we notice the woman deep in the alleyway.

Vermeer — *Young Woman Reading a Letter*

Vermeer's placid scenes also have an air of mystery. Something is being revealed to the girl, but we don't know what it is. She is reading a letter. From whom? A lover? A father away at sea? Not even taking time to sit down, she reads it intently, with parted lips and a bowed head. It must be important.

Again, Vermeer has framed off a moment of everyday life. But within this small world are hints of a wider, wilder world. The light coming from the left is obviously from a large window, giving us a whiff of a much broader world outside. The map hangs prominently, reminding us of travel to exotic lands, most likely where the sender of the letter is.

Vermeer — *The Love Letter*

There's a similar theme here. The curtain is parted, and we see through the doorway into one world, then through the seascape on the back wall to the wide ocean. The mysterious letter brought by the servant intrudes like a pebble dropped into the tide pool of Vermeer's quiet world.

● *Room 223 tells the history of Rembrandt's* Night Watch.

The Night Watch History Room

Pause here and let your retina muscles unclench. We'll go from Vermeer's tiny canvases to the dramatic sweep of Rembrandt. The displays tell about the painting, hanging, cleaning, and chopping up of this controversial work. There's a small-scale copy showing the original dimensions before the sides were lopped off and lost, putting the two lead characters in the center and causing the work to become more static than intended.

● *The glass door leads into the large* Night Watch *room. The best viewing spot is to the right of center. This is the angle Rembrandt had in mind when he designed it for its original location.*

Rembrandt — Later Works

In our last episode, we left Rembrandt at the height of fame, wealth, and happiness. He may have had it all, but not for long. We'll see how disappointments in his personal life added a new wisdom to his work.

The Night Watch. *Rembrandt makes this much more than a group portrait. It's an action scene, capturing the can-do spirit of the Golden Age.*

Rembrandt — The Night Watch

This is Rembrandt's most famous—though not necessarily greatest—painting. Done in 1642 when he was 36, it was one of his most important commissions—a group portrait of a company of Amsterdam's civic guards to hang in their meeting hall.

This is an action shot. The guardsmen (who, by the 1640s, were really only an honorary militia of rich bigwigs) are spilling into the street from a large doorway in the back. It's all for one and one for all as they rush to the rescue of Amsterdam. Flags are flying, the drummer beats a march cadence, the soldiers grab lances and load their muskets. In the center, the commander steps forward energetically with a hand gesture that seems to say, "What are we waiting for? Let's move out!"

Why is *The Night Watch* so famous? Compare it with the less famous group portraits on either side. Every face is visible. Everyone is well lit, flat, and flashbulb-perfect. These people paid good money to have their mug preserved for posterity, and they wanted it right up front. These colorful, dignified, and relaxed works are certainly the work of a master ... but not quite masterpieces.

By contrast, Rembrandt rousted the Civic Guards off their fat duffs.

He took posers and turned them into warriors. He turned a simple portrait into great art.

By adding movement and depth to an otherwise static scene, Rembrandt caught the optimistic spirit of Holland in the 1600s. Their war of independence from Spain was heading to victory and their economy was booming. These guardsmen on the move epitomize the proud, independent, upwardly mobile Dutch.

The Night Watch, contrary to common myth, was a smashing success in its day. However, there are elements in it that show why Rembrandt soon fell out of favor as a portrait painter. He seemed to spend as much time painting the dwarf and the mysterious glowing girl with a chicken (the very appropriate mascot of this "militia" of shopkeepers) than he did the faces of his employers.

(OK, some *Night Watch* scuttlebutt: First off, "*The Night Watch*" is a misnomer. It's a daytime scene, but over the years, as the preserving varnish darkened and layers of dirt built up, the sun set on this painting and it got its popular title. At one point, the painting was cropped to fit a smaller room, and the missing pieces were lost for good. During World War II, it was rolled up and hidden for five years. More recently, a madman attacked the painting, slicing the captain's legs (now repaired skillfully. The madman committed suicide at the police station that night.)

Rembrandt's life darkened long before his *Night Watch* did. This work marks the peak of Rembrandt's popularity ... and the beginning of his fall from grace. The commissions came more slowly. The money ran out. His wife, Saskia, died. His mother died. One by one his sons died. He had to auction off his paintings and furniture to pay debts. He moved out of his fine house to humble lodgings. He became bitter, disappointed, and disillusioned.

He painted masterpieces. Free from the dictates of employers whose taste was in their mouths, he painted what he wanted, how he wanted it. Rembrandt goes beyond mere craftsmanship to probe into and draw life from the deepest wells of the human soul.

● *In the long gallery, near* The Night Watch, *you'll find ...*

Rembrandt — *St. Peter's Denial* (1660)

Jesus has been arrested as a criminal. Here, his disciple Peter has followed him undercover to the prison to check on the proceedings. The young girl recognizes Peter and asks him, "Don't you know Jesus?" Peter, afraid of being arrested by the Romans, denies it.

Here we see Peter as he answers the girl's question. He must decide where his loyalties lie. With the Roman soldier who glares at him suspiciously from the left, not buying Peter's story at all? Or with his doomed master in the dark background on the right looking knowingly over his shoulder, understanding Peter's complicated situation? Peter must choose. The confusion and self-doubt are written all

over his face. He has told his lie and now he's stuck with it.

The strong contrasts of light and dark heighten the drama of this psychologically tense scene. The soldier is a blotch of brown. Jesus is a distant shadowy figure, a lingering presence in Peter's conscience. The center of the picture is the light shining through the girl's translucent fingers, glowing like a lamp as she casts the light of truth on Peter. Peter's brokenhearted betrayal and sense of guilt could only have been portrayed by an older, wiser—and perhaps himself guilt-ridden—Rembrandt.

Rembrandt — *The Jewish Bride*

Another melancholy though touching painting is the uncommissioned portrait known as *The Jewish Bride*. This is a truly human look at the relationship between two people in love. The man gently draws the woman toward him. She's comfortable enough with him to sink into thought, but she still reaches up unconsciously to return the gentle touch. The touching hands form the center of this somewhat sad but yes-saying work. Van Gogh said: "Rembrandt alone has that tenderness—the heart-broken tenderness."

Rembrandt — *De Staalmeesters* (1662)

While commissions were rare, Rembrandt could still paint a portrait better than anyone. Here, in the painting made famous by Dutch Masters cigars, he catches the Draper's Guild in a natural but dig-

nified pose (except, perhaps, for the guy who looks like he's sitting on his friend's lap). They've gathered around a table to examine the company's books. They look up spontaneously, as though we've just snapped our fingers to catch their attention. It's as natural as a snapshot, though radiographs show Rembrandt made many changes in posing them perfectly. Even in this simple portrait we feel we can read the guild members' personalities in their faces.

Rembrandt — *Self-Portrait as the Apostle Paul* (1661)

Perhaps Rembrandt's greatest legacy is his many self-portraits. They show us the evolution of a great painter's style as well as the progress of a genius' life. For Rembrandt, the two were intertwined.

Compare this later self-portrait with the youthful, curious Rembrandt of age 22 we saw earlier. This man has seen it all—success, love, money, fatherhood, loss, poverty, death. He took these experiences and wove them into his art. Rembrandt died poor and misunderstood, but he remained very much his own man to the end.

12 Van Gogh Museum

The Van Gogh Museum (we say "van-GO," the Dutch say "van-GOCK") is a cultural high even to those "not into art." It's a short, well-organized, and user-friendly look at the art of one fascinating man. If you like bright-colored landscapes in the Impressionist style, you'll like this museum. If you enjoy finding deeper meaning in works of art, you'll really love it. The mix of van Gogh's creative genius, his tumultuous life, and the tourist's determination to find meaning in it makes this museum as much a walk with Vincent as with his art.

NATIONAL MUSEUM VINCENT VAN GOGH

Note: The Van Gogh Museum will close for renovation from September 1, 1998, to April 23, 1999. During this time, some of van Gogh's art will be displayed in the south wing of the Rijksmuseum.

Hours: Daily 10:00–17:00, closed only on January 1.

Cost: 12.50 guilders, discounts for those under 17 and with one ear.

Tour length: One hour

Getting there: If you're visiting before mid-April, 1999, go to the south wing of the Rijksmuseum. Starting April 24, 1999, follow the tourists 400 yards behind the Rijksmuseum to the Van Gogh Museum or ride trams 2 or 5 from the station to first stop past the Rijksmuseum.

Information: The information desk rents audio players for seven guilders. The bookstore is understandably popular with several good basic "Vincent" guidebooks. The museum has a fine reading room and library on entry level. Tel. 020/570-5200.

Cloakroom: Free.

Photography: No cameras allowed.

Cuisine art: The terrace cafeteria (soup, salads, sandwiches) is pricey.
Starring: Take it, Vincent.

Note: this map shows the layout of the Van Gogh Museum, not the layout of the temporary exhibition (Sept. 1, '98–April 1, '99) in the south wing of the Rijksmuseum.

ORIENTATION

The core of the museum and this entire *Mona* tour is on a single floor, one flight up. The bookstore, cafeteria, and study room are on the

OVERVIEW—2ND FLOOR

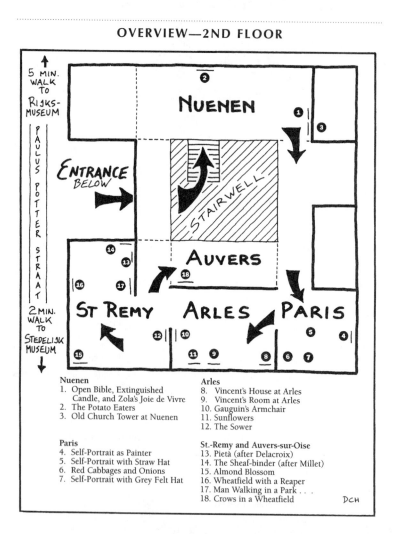

Nuenen
1. Open Bible, Extinguished Candle, and Zola's Joie de Vivre
2. The Potato Eaters
3. Old Church Tower at Nuenen

Paris
4. Self-Portrait as Painter
5. Self-Portrait with Straw Hat
6. Red Cabbages and Onions
7. Self-Portrait with Grey Felt Hat

Arles
8. Vincent's House at Arles
9. Vincent's Room at Arles
10. Gauguin's Armchair
11. Sunflowers
12. The Sower

St.-Remy and Auvers-sur-Oise
13. Pietà (after Delacroix)
14. The Sheaf-binder (after Millet)
15. Almond Blossom
16. Wheatfield with a Reaper
17. Man Walking in a Park . . .
18. Crows in a Wheatfield

DCH

ground floor. The top two floors contain more van Goghs, including his drawings, works by his friends and colleagues like Gauguin and Toulouse-Lautrec, and temporary exhibits by more recent artists.

The paintings on the second floor are arranged chronologically, taking us through the changes in van Gogh's life and styles. Some background on Vincent's star-crossed life makes the museum even better, so I've included liberal doses of biographical material. The paintings are divided into five periods of his life proceeding clockwise around the floor.

● *Before heading upstairs to the paintings, find a quiet spot to read the following.*

VINCENT VAN GOGH

"I am a man of passions ... "

You can see van Gogh's canvases as a series of suicide notes ... or as the record of a life full of beauty—too full of beauty. He attacked life with a passion, experiencing life's highs and lows more intensely than the average person. The beauty of the world overwhelmed him and its ugliness struck him as only another dimension of beauty. He tried to absorb all of life, good and bad, and channel it onto a canvas. The frustration of this overwhelming task drove him to madness. If all this is a bit overstated—and I guess it is—it's an attempt to show the emotional impact van Gogh's works have had on many people, myself included.

Van Gogh's life and art were one. His style changed with his circumstances and changing mood. As with Rembrandt, a little knowledge of his life makes the art come alive. For each painting I'll give a little background material and let the work itself say the rest. Since the museum divides his life and art into distinct periods, let's do the same.

Early Years (1853–1883) — Wandering

Vincent was a pastor's son from a small Dutch town. At 16 he went to work as a clerk for an art dealership. But his two interests, art and religion, distracted him from his dreary work and, after several years, he was finally fired.

The next 10 years are a collage of dead ends as he travels Northern Europe pursuing one path after another. He'd launch into each project with incredible energy, then get disillusioned and move on to something else: teacher at a boarding school, assistant preacher, bookstore apprentice, preacher again, theology student, English student, literature student, art student. He bounces around England, France, Belgium, and Holland. He falls in love but is rejected for someone more respectable. He quarrels with his family and is exiled. He lives with a prostitute and her daughter, offending the few friends he has. Finally, in his late twenties, worn out, flat broke, and in poor health, he returns to his family in Nuenen and makes peace. He starts to paint.

● Climb the stairs to the second floor, entering van Gogh's Nuenen period.

Nuenen (Dec. 1883–Nov. 1885) — Poverty and Religion

These dark grey canvases show us the hard, plain existence of the rural southern Netherlands. We see simple buildings, bare or autumn trees, and overcast skies, a world where it seems spring will never arrive. What warmth there is comes from the sturdy, gentle people themselves.

The style is crude—van Gogh couldn't draw very well, nor would he ever be a great technician. The paint is laid on thick, as though painted with Nuenen mud. The main subject is almost always dead center, with little or no background, so there's a claustrophobic feeling. We are unable to see anything but the immediate surroundings.

The Potato Eaters (1885)

"Those that prefer to see the peasants in their Sunday-best may do as they like. I personally am convinced I get better results by painting them in their roughness ... If a peasant picture smells of bacon, smoke, potato steam—all right, that's healthy."

Van Gogh had dabbled as an artist during his wandering years, sketching things around him and taking a few art classes, but it wasn't until he was 30 that he threw himself into it with abandon.

He painted the poor working peasants. He had worked as a lay minister among the poorest of the poor, peasants and miners. He joined them at work in the mines, taught their children, and even gave away his own few possessions to help them. The church authorities finally dismissed him for "excessive zeal," but he came away understanding the poor's harsh existence and the dignity with which they bore it.

Still Life with Bible (1885)
"I have a terrible need of—shall I say the word?—religion. Then I go out and paint the stars."

A Bible and a book titled *Lust for Life*—these two things dominated van Gogh's life. In his art he tried to fuse his religious upbringing with his love of the world's beauty. He lusted after life with a religious fervor. The burned-out candle tells us of the recent death of his father.

The Old Church Tower in Nuenen (1885)
The crows circle above the local cemetery of Nuenen. Soon after his father's death, van Gogh—in poor health and depressed—moves briefly to Antwerp. He then decides to visit his brother Theo, an art dealer living in the art capital of the world. Theo's support—financial and emotional—allows Vincent to spend the rest of his short life painting. He moves from rural, religious, poor Holland to ... Paris, the City of Light. Vincent van Gone.

● *Cross to the opposite side of the stairwell.*

Paris (March 1886–Feb. 1888) — Impressionism
Whoa! Whip out the sunglasses! The colors! The sun begins to break through, lighting up everything he paints. His landscapes are more spacious, with plenty of open sky, giving a feeling of exhilaration after the closed, dark world of Nuenen.

Vincent tries his hand at the Impressionist technique of building a scene using dabs of different colored paint. In fact, he tries many techniques, painting many different subjects—country scenes, city scenes, cafés, people, even Japanese prints, which were in vogue.

Self-Portrait at the Easel (1888)
"I am now living with my brother Vincent who is studying the art of painting with indefatigable zeal."

— Theo to a friend

Here Vincent proudly displays his new palette full of bright new colors. A whole new world of art—and life—is opening up to him.

In the cafés and bars of Paris' bohemian Montmarte district, van Gogh meets the revolutionary Impressionists. He rooms with Theo and becomes friends with other struggling young painters, like Gauguin and Toulouse-Lautrec. His health improves, he becomes more sociable, has an affair with an older woman, and is generally happy.

He signs up to study under a well-known classical teacher, but quits after only a few classes. He can't afford to hire models, so he roams the streets with sketch pad in hand and learns from his Impressionist friends.

The Impressionists emphasized getting out of the stuffy studio and setting up the canvas outside on the street or in the countryside to paint the play of sunlight off the trees, buildings, and water.

At first van Gogh copied from the Impressionist masters. In nearby paintings you'll see garden scenes like Monet's, café snapshots like Degas', "block prints" like the Japanese masters', and self-portraits … like nobody else's.

Various Self-Portraits (1887)

"You wouldn't recognize Vincent, he has changed so much … The doctor says that he is now perfectly fit again. He is making tremendous strides with his work … He is also far livelier than he used to be and is popular with people."
—Theo to their mother

The shimmering effect from Impressionist paintings comes from the technique of placing dabs of different colors side by side on the canvas. At a distance, the two colors blend in the eye of the viewer to become a third color. For example, here van Gogh uses separate strokes of blue, yellow, green, and red to create a brown beard—but a brown that throbs with excitement.

Still Lifes, such as *Red Cabbages and Onions* (1887)

He quickly develops his own style— thicker paint, broad, swirling brush strokes, and brighter clashing colors that make even inanimate objects seem to vibrate with life. The many different colors are supposed to blend together, but you'd have to back up to Belgium before these colors resolve.

Self-Portrait with Grey Felt Hat

"He has painted one or two portraits which have turned out well, but he insists on working for nothing. It is a pity that he shows no desire to earn some money because he could easily do so here. But you can't change people."

—Theo to their mother

Despite his new sociability, van Gogh never quite fit in with his Impressionist friends. He was developing into a good painter, and was anxious to strike out on his own. Also, he thought the social life of the big city was distracting him from serious work. In this painting, his face screams out from a swirling background of molecular activity. Van Gogh wanted peace and quiet where he could throw himself into his work completely. He heads for the sunny south of France.

Arles (Feb. 1888–May 1889) — Sunlight, Beauty, and Madness

Winter was just turning to spring when he arrived in Arles near the French Riviera. After the dreary Paris winter, the colors of springtime overwhelmed him. The blossoming trees inspired him to paint canvas after canvas, pulsing with new life and drenched in sunlight.

Vincent's House at Arles — The Yellow House (1888)

"It is my intention ... to go temporarily to the South, where there is even more color, even more sun."

He rents this house with the green shutters. Look at that blue sky! He paints in a frenzy, working feverishly to try and take it all in. He is happy and productive.

Vincent's Room at Arles (1888)

"I am a man of passions, capable of and subject to doing more or less foolish things—which I happen to regret, more or less, afterwards."

But Vincent is alone, a stranger in Provence. And that has its down side. Vincent swings from flurries of ecstatic activity to bouts of great loneliness. Like anyone traveling alone he experiences those high highs and low lows. This narrow room that's almost folding in on him must have seemed like a  prison cell at times. (Psychologists point out that most everything in this painting comes in pairs—two chairs, two paintings, a double bed squeezed down to a single—indicating his desire for a mate. Hmm.)

He invites his friend Gauguin to join him, envisioning a sort of artists' colony in Arles. He spends months preparing a room upstairs for Gauguin's arrival.

Gauguin's Armchair (1888)

"Empty chairs—there are many of them, there will be even more, and sooner or later, there will be nothing but empty chairs."

Gauguin arrives. At first they get along great, painting and carousing. But then things go bad. They clash over art, life, and personalities. Van Gogh, enraged during an argument, pulls out a knife and waves it in Gauguin's face. Gauguin takes the hint and quickly leaves town. Vincent is horrified at himself. In a fit of remorse and madness, he mutilates his own ear.

Sunflowers (1889)

"The worse I get along with people the more I learn to have faith in Nature and concentrate on her."

The people of Arles realize they have a madman on their hands, and the local vicar talks him into admitting himself to a mental hospital. Vincent writes to Theo: "Temporarily I wish to remain shut up, as much for my own peace of mind as for other people's."

Even a simple work like these *Sunflowers* (one of a half-dozen Vincent painted) bursts with life. Different people see different things in the *Sunflowers*. Is it a happy mood or a melancholy one? Take your own emotional temperature.

The Sower (1888)

A dark, silhouetted figure sows seeds in the burning sun. It's late in the day. The heat from the sun, the source of all life, radiates out in thick swirls of paint. The sower must be a hopeful man, because the field looks slanted and barren. Someday, he thinks, the seeds he's planting will grow into something great, like the tree that slashes diagonally across the scene—tough and craggy, but with small optimistic blossoms.

Vincent had worked sowing the Christian gospel in a harsh environment (see Mark 4:1–9). Now in Arles, ignited by the sun, he flung his artistic seeds to the wind, hoping.

Saint-Remy (May 1889–1890) — The Mental Hospital

In the mental hospital, he continues to paint whenever he's well enough. He can't go out as often, so he copies from books, making his own distinctive versions of works by Rembrandt, Delacroix, Millet, and others.

We see a change from bright, happy landscapes to more introspective subjects. The colors are less bright and more surreal, the brushwork even more furious. The strong outlines of figures are twisted and tortured.

Pietà (after Delacroix)

It's evening after a thunderstorm. Jesus has been crucified, and the corpse lies at the mouth of a tomb. Mary, whipped by the cold wind, holds her empty arms out in despair and confusion. She is the tender mother who receives us all in death as though saying, "My child, you've been away so long—rest in my arms."

At first the peace and quiet of the asylum do van Gogh good and his health improves. Occasionally he's allowed outside to paint the gardens and landscapes. Meanwhile, the paintings he has sent to Theo begin to attract attention in Paris for the first time. A woman in Brussels buys one of his canvases—the only painting he ever sold during his lifetime. Nowadays, a *Sunflowers* sells for $40 million.

The Sheaf-binder (after Millet)

"I want to paint men and women with that something of the eternal which the halo used to symbolize ... "

Van Gogh's compassion for honest laborers remained constant since his work with Belgian miners. These sturdy folk with their curving bodies wrestle as one with their curving wheat. The world van Gogh sees is charged from within by spiritual fires, twisting and turning, matter turning into energy and vice versa.

The fits of madness return. During these spells he loses all sense of his own actions. It means he can't paint, the one thing he feels driven to do. He writes to Theo: "My surroundings here begin to weigh on me more than I can say—I need air. I feel overwhelmed by boredom and grief."

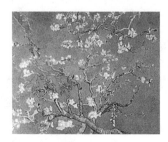

Almond Blossom

They make plans to move him north to Auvers, a small town near Paris where he can stay at a hotel under a doctor-friend's supervision. On the way there, he visits Theo. Theo's wife had just had a baby, which they named Vincent. Van Gogh shows up with this painting under his arm as a birthday gift. Theo's wife later recalls: "I had expected a sick man, but here was a sturdy, broad-shouldered man with a healthy color, a smile on his face, and a very resolute appearance."

Wheatfield with a Reaper

"I have been working hard and fast in the last few days. This is how I try to express how desperately fast things pass in modern life."

The harvest is here. The time is short. There's much work to be done. A lone reaper works uphill, scything through a swirling wheatfield, cutting slender paths of calm.

Man Walking in a Park with Falling Leaves

" … a traveler going to a destination that does not exist … "

The stark brown trees are blown by the wind. A solitary figure (who?) winds along a narrow, snaky path as the wind blows leaves on him. The colors are surreal—blue, green, and red tree trunks with heavy black outlines. A road runs away from us, heading nowhere.

Auvers (May–July 1890) — Flying Away

"The bird looks through the bars at the overcast sky where a thunderstorm is gathering, and inwardly he rebels against his fate. 'I am caged, I am caged, and you tell me I have everything I need! Oh! I beg you, give me liberty, that I may be a bird like other birds.' A certain idle man resembles this idle bird ... "

In his new surroundings he continues painting, interrupted by spells that swing from boredom to madness. His letters to Theo are generally optimistic, but he worries that he'll succumb completely to insanity and never paint again. The final landscapes are walls of bright, thick paint.

Crows in a Wheatfield (1890)

"This new attack ... came on me in the fields, on a windy day, when I was busy painting."

On July 27, Vincent leaves his hotel, walks out to a nearby field and puts a bullet through his chest.

This is the last painting Vincent finished. We can try to search the wreckage of his life for the black box explaining what happened, but there's not much there. His life was sad and tragic, but the record he left is one not of sadness but of beauty. Intense beauty.

The wind-blown wheatfield is a nest of restless energy. Scenes like this must have overwhelmed van Gogh with their incredible beauty— too much too fast with no release. The sky is dark blue, almost night-time, barely lit by two suns boiling through the deep ocean of blue. The road starts nowhere, leads nowhere, disappearing into the burning wheatfield. Above all of this swirling beauty fly the crows, the dark ghosts that had hovered over his life since the cemetery in Nuenen.

VENICE

St. Mark's Cathedral and the Doge's Palace

Accademia

E choes of a time when Venice was Europe's economic superpower still bounce down the lush halls of the Doge's Palace, around the gilded domes of St. Mark's basilica and through the rich paintings of the Accademia. With a huff and a puff from *Rick Steves' Mona Winks,* Europe's best-preserved big city once again becomes that most serene (hedonistic, mysterious, and lavish) republic.

13 St. Mark's Cathedral and the Doge's Palace

Venice was once Europe's richest city. As middleman in the trade between Asia and Europe, it reaped wealth from both sides. In 1450, Venice had 150,000 citizens (far more than Paris), and a gross "national" product 50 percent greater than the entire country of France. The rich Venetians learned to love the good life—silks, spices, and jewels from the East, crafts from northern Europe, good food and wine, fine architecture, music, gaiety, and laughter. Venice was a vibrant city full of impressed visitors, palaces, and glittering canals. Five centuries after its "fall," Venice is all of these still, with the added charm of romantic decay. In this tour we'll spend a couple of hours in the political and religious heart of this Old World superpower.

DOGE'S PALACE (PALAZZO DUCALE)

Hours: Daily 9:00–19:00 April–October, 9:00–17:00 November–March, last entrance 90 minutes before closing. Closed Jan. 1, May 1, Dec. 25.

Cost: 17,000 L, 9,000 L students, 3,000 L kids 6–14 years old. Admission includes entry to the Correr Museum on city history (entry on square opposite St. Mark's Church).

Information: There are no English descriptions. Guidebooks are on sale in the bookshop. Audiophone tours of the palace are rentable for 7,000 L (unnecessary with this book). WC in courtyard near palace exit.

Starring: Tintoretto and the Doges.

BASILICA DI SAN MARCO

Hours: Monday–Saturday 9:45–19:30, Sunday 14:00–17:00, interior beautifully lit 14:00–17:00 on Sunday. Shorter hours off-season.

Cost: The church is free. The treasury, altarpiece, and loggia with horses cost 4,000 L each. Strict dress code enforced (no shorts or bare shoulders).

Getting there: Signs all over town point to San Marco. It's on Piazza San Marco, near the Grand Canal. Vaporetto stop: San Marco.

Information: Guidebooks in church atrium bookstand. Public pay WC just beyond far end of square.

Starring: St. Mark, Byzantium, Sansovino.

PIAZZA SAN MARCO

Bride of the Sea

● *Sit on the steps at the far end of the square (away from the church).*

Imagine this square full of water with gondolas floating where people are now sipping coffee at the café tables. That happens every so often at very high tides, a reminder that Venice and the sea are intertwined.

Venetian wealth came from sea trading. As middleman between Europe and the East (the Moslem world of Turkey and the Middle East), Venice became the wealthiest city in Europe. In St. Mark's Square, the exact center of this East-West axis, we see both the luxury and the mix of Eastern and Western influences.

Basilica San Marco dominates the square with its Greek-Byzantine style domes and glowing mosaics. Mark Twain said it looked like "a warty bug taking a walk." To the left and right stand the government offices that administered the Venetian Empire's vast network of trading outposts. On the left are the "Old" offices, built in 1530 in solid Renaissance style. The "New" offices on the right from a century later are a little heavier and more ornamented, mixing various arches, columns, and statues in the Baroque style.

● *Behind you, you'll find the public WC, the post office, American Express office, and a Tourist Info office. Another is on the canal (see map). With Venice's inconsistent opening hours, it's wise to confirm your sightseeing plans here.*

Walk to the center of the square—to the cool shadow of the bell tower, or Campanile.

The Piazza

The square is big, but it feels intimate. Napoleon called it "the most beautiful drawing room in Europe." We have Napoleon himself to

PIAZZA SAN MARCO

```
           DOGE'S      BRIDGE
           PALACE      OF SIGHS

              BASILICA    COURT-
     CLOCK    S. MARCO    YARD           B A S I N
     TOWER
                          COLUMNS        O F
TO
RIALTO                  PIAZZETTA
   MERCERIA   FLAGPOLES                  S A N

                                         M A R C O
              CAMPANILE +
              LOGGETTA
     OLD                   NEW
     OFFICES               OFFICES

              PIGEONS                    VAPORETTO
   N          NAPOLEON'S   TOURIST       STOP
              WING         OFFICE
                                         TO RIALTO +
              POST  WC                   TRAIN STN.
 DCH                        TO           VIA GRAND
                            ACCADEMIA    CANAL
```

thank for the intimate feel. He built the final wing, opposite the church.

For architecture buffs, here's three centuries of styles, bam, side by side, *uno due tre*, for easy comparison: (1) Old wing, Renaissance, (2) New wing, Baroque, (3) Napoleon's wing, Neoclassical—a return to simpler, more austere classical columns and arches. Napoleon's architects tried to make his wing bridge the styles of the other two. But it turned out a little too high for one side and not enough for the other. Nice try.

● *Meet you at the center flagpole in front of the church. If you're real tired, make your homebase on a bench at the foot of the Campanile, the tall brick bell tower. Watch out for pigeon speckle.*

Basilica San Marco — Exterior

Mark was the author of one of the four Bible books telling the story

of Jesus' life (Matthew, Mark, Luke, and John). Seven centuries after his death his holy body was in Moslem-occupied Alexandria, Egypt. Two visiting merchants of Venice "rescued" the body from the infidels and spirited it away to Venice, giving the fast-growing city instant religious status. They made Mark the patron saint of the city, and you'll see his symbol, the winged lion, all over Venice. (Find four in 20 seconds.)

Above the door on the far left of the church is a mosaic of the

event that put Venice on the pilgrimage map. The *Transporting of St. Mark* shows two men in the center (with crooked staffs) entering the church bearing a coffin with the body. Mark looks grumpy from the long voyage.

The original church was built (over Mark's dead body) in the ninth century. The structure we see was begun in the 11th century with changes made throughout Venice's glory days. In this mosaic, one of the oldest, you can see the church as it looked in the 13th century—even with its famous bronze horses on the balcony. True to its founding, the church is built with columns, stones, and decorations looted from buildings throughout the Venetian empire. The style has been called "Early Ransack."

Along with Mark's bones, the four bronze horses over the central doorway are the most famous bit of booty. The Venetians stole them from their fellow Christians during the looting of Constantinople and brought them to San Marco. Napoleon stole the horses away to Paris—the French later returned them. (Copies top the arch next to the Louvre.) The horses we see overlooking St. Mark's Square are also copies, but you can visit the impressive originals housed inside church museum (upstairs).

The Clock Tower

Two bronze Moors (African Moslems), "rescued" from who knows where, stand atop the clock tower. At the top of each hour they swing their giant clappers. The dial shows the 24 hours, the signs of the zodiac, and the phases of the moon. Above it is the world's first digital clock, which changes every five minutes. There are both Roman numerals and Arabic numerals. And of course, there's a lion of St. Mark with alert wings looking down on the crowded square.

Campanile

The original Campanile (pron: camp-ah-NEE-lay), or bell tower, was a marvel of 10th-century architecture until the 20th century, when it toppled into the center of the Piazza. It had groaned ominously the night before, sending people in the cafés scurrying. The next morning ... crash!

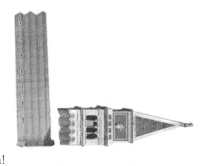

The Campanile fell in 1902 and was rebuilt 10 years later complete with its golden angel on top facing the breeze. You can ride a lift to the top for the best view of Venice. Notice the photo of the crumpled tower on the wall just before you enter the elevator. The ride is glassed in, stuffy, and crowded at times but worth it.

● *Sit at the base of the Campanile and face the water. The small square between the church and the water is ...*

The Piazzetta

This "Little Square" is framed by the Doge's Palace on the left and the Old Library on the right. In former days it used to be closed off to the general public for a few hours a day so that government officials and bigwigs could gather in the sun to strike shady deals.

The two large 12th-century columns near the water were looted from Constantinople. These columns were used to string up and torture criminals so the public could learn its lessons vicariously. There's a winged lion on top of one of them, the symbol of St. Mark, Venice's patron saint. The other shows St. Theodore, the former patron saint who was replaced when they got hold of Mark. I guess stabbing crocodiles in the back isn't classy enough for an upwardly mobile world power.

Venice was the "Bride of the Sea" because she was dependent on sea trading for her livelihood. This "marriage" was celebrated annually by the people. The Doge, in full regalia, boarded a ritual boat here at the edge of the Piazzetta and sailed out into the canal. There a vow was made and he dropped a jewelled ring into the water to seal the marriage.

In the distance, across the Grand Canal, is one of the grandest scenes in the city, the Church of San Giorgio Maggiore. The church was designed by the late-Renaissance architect Palladio.

Speaking of architects, I will for the next second-and-a-half: Sansovino. The Old Offices, the Old Library, and the delicate Loggetta you're sitting under (at the base of the Campanile) were all designed by him. Take 10 steps

toward the Doge's Palace, turn around and you can see all three of these at once. More than any single man, he made Piazza San Marco what it is.

When Venice floods, the puddle appears first around round, white pavement stones like the one between the Loggetta and the Doge's Palace.

● *Head to the water's edge and turn left. Stop in the middle of the first bridge and look inland.*

The Bridge of Sighs

On your left is the Doge's Palace where the government doled out justice. On the right were the prisons. (Don't let the palatial façade fool you—see the bars on the windows?) Prisoners sentenced in the palace crossed to the prisons by way of the covered bridge in front of you. From this bridge they got their final view of sunny, joyous Venice before entering the black and dank prisons. They sighed.

Venice has been a major tourist center for four centuries. Anyone who ever came here has stood on this very spot, looking at the Bridge of Sighs. Lean on the railing leaned on by everyone from Casanova to Byron to Hemingway.

● *Sigh. Then return to the flagpole in front of the basilica.*

BASILICA SAN MARCO

St. Mark's Cathedral is a treasure chest of booty looted during Venice's glory days. That's only appropriate for a church built on the bones of a stolen saint. The first church built over the relics burned down in 976, so what we see dates largely from the 11th century. Succeeding generations plastered it with columns, doors, mosaics, and statues plundered by centuries of conquest and aggressive trading.

BASILICA SAN MARCO

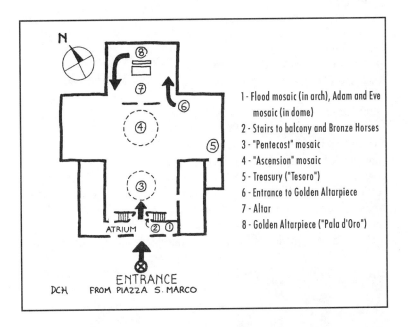

N

1 - Flood mosaic (in arch), Adam and Eve mosaic (in dome)
2 - Stairs to balcony and Bronze Horses
3 - "Pentecost" mosaic
4 - "Ascension" mosaic
5 - Treasury ("Tesoro")
6 - Entrance to Golden Altarpiece
7 - Altar
8 - Golden Altarpiece ("Pala d'Oro")

ATRIUM

DCH   ENTRANCE
FROM PIAZZA S. MARCO

The façade shows this crazy mix of East and West. The doorways are massive Romanesque (European) arches but lined with marble columns from Eastern buildings. The mosaics are mostly Venetian designs but executed by Greek craftsmen. There's sculpture from Constantinople, columns from Alexandria, and capitals from Sicily. The upper story has some pointed Gothic-style arches, while the whole affair is topped by Greek domes with their onion-shaped caps. What's amazing isn't so much the variety as the fact that the whole thing kind of comes together in a bizarre sort of harmony. It remains simply the most unique church in Europe, a church that, as Goethe said, "can only be compared with itself."

● *Enter through the central door—a sixth-century bronze-paneled Byzantine job. Turn right in the atrium (the entry hall) and drop anchor under the last dome.*

The Atrium Mosaics

St. Mark's is famous for its mosaics. Some of the oldest and finest are here in the atrium. Mosaics are made of small cubes of glass or stone pressed into wet plaster. Their popularity spread from ancient Rome to the Greek-speaking world through Constantinople. Byzantine

churches perfected the gold background effect by baking gold leaf
right into the tiny cubes of glass.

Medieval mosaics were teaching
aids to tell Bible stories to the illiterate masses. Today's literate masses
have trouble reading them, so let's
look at two simple examples.

In the arch next to the dome is the story of Noah and the Great
Flood. If you face the Piazza you'll see (on top) Noah building the
Ark. Below that are three scenes of Noah putting all species of animals
into the Ark, two by two. Turning around and facing the church interior, you'll see the Flood in full force, drowning the wicked. Noah
sends out a dove twice to see if there's any dry land to dock at. He
finds it, leaves the Ark with a gorgeous rainbow overhead and offers a
sacrifice of thanks to God. Easy, huh?

Now that our medieval literacy rate has risen, let's try the story that

rings the bottom of the dome—Adam
and Eve in the Garden of Eden. Stand
right under the dome facing the
church, crane your neck, and read
clockwise around the dome:

(1) Adam names the animals; (2) God
creates Eve from a spare rib, and (3)
presents her to Adam; (4) Eve is tempted by the serpent; (5) she picks and
gives the forbidden fruit to Adam; (6) they realize that they're naked
and (7) in shame, try to hide from God; (8) God finds them and (9)
lectures them; (10) He gives them clothes and (11) pushes them out
into the real world where they have to work for a living.

● *Enter the church through the central door past the gaily dressed guard
who makes sure all who enter have covered legs and shoulders. There are
benches along the back wall to both sides of the entry, but wait a second.*

While your eyes adjust to the dark, get a feel for the church. Before
reading on, walk up to the center of the church and back. Notice the
floor plan of four equal arms radiating from the center. Meet you back
here at the bench.

The Greek Cross Floor Plan

Western Christianity focuses on the death of Jesus; Eastern
Christianity focuses on his resurrection. That's why most Western
European churches have so many crucifixes, and even the shape of

the church itself is often in the form of a crucifix. But look around St. Mark's—not many crucifixes. And the floor plan is not the Latin Cross symbolizing the crucifixion but the Greek Cross (+), symbolizing perfection.

Topping the Greek Cross are five domes—one large one in the center and one over each arm, or transept. These are decorated with golden mosaics in the Byzantine style, though many were designed by Italian Renaissance and later artists. The entire upper part is in mosaic (imagine paving a football field with contact lenses). The often-overlooked lower walls are in beautiful marble.

The overall effect is one of "mystical, golden luminosity." It's a subtle effect, one that grows on you, especially as the filtered light changes. There are more beautiful churches, bigger, more overwhelming and even more holy, but none are as stately.

● *Find the chandelier near the central doorway (in the shape of a "Greek Cross" cathedral space station), and run your eyes up the support chain to the dome above.*

The Mosaics

This dome has one of the oldest mosaics in the church, from around 1125. The scene is the Pentecost. The Holy Spirit in the form of a dove sends out tongues of fire—the miracle of speaking in tongues, looking like a red horn on each head—to the 12 Apostles

below. (As the poet Yeats described it: "O sages standing in God's holy fire as in the gold mosaic of a wall, come from the holy fire … and be the singing-masters of my soul.") While the mosaics in the Atrium were from the Old Testament, we've now entered the new age of the New Testament.

● *Walk up the aisle again to the central dome. Take a seat against a pillar. The corner seat is ideal.*

Central Dome Mosaic

You've probably noticed that the floor is also mosaics, mostly geometrical designs and animals. You've also noticed it rolls like the sea. Venice is sinking—and shifting—creating these cresting waves of stone.

Gape upwards. The mosaic in the central dome is, again, not the death of Jesus, but *The Ascension* into heaven after the Resurrection. This isn't the dead, crucified mortal Jesus shown in most churches, but a powerful god, the Creator of All, seated on a crescent moon in the center of starry heaven solemnly giving us his blessing. Below him is Mary (with shiny golden Greek crosses on each shoulder and looking ready to play patty-cake) flanked by two winged angels and the 12 Apostles.

Sailing to Byzantium

For centuries Constantinople (modern Istanbul) was the greatest city in Europe. In A.D. 330, the Emperor Constantine moved the Roman Empire's capital to the newly built city of Constantinople, taking with him Rome's best and brightest. While the city of Rome decayed and fell, the Eastern half of the Empire lived on, speaking the Greek language and adopting a more Oriental outlook.

Venetian traders tapped the wealth of this culture during the Crusades, the series of military expeditions to "save" the holy city of Jerusalem from the Moslems. In the Fourth Crusade, in 1204, when Constantinople was threatened by the Turks, they appealed to their fellow Christians in the West for help. The Pope launched a Crusade, the armies marched, they fought the Turks, drove the savage infidel beasts away, entered the city ... and proceeded to loot it themselves. (This was, at least until the advent of TV evangelism, perhaps the lowest point in Christian history.) Among the treasures shipped back to Venice were the bronze horses and many of the artifacts in the Treasury.

Consider checking out the Treasury and the Golden Altarpiece (Pala d'Oro). This is your best chance outside of Istanbul or Ravenna to experience the glory of the Byzantine civilization. The Treasury entrance is in the right transept. The Altarpiece is in the apse, behind the high altar. Of the three separate admissions you'll encounter in this church, I'd prioritize in this order: Loggia and horses (see below), Golden Altarpiece, Treasury.

● *The Treasury (Tesoro) is at the far corner of the right transept.*

Treasury

You'll see Byzantine chalices, silver reliquaries, monstrous monstrances (for displaying the Communion wafer), the marble *Chair of St. Mark*, and icons done in gold, silver, enamels, agate, studded with precious gems, and so on. This is marvelous handiwork, but all the more marvelous because many were done in A.D. 500, when Western Europe was still rooting in the mud.

● *Exiting the Treasury, cross the right transept to the Golden Altarpiece entrance. On the way, notice the door under the rose window at the end of the transept. This was the Doge's private entrance direct from the Doge's Palace. Follow the crowds behind the altar. Read as you shuffle on.*

Golden Altarpiece (Pala d'Oro)

The first thing you see after showing your ticket is the high altar itself (under the stone canopy). Beneath this lies the body of Mark, the Gospel writer (the tomb, through the grate under the altar, says "Marxus").
Legend has it that before he died he visited Venice, where an angel promised him he could rest his weary bones when he died. Hmm. Shhh.

Above the altar is a marble canopy. The four supporting columns are wonderful and mysterious—scholars don't even know whether they're from fifth-century Byzantium or 13th-century Venice! I spent as much time looking at the funny New Testament scenes carved in them as at the Golden Altarpiece with its crowds and glaring lights. (On the right-hand pillar closest to the Altarpiece, fourth row from the bottom—is that a genie escaping from a bottle while someone tries to stuff him back in?)

The Golden Altarpiece is a dazzling golden wall made of 80 Byzantine enamels decorated with religious scenes set in gold and studded with rubies, emeralds, sapphires, pearls, amethysts, and topaz. Byzantine craftsmen made this for the Doges over the course of several centuries (976–1345). It's a bit much to take in all at once, but one figure you might recognize is in the center of the lower half—Jesus as Creator of All, similar to the mosaic in the main dome—with Matthew, Mark, Luke, and John around him. Once you've looked at some of the individual scenes, back up as far as this small room will let you, and just let yourself be dazzled by the "whole picture"—this "mosaic" of Byzantine greatness.

The Bronze Horses and View of the Piazza

● *The staircase up to the bronze horses is in the Atrium near the main entrance. The sign says "Loggia dei Cavalli, Museo."*

Your ticket gives you admission to:

(1) A small museum with fragments of mosaics that you can examine up close.

(2) An upstairs gallery with an impressive top-side view of the church interior with its mosaic wallpaper.

(3) The Loggia, the balcony overlooking Piazza San Marco. Nice view, fun pigeon- and people-watching.

(4) The Bronze Horses. You can walk among the copies on the Loggia with their "1978" date on the hoof. Then go inside to a room with the real things. Very impressive. Stepping lively in pairs with smiles on their faces, they exude energy and exuberance. Originally gilded bronze, you can still see some streaks of gold.

These horses have done some traveling in their day. Made in the time of Alexander the Great, they were taken by Nero to Rome. Constantine took them to his new capital in Constantinople. The Venetians then stole them from their fellow Christians during the looting of noble Constantinople and brought them to San Marco.

What goes around comes around, and Napoleon came around and took the horses when he conquered Venice in 1797. They stood atop a triumphal arch in the Louvre courtyard until Napoleon's empire was "blown-aparte" and they were returned to their "rightful" home.

(What Goes Around Comes Around Dept., P.S.: The horses were again removed from their spot when attacked by their most dangerous enemy yet—20th-century man. The threat of oxidation from pollution sent them running for cover inside the church.)

THE DOGE'S PALACE

Venice is a city of beautiful façades—palaces, churches, carnival masks—that can cover darker interiors of intrigue and decay. The Doge's Palace with its frilly pink exterior hides the fact that "the Most Serene Republic" (as it called itself) in its heyday was far from serene.

The Doge's Palace housed the fascinating government of this rich and powerful Empire. It also served as the home for the Venetian ruler known as the Doge (pron: DOJE-eh), or Duke. For four centuries (about 1150–1550) this was the most powerful half-acre in Europe. The Doges wanted it to reflect the wealth of the Republic, impressing visitors and serving as a reminder that the Venetians were number one in Europe.

The Exterior

"The Wedding Cake," "The Table Cloth," or "The Pink House" is also sometimes known as the Doge's Palace. The style is called Venetian Gothic, and the arches and windows come to a point like Gothic arches, but the upper half has an Eastern, Islamic flavor with its abstract patterns. The columns originally had bases on the bottoms, but these were covered over as the columns sank. If you compare this delicate, top-heavy structure with the massive fortress palaces of Florence, you realize the wisdom of building a city in the middle of the sea—you have no natural enemies except gravity.

The palace was originally built in the 800s, but most of what we see came after 1300 as it was expanded to meet the needs of the Empire. Each Doge wanted to leave his mark on history with a new wing. But so much of the city's money was spent on the building that finally a law was passed levying an enormous fine on anyone who even mentioned any new building. That worked for a while, until one brave and wealthy Doge proposed a new wing, paid his fine ... and started building again.

● *Enter the Doge's Palace from the canal side. Included in your admission is a new ground floor museum. After exploring this, you'll cross an inner courtyard to the base of a big staircase closer to the basilica.*

Imagine yourself as a foreign dignitary on business to meet the Doge. Ahead of you is the grand staircase with two nearly nude statues of, I think, Moses and Paul Newman. The Doge and his aides would be waiting for you at the top. No matter who you were, you'd have to hoof it up—the powerful Doge would descend the stairs for no one.

You'll notice that the entry hall ceiling alternates between Gothic pointed-arch vaulting and round Roman arches. Much of the palace was built on the cusp between medieval and Renaissance.

● *Go up the tourists' staircase and look out over the courtyard (and the backside of Paul Newman). From here on it's hard to get lost (though I've managed). It's a one-way system, so just follow the arrows.*

The Courtyard

You have a Doge's-eye view of the courtyard. Ambassadors would walk up this staircase to bow to you. The Doge was something like an "elected king"—which makes sense only in the "dictatorial republic" that was Venice. Technically he was just a noble selected by other nobles to carry out their laws and decisions. Gradually, though, the Doges extended their powers and ruled more like divine-right kings, striking the fear of death in all who opposed them.

Ahead of you on the right, notice that the palace is attached right to St. Mark's Cathedral. You can see the ugly brick of both structures—the stern inner structure without its painted-lady veneer of marble. On this tour we'll see the sometimes harsh inner structure of this outwardly serene Republic.

● *Head down the loggia to the entrance to the Golden Staircase leading to the Doge's residence on the first landing and on to the actual palace at the top.*

The Golden Staircase

The palace was propaganda, designed to impress visitors. This gilded-ceiling staircase was something for them to write home about.

The first floor is where the Doge actually lived. Wander around these sumptuous rooms before continuing upstairs. Despite his great power, the Doge had to obey one iron-clad rule—he and his family had to leave their own home and live in the Doge's Palace. Poor guy.

● *Go up the first step of steps. At the middle landing, go straight (not right) up toward stained-glass windows, then make a U-turn to the right and go up more stairs to …*

The "Atrio Quadrato"

Look at the ceiling painting, *Justice Presenting the Sword and Scales to Doge Girolano* by Tintoretto. It's a masterpiece by one of the late-Renaissance greats. So what? May as well adopt the "so what" attitude now because you'll get it sooner or later. There's so much great art here by great painters—mostly Tintoretto and Veronese—that you can't possibly appreciate it all. Best to enjoy it not as museum art but as palace wallpaper.

● *Enter the next room.*

Room of the Four Doors

This was the central clearinghouse for all the goings-on in the palace. Visitors trying to see the Doge or any other government official presented themselves here. The three other doors then led to their destination—the executive, legislative, or judicial branch of government.

The room was designed by Palladio, the architect who did the impressive San Giorgio Maggiore Church you see almost floating across the Grand Canal from St. Mark's Square. On the intricate stucco ceiling notice the feet of the women dangling down below the edge (above the windows), a typical Baroque technique of creating the illusion of 3-D.

DOGE'S PALACE—EXECUTIVE AND LEGISLATIVE

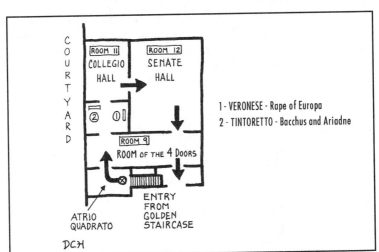

```
C
O    ROOM 11    ROOM 12
U    COLLEGIO   SENATE
R    HALL       HALL
T
Y              1 - VERONESE - Rape of Europa
A    ②   ①    2 - TINTORETTO - Bacchus and Ariadne
R
D    ROOM 9
     ROOM OF THE 4 DOORS

     ⊗  ▥

         ENTRY
         FROM
  ATRIO   GOLDEN
  QUADRATO STAIRCASE

DCH
```

On the wall is a painting by (ho-hum) Titian showing a Doge kneeling with great piety before a woman embodying Faith holding the Cross of Jesus. Notice old Venice in the misty distance under the cross. This is one of many paintings you'll see of Doges in uncharacteristically humble poses—paid for, of course, by the Doges themselves.

● *Enter the small room with the big fireplace. With your back to the fireplace, face the two paintings on the opposite wall ...*

The "Ante-Collegio"

It took a big title or bribe to get in to see the Doge. But first you were told to wait here, combing your hair, adjusting your robe, popping a Certs, and preparing the gifts you'd brought. While you cooled your heels and warmed your hands at the elaborate fireplace, you might look at some of the paintings—among the finest in the palace, worthy of any museum in the world.

The Rape of Europa by Veronese (opposite the window) shows the luxury and sensuality of Venice at its peak. The Venetian Renaissance looked back to pagan Greece and Rome for subjects to paint, a big change from the saints and crucifixions of the Middle Ages. Here Zeus, the king of the Greek gods, appears in the form of a bull to carry off a beautiful earthling. This is certainly no medieval condemnation of sex and violence, but a celebration in cheery pastel colors of the earthy, optimistic spirit of the Renaissance.

Tintoretto's *Bacchus and Ariadne* (next to the window) is another colorful display of Venice's sensual tastes. The god of wine offers a ring to the mortal Ariadne who's being crowned with stars. The ring is the center of a spinning wheel of flesh with the three arms like spokes.

But wait, the Doge is ready for us. Let's go in.

● *Enter the next room.*

The Collegio (Executive Branch)

Surrounded by his counselors, the Doge would sit on the platform at the far end to receive ambassadors who laid their gifts at his feet and pled their country's case. The gifts were often essentially tribute from lands conquered by Venetian generals. All official ceremonies, such as ratifying treaties, were held here.

At other times it was the private meeting room of the Doge and his cabinet to discuss secrets of state, proposals to give the legislature, or negotiations with the Pope. The wooden benches around the sides where they sat are original. The clock on the wall is a backward-running 24-hour clock with Roman numerals and a sword for hands.

The ceiling is 24-carat gold with paintings by Veronese. These are not frescoes (painting on wet plaster) like in the Sistine Chapel but actual canvases painted here on earth and then placed on the ceiling. Venice's humidity would have melted frescoes like so much mascara within years. Check out the painting of the woman with the spider web (on the ceiling, opposite the big window). This was the Venetian symbol of "Discussion." You can imagine the many intricate webs of truth and lies woven in this room by the Doge's sinister nest of advisers.

● *Enter the large Senate Room.*

The Senate Chamber (Legislative Branch)

This was the center of the Venetian government. Venice was technically a republic ruled by the elected Senate that met here, though its power was gradually overshadowed by the Doge and, later, the Council of Ten. This body of 60 annually elected senators, chaired by the Doge, debated and passed laws, and made declarations of war in this room. Senators would speak from the podium between the windows.

Tintoretto's *Triumph of Venice* on the ceiling (center) shows the city in all its glory. Lady Venice is up in heaven with the Greek gods while barbaric lesser nations swirl up to give her gifts and tribute. Do you get the feeling the Venetian aristocracy was proud of its city?

On the wall are two large clocks with the signs of the zodiac and phases of the moon. The senators shared one of them with the Doge next door, explaining the mystery of time reversal. And there's one final oddity in this room, in case you hadn't noticed it yet. In one of the wall paintings (above the entry door), there's actually a Doge ... not kneeling.

● *Pass again through the Room of the Four Doors, then around the corner into the large hall with a semi-circular platform at the far end.*

Room of the Council of Ten (Judicial Branch)

Venice's worldwide reputation for swift, harsh, and secret justice came from the dreaded Council of Ten. This group consisting of the Doge and other elected officials dealt out justice for traitors, murderers, and "morals" violators.

Slowly they developed into a CIA-type unit with their own force of policemen, guards, spies, informers, and even assassins. They had their own budget and were accountable to no one, soon making them the *de facto* ruling body of the "Republic." No one was safe from the spying eye of the "Terrible Ten." If you were even suspected of disloyalty or troublemaking you could be swept off the streets, tried, judged, and thrown into the dark dungeons in the palace for the rest of your life without so much as a Miranda warning.

DOGE'S PALACE—JUDICIAL

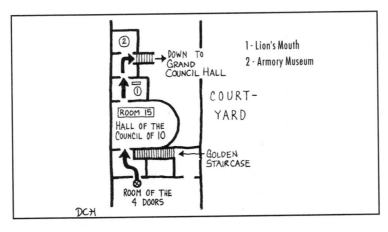

It was in this room that the Council met to decide punishments—who lived, died, was decapitated, tortured, or merely thrown in jail. The small, hard-to-find door leading off the platform (to the right) leads through secret passages to the prisons and torture chambers.

The large central oval ceiling painting by Veronese (a copy of the original stolen by Napoleon and still in the Louvre) shows *Jupiter Descending from Heaven to Strike Down the Vices*, redundantly informing the accused that justice in Venice was swift and harsh.

The dreaded Council of Ten was, of course, eventually disbanded. Today, their descendants enforce the dress code for tourists entering St. Mark's.

● *Pass through the next room noticing the "Lion's Mouth" (on both sides of the exit door). These letterboxes, known as Lions' Mouths because some had a lion's head, are scattered throughout the palace. Anyone who had a complaint or suspicion about anyone else could accuse him by simply dropping a slip of paper in the mouth. This set the blades of justice turning inside the palace. The Armory Museum is up the stairs.*

Armory Museum

The aesthetics of killing is beyond me, but I must admit I've never seen a better collection of halberds, falchions, ranseurs, mulchers, targes, morions, and brigandines in my life. (One of these words is a fake.) The stock of weapons in these three rooms makes you realize the important role the military played in keeping open the East-West trade lines.

In the fourth room, you'll see artistic shields, a midget's armor, old globes, and old quivers (but no mulchers). Squint out the window at the far end. It's Palladio's San Giorgio again and Venice's Lido (beach) in the distance. To the right, the tall glass case contains a tiny crossbow, some torture devices (including an effective-looking thumbscrew), "the devil's box" (a clever item that could fire in four directions at once), and a chastity belt. These "iron breeches" were worn by the wife of the Lord of Padua. On your way out you'll pass a very, very early attempt at a machine gun.

● *Go downstairs, turn left and pass through the long hall with a wood-beam ceiling. Now turn right and open your eyes as wide as you can …*

Hall of the Grand Council

It took a room this size to contain the grandeur of the Most Serene Republic. This huge room (180 feet long) could accommodate up to 2,000 people at one time—the nobility who were the backbone of the Empire. In theory, the Doge, the Senate, and the Council of Ten were subordinate to the Grand Council. They were elected from among its ranks.

Once the Doge was elected he was presented to the people of Venice from the balcony on the far end of the room (Salla dello Scrutino) that overlooks the Piazzetta. A noble would announce, "Here is your Doge, if it pleases you." That was fine until one time when the people weren't pleased. From then on they just said, "Here is your Doge."

Ringing the hall near the ceiling are portraits in chronological order of 76 Doges. The one at the far end that's blacked out is the notorious Doge Falier, who opposed the will of the Grand Council. He was tried for treason and beheaded. Ironically, the Doge whose memory they tried to blot out is now the best remembered. Fame is great—infamy is better.

On the wall over the Doge's throne is Tintoretto's monsterpiece, *Paradise*, the largest oil painting in the world. At almost 1,700 square feet, I could slice it up and wallpaper my entire apartment with enough left over for place mats.

Christ and Mary are at the top of heaven surrounded by 500 saints who ripple out in concentric rings. Tintoretto worked on this in the last years of his long life. On the day it was finished, his daughter died. He got his brush out again and painted her as saint #501. She's dead center with the blue skirt, hands clasped, getting sucked up to heaven. (At least that's what an Italian tour guide told me.)

The rest of the room's paintings show great moments in Venice's glory days of military conquest. Veronese's *The Apotheosis of Venice* (on the ceiling at the Tintoretto end) is a typically unsubtle work showing Lady Venice being crowned a goddess by an angel.

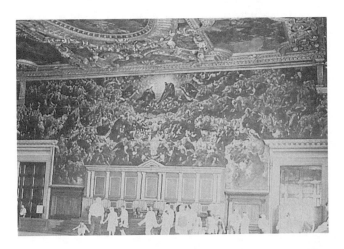

Actually, the Venetians were looking back to better times before the series of military defeats that began their city's decline. One by one the Turks gobbled up Venice's trading outposts. In the West the rest of Europe ganged up on Venice to reduce her power. To top it off, by 1500 Portugal had broken Venice's East-West trade monopoly by finding a sea route to the East around Africa. From 1500 to 1800 Venice remained a glorious city but not the great world power she once was.

Out the windows is a fine view of the domes of the basilica and the palace courtyard below. There's Paul Newman again, and the ugly brick walls and the round- and pointed-arched arcades.

● Read the intro to the prisons here in the Grand Council Hall, where there are more benches and fewer rats.

The Prisons
The palace had its own dungeons. The Doges could sentence, torture, and jail political opponents in the privacy of their own home. The most notorious cells were "the Wells" in the basement, so-called because they were deep, wet, and cramped.

By the 1500s, the Wells were full of political prisoners. New prisons were built across the canal to the east of the palace and connected with a covered bridge—covered so they could still imprison opponents without public knowledge.

● Exit the Grand Hall (next to the monsterpiece) and pass through a series of rooms and once-secret passages, following signs for "Ponte dei Sospiri/Prigioni," through the covered Bridge of Sighs over the canal to the "New" Prisons.

Medieval justice was harsh. The cells consisted of cold stone with heavily barred windows, a wooden plank for a bed, a shelf, and a bucket. (My question—what did they put on the shelf?)

Circle the cells. Notice the carvings made by prisoners on some of the stone windowsills of the cells. My favorites are on the second cell in the far corner of this building.

The Bridge of Sighs
Criminals were tried and sentenced in the palace, then marched across the canal here to the dark prisons. On this bridge they got their one last look at Venice. They gazed out at the sky, the water, the beautiful buildings.

● Cross back over the Bridge of Sighs, pausing to look through the marble-trellised windows at all the tourists and San Giorgio Church. Have one last sigh.

14 *Accademia*

The main sight to see in Venice is Venice. If you only have a day in Venice, I'm a little hesitant to recommend visiting the Accademia (pron: ack-uh-DAY-mee-uh).

Still, the Accademia is the greatest museum anywhere for Venetian Renaissance art and a good overview of painters whose works you'll see all over town. Venetian art is underrated and, I think, misunderstood. It's nowhere near as famous today as the work of the florescent Florentines, but it's livelier, more colorful, and simply more fun.

GALLERIE DELL' ACCADEMIA

Hours: Monday 9:00–14:00, Tuesday–Saturday 9:00–22:00, Sunday 9:00–20:00. Shorter hours off-season. Afternoons and evenings are less crowded with shorter lines.

Cost: 12,000 L

Tour length: One hour

Getting there: Walk 15 minutes from San Marco, following signs to "Accademia." The museum faces the Grand Canal, just over a wooden bridge. Vaporetto stop: Accademia.

Information: Precious little. Tel. 041-522-2247. *Note*: The Peggy Guggenheim museum of modern art is a five-minute walk east along the Grand Canal. Housed in a small palace on the Grand Canal, it's an excellent collection, well-displayed, and a great introduction to nearly every major movement in modern art (read chapter 22 on Modern Art for more information).

Anticipated Changes: In 2000, the Accademia will expand into the adjacent school. Currently only 300 of the Accademia's 2,000 paintings are on view.

Cuisine art: Eateries (Bar Accademia Foscarini) and snack stands nearby.

Starring: Titian, Veronese, Giorgione, Tintoretto.

ACCADEMIA—OVERVIEW

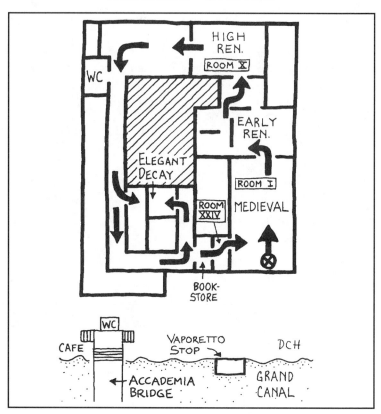

VENICE —
SWIMMING IN LUXURY

● *Buy your ticket, check your bag, and head upstairs to a large hall filled with gold-leaf altarpieces. Immediately past the turnstile, turn left, enter the small Room XXIV, and take a seat.*

The Venetian love of luxury shines through in Venetian painting. We'll see grand canvases of colorful, spacious settings peopled with happy Venetians in luxurious clothes having a great time. Even in solemn religious works, the Venetian love of color and beauty is obvious.

We'll work chronologically from medieval days to the 1700s. But before we start at the medieval beginning, let's sneak a peak at a work by the greatest Venetian Renaissance master, Titian.

Titian (Tiziano Vecellio) —
Presentation of the Virgin

This work is typical of Venetian Renaissance art. Here and throughout this museum, you will find: (1) bright, rich color, (2) big canvases,

(3) Renaissance architectural backgrounds, (4) slice-of-life scenes of Venice (notice the market woman in the foreground selling eggs), and (5) three-dimensional realism.

The scene is the popular "Biblical" story (though it's not in the Bible) of the child Mary, later to be the mother of Jesus, being presented to the high priest in Jerusalem's temple. But here the religious scene is more an excuse for a grand display of Renaissance architecture and colorful robes.

The painting is a parade of colors. Titian (pron: TEESH-un) leads you from color to color. First, the deep blue sky and mountains in the background. Then down to the bright red robe of one of the elders. Then you notice the figures turning and pointing at something. Your eye follows up the stairs to the magnificent jewelled robes of the priests.

But wait! What's that along the way? In a pale blue dress that sets her apart from all the other colored robes, dwarfed by the enormous staircase and columns is the tiny, shiny figure of the child Mary almost floating up to the astonished priest. She is unnaturally small, towered over by the priests, and easily overlooked at first glance. When we finally notice her, we realize all the more how delicate she is, a fragile flower amid the hustle, bustle, and epic grandeur. Venetians love this painting and call it, appropriately enough, "the Little Mary."

Now that we've gotten a taste of Renaissance Venice at its peak, let's backtrack and see some of Titian's predecessors.

● *Return to Room I, stopping at a work near the turnstile of Mary and baby Jesus.*

MEDIEVAL

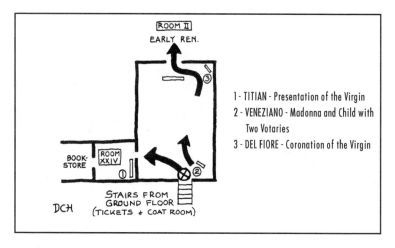

ROOM II
EARLY REN.

1 - TITIAN - Presentation of the Virgin
2 - VENEZIANO - Madonna and Child with Two Votaries
3 - DEL FIORE - Coronation of the Virgin

BOOK-STORE
ROOM XXIV

STAIRS FROM GROUND FLOOR
DCH (TICKETS & COAT ROOM)

Medieval — Pre-3-D

Medieval painting like you see in this hall was religious. The point was to teach Bible stories and doctrines to the illiterate masses by using symbolism. This art then is less realistic, less colorful, and less dramatic than later Renaissance art. Look around the hall and you'll see a lot of gold in the paintings. Medieval Venetians, with their close ties to the East, borrowed techniques like gold-leafing from Byzantine (modern Istanbul) religious icons.

Veneziano — *Madonna and Child with Two Votaries (Madonna e Bambino con Due Votari)*

There's a golden Byzantine background of heaven, and the golden haloes let the illiterate masses know that these folks are holy. The child Jesus is a baby in a bubble, an iconographical symbol of his "aura" of holiness.

Notice how two-dimensional and unrealistic this painting is. The size of the figures reflects their religious importance, not their actual size—Mary is huge, being both the mother of Christ as well as "Holy Mother Church." Jesus is next, then the two angels crowning Mary. Finally, in the corner, are two mere mortals kneeling in devotion.
● *In the far right corner of the room you'll find ...*

Jacobello del Fiore — *Coronation of the Virgin*

This swarming beehive of saints is an attempt to cram as much information as possible into one space. The architectural setting is a clumsy attempt at three-dimensionality. The saints are simply stacked one on top of the other rather than receding into the distance as they would in real life.

● *Enter Room II at the far end of this hall.*

Early Renaissance (1450–1500)

Only a few decades later artists rediscovered the natural world and how to capture it on canvas. With this Renaissance, or "rebirth," of the arts and attitudes of ancient Greece and Rome, painters took a giant leap forward. They weeded out the jumble of symbols and fleshed out cardboard characters into real people.

Giovanni Bellini — *Holy Conversation (Retable di San Giobbe)*

One key to the Renaissance was balance. Here Giovanni Bellini (pron: bell-EEN-ee) takes only a few figures, places them in a spacious architectural setting, and balances them half on one side of Mary and half on the other. The overall effect is one of calm and serenity rather than the

EARLY RENAISSANCE

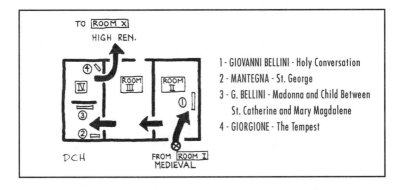

TO ROOM X
HIGH REN.

1 - GIOVANNI BELLINI - Holy Conversation
2 - MANTEGNA - St. George
3 - G. BELLINI - Madonna and Child Between
    St. Catherine and Mary Magdalene
4 - GIORGIONE - The Tempest

DCH

FROM ROOM I
MEDIEVAL

hubbub of the "Coronation" we just saw. Look at St. Sebastian—even arrows can't disturb the serenity.

This is a religious scene—a mythical meeting of Mary and the baby Jesus with saints. Left to right, you'll find Saints Francis (founder of an order of medieval monks), John the Baptist, Job, Dominic (founder of another order of monks), Sebastian, and Louis. But Bellini is more interested in pleasing the eye than teaching Church doctrine.

The painting has three descending arches. The top one is the Roman arch above the scene. Below that is a pyramid-shaped "arch" formed by the figures themselves, with Mary's head at the peak. Still lower is a smaller arch formed by the three musician angels. Subconsciously, this creates a mood of spaciousness, order, and balance.

Bellini was the teacher of two more Venetian greats, Titian and Giorgione. His gift to the Venetian Renaissance was the "haze" he put over his scenes, giving them an idealized, glowing, serene—and much copied—atmosphere.

● *Climb the small staircase, pass through Room III and into the small Room IV.*

Mantegna —
St. George (San Giorgio)

This Christian warrior is essentially a Greek nude sculpture with armor painted on. Notice his stance with the weight resting on one leg (*contrapposto*), the same as a classical sculpture or Michelangelo's *David* or an Italian guy trying to look cool on the street-corner. Also, Mantegna (pron: mon-TAIN-ya) has placed him in a doorway that's really just an architectural niche designed for a classical statue.

The Renaissance began in Florence among sculptors and architects. Even the painters were sculptors, "carving" out figures (like this) with sharp outlines, then filling them in with color. *St. George* is different in that respect from other works in the museum. It has a harder Florentine edge to it compared with the hazy Venetian outlines of Bellini.

St. George typifies Renaissance balance—a combination of stability and movement, alertness and relaxation, humility and proud confidence. With the broken lance in his hand and the dragon at his feet, George is the strong Renaissance Man slaying the medieval dragon of superstition and oppression.

● *Find three women and a baby.*

Bellini — *Madonna and Child Between*
St. Catherine and Mary Magdalene

In contrast to Mantegna's sharp three-dimensionality, this is just three heads on a flat plane with a black backdrop. Their features are soft, hazy, atmospheric, glowing out of the darkness as though lit by the soft light of a candle. It's not sculptural line that's important here, but color—warm, golden, glowing flesh tones.

Bellini painted dozens of Madonna-and-Childs in his day. (Others are nearby.) This Virgin Mary's pretty, but it can't compare with the sheer idealized beauty of Mary Magdalene (on the right). With her hair down like the prostitute she was, yet with a childlike face, thoughtful and repentant, this is the perfect image of the innocent woman who sinned by loving too much.

● *Around the partition, you'll find ...*

Giorgione — *The Tempest*

It's the calm before the storm. The atmosphere is heavy, luminous but ominous. There's a sense of mystery. Who is the woman suckling her baby in the middle of the countryside? And the soldier, is he spying on her or protecting her? Do they know that the serenity of this beautiful landscape is about to be shattered by an approaching storm?

The mystery is heightened by contrasting elements. The armed soldier contrasts with the naked lady with her baby. The austere ruined columns contrast with the lusciousness of Nature. And, most important, the stillness of the foreground scene is in direct opposition to the threatening storm in the background.

Giorgione (pron: jor-JONE-ee) was as mysterious as his few paintings, yet he left a lasting impression. A student of Bellini, he learned to use haziness to create a melancholy mood of beauty in his work,. But nothing beautiful lasts. Flowers fade, Mary Magdalenes grow old, and, in *The Tempest*, the fleeting stillness of a rare moment of peace is about to be shattered by the slash of lightning—the true center of the composition.

● *Exit and turn left, passing through the long Room VI and up the steps to the large Room X.*

Venetian High Renaissance —
Titian, Veronese, Tintoretto (1500–1600)

Veronese —
Feast of the
House of Levi

Parrrrty!! Stand about ten yards from this enormous canvas, to where it just fills your field of vision ... and hey, you're invited. Venice loves the good life, and the party's in full swing. You're in a huge room with a great view of Venice. Everyone's dressed to kill in brightly colored silks. Conversation roars and the servants bring on the food and drink.

This captures the Venetian attitude (more love, less attitude) as well as the style of Venetian Renaissance painting. Remember: (1) bright colors, (2) big canvases, (3) Renaissance architectural settings, (4) scenes of Venice life, and (5) three-dimensional realism. Painters had mastered realism and now gloried in it.

The Feast of the House of Levi is, believe it or not, a religious work painted for a monastery. The original title was *The Last Supper*. In the center of all the wild goings-on, there's Jesus, flanked by his disciples, sharing a final meal before his crucifixion.

This festive feast shows the optimistic spirit of pagan Greece and Rome that was reborn in the Renaissance. Life was a good thing, beauty was to be enjoyed, and man was a strong, good creature capable of making his own decisions and planning his own life. Yet to Renaissance Men and Women this didn't exclude religion. To them, the divine was

HIGH RENAISSANCE

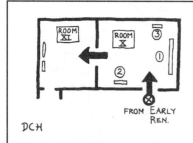

1 - VERONESE - Feast of the House of Levi
2 - TITIAN - Pieta
3 - TINTORETTO - Transporting of St. Mark's Body

DCH

expressed through natural beauty. God was glorified by glorifying man, His greatest creation. Humanism was an expression of devotion.

Uh-uh, said the Church. In their eyes, the new humanism was the same as the old atheism. The false spring of the Renaissance froze quickly after the Reformation, when half of Europe left the Catholic Church and became Protestant. The Church pulled in the wagons and stamped out any hint of free "pagan" thought that might encourage more deserters.

Veronese (pron: var-o-NAY-zee) was hauled before the Inquisition. What did he mean by painting such a bawdy Last Supper? With dwarf jesters? And apostles picking their teeth? And half-dressed ladies? And dogs? And a black man, God forbid? And worst of all, some German soldiers—that is, Protestants (gasp!)—at the far right!

Veronese argued that it was just artistic license, so they asked to see his—it had expired. But the solution was simple. Rather than change the painting, just fine-tune the title. *Si, no problema. The Last Supper* became the *Feast of the House of Levi.*

Titian — *Pietà*

The Counter-Reformation affected even the great Titian in his last years. Titian was perhaps the most famous painter of his day—even more famous than Michelangelo. He was a great portrait painter and a friend of the dukes, kings, and popes he painted. He was cultured, witty, a fine musician, and businessman—an all-around Renaissance kind of guy. The story goes that he once dropped his brush while painting a portrait of the Emperor Charles V, the most powerful man in Europe. Charles stooped and picked it up for him, a tribute to Titian's stature and genius.

Titian was 99 years old when he painted this. He had seen the birth, rise, and decline of the Renaissance. Remember "Little Mary," the colorful, exuberant Titian painting we saw at the beginning, done at the height of the Renaissance? Now the canvas is darker, the mood more somber. Jesus has just been executed, and his followers have removed his body from the cross. They grieve over it before burying it. Titian painted this to hang over his own tomb.

There are some Renaissance elements, but they create a whole different mood—the optimism is gone. Jesus is framed by a sculpture niche like Mantegna's confident *St. George*, but here the massive

Roman architecture overpowers the figures, making them look puny and helpless. The lion statues are downright fierce and threatening. Instead of the clear realism of Renaissance paintings, Titian has used rough, messy brushstrokes, a technique that would be picked up by the Impressionists three centuries later. Instead of simple Renaissance balance, Titian has added a dramatic compositional element—starting with the lion at lower right, a line sweeps up diagonally along the figures, culminating in the grief-stricken Mary Magdalene who turns away, flinging her arm in despair.

Finally, the kneeling figure of Joseph of Arimathea is a self-portrait of the aging Titian himself, tending to the corpse of Jesus, who symbolizes the once-powerful, now-dead Renaissance Man.

● *Head for the opposite wall, last painting on the right.*

Tintoretto — *The Transporting of St. Mark's Body (Trafugamento del Corpo di San Marco)*

This is the event that put Venice on the map, painted in the dramatic, emotional style that developed after the Renaissance. Tintoretto would have made a great black-velvet painter. His colors burn with a metallic sheen, and he does everything possible to make his subject popular with common people.

In fact, Tintoretto was a common man himself, self-taught, who took only a few classes from Titian before striking out on his own. He sold paintings in the marketplace in his youth and insisted on living in the poor part of town even after he got famous.

Tintoretto has caught the scene at its most dramatic moment. The Moslems in Alexandria are about to burn Mark's body (there's the smoke from the fire in the center) when suddenly a hurricane appears miraculously, sending them running for cover. (See the wisps of baby angel faces in the storm, blowing on the infidels? Look hard, on the left-hand side.) Meanwhile, the Venetian merchants whisk the body away.

Tintoretto makes us part of the action. The square tiles in the courtyard run straight away from us, an extension of our reality, as though we could step right into the scene—or the merchants could carry Mark into ours.

Tintorettos abound here, in the next room, and throughout Venice. Look for these characteristics, some of which became standard features of Baroque art that followed the Renaissance: (1) heightened drama, vio-

ELEGANT DECAY

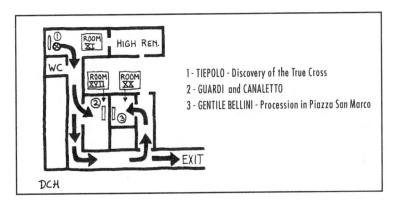

1 - TIEPOLO - Discovery of the True Cross
2 - GUARDI and CANALETTO
3 - GENTILE BELLINI - Procession in Piazza San Marco

lent scenes, strong emotions; (2) elongated bodies; (3) strong contrasts between dark and light; (4) vibrant colors; (5) diagonal compositions.

● *Spend some time in this room, the peak of Venice and the climax of the museum. After browsing, enter the next large room and find a large round painting.*

Elegant Decay (1600–1800)

G. B. Tiepolo — *Discovery of the True Cross*

Tiepolo was the last of the great colorful, theatrical Venetian painters. He took the colors of Titian, the grand settings of Veronese, and the dramatic angles of Tintoretto and plastered them on the ceilings of Europe. His best known works are the ceiling decorations in Baroque palaces like the Royal Palace of Madrid and the Wurzburg Residenz in Germany.

Tiepolo was a master of illusion. His works look as though they open up into heaven. Saints and angels cavort overhead as we peek up their robes. His strongly "foreshortened" figures are masterpieces of technical skill, making us feel like the heavenly vision is taking place right above us. Think back on those clumsy attempts at three-dimensionality we saw in the medieval room, and realize how far painting has come.

Nearby is Luca Giordano's *Crucifixion of St. Peter,* which also uses a dramatic angle to place us in the thick of the scene—right at the foot of the upside-down cross. The violent subject, rippling muscles and heightened emotion are Baroque at its Baroque-iest.

● *Works of the later Venetians are in rooms branching off the long corridor*

to your left. Walking down the corridor, the first right leads to the WC.
Stop in Room XVII, the first door on the left.

Canaletto and Guardi

By the 1700s Venice had retired as a world power and become Europe's #1 tourist attraction. Wealthy offspring of the nobility traveled here to soak up its art and culture. They wanted souvenirs, and what better memento than a picture of the city itself?

Guardi and Canaletto painted "postcards" for visitors who lost their heart to the romance of Venice. The city produced less art ... but was art. Here are some familiar views of a city that has aged gracefully.

Canaletto gives us a camera's-eye perspective on the city, while Guardi sweetens it up. In Guardi's *The Island of S. Giorgio Maggiore* (right in front of you as you enter Room XVII), we see that familiar view across the water from St. Mark's Square. Guardi has caught the play of light at twilight, the shadows on the buildings, the green of the water and sky, the pink light off the distant buildings, the Venice that exists in the hearts of lovers—an Impressionist work a century ahead of its time.

● *Follow the corridor, turning left at the end. Then take your first left,*
then left again. Are you in Room XX?

Gentile Bellini — Procession in Piazza San Marco (*Processione in Piazza San Marco*)

A fitting end to our tour is a look back at Venice in its heyday. This wide-angle view by Giovanni's big brother—more than any human eye could take in at once—reminds us how little Venice has changed over the centuries. There's St. Mark's gleaming gold with mosaics; the three flagpoles out front; the old Campanile is on the right; the Doges' Palace. (But there's no clock tower with the two bronze Moors yet.) Every detail is in perfect focus regardless of its distance from us, presented for our inspection. Take some time to linger over this and the other views of old Venice in this room. Then get outta here and enjoy the real thing.

● *To exit, backtrack to the main corridor and turn left past the bookstore.*
Say ciao to Titian's Little Mary on the way out.

FLORENCE

The Renaissance Walk

Uffizi Gallery

Bargello

*A*s the birthplace of the Renaissance, Florence gave us enough great art to overwhelm a Medici. With a little help from *Mona*, you'll squint into Dante's inferno, look *David* straight in the eyes, and sway to the seductive rhythm of Botticelli's *Birth of Venus*. From Michelangelo to Leonardo, from cappuccino to the best *gelati* in Italy, the art of Florence is a non-stop joy.

15 Florence— The Renaissance Walk

After centuries of labor, Florence gave birth to the Renaissance. Great and rich as Florence may be, it's easily covered on foot, and while "you could spend a lifetime here," let's pretend we've got eight hours—three for a walk through the old town, from *David* to the Duomo to the river, an hour for the Bargello (top statues), two for the Uffizi (best Italian painting anywhere), an hour for lunch, and an hour for lines (try to reserve ahead at the Uffizi—see Uffizi chapter for specifics). Start with the walk (but keep the opening hours in mind).

THE RENAISSANCE SIGHTS OF DOWNTOWN FLORENCE (FIRENZE)

Accademia—(Michelangelo's *David*)—Tuesday–Saturday 8:30–22:00, Sunday and holidays 8:30–20:00, closed Monday, last entry 30 minutes before closing, 12,000 L (groups from Albania and many places other than the U.S. get a discount). Shorter hours off-season.

The Duomo—(cathedral)—Monday–Saturday 10:00–17:00, Sunday and holidays 13:00–17:00, first Saturday of the month 10:00–15:30, free.

Giotto's Tower—Daily 9:00–18:50, shorter hours off-season, last entry 40 minutes before closing, 10,000 L.

Baptistery—Interior open Monday–Saturday 13:30–18:30, Sunday 8:30–13:30, 5,000 L. The famous Baptistery bronze doors are outside, always "open."

Museo del Opera del Duomo—(Piazza del Duomo #9)—Monday–Saturday 9:00–18:50, Sunday 9:00–13:20. 10,000 L (open Monday when other museums are closed).

Photography: Cameras without a flash are generally okay.

Tour length: Three hours

Getting there: The Accademia is a 15-minute walk from the train station, 10 from the cathedral (down via Ricasoli). Taxis are reasonable.

Information: Info office is at the station (try to pick up the update of current museum hours). Two fine bookshops across from the Accademia. Accademia tel. 055-238-8609.

Misc.: WCs in Accademia (downstairs near ticket booth) and in restaurants all along the walk. The Accademia is most crowded on Sunday, Tuesday, and right at 9:00.

Starring: Michelangelo, Brunelleschi, and Ghiberti.

ORIENTATION

The Duomo, the cathedral with the distinctive red dome, is the center of Florence and the orientation point for this walk. If you ever get lost, home's the dome.

Our slightly-more-than-half-mile walk past Florence's top sights runs from the Accademia (where Michelangelo's *David* is), past the Duomo, down Florence's main pedestrian-only street to the Arno River.

We'll start at the Accademia (long blocks north of the Duomo), though you could easily start at the Duomo and visit the Accademia later.

● *Head to the Accademia. If there's a line, as you shuffle your way along, notice the perspective tricks on the walls of the ticket room.*

The Florentine Renaissance (1400–1550)

In the 13th and 14th centuries, Florence was a powerful center of banking, trading, and textile manufacturing. The resulting wealth fertilized the cultural soil. Then came the Black Plague of 1348. Over half the people died, but the infrastructure remained strong, and the city rebuilt stronger than ever. Led by Florence's chief family, the art-crazy Medicis, and with the natural aggressive and creative spirit of the Florentines, it's no wonder the long-awaited Renaissance finally took root here.

The Renaissance—the "rebirth" of Greek and Roman culture that swept across Europe—started around 1400 and lasted about 150 years. In politics, the Renaissance meant democracy. In science, a renewed interest in exploring nature. The general mood was optimistic and "humanistic," with a confidence in the power of the individual.

In medieval times, poverty and ignorance had made life "nasty, brutish, and short" (for lack of a better cliché). The church was the people's opiate, and their lives were only a preparation for a happier time in heaven after leaving this miserable vale of tears.

Medieval art was the church's servant. The most noble art form was architecture—churches themselves—and other arts were considered most worthwhile if they embellished the house of God. Painting and sculpture were narrative and symbolic, basically there to tell Bible stories to the devout and illiterate masses.

As prosperity rose in Florence, so did people's confidence in life and themselves. Middle-class craftsmen, merchants, and bankers felt they could control their own destinies, rather than being at the whims of nature. They found much in common with the ancient Greeks and Romans, who valued logic and reason above superstition and blind faith.

Renaissance art was a return to the realism and balance of Greek and Roman sculpture and architecture. Domes and round arches replaced Gothic spires and pointed arches. In painting and sculpture, Renaissance artists strove for realism. Merging art and science, they used mathematics, the laws of perspective, and direct observation of nature to paint the world on canvas.

This was not an anti-Christian movement, though it was a logical and scientific age. Artists saw themselves as an extension of God's creative powers. At times, the church even supported the Renaissance and commissioned many of its greatest works. Raphael frescoed Plato and Aristotle to the walls of the Vatican. But for the first time we also find rich laymen who want art simply for art's sake.

After 1,000 years of waiting, the smoldering fires of Europe's classical heritage broke out in flames in Florence.

The Accademia — Michelangelo's David

Start with the ultimate. When you look into the eyes of Michelangelo's *David*, you're looking into the eyes of Renaissance Man. This 14-foot symbol of divine victory over evil represents a new century and a whole new Renaissance outlook. This is the age of Columbus and Classicism, Galileo and Gutenberg, Luther and Leonardo—of Florence and the Renaissance.

In 1501, Michelangelo Buonarotti, age 26, a Florentine, was commissioned to carve a large-scale work for the Duomo. He was given a block of marble that other sculptors had rejected as too tall, shallow and flawed to be of any value. But Michelangelo picked up his hammer and chisel, knocked a knot off what became David's heart and started to work.

The figure comes from a Bible story. The Israelites, God's chosen people, are surrounded by barbarian warriors led by a brutish giant named Goliath who challenges the Israelites to send out someone to fight him. Everyone is afraid except one young shepherd boy—David. Armed only with a sling, which he throws over his shoulder, David picks up some stones in his other hand and heads out to face Goliath.

The statue captures David as he's sizing up his enemy. He stands relaxed but alert, leaning on one leg in a classical pose. In his powerful right hand he fondles the stones he'll fling at the giant. His gaze is steady—searching with intense concentration, but also with extreme confidence. Michelangelo has caught the precise moment when David is saying to himself: "I can take this guy."

David is a symbol of Renaissance optimism. He's no brute but a civilized, thinking individual who can grapple with and overcome problems. He needs no armor, only his God-given body and wits. Look at his right hand, with the raised veins and strong, relaxed fingers. Many complained that it was too big and overdeveloped. But this is the hand of a man with the strength of God. No mere boy could slay the giant. But David, powered by God, could ... and did.

Originally, the statue was commissioned to go on top of the church, but the people loved it so much they put it next to the Palazzo Vecchio on the main square where a copy stands today. (If the relationship between the head and body seems a bit out of proportion, remember, Michelangelo designed it to be seen "correctly" from far below the rooftop of a church.)

Florentines could identify with David. Like David, they considered themselves God-blessed underdogs fighting their city-state rivals. In a deeper sense they were civilized Renaissance people slaying the ugly giant of medieval superstition, pessimism and oppression.

● *A fine bust of an older, brooding Michelangelo (by Volterra) looks on.* David *stands under a wonderful Renaissance dome. Hang around awhile. Lining the hall leading up to* David *are other statues by Michelangelo—his* Prisoners (Prigioni), St. Matthew, *and a* Pietà.

Prisoners

These unfinished figures seem to be fighting to free themselves from the stone. Michelangelo believed the sculptor was a tool of God, not creating but simply revealing the powerful and beautiful figures He put in the marble. Michelangelo's job was to chip away the excess, to reveal. He needed to be in tune with God's will, and whenever the spirit came upon him, Michelangelo worked in a frenzy, often for days on end without sleep.

The *Prisoners* give us a glimpse at this fitful process, showing us the restless energy of someone possessed, struggling against the rock that binds them. Michelangelo was known to shout at his figures in frustration: "Speak!" You can still see the grooves from the chisel and you can picture Michelangelo hacking away in a cloud of dust. Unlike most sculptors, who built a model then marked up their block of marble to know where to chip, Michelangelo always worked free-hand, starting from the front and working back. These figures emerge from the stone (as his colleague Vasari put it) "as though surfacing from a pool of water."

The *Prisoners* were designed for the tomb of Pope Julius II (who also commissioned the Sistine Chapel ceiling). Michelangelo may have abandoned them simply because the project itself petered out, but he may have left them unfinished deliberately. Having satisfied himself that he'd accomplished what he set out to do, and seeing no point in polishing them into their shiny, finished state, he went on to a new project.

As you study the *Prisoners*, notice Michelangelo's love of and understanding of the human body. His greatest days were spent sketching the muscular, tanned, and sweating bodies of the workers in the Carrara marble quarries. Here, the prisoners' heads and faces are the least-developed part—they "speak" with their poses.

Pietà

In the unfinished *Pietà* (the threesome closest to *David*), Michelangelo emphasises the theological point of any pietà, Christ's death, by emphasizing the heaviness of Jesus' dead body. Christ's massive arm is almost the size of his bent and broken legs. By stretching his body—if he stood up he'd be seven feet tall—its weight is exaggerated.

● *Leaving the Accademia (possibly after a look at its paintings, including two Botticellis), turn left and walk 10 minutes to the Duomo. The dome of the Duomo is best viewed just to the right of the façade on the corner of the pedestrian-only street (see map).*

THE DUOMO

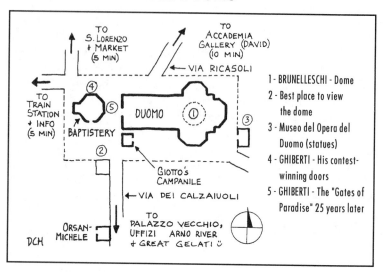

TO
S. LORENZO
+ MARKET
(5 MIN)

TO
ACCADEMIA
GALLERY (DAVID)
(10 MIN)

← VIA RICASOLI

TO
TRAIN
STATION
+ INFO
(5 MIN)

④

⑤

DUOMO   ①

③

BAPTISTERY

②

GIOTTO'S
CAMPANILE

← VIA DEI CALZAIUOLI

ORSAN-
MICHELE

TO
PALAZZO VECCHIO,
UFFIZI   ARNO RIVER
+ GREAT GELATI ☺

DCH

1 - BRUNELLESCHI - Dome
2 - Best place to view
the dome
3 - Museo del Opera del
Duomo (statues)
4 - GHIBERTI - His contest-
winning doors
5 - GHIBERTI - The "Gates of
Paradise" 25 years later

The Duomo — Florence's Cathedral

The dome of Florence's cathedral helped kick off the Florentine Renaissance by inspiring other artists to great things. The big but unremarkable church itself (nicknamed the Duomo) is Gothic, built in the Middle Ages by architects who left it unfinished—with a big hole in the roof. In the 1400s, the architect Brunelleschi was called on to finish the job. Brunelleschi capped the church with a Roman-style dome—a tall, self-supporting dome as grand as the ancient Pantheon—which he had studied intensely.

He used a dome within a dome. First he built the grand white skeletal ribs, which you can see, then he filled them in with interlocking bricks. The dome grew igloo-style, supporting itself as it proceeded from the base upward. When they reached the top, Brunelleschi arched the ribs in and "nailed" them in place with the lantern. His dome, built in only 14 years, was the largest since Rome's Pantheon.

Brunelleschi's dome was the wonder of the age, the model for many domes to follow including Michelangelo's dome of St. Peter's in Rome.

People gave it the ultimate compliment saying "not even the ancients could have done it." When Michelangelo set out to construct the dome of St. Peter's he said, "I'll make its sister ... bigger, but not more beautiful" than the dome of Florence.

Giotto's Tower

You can climb the dome, but the bell tower (to the right of the façade) is easier and rewards you with a better view. Giotto, like any good Renaissance genius, wore several artistic hats. Considered the father of modern painting, he designed this 274-foot tall bell tower for the Duomo two centuries before the age of Michelangelo. In his day Giotto was called the ugliest man to ever walk the streets of Florence, but he left the city what, in our day, many call the most beautiful bell tower in all of Europe.

The ornate neo-Gothic front of the church is from the 1870s and is generally ridiculed. (While one of this book's authors thinks it's the most beautiful church façade this side of heaven, the other one naively agrees with those who call it "the cathedral in pajamas.") Thin marble sheets cover the brick construction, decorating the entire exterior. The inside is worth a walk only for its coolness and to notice how bare the terrible flood of 1966 left it.

Either now or later, you may want to visit the wonderful Museo dell' Opera del Duomo (museum of the cathedral, across the street, behind the church). In it you will see Brunelleschi's wooden model of his dome, a fine collection of Donatello statues, and a late *Pietà* by Michelangelo (on the second floor). According to most tour guides, the head of Nicodemus (the old guy on top) is a self-portrait of the aging Michelangelo.

● *The Baptistery is the small octagonal building in front of the church.*

Baptistery — Ghiberti's Bronze Doors

Florence's Baptistery is dear to the soul of the city. The locals, eager to link themselves to the classical past, believed (wrongly) that this was a Roman building. It *is* Florence's oldest building (10th century). Most festivals and parades either started or ended here. Go inside for a fine example of pre-Renaissance mosaic art (1300s).

The Last Judgment on the ceiling gives us a glimpse of the medieval worldview. Life was a preparation for the afterlife, when you would

be judged good or bad, black or white, with no in-between. Christ, peaceful and reassuring, would bless you with heaven (on His right hand) or send you to hell (at the base of the ceiling, to Christ's left) to be tortured by demons and gnashed between the teeth of monsters. This hellish scene looks like something

right out of the *Inferno* by Dante ... who was dipped into the baptismal waters right here.

The Baptistery's bronze doors bring us out of the Middle Ages and into the Renaissance. Florence had great civic spirit, with different guilds and merchant groups embellishing their city with great art. For the Baptistery's north doors (on the right side as you face the Baptistery with the Duomo at your back), they staged a competition for the commission. All the greats entered, and 25-year-old Lorenzo Ghiberti won easily, beating out heavyweights like Donatello and Brunelleschi (who, having lost the Baptistery gig, was free to go to Rome, study the Pantheon and, later, design the Duomo). The entries of Brunelleschi and Ghiberti are in the Bargello, where you can judge them for yourself.

Later, in 1425, Ghiberti was given another commission, for the east doors (facing the church), and this time there was literally no contest. The bronze panels of these doors (the ones with the crowd of tourists looking on) are the doors Michelangelo said were fit to be the Gates of Paradise. (These panels are copies. The originals are in the nearby Museo del Duomo.) Here we see how the Renaissance was a merging of art and science. Realism was in, and Renaissance artists used math, illusion, and dissection to get it.

The "Jacob and Esau" panel (just above eye level on the left) is a good example of how the artist used receding arches, floor tiles, and bannisters to create a background for a realistic scene. The figures in the foreground stand and move like real people, telling the Bible story with human details. Amazingly, this spacious, three-dimensional scene is made from bronze only a few inches deep.

Ghiberti spent 27 years (1425–1452) working on these panels. That's him in the center of the door frame, atop the second row of panels—the guy on the left with the shiny bald head.

● *Facing the Duomo, turn right onto the pedestrian-only street that runs from here towards the Arno River.*

Via dei Calzaiuoli

The pedestrian-only Via dei Calzaiuoli leads from the Duomo to Florence's main square and the Uffizi Gallery. This was "Main Street" of the ancient Roman camp that became Florence. Throughout the city's history, this street has connected the religious center (where we are now) with the political center (where we're heading), a ten-minute walk away. In the last decade traffic jams have been replaced by potted plants, and this is a pleasant place to stroll, people-watch, window-shop, catch the drips on your ice cream cone, and wonder why American cities can't become pedestrian-friendly.

Two blocks past the Duomo at the intersection of Via dei Calzaiuoli and Via degli Speziali, look right to see an archway, the original entrance to the city. Look left if you're in the mood for some of the world's best edible art, and drop by an ice cream parlor called "Festival del Gelato" for a cup of their famous *gelato*.

Gelati tips: *Nostra Produzione* and *Produzione Propia* mean they make it on the premises. Also, metal tins rather than the normal white plastic indicate it's most likely homemade.

Orsanmichele Church— Florence's Medieval Roots

The Orsanmichele Church (at the intersection with Via dei Tavolini) provides an interesting look at Florentine values. It's a combo church/grainery. Originally this was an open *loggia* (covered porch) with a huge warehouse upstairs to store grain to feed the city during seiges. The arches of the loggia were artfully filled in and the building gained a new purpose—a church.

The entrance to the church is on the opposite side of the building, one short block off Via del Calzaiuoli. Step inside and find the pillars with spouts in them (about two feet off the ground) for delivering

ORSANMICHELE CHURCH

```
                  TO  PALAZZO
                      VECCHIO
                    & UFFIZI

              VIA  LAMBERTI
  V
  I
  A
                                    WOOL
  C                                 MERCHANT's
  A            ┌───┐  ①             GUILD          1 - Tabernacle
  L            │   │
  Z            └───┘                               2 - DONATELLO - St. Mark
  A
  I                                                3 - NANNI - Four Saints
  U
  O     ②                                          4 - DONATELLO - St. George
  L
  I               ③ ─ ④
              VIA  ORSANMICHELE

  DCH      FROM  DUOMO
```

grain from the storage rooms upstairs. Stand before the Gothic taber-
nacle. Drop a coin in the box to buy a minute of light. Notice its
medieval elegance, color, and disinterest in depth and realism. This
is a wonderfully medieval scene—Florence in 1350. Remember the
candle-lit medieval atmosphere that surrounds this altarpiece as you
view similar altarpieces out of context in the Uffizi Gallery.

Back outside, circle the church. Each niche was filled with an
important statue. In Gothic times, statues were set deeply in the
niches, simply embellishing the house of God. Here we see statues
(as restless as man on the verge of the Renaissance) stepping out

from the protection of the
church. Donatello's *St. Mark*
(in the far right niche as you
face the church), is a fine
example of the new Renaissance style and advances.
Notice his classical *contrapposto* (weight on one foot)
stance. And, even fully
clothed, you know his anatomy is fully there.

Donatello's great *St. George*
(around the right side of the
church) is alert, stepping out,

PALAZZO VECCHIO

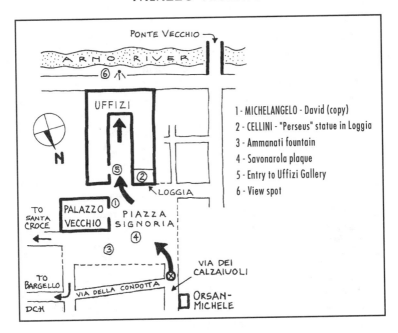

PONTE VECCHIO

ARNO RIVER

⑥

UFFIZI

N

⑤ ②

LOGGIA

TO SANTA CROCE

PALAZZO VECCHIO ①

PIAZZA SIGNORIA

④

③

TO BARGELLO

VIA DELLA CONDOTTA

VIA DEI CALZAIUOLI

ORSAN-MICHELE

DCH

1 - MICHELANGELO - David (copy)
2 - CELLINI - "Perseus" statue in Loggia
3 - Ammanati fountain
4 - Savonarola plaque
5 - Entry to Uffizi Gallery
6 - View spot

announcing the new age with its new outlook. (The original statue is in the Bargello.) Compare this Renaissance-style St. George, on the right, with the smaller-scale, deeply set, and less sophisticated *Four Saints* statue to its left.

Below some of the niches you'll find the symbols of various guilds and groups that paid for the art, like the carpenters guild below the *Four Saints*. At the back of the church is the headquarters of the wool merchants guild—just another rich old building rotting in the shadow of the Florentine superstars.

● *The House of Dante and Florence's best collection of sculpture, the Bargello (see chapter 16), are just down Via del Tavolini. But let's continue down the mall 50 more yards, to the huge and historic square.*

Palazzo Vecchio — Florence's Political Center

Via dei Calzaiuoli empties into the main civic center of Florence, with the Palazzo Vecchio, the

Uffizi Gallery, and the marble greatness of old Florence littering the cobbles. This square still vibrates with the echoes of Florence's past—executions, riots, and great celebrations. Today it's a tourist's world with pigeons, postcards, horsebuggies, and tired hubbies.

Stand in the center. Before you towers the Palazzo Vecchio, the Medicis' palatial city hall—a fortress designed to contain its riches and survive the many riots that went with local politics. The windows are just beyond the reach of angry stones, the tower was a handy lookout, and justice was doled out sternly on this square. The original *David*

once stood (until 1873) where the replica stands today. During one riot, a bench was thrown out of a palace window and knocked *David*'s arm off.

To the right is the Loggia, once a forum for public debate but later, when the Medici figured good art was more desirable than free speech, it was turned into an outdoor sculpture gallery. Notice the squirming Florentine themes—conquest, dominance, rapes, and severed heads. Benvenuto Cellini's *Perseus*, the Loggia's most noteworthy piece, shows the Greek hero who decapitated the snake-headed Medusa. They say Medusa was so ugly she turned humans who looked at her to stone—though one of this book's authors thinks she's kinda cute.

● *Step past the replica* David *through the front door into the Palazzo Vecchio's courtyard.*

This palace replaced the Bargello as Florence's civic center. You're surrounded by art for art's sake—a statue frivolously marking the courtyard's center, and ornate walls and columns. Such luxury was a big change 500 years ago.

● *The Palazzo is not worth touring on a quick visit like ours. Return to the square and head right as you leave the palace door, over towards the big fountain by Ammanati that Florentines (including Michelangelo) consider a huge waste of marble—though one of this book's authors ...*

Find the round bronze plaque in the cobbles 10 steps in front of the fountain.

Savonarola

The Medici family was briefly thrown from power by an austere monk named Savonarola, who made Florence a theocracy. He organized huge rallies here on the square where he preached, lit by roaring bonfires. While children sang hymns, the devout brought their rich "vanities" and threw them into the flames.

But not everyone wanted a return to the medieval past. The Medici fought back, and they arrested Savonarola. For two days, they tortured him, trying unsuccessfully to persuade him to see their side of things. Finally, as the plaque says, "On this spot where Savonrola once had the decadence and vanities of Florence burned, Savonarola himself was burned to death" ... in the year "MCCCCXCVIII" (1498, I think).

● *Stay cool, we have 100 yards to go. Follow the gaze of the fake David into the courtyard of the two-toned horseshoe-shaped building ...*

Uffizi Courtyard — The Renaissance Hall of Fame

The top floor of this building, known as the Uffizi ("offices") during Medici days, is filled with the greatest collection of Florentine painting anywhere. It's one of Europe's top four or five galleries (see next chapter).

The Uffizi courtyard, filled with merchants and hustling young artists, is watched over by statues of the great figures of the Renaissance. Tourists zero in on the visual accomplishments of the Renaissance—they show best on a postcard. Let's pay tribute to the non-visual Renaissance as well as we wander through Florence's Hall of Fame.

● *Stroll down the left side of the courtyard from the Uffizi entrance to the river, noticing ...*

(1) Lorenzo the Magnificent (next to the Uffizi entrance)—excelling in everything but modesty, he set the tone for the Renaissance—great art patron and cunning broker of power; (2) Giotto (he died from the plague, this statue looks posthumous); (3) Donatello, holding his hammer and chisel; (4) Leonardo da Vinci; (5) Michelangelo, pondering the universe and/or stifling a belch; (6) Dante, considered the father of the Italian language. He was the first Italian to write a popular work (*The Divine Comedy*) in non-Latin, using the Florentine dialect which  soon became "Italian" throughout the country; (7) the poet Petrarch; (8) Boccaccio, author of *The Decameron*; (9) the devious-looking Machiavelli, whose book, *The Prince*, taught "Machiavellian" ends-justifies-the-means thinking, paving the way for the slick and cunning politics of today; and finally, (10) Amerigo Vespucci (in the corner nearest the river), an explorer who gave his name to a fledgling New World.

● *Finish our walk at the Arno River, overlooking the Ponte Vecchio.*

Ponte Vecchio

Before you is the Ponte Vecchio (Old Bridge). A bridge has spanned this narrowest part of the Arno since Roman times. In the 1500s the Medici booted the butchers and tanners and installed the gold-and silversmiths you'll see and be tempted by today. (A fine bust of the greatest goldsmith, Cellini, graces the central point of the bridge.) Notice the Medici's protected and elevated passageway that led from the Palazzo Vecchio through the Uffizi, across the Ponte Vecchio, and up to the immense Pitti Palace, four blocks beyond the bridge. During WWII the local German commander was instructed to blow the bridge up. But even some Nazis appreciate history—he blew up the buildings at either end, leaving the bridge impassable but intact. *Grazie.*

More Michelangelo

One more "must-see" sight and I'm history. But if you're a fan of earth's greatest sculptor, you won't leave Florence until there's a check next to each of these:

- Bargello Museum (Several Michelangelo sculptures. See chapter 16.)
- Duomo Museum (Another moving *Pietà*. Located behind the Duomo at #9.)
- Medici Chapel (The *Night* and *Day* statues, plus others done for the Medici tomb. Located at Church of S. Lorenzo.)
- Laurentian Library (He designed the entrance staircase. Located at Church of S. Lorenzo.)
- Uffizi Gallery (A rare Michelangelo painting. See chapter 16.)
- Casa Buonarotti (A house Michelangelo once owned, at Via Ghibellina 70, with some early works.)
- Michelangelo's tomb (Church of Santa Croce.)

16 Uffizi Gallery

In the Renaissance, Florentine artists rediscovered the beauty of the natural world. Medieval art had been symbolic, telling Bible stories. Realism didn't matter. But Renaissance people saw the beauty of God in Nature and the human body. They used math and science to capture the natural world on canvas as realistically as possible.

The Uffizi Gallery (pron: oo-FEEDZ-ee) has the greatest overall collection anywhere of Italian painting. We'll trace the rise of realism and savor the optimistic spirit that marked the Renaissance.

My eyes love things that are fair,
and my soul for salvation cries.
But neither will to Heaven rise
unless the sight of Beauty lifts them there.
—Michelangelo

GALLERIA DELL' UFFIZI

Hours: Tuesday–Saturday 8:30–22:00, Sunday and holidays 8:30–20:00, closed Monday, shorter hours off-season. Last entry 45 minutes before closing. Hours can be erratic, lines can be very long. It's worth reserving in advance—either in person at the museum or by phone at 055-294-883 (2,400 L fee added per ticket; book by phone, pay in cash when you pick up ticket). The Uffizi can be hot and mobbed—16:00 or 17:00 is relatively cool and quiet.

Cost: 12,000 L

Tour length: Two hours

Getting there: On the Arno River near the Palazzo Vecchio and Ponte Vecchio, a 15-minute walk from the station.

Information: Only books from street vendors. Nothing inside. Decent card and bookshop at exit. Only one WC, near exit.

Cloakroom: At the start, far from the finish.

Photography: Cameras without flash are okay.

Cuisine art: The snack bar at the end of the gallery has salads, desserts, fruit cups, and a great terrace with a Duomo/Palazzo Vecchio view. A cappuccino here is one of Europe's great $2 treats.

Starring: Botticelli, Venus, Raphael, Giotto, Titian, Leonardo, and Michelangelo.

ORIENTATION

● *Buy your ticket, then take the lift or walk up the four flights of the "Monumental" staircase to the top floor. Your brain should be fully aerated from the hike up. Past the ticket-taker, look out the window.*

The U-ffizi is U-shaped, running around the courtyard. The entire collection is on this one floor, displayed chronologically. This left wing contains Florentine painting from medieval to Renaissance times. The right wing (which you can see across the courtyard) has Roman and Venetian High Renaissance, the Baroque that followed, and a café terrace facing the Duomo. Connecting the two wings is a short corridor with sculpture. We'll concentrate on the Uffizi's forte, the Florentine section, then get a taste of the art it inspired.

● *Down the hall, enter the first door on the left and face Giotto's giant* Madonna and Child.

MEDIEVAL — WHEN ART WAS AS FLAT AS THE WORLD (1200–1400)

Giotto — *Madonna and Child (Madonna col Bambino Gesu, Santi e Angeli)*

For the Florentines, "realism" meant "three-dimensionality." In this room, pre-Renaissance paintings show the slow process of learning to paint a 3-D world on a 2-D canvas.

Before concentrating on the Giotto, look at some others in the room. First look at the crucifixion on your right (as you face the Giotto). This was medieval three-dimensionality—paint a crude two-dimensional work … then physically tilt the head forward. Nice try.

UFFIZI GALLERY—OVERVIEW

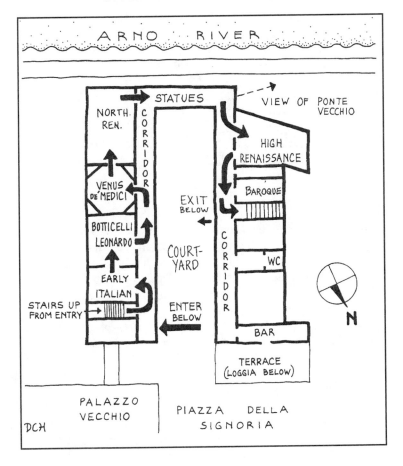

The three Madonna-and-Bambinos in this room were all painted within a few decades of each other around the year 1300. The one on the left (as you face Giotto), by Duccio, is the most medieval and two-dimensional. There's no background. The angels are just stacked one on top of the other, floating in an unreal space. Mary's throne is crudely drawn—the left side is at a three-quarters angle while the right is practically straight on. Mary herself is a wispy cardboard-cutout figure seemingly floating a half-inch above the throne.

On the opposite wall, Cimabue's is a vast improvement. The large throne creates an illusion of depth. Mary's foot actually sticks out toward us. Still, the angels are stacked like sardines, serving as a pair of heavenly bookends.

EARLY ITALIAN—GIOTTO AND MEDIEVAL

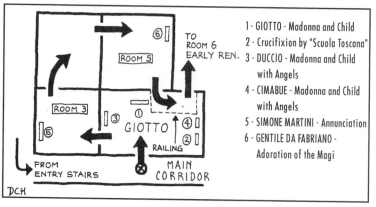

1 - GIOTTO - Madonna and Child
2 - Crucifixion by "Scuola Toscana"
3 - DUCCIO - Madonna and Child with Angels
4 - CIMABUE - Madonna and Child with Angels
5 - SIMONE MARTINI - Annunciation
6 - GENTILE DA FABRIANO - Adoration of the Magi

Now let's look at the Giotto. Giotto (pron: ZHOTT-oh) creates a space and fills it. Like a set designer he builds a three-dimensional "stage"—the canopied throne—then peoples it with real beings. We know the throne has depth because there are angels in front of it and prophets behind. The steps leading up to it give even more depth. But the real triumph here is Mary herself—big and monumental, like a statue. Beneath her robe she has a real live body—her knees and breasts stick out at us. This three-dimensionality was revolutionary in its day, a taste of the Renaissance a century before it began.

Giotto was one of the first "famous" artists. In the Middle Ages, artists were mostly unglamorous craftsmen, like carpenters or cable-TV repairmen. They cranked out generic art and could have signed their work with a bar code. Giotto was the first to be recognized as a genius, a unique individual. He died in a plague which devastated Florence. If there had been no plague, would the Renaissance have started 100 years earlier? No.

● *Enter Room 3, to the left of Giotto.*

Simone Martini — *Annunciation (Annunciazione con I Santi Ansano e Giulitta)*

After Giotto's spasm of Renaissance-style realism, painting returned to two-dimensionality for the rest of the 1300s. But several medieval artists (including this one from Siena) eased Florence into the Renaissance.

Martini's *Annunciation* has medieval features you'll see in many of the paintings in the next few rooms: (1) religious subject; (2) gold background; (3) two-dimensionality; (4) meticulous details.

This is not a three-dimensional work. But remember, this was medieval, so the point was not to recreate reality but to teach religion, especially to the illiterate masses. Martini boiled things down to the basic figures needed to get the message across: (1) The angel appears to sternly tell (2) Mary that she'll be the mother of Jesus. In the center is (3) a vase of lilies, a symbol to tell us Mary is pure. Above is the (4) Holy Spirit as a dove about to descend on her. If the symbols aren't enough to get the message across, Martini has spelled it right out for us: "Hail, favored one, the Lord is with you." Mary doesn't look exactly pleased as punch.

This isn't a beautiful Mary or even a real Mary. She's a generic woman without distinctive features. We know she's pure—not from her face but only because of the halo and symbolic flowers. Before the Renaissance, artists didn't care about the beauty of individual people.

● *Pass through the next room, full of golden altarpieces, stopping at the far end of Room 5.*

Gentile da Fabriano — *Adoration of the Magi (Adorazione dei Magi)*

Look at the incredible detail of the Three Kings' costumes, the fine horses, the cow in the cave. This work is crammed with realistic details—but it's still far from realistic. The point was to tell a story.

● *Exit to your right and hang a U-turn left into Room 6.*

EARLY RENAISSANCE (MID-1400s)

Uccello — *The Battle of San Romano (La Battaglia di S. Romano)*

In the 1400s painters worked out the problems of painting realistically. They concentrated on "perspective" (using mathematics to create the illusion of three-dimensionality) and how to paint the human body.

Paolo Uccello almost literally went crazy trying to conquer the problem of perspective. He was a man obsessed with the three dimensions (thank God he was born before Einstein discovered one more). This canvas is not so much a piece of art as an exercise in

perspective. Uccello (pron: oo-CHELL-o) has challenged himself with every possible problem.

The broken lances at left set up a 3-D "grid" in which to place this crowded scene. The fallen horses and soldiers are experiments in "foreshortening"—shortening the things that are farther away from us to create the illusion of distance. Some of the figures are definitely A-plus material, like the fallen grey horse in the center and the white horse at right riding away. But some are more like B-minus work—the kicking red horse's legs look like hamhocks at this angle, and the fallen soldier at far right would only be four feet tall if he stood up.

And then there's the D-minus "Are-you-on-drugs?" work. The converging hedges in the background create a nice illusion of a distant hillside maybe 75 or 100 yards away. So what are those soldiers the size of the foreground figures doing there? And jumping the hedge, is that a 40-foot rabbit? Uccello got so wrapped up in three-dimensionality he kind of lost ... perspective.

● *Enter Room 8.*

Fra Filippo Lippi — *Madonna and Child with Two Angels (Madonna col Bambino e Due Angeli)*

Compare this Mary with the generic female in Martini's *Annunciation.* We don't need the wispy halo over her head to tell us she's holy—she radiates sweetness and light from her divine face. Heavenly beauty is expressed by a physically beautiful woman.

Fra (Brother) Lippi was a monk who lived a less-than-monkish life. He lived with a nun who bore him two children. He spent his entire life searching for the perfect Virgin. Through his studio passed Florence's prettiest girls, many of whom decorate the walls here in this room.

Lippi painted idealized beauty, but his models were real flesh-and-blood human beings. You could look through all the thousands of

EARLY RENAISSANCE

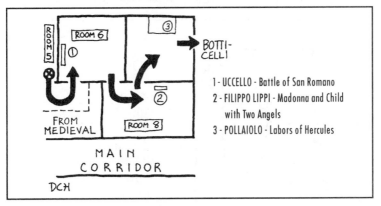

1 - UCCELLO - Battle of San Romano
2 - FILIPPO LIPPI - Madonna and Child
with Two Angels
3 - POLLAIOLO - Labors of Hercules

paintings from the Middle Ages and not find anything so human as the mischievous face of one of Lippi's little angel boys.

● *Enter Room 9. Take a look at the two small works by Pollaiolo in the glass case between the windows.*

Pollaiolo — *Labors of Hercules (Fatiche di Ercole)*

While Uccello worked on perspective, Pollaiolo studied anatomy. In medieval times, dissection of corpses was a sin and a crime (the two were one then), a desecration of the human body which was the temple of God. But Pollaiolo was willing to sell his soul to the devil for artistic knowledge. He dissected.

These two small panels are experiments in painting anatomy. The poses are the wildest imaginable, excuses to see how the muscles twist and tighten.

There's something funny about this room that I can't put my finger on … I've got it—no Madonnas. Not one. We've seen how Early Renaissance artists worked to conquer reality. Now let's see the fruits of their work, the flowering of Florence's Renaissance.

● *Enter the large Botticelli room and take a seat.*

FLORENCE — THE RENAISSANCE BLOSSOMS (1450–1500)

Florence in 1450 was in a firenz-y of activity. There was a can-do spirit of optimism in the air, led by prosperous merchants and bankers

FLORENCE—THE RENAISSANCE BLOSSOMS

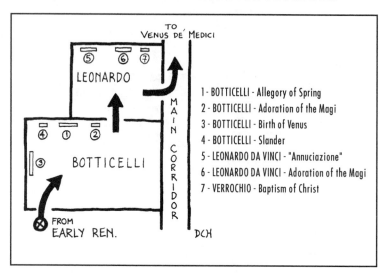

TO
VENUS DE' MEDICI

⑤ ⑥ ⑦

LEONARDO

MAIN CORRIDOR

④ ① ②

⑨   BOTTICELLI

FROM
EARLY REN.

DCH

1 - BOTTICELLI - Allegory of Spring
2 - BOTTICELLI - Adoration of the Magi
3 - BOTTICELLI - Birth of Venus
4 - BOTTICELLI - Slander
5 - LEONARDO DA VINCI - "Annunciazione"
6 - LEONARDO DA VINCI - Adoration of the Magi
7 - VERROCHIO - Baptism of Christ

and a strong middle class. The government was reasonably democratic, and Florentines saw themselves as citizens of a strong Republic like ancient Rome. Their civic pride showed in the public monuments and artworks they built. Man was leaving the protection of the church to stand on his own two feet.

Lorenzo de Medici, head of the powerful Medici family, epitomized this new humanistic spirit. Strong, decisive, handsome, poetic, athletic, sensitive, charismatic, intelligent, brave-clean-and-reverent Lorenzo was a true Renaissance Man deserving the nickname he went by—"the Magnificent." He gathered Florence's best and brightest around him for evening wine and discussions of great ideas. One of this circle was the painter Botticelli (pron: bott-i-CHELL-ee).

Botticelli —
Allegory of Spring
(Allegoria dell Primavera)

Here is the Renaissance in its first bloom, its "springtime" of innocence. Madonna is out, Venus is in. Adam and Eve hiding their nakedness are out, glorious flesh is in. This is a return to the pre-

Christian pagan world of classical Greece where things of the flesh are not sinful. But this is certainly no orgy—just fresh-faced innocence and playfulness.

It's springtime in a citrus grove. The winds of spring blow in (Mr. Blue at right) causing Flora to sprout flowers from her lips. Meanwhile the figure of Spring walks by spreading flowers from her dress. At the left are Mercury and the Three Graces, dancing a delicate maypole dance. The Graces may be symbolic of the three forms of love—love of beauty, love of people, and sexual love, suggested by the raised intertwined fingers. (They forgot love of peanut-butter-on-toast.) In the center stands Venus, the Greek goddess of love. Above her flies a blindfolded Cupid, happily shooting his arrows of love without worrying who they'll hit.

Botticelli has painted a scene of exquisite beauty. The lines of the bodies, especially of the Graces in their see-through nighties, have pleasing S-like curves. The faces are idealized but have real human features. There's a look of thoughtfulness and even melancholy in the faces—as though everyone knows that the innocence of spring must soon pass.

● *Look at the next painting to the right.*

Botticelli — *Adoration of the Magi* (*Adorazione dei Magi*)

Here's the rat pack of confident young Florentines who reveled in the optimistic pagan spirit—even in a religious scene. Botticelli included himself among the adorers, looking vain in the yellow robe at far right. Lorenzo's the Magnificent-looking guy at the far left.

Botticelli — *Birth of Venus* (*Nascita di Venere*)

This is the purest expression of Renaissance beauty. Venus' naked body is not sensual but innocent. Botticelli thought that physical beauty was a way of appreciating God. Remember Michelangelo's poem: souls will never ascend to Heaven " … unless the sight of Beauty lifts them there."

According to myth, Venus was born from the foam of a wave. Still only half-awake, this fragile newborn beauty is kept afloat on a clam shell while the winds come to blow her to shore, where her maiden waits to cover her. The pose is the same S-curve of classical statues (as we'll soon see). Botticelli's pastel colors make the world itself seem fresh and newly born.

The details show Botticelli's love of the natural world—Venus' wind-blown hair, the translucent skin, the braided hair of her hand-maiden, the slight ripple of the wind's chest muscles, and the flowers tumbling in the slowest of slow motions, suspended like musical notes, caught at the peak of their brief but beautiful life.

Mr. and Mrs. Wind intertwine—notice her hands clasped around his body. Their hair, wings, and robes mingle like the wind. But what happened to those toes?

● *"Venus on the Half-shell" (as many tourists call this) is one of the masterpieces of Western art. Take some time with it. Then find the small canvas on the wall to the right, near* La Primavera.

Botticelli —
Slander (La Calumnia)

The spring of Florence's Renaissance had to end. Lorenzo died young. The economy faltered. Into town rode the monk Savonarola preaching medieval hellfire and damnation for those who embraced the "pagan" Renaissance spirit. "Down, down with all gold and decoration," he roared. "Down where the body is food for the worms." He presided over huge bonfires where the people threw in their fine clothes, jewelry, pagan books ... and paintings.

Botticelli listened to Savonarola. He burned some of his own paintings and changed his tune. The last works of his life were darker, more somber and pessimistic of humanity.

Slander spells the end of the Florentine Renaissance. The setting is classic Brunelleschian architecture, but look what's taking place beneath those stately arches. These aren't proud Renaissance Men and Women but a ragtag, medieval-looking bunch, squatters in an abandoned hall of justice. Here in this chaotic Court of Thieves the accusations fly and everyone is condemned. The naked man pleads for mercy but the hooded black figure, a symbol of his execution, turns away. Once-proud Venus—straight out of *The Birth of Venus*—looks up to heaven as if to ask "What has happened to us?" The classical statues in their niches look on in disbelief.

The German poet Heine said, "When they start by burning books, they'll end by burning people." Savonarola, after four short years of power, was burned on his own bonfire in the Piazza della Signoria, but by then the city was in shambles. The first flowering of the Renaissance was over.

● *Enter the next room.*

Leonardo da Vinci — *Annunciation*

A scientist, architect, engineer, musician, and painter, Leonardo was a true Renaissance Man. He worked at his own pace rather than to please an employer, so he often left works unfinished. The two in this room aren't his best, but even a lesser Leonardo is enough to put a museum on the map, and they're definitely worth a look.

Think back to Martini's *Annunciation* to realize how much more natural, relaxed, and realistic Leonardo's is. He's taken a miraculous event—an angel appearing out of the blue—and made it seem almost commonplace. He constructs a beautifully landscaped "stage" and puts his characters in it. Gabriel has walked up to Mary and now kneels on one knee like an ambassador, saluting her. Look how relaxed his other hand is draped over his knee. Mary, who's been reading, looks up with a gesture of surprise and curiosity. Leonardo has taken a religious scene and presented it in a very human way.

Look at the bricks on the right wall. If you extended lines from them, the lines would all converge at the center of the painting, the distant blue mountain. Same with the edge of the sarcophagus and the railing. Subconsciously, this subtle touch creates a feeling of balance, order and spaciousness.

Leonardo — *Adoration of the Magi (unfinished)*

Leonardo's human insight is even more apparent here. The poor kings are amazed at the Christ child—even afraid of him. They scurry around like chimps around fire. This work is as agitated as the *Annunciation* is calm, giving us an idea of Leonardo's range. Leonardo was pioneering a new era of painting, showing not just the outer features but the inner personality.

The next painting to the right, *Baptism of Christ,* is by Verrochio, Leonardo's teacher. Legend has it that Leonardo painted the angel on the far left when he was only 14 years old. When Verrochio saw that some kid had painted an angel better than he ever would ... he hung up his brush for good.

Florence saw the first blossoming of the Renaissance. But when the cultural climate turned chilly, artists flew south to warmer climes. The Renaissance shifted to Rome.

● *Exit into the main corridor. Breathe. Sit. Admire the ceiling. Look out the window. See you in five.*

Back already? Now continue down the corridor and turn left into the octagonal Venus de' Medici *room. You'll recognize it by the line outside—they only allow 25 people in at a time. Read while you wait. If you skip this because of the line you'll be missing the next five rooms, which include masterpieces by Dürer (including his* Adam *and* Eve)*, Memling, Holbein, Giorgione, and others.*

CLASSICAL SCULPTURE

If the Renaissance was the foundation of the modern world, the foundation of the Renaissance was classical sculpture. Sculptors, painters, and poets alike turned for inspiration to these ancient works as the epitome of balance, 3-D, human anatomy, and beauty. While the best collection of Renaissance sculpture is in the nearby Bargello, these classical statues illustrate nicely what a profound effect the art of the ancient world had on Renaissance artists.

The *Venus de' Medici*, or *Medici Venus (Venere de' Medici)*, ancient Greece

Is this pose familiar? Botticelli's *Birth of Venus* has the same position of the arms, the same S-curved body and the same lifting of the right

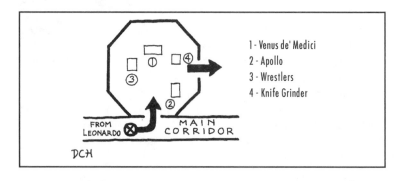

CLASSICAL SCULPTURE

1 - Venus de' Medici
2 - Apollo
3 - Wrestlers
4 - Knife Grinder

FROM LEONARDO ⊗
MAIN CORRIDOR

DCH

leg. A copy of this statue stood in Lorenzo the Magnificent's garden where Botticelli used to hang out. This one is a Roman copy of the lost original by the great Greek sculptor Praxiteles.

Perhaps more than any other work of art this statue has been the epitome of both ideal beauty and sexuality. In the 18th and 19th centuries, sex was "dirty," so the sex drive of cultured aristocrats was channeled into a love of pure beauty. Wealthy sons and daughters of Europe's aristocrats made the pilgrimage to the Uffizi to complete their classical education ... where they swooned in ecstasy before the cold beauty of this goddess of love.

Louis XIV had a bronze copy made. Napoleon stole her away to Paris for himself. And in Philadelphia in the 1800s, a copy had to be kept under lock and key to prevent the innocent from catching the Venere-al disease. At first, it may be difficult for us to appreciate such passionate love of art, but if any generation knows the power of sex to sell something—be it art or underarm deodorant—it's ours.

The Other Statues

The Medici Venus is a balanced, harmonious, serene statue from Greece's "Golden Age" when balance was admired in every aspect of life. Its "male" counterpart is on the right, facing Venus. *Apollino* (a.k.a. "Venus with a Penis") is also by the master of smooth, cool lines, Praxiteles.

The other works are later Greek (Hellenistic) when quiet balance was replaced by violent motion and emotion. *The Wrestlers* to the left of Venus is a study in anatomy and twisted limbs—like Pollaiolo's paintings a thousand years later.

The drama of *The Knife Grinder* to the right of Venus stems from the off-stage action—he's sharpening the knife to flay a man alive.

● *Exit the Tribune room passing through five rooms of masterpieces. In the second room, check out the two portraits (on the left) of Martin Luther by his friend Lukas Cranach. Exit to a great view of the Arno. Stroll through the sculpture wing.*

The Sculpture Wing

A hundred years ago no one even looked at Botticelli—they came to the Uffizi to see the sculpture collection. Why isn't the sculpture as famous now? Stop at the *Boy Pulling a Spine from His Foot* on your left. This is a famous statue, right? And it must be old because the label says "UN ORIGINAL" in big block letters. But now read the fine print—the tiny little "da" in front. It's not an original at all, but a copy "from" (*da*) an original ... which is in Rome.

● *There are benches at the other end of the wing with a great view.*

View of the Arno

Enjoy Florence's best view of the Arno and the Ponte Vecchio. You can also see the red-tiled roof of the Vasari Corridor, the "secret" passage connecting the Palazzo Vecchio, the Uffizi, the Ponte Vecchio, and the Pitti Palace on the other side of the river (not visible from here)—a half-mile in all. This was the private walkway, wallpapered in great art, for the Medici family's commute from home to work.

As you appreciate the view remember that it's this sort of pleasure that Renaissance painters wanted you to get from their paintings. For them, a canvas was a window you looked through to see the wide world.

We're headed down the home stretch now. If your feet are killing you and it feels like torture, remind yourself it's a pleasant torture and smile ... like the statue next to you.

● *In the far corridor, turn left into the first room (#25) and grab a blast of cold from the air-conditioner vent below the chairs to the left.*

HIGH RENAISSANCE — MICHELANGELO, RAPHAEL, TITIAN (1500–1550)

Michelangelo —
Holy Family (Sacra Famiglia)

This is the only completed easel painting by the greatest sculptor in history. Florentine painters were sculptors with brushes. This shows it. Instead of a painting it's more like three clusters of statues with some clothes painted on. The main subject is the holy family—Mary, Joseph, and baby Jesus—and in the background are two groups of nudes looking like classical statues. The background represents the old pagan world, while Jesus in the foreground is the new age of Christianity. The figure of young John the Baptist at right is the link between the two.

Michelangelo was a Florentine—in fact he was like an adopted son of the Medicis who recognized his talent—but much of his greatest work

HIGH RENAISSANCE

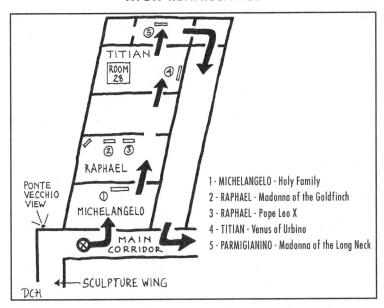

TITIAN
ROOM 28

⑤

④

② ③

RAPHAEL

PONTE VECCHIO VIEW

① MICHELANGELO

MAIN CORRIDOR

⊗

SCULPTURE WING

DCH

1 - MICHELANGELO - Holy Family
2 - RAPHAEL - Madonna of the Goldfinch
3 - RAPHAEL - Pope Leo X
4 - TITIAN - Venus of Urbino
5 - PARMIGIANINO - Madonna of the Long Neck

was done in Rome as part of the Pope's face-lift of the city. We can see here some of the techniques he used on the Sistine Chapel ceiling that revolutionized painting—monumental figures, dramatic angles (we're looking up Mary's nose), accentuated rippling muscles, and bright clashing colors (all the more apparent since both this work and the Sistine have been recently cleaned). These added an element of dramatic tension lacking in the graceful work of Leonardo and Botticelli.

Michelangelo painted this for Angelo Doni for 70 ducats. When the painting was delivered, Doni tried to talk Michelangelo down to 40. Proud Michelangelo took the painting away, and wouldn't sell it until the man finally agreed to pay double ... 140 ducats.

● *Enter Room 26.*

Raphael (Raffaello Sanzo) — *Madonna of the Goldfinch (La Madonna del Cardellino)*

Raphael (pron: roff-eye-ELL) perfected his craft in Florence, following the graceful style of Leonardo. Like Leonardo, he adds the human touch to a religious subject. In typical Leonardo fashion, this group of Mary, John the Baptist, and

Jesus is arranged in the shape of a pyramid with Mary's head at the peak. It's a tender scene painted with warm colors and a hazy background that matches the golden skin of the children.

The two halves of the painting balance perfectly. Draw a line down the middle, through Mary's nose and down through her knee. On the left is John the Baptist balanced by Jesus on the right. Even the trees in the background balance each other, left and right. These things aren't immediately noticeable, but they help create the subconcious feeling of balance and order that reinforce the atmosphere of maternal security in this domestic scene—pure Renaissance.

Raphael — *Leo X and Cardinals (Leone X con i Cardinali)*

Raphael was called to Rome at the same time as Michelangelo, working next door while Michelangelo did the Sistine ceiling. Raphael peeked in from time to time, learning from Michelangelo's monumental, dramatic figures. His later work is grittier and more realistic than the idealized, graceful, and "Leonardesque" Madonna. Pope Leo is big like a Michelangelo statue. And Raphael captures some of the seamier side of Vatican life in the cardinals' eyes— shrewd, suspicious, and somewhat cynical. With Raphael, the photographic realism pursued by painters ever since Giotto was finally achieved.

The Florentine Renaissance ended in 1520 with the death of Raphael. Raphael (see his self-portrait to the left of the Madonna) is considered both the culmination and conclusion of the Renaissance. The realism, balance, and humanism we associate with the Renaissance are all found in Raphael's work. He combined the grace of Leonardo with the power of Michelangelo. With his death, the Renaissance shifted again—to Venice.

● *Return to the corridor and go to room 35.*

Titian (Tiziano) — *Venus of Urbino (La Venere di Urbino)*

Compare this Venus with Botticelli's newly hatched Venus and you get a good idea of the difference between the Florentine and Venetian Renaissance. Botticelli's was pure, innocent, and otherworldly. Titian's should have a staple in her belly-button. This isn't a Venus, it's a cen-

terfold—with no purpose but to please the eye and other organs. While Botticelli's allegorical Venus is a message, this is a massage.

Titian and his fellow Venetians took the pagan spirit pioneered in Florence and carried it to its logical hedonistic conclusion. Using bright rich colors, they captured the luxurious life of happy-go-lucky Venice.

Remember how balanced Raphael's *Madonna of the Goldfinch* was? Every figure on one side had a balancing figure on the other. Titian balances his painting a different way—with color. The canvas is split down the middle by the curtain. The left half is dark, the right half warmer. The two halves are connected by a diagonal slash of luminous gold—the nude woman.

By the way, visitors from centuries past also panted in front of this Venus. The poet Byron called it "*the* Venus." With her sensual skin, hey-sailor look and suggestively placed hand, she must have left them blithering idiots.

● *Find the n-n-n-next painting.*

Parmigianino — Madonna of the Long Neck (Madonna dal Collo Lungo)

Raphael, Michelangelo, Leonardo, and Titian mastered reality. They could place any scene onto a canvas with photographic accuracy. How could future artists top that?

"Mannerists" like Parmigianino tried to by going beyond realism, exaggerating it for effect. Using brighter colors and elongated figures (two techniques explored by Michelangelo) they created scenes more elegant and more exciting than real life.

By stretching the neck of his Madonna, Parmigianino (pron: like the cheese) gives her an unnatural swan-like beauty. She has the same pose and position of hands as Botticelli's *Venus* and the *Venus de' Medici*. Her body forms an arcing S-curve—down her neck as far as her elbow, then back the other way along Jesus' body to her knee, then down to her foot. The baby Jesus seems to be blissfully gliding down this slippery-slide of sheer beauty.

● *Pass through several rooms, returning to the main corridor where, by the window, you'll see the famous* Venus de' Mallard *statue.*

THE REST OF THE UFFIZI

As art moved into the Baroque period, artists took Renaissance real-ism and exaggerated it still more—more beautiful, more emotional, or more dramatic. There's lots of great stuff in the following rooms, and I'd especially recommend Tintoretto's *Leda*, the enormous canvases of Rubens, and the shocking ultra-realism of Caravaggio's *Bacchus* and *Abraham Sacrificing Isaac*.

● *But first (or last, if your little uffizis hurt), head to the end of the cor-ridor for a true aesthetic experience.*

The Little Cappuchin Monk (Cappuccino) — anonymous Italian

This drinkable art form, born in Italy, is now enjoyed all over the world. It's called *The Little Cappuchin Monk* because its frothy milk foam gives the coffee a light-and-dark-brown look like the two-toned cowls of the Cappuchin order. Drink it on the terrace in the shadow of the towering Palazzo Vecchio and argue Marx and Hegel—was the Renaissance an economic phenomenon or a spiritual one? *Salute.*

17 Bargello

The Renaissance began with sculpture. The great Florentine painters were "sculptors with brushes." You can see the birth of this revolution of 3-D in the Bargello (pron: bar-JELL-oh), which boasts the best collection of Florentine sculpture. It's a small, uncrowded museum, and a pleasant break from the intensity of the rest of Florence.

MUSEO NAZIONALE IN THE BARGELLO

Hours: Generally daily 8:30–13:50 *but* closed the first, third, and fifth Sunday of the month and the second and fourth Monday. Last entry 30 minutes before closing.

Cost: 8,000 L

Tour length: One hour

Getting there: Five-minute walk northeast of Uffizi. Facing the Palazzo Vecchio, head to the far left corner of the square. Go left at Canto de Giugni (at Ristorante Cavallino), then right onto Via della Condotta. Go two blocks and look kitty-corner to the left for a rustic brick building with a spire that looks like a baby Palazzo Vecchio. If lost ask, *"Doe-vay bar-jello?"*

Information: None.

Photography: Cameras without flash are okay.

Starring: Michelangelo, Donatello, Brunelleschi, Ghiberti, and four different *Davids.*

ORIENTATION — SCULPTURE IN FLORENCE

● *Buy your ticket and take a seat in the courtyard.*

The Bargello, built in 1255, was Florence's city hall. The heavy fortifications tell us that politics in medieval Florence had its occupational hazards. After the administration shifted to the larger Palazzo Vecchio, this became a police station (*bargello*) and then a prison.

The Bargello, a three-story rectangular building, surrounds this cool and peaceful courtyard. The best statues are found in two rooms—one on the ground floor at the foot of the stairs, and another one flight up, directly above it. We'll proceed logically in a chrono- kind of way.

But first, meander around this courtyard and get a feel for sculpture in general and rocks in particular. Sculpture is a much more robust art form than painting. Think of the engineering problems alone of moving these stones from a quarry to an artist's studio. Then the sheer physical strength of chiseling away for hours on end. A sculptor must be powerful yet delicate, controlling the chisel to chip out the smallest details. Think of Michelangelo's approach to sculpt- ing—he wasn't creating a figure but only liberating it from the rock that surrounded it.

If the Renaissance is humanism, then sculpture is the perfect medi- um to express it. It shows the human form, standing alone, indepen- dent of church, state, or society.

Finally, a viewing note. Every sculpture has an invisible "frame" around it—the stone block it was cut from. Visualizing this frame helps you find the center of the composition.

● *Climb the courtyard staircase to the next floor up and turn right into the large Donatello room. Pause at Donatello's painted bust of Niccolo de Uzzano.*

DONATELLO ROOM

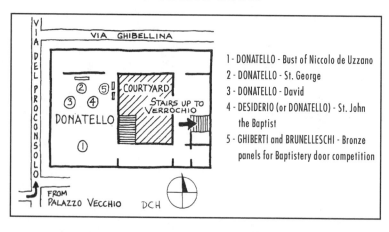

1 - DONATELLO - Bust of Niccolo de Uzzano

2 - DONATELLO - St. George

3 - DONATELLO - David

4 - DESIDERIO (or DONATELLO) - St. John the Baptist

5 - GHIBERTI and BRUNELLESCHI - Bronze panels for Baptistery door competition

Donatello (1386–1466)

Donatello was the first great Renaissance genius, a model for Michelangelo and others. He mastered realism, creating the first truly lifelike statues of people since ancient times. Donatello's work is highly personal. Unlike the ancient Greeks, he often sculpted real people, not idealized versions of pretty gods and goddesses. Some of these people are downright ugly. In the true spirit of Renaissance humanism, Donatello was the first to appreciate the beauty of flesh-and-blood human beings—even ordinary ones like *Niccolo de Uzzano* here.

Donatello's personality was also a model for later artists. He was moody and irascible, purposely setting himself apart from others in order to concentrate on his sculpting. He developed the role of the "mad genius" that Michelangelo would later perfect.

● *At the far end of the room,* St. George *stands in a niche in the wall.*

Donatello — *St. George* (1416)

A century before Michelangelo sculpted his famous *David*, this was the unofficial symbol of Florence. George, the Christian slayer of dragons, was just the sort of righteous warrior that proud Renaissance Florentines could rally around in their struggles with nearby cities. He stands on the edge of his niche looking out alertly with the same relaxed intensity and determination that Michelangelo used for his *David*. This is the original marble statue. A bronze version stands in its original niche at Orsanmichele Church. The relief panel below shows George doing what he's been pondering.

● *On the floor to your left you'll find …*

Donatello — *David* (c. 1430)

This boyish-approaching-girlish *David* is quite a contrast with Michelangelo's powerful version at the Accademia. Donatello's smooth-skinned warrior sways gracefully, poking his sword playfully at the severed head of the giant Goliath. He has a *contrapposto* stance similar to Michelangelo's, resting his weight on one leg in the classical style, but it gives him a feminine rather than masculine look. Gazing into his coy eyes is a very different experience from confronting Michelangelo's tough Renaissance Man.

This *David* paved the way for Michelangelo's. Europe hadn't seen a free-standing male nude like this in a thousand years. In the Middle Ages, the human body was considered a dirty thing, a symbol of man's weakness, something to be covered up in shame. The church prohibited exhibitions of nudity like this one and certainly would never decorate a church with it. But in the Renaissance, a new class of rich and powerful merchants appeared that bought art for their own personal enjoyment. This particular statue stood in the courtyard of the Medici's palace ... where Michelangelo, practically an adopted son, grew up admiring it.

This is the first of four different *Davids* in the Bargello: (1) This one, (2) another version by Donatello—look over your left shoulder, (3) Verrochio's *David* upstairs (which we'll visit),
and (4) Michelangelo's other unfinished version we'll see downstairs. Compare and contrast the artists' styles as you see them. How many ways can you slay a giant?

● St. John the Baptist, *done in the style of Donatello, is to the right of* David #1.

Desiderio da Settignano (or Donatello) — *St. John the Baptist (S. Giovanni Battista)*

John the Baptist was the wild-eyed wildcat prophet who lived in the desert preaching, eating bugs and honey, and baptizing Saviors of the World. Donatello, the mad prophet of the coming Renaissance, might have identified with this original eccentric.

● *On the wall you'll find some bronze relief panels. Don't look at the labels just yet.*

Ghiberti and Brunelleschi — Baptistery Door Competition Entries (two different relief panels, titled *Il Sacrificio di Abramo)*

These two versions of *Abraham Sacrificing Isaac* were finalists in the contest (1401) held to decide who would do the bronze doors of the Baptistery. (Donatello also entered but lost.) Ghiberti eventually won and later did the doors known as the Gates of Paradise. Brunelleschi lost—fortunately for us—freeing him to design the Duomo's dome.

You be the judge. Here are the two finalists for the Baptistery door competition—Ghiberti's and Brunelleschi's. Which do you like the best?

(Ghiberti's, on the left, won.)

Both artists catch the crucial moment when Abraham, obeying God's orders, prepares to slaughter and burn his only son as a sacrifice. At the last moment—after Abraham passed this test of faith—an angel of God appears to stop the bloodshed.

One panel is clearly better than the other. Composition: One is integrated and cohesive, the other a balanced knick-knack shelf of segments. Human drama: One has bodies and faces that speak. The boy's body is a fine classical nude in itself, so real and vulnerable. Abraham's face is intense and ready to follow God's will. Perspective: An angel zooms in from out of nowhere to save the boy in the nick of time.

● *Exit the Donatello room through the same door you entered. Cross to the opposite side of the courtyard, then take your first left and climb the red-carpeted stairs to the next floor. At the top of the stairs, turn left, then left again. Verrochio's* David *stands in the center of the room.*

Verrochio — *David* (c. 1470)

Verrochio is best known as the teacher of Leonardo da Vinci, but he was also the premier sculptor between the time of Donatello and Michelangelo. This saucy, impertinent *David* is more masculine than Donatello's, but a far cry from Michelangelo's monumental version. He leans on one leg, but it's not a firm, commanding stance but a nimble one (especially noticeable from behind). The artist is clearly contrasting the smug smile of the victor with Goliath's "Oh, have I got a headache" expression.

● *Nearby is a room of glass cases filled with small statues. In the center of the room, you'll find …*

Pollaiuolo — *Hercules and Antaeus (Ercole e Anteo)*

Antaeus was invincible as long as he was in contact with the earth, his mother. So Hercules just picked him up like a Renaissance Hulk Hogan and crushed him to death.

More than any early artist from this period, Pollaiuolo studied the human body in motion. These figures are not dignified Renaissance Men, but brutish, violent, animal-like beasts. Yet in this tangled pose of flailing arms and legs there still is a Renaissance sense of balance—all the motion spins around the center of gravity where their bodies grind together.

● *In the glass cases, you'll see small-scale versions of the* Mercury *we'll soon see. Poke around, then descend back to the courtyard on the ground floor. The final room we'll see is through the door to your left at the bottom of the stairs.*

Lesser Michelangelos

Michelangelo — *Bacchus (Bacco)* (c. 1497)

Maybe Michelangelo had a sense of humor after all. Compare this tipsy Greek god of wine with his sturdy, sober *David*, begun two years later. *Bacchus* isn't nearly so muscular, so monumental … or so sure on his feet. Hope he's not driving. The pose, the smooth muscles, and curving belly and hip look more like Donatello's boyish *David*.

This is Michelangelo's first major commission. He often vacillated between showing man as strong and noble, and as weak and perverse. This isn't the nobility of the classical world, but the decadent side of orgies and indulgence.

● *Just to the left you'll find …*

Michelangelo — *Bruto* (1540)

Another example of the influence of Donatello is this so-ugly-he's-beautiful bust by Michelangelo. His rough intensity gives him the look of a man who has succeeded against all

GROUND FLOOR

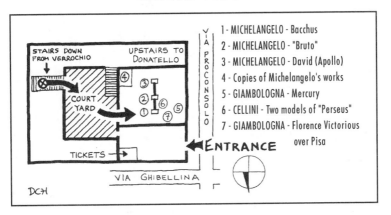

STAIRS DOWN FROM VERROCHIO

UPSTAIRS TO DONATELLO

COURT YARD

TICKETS →

VIA PROCONSOLO

VIA GHIBELLINA

◄ENTRANCE

DCH

1 - MICHELANGELO - Bacchus

2 - MICHELANGELO - "Bruto"

3 - MICHELANGELO - David (Apollo)

4 - Copies of Michelangelo's works

5 - GIAMBOLOGNA - Mercury

6 - CELLINI - Two models of "Perseus"

7 - GIAMBOLOGNA - Florence Victorious over Pisa

odds, a dignity and heroic quality that would be missing if he were too pretty.

The subject is Brutus, the Roman who, for the love of liberty, murdered his friend and dictator, Julius Caesar (*Et tu ... ?*). Michelangelo could understand this man's dilemma. He himself had close ties to the Medicis, his adopted family, who could also be corrupt and tyrannical.

So he gives us two sides of a political assassin. The right profile (the front view) is heroic. But the hidden side, with the drooping mouth and squinting eye, makes him more cunning, sneering, and ominous.

Michelangelo —
David (also known as *Apollo*)

This is the last of the *Davids* in the Bargello, a good time to think back on those we've seen: Donatello's girlish, gloating *David*; Verrochio's boyish, impish version; and now this unfinished one by Michelangelo. Michelangelo certainly learned from these earlier versions, even copying certain elements, but what's truly amazing is that his famous *David* in the Accademia is so completely different—so much larger than life in every way—from the earlier attempts.

In the glass cases in the corner are small-scale copies of some of Michelangelo's most famous works. Back near the entrance there's a bust of Michelangelo, capturing his broken nose and brooding nature.

● *On the other side of the room ...*

Giambologna — *Mercury*

Catch this statue while you can—he's got flowers waiting to be delivered. Despite all the bustle and motion, *Mercury* has a solid Renaissance core: the line of balance that runs straight up the center, from toes to nose to fingertip. Back down at the toes, notice the cupid practicing up for the circus.

Cellini — Two Small Models of Perseus (Perseo)

The life-size statue of Perseus slaying the Medusa, located in the open-air Loggia next to the Palazzo Vecchio, is cast bronze. Cellini started with these smaller models in wax and bronze to get the difficult process down. When it came time to cast the full-size work, everything was going fine ... till he realized he didn't

have enough metal! He ran around the studio, gathering up pewterware and throwing it in, narrowly avoiding a messterpiece.

Giambologna — *Florence Victorious over Pisa (Firenze Vittoriosa su Pisa)*

This shows the fierce Florentine chauvinism born in an era when Italy's cities struggled for economic and political dominance ... and Florence won.

ROME

A Walk Through Ancient Rome

St. Peter's

The Vatican Museum

*A*t its peak the word "Rome" meant civilization itself. And the grandeur of ancient Rome survives today, Vatican-style. The "Caesar Shuffle" winds through people, cats, and traffic from one magnificent sight to another, culminating with St. Peter's and the Vatican City. From the Colosseum to the *Pietà* to the spanking new Sistine Chapel, Rome is fit for a caesar, a pope, and a wide-eyed, well-prepared tourist.

18 A Walk Through Ancient Rome

Rome has many layers—modern, Baroque, Renaissance, Christian—but let's face it, "Rome" is Caesars, gladiators, chariots, centurions, "*Et tu, Brute*," trumpet fanfares, and thumbs up or thumbs down. That's the Rome we'll look at. On our "Caesar Shuffle" we'll see the downtown core of ancient Rome, from the Colosseum, through the Forum, over the Capitol Hill and to the Pantheon.

COLOSSEO, FORO ROMANO, MAMERTINUM, CAMPIDOGLIO, PANTHEON

Hours and Cost:

Colosseum—In summer Monday–Saturday 9:00–18:00, Sunday 9:00–13:00; off-season Monday–Saturday 9:00–15:00, Sunday 9:00–13:00; 10,000 L.

Forum—In summer Monday–Saturday 9:00–18:00, Sunday 9:00–13:00; off-season Monday–Saturday 9:00–15:00, Sunday 9:00–13:00. Entrance to the Forum is free, to Palatine Hill 12,000 L.

Mamertine Prison—9:00–12:00, 14:00–18:00 (donation, 1,000 L).

Pantheon—9:00–18:30, Sunday 9:00–13:00, free.

Note: Hours are notoriously unreliable in Rome. Call the tourist office at 06-4889-9255, 06-4889-9253, or 06-487-1270 to confirm.

Tour length: Four hours

Getting there: Subway to Metro stop "Colosseo," or taxi.

Information: No info service, only guidebooks from street vendors. The excellent *Rome: Past and Present* book has overlay reconstructions of many of the monuments on this tour (pay 13,000–15,000 L, not the 20,000 L list price).

Theft alert: You might be accosted by street thieves (usually mothers with

babies or 8- to 15-year-olds) who pretend to beg but can strip you bare.
Cuisine art: Restaurants near Victor Emmanuel Monument, and good self-service cafeteria at Largo Argentina near the Pantheon. Bring a water bottle and consider a picnic lunch. Forum has drinking fountains.

ROME WALK—OVERVIEW

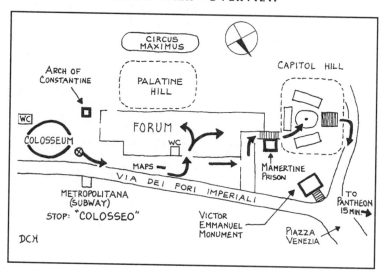

ROME — REPUBLIC AND EMPIRE (500 B.C.–A.D. 500)

Ancient Rome spanned a thousand years, from 500 B.C. to A.D. 500. In that thousand years Rome expanded from a small tribe of barbarians to ruler of a vast empire, then dwindled slowly to city size again. The first 500 years, when Rome's armies made her ruler of the Italian peninsula and beyond, Rome was a republic governed by elected senators. The next 500 years of world conquest and eventual decline, Rome was an empire ruled by a dictator backed by the military.

Julius Caesar bridged the Republic and the Empire. This ambitious general and politician, popular with the people because of his military victories and charisma, suspended the constitution and assumed dictatorial powers (around 50 B.C.). He was assassinated by a conspiracy of senators. His adopted son Augustus succeeded him, and soon

"Caesar" was not just a name but a title. Emperor Augustus ushered in the Pax Romana, or Roman peace (A.D.1–200), when Rome reached her peak, controlling an empire stretching even beyond Eurail—from Scotland to Egypt, from Turkey to Morocco.

The Colosseum

● *View the Colosseum from the Forum fence near the grassy patch across the street from the "Colosseo" subway station.*

Built when the Empire was at its peak (A.D. 80), this represents Rome at its grandest. The Flavian Amphitheater (its real name) was an arena for gladiator contests and public spectacles. When killing became a spectator sport, the Romans wanted to share the fun with as many people as possible. They did this by sticking two Greek theaters together. The outside (the grassy patch) was decorated with a 100-foot bronze statue that gleamed in the sunlight. The final structure was colossal, a "coloss-eum," the wonder of its age. It could accommodate 50,000 roaring fans (100,000 thumbs).

The Romans pioneered the use of the rounded arch and concrete, enabling them to build on this colossal scale. They made a shell of brick, then filled it in with concrete. Inside, you'll see this clearly among the ruins. Iron pegs held the larger stones together—notice the small holes that pockmark the sides. When it was done, the whole thing was faced with shining travertine marble (still visible on the very upper level).

The exterior says a lot about the Romans. They were great engineers, not artists. While the essential structure is Roman, the façade is Greek, decorated with the three types of Greek columns—Doric on bottom, Ionic in the middle, and Corinthian on top. Originally copies of Greek statues stood in the arches of the upper two stories. The Colosseum was designed to be functional more than beautiful. If ancient Romans visited the United States today as tourists, they'd send home postcards of our greatest works of "art"—freeways.

Only a third of the original Colosseum remains. Earthquakes destroyed some of it, but most was carted off as easy pre-cut stones for other buildings during the Middle Ages and Renaissance.

● *Enter by the west entrance—to your right, past the Arch of Constantine. Buy your ticket and go inside. Move up to a railing overlooking the arena.*

Interior

You're on arena level. What we see now are the underground passages beneath the playing surface. The oval-shaped arena (86 by 50 yards) was originally covered with boards, then sprinkled with sand (Latin word: *arena*). Like modern stadiums, the spectators ringed the playing area. The brick masses around you supported the first small tier of seats, and you can see two larger slanted supports higher up. A few marble seats survive on the opposite side. Wooden beams stuck out from the top to support an enormous canvas awning which could be hoisted across by armies of sailors to provide shade for the spectators—the first domed stadium.

"Hail, Caesar! We who are about to die salute you!" The gladiators would enter the arena from the west end (to your left), parade around to the sound of trumpets, stop at the emperor's box at the "50-yard-line" on the right (where you're standing), raise their weapons, shout this salute … and the fights would begin. The fights pitted men against men, men against beasts, and beasts against beasts.

The gladiators were usually slaves, criminals, or poor people who got their chance for freedom, wealth, and fame in the ring. They learned to fight in training schools then battled their way up the ranks. The best were rewarded like our modern sports stars with fan clubs, great wealth, and product endorsements.

The animals came from all over the world—lions, tigers, bears, oh my, crocodiles, elephants, and hippos (not to mention exotic human "animals" from the "barbarian" lands). They were kept in cages beneath the arena floor, then lifted up in elevators where they'd pop out from behind blinds into the arena—the gladiator didn't know where, when, or by what he'd be attacked. Nets ringed the arena to protect the crowd. The stadium was inaugurated with a 100-day festival in which 2,000 men and 9,000 animals were killed. Colosseum employees squirted perfumes around the stadium to mask the stench of blood. For a lighthearted change of pace between events, the fans watched dogs bloody themselves fighting porcupines.

If a gladiator fell helpless to the ground, his opponent would approach the emperor's box and ask—should he live or die? Sometimes the emperor left the decision to the crowd, who would judge based on how valiantly the man had fought. They would make their decision—thumbs up (Latin word: *siskel*) or thumbs down (*ebert*).

And Christians? Did they throw Christians to the lions like in the movies? Christians were definitely thrown to the lions, made to fight gladiators, crucified, and burned alive … but probably not here in this particular stadium. Maybe, but probably not.

Rome was a nation of warriors which built an empire on conquest. The battles fought against Germans, Egyptians, barbarians, and strange animals were played out daily here in the Colosseum for the benefit of city-slicker bureaucrats who got vicarious thrills watching brutes battle to the death. The contests were always free, sponsored by politicians to buy votes or to keep Rome's growing mass of unemployed rabble off the streets.

● *With these scenes in mind, wander around. Climb to the upper deck for a more colossal view (stairs near the exit).*

As you exit, the Roman Forum is directly in front of you, the subway stop is on your right, and the Arch of Constantine is on your left.

Arch of Constantine

If you are a Christian, were raised a Christian, or simply belong to a so-called "Christian nation," ponder this arch. It marks one of the great turning points in history—the military coup that made us all Christians. In A.D. 312 an upstart general named Constantine defeated the Emperor Maxentius in one crucial battle. The night before, he'd seen a vision of a cross in the sky. Constantine became Emperor and promptly legalized Christianity. With this one battle, a once-obscure Jewish sect with a handful of followers was now the state religion of the entire Western world. In the year A.D. 300 you could be killed for being a Christian—by 400 you could be killed for not being one. Church enrollment boomed.

By the way, don't look too closely at the reliefs decorating this arch. By the fourth century Rome was on its way down. Rather than struggle with original carvings, the makers of this arch plugged in bits and pieces scavenged from existing monuments. It's newly restored and looking great. But any meaning read into the stone will be very jumbled.

● *The entrance to the Roman Forum is 300 yards west along busy Via dei Fori Imperiali (which Mussolini had built for a military parade boulevard and to clear a visual path from his office, at one end, to the Colosseum at the other). The low-profile entrance building is on the left, in a small square called "Largo Romolo e Remo." Remember, there are other "Forums" nearby—you're looking for "Foro Romano."*

About halfway along the way to the Forum, pause at the four maps on the wall to the left.

Maps Showing the Growth of Rome

In the first map (eighth century B.C.), "Rome" is just the city itself, a tiny white dot. Next (146 B.C.), they've conquered Spain and Greece. More important, they've defeated their arch-rivals across the Mediterranean, the Carthaginians, in the Punic Wars. The third map (A.D. 1) is from the time of Augustus, the first emperor. Finally (A.D. 100), we see Rome at its greatest expanse, as far north as Scotland, as far east as Mesopotamia. They affectionately nicknamed the Mediterranean "Our Lake."

● *Enter the forum—it's free (WCs on the left after you enter). Walk down the ramp, then go right about 20 yards. Find a seat on a piece of rubble. I know it's hot, but Roman history is most enjoyable when consumed while sitting on a broken slice of column. Sit with your back to the entrance.*

Roman Forum (Foro Romano) — Heart of the Empire

The Forum was the political, religious, and commercial center of the city. Rome's most important temples and halls of justice were here. This was the place for religious processions, elections, important speeches, and parades by conquering generals. As Rome's empire expanded, these few acres of land became the center of the civilized world.

The hill ahead of you and slightly to the left, with all the trees (the south border of the Forum), is the Palatine Hill where Rome started in 753 B.C. According to legend, twin brothers named Romulus (Rome) and Remus were orphaned in infancy and raised by a she-wolf on top of the Palatine. Growing up, they found it hard to get dates. So they and their cohorts attacked the nearby Sabine tribe, fought them here in this valley, and kidnapped the women. After they made peace, the marshy valley became the meeting place and then the trading center for the scattered tribes on the surrounding hillsides. Rome was born right here.

The valley is rectangular, running roughly east-west. At the far east end (to the left, out of sight) is the Colosseum. To the right rises the Capitol Hill. Running left to right at your feet is the rocky path known as the Via Sacra, main street of ancient Rome, which runs down to the right past the large brick Senate building (Curia) to the well-preserved Arch of Septimius Severus.

THE FORUM

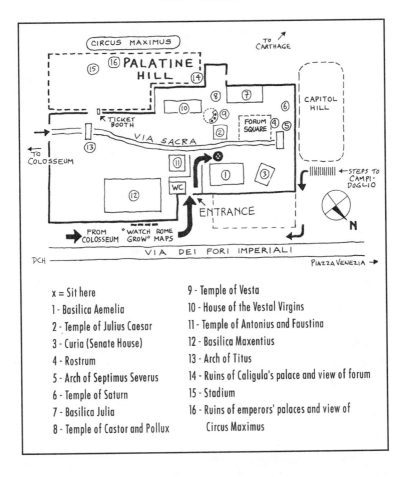

x = Sit here

1 - Basilica Aemelia

2 - Temple of Julius Caesar

3 - Curia (Senate House)

4 - Rostrum

5 - Arch of Septimus Severus

6 - Temple of Saturn

7 - Basilica Julia

8 - Temple of Castor and Pollux

9 - Temple of Vesta

10 - House of the Vestal Virgins

11 - Temple of Antonius and Faustina

12 - Basilica Maxentius

13 - Arch of Titus

14 - Ruins of Caligula's palace and view of forum

15 - Stadium

16 - Ruins of emperors' palaces and view of Circus Maximus

The original Forum, or main square, was the flat patch about the size of a football field stretching out to the right. Surrounding it were once temples, law courts, government buildings, and triumphal arches.

The Forum is now rubble, no denying it. We'll have to raise our imaginations to near-psychedelic levels in order to turn these ruins into temples.

The Forum's Main Square

The Forum Square was the busiest, most crowded—and often the seediest—section of town. Besides the senators, politicians, and currency

*The **Forum Square** (existing rubble in dark), as viewed from the Forum entrance toward Capitol Hill. For 500 years this square, surrounded by temples and government buildings, was the center of the Western world.*

exchangers, there were even sleazier types—souvenir hawkers, fortunetellers, gamblers, slave marketers, drunkards, hookers, lawyers, and tour guides.

Imagine the Forum in its prime: blinding white marble buildings with 40-foot columns and shining bronze roofs. Rows of statues, painted in realistic colors. Chariots rattling down the Via Sacra. Mentally replace tourists in T-shirts with tribunes in togas. Imagine the buildings towering and the people buzzing around you while an orator gives a rabble-rousing speech from the Rostrum. If things still look like just a pile of rocks, at least tell yourself, "But Julius Caesar once leaned against these rocks."

● *Cross the Via Sacra and wander a few steps to your left for a closer look at the rubble of ...*

The Temple of Julius Caesar (Templo del Divo Giulio)

The square changed dramatically—as did Rome itself—with the coming of Julius Caesar (50 B.C.). He cleared out many of the wooden market stalls and began to ring the square with even grander buildings. (Caesar's house was located right behind the temple, near that clump of trees.)

However, not everyone liked his urban design or his politics. When he tried to assume dictatorial powers, he was ambushed and stabbed to death by a conspiracy of senators, including his friend Brutus (*Et tu, Bruté*?).

The funeral was held on the steps of this temple, facing the main square. The citizens gathered and speeches were made. Mark Antony stood up to say (in Shakespeare's words), "Friends, Romans, countrymen, lend me your ears. I come to bury Caesar, not to praise him." When Caesar's body was burned, the citizens who had loved him threw anything at hand on the fire, requiring the fire department to come put it out. Then the very people who had killed him rededicated this temple in his name, making him the first Roman to be a god.

● *Head down the Via Sacra towards the arch of Septimius Severus. Stop at the big, well-preserved brick building with the triangular roof. If the door's open, look in.*

The Curia

Rome prided itself on being a republic. Early in their history, they threw out the king and established rule by elected representatives. Each Roman citizen was free to speak his mind and have a say in public policy.

The Senate House (Curia) was the most important political building in the Forum. Three hundred senators, elected by the citizens of Rome, met here to debate and create the laws of the land. Their wooden seats once circled the building in three tiers, with the far end as the Senate president's podium. The marble floor is from ancient times. Even when emperors became the supreme authority, the Senate was a power to be reckoned with. (Note: Although Julius Caesar was assassinated on the steps of the Senate, it wasn't here—the Senate was temporarily meeting across town.)

A statue and two reliefs inside the Curia help build our mental image of the Forum. The statue, made of porphyry in about A.D. 100, with its plugged-in head, arms, and feet missing, was a tribute to an emperor, probably Hadrian or Trajan. The two relief panels may have decorated the Rostrum. One shows a government amnesty on debt with people burning their debt records while the other shows intact architecture and the latest fashion in togas.

● *Go back down the Senate steps to the metal guardrail and look right to a wall marked ...*

Rostrum (Rostri)

Nowhere was Roman freedom more apparent than at this "Speaker's Corner." Here is where Rome's orators great and small tried to draw a crowd and sway public opinion. Men like Cicero railed against the corruption and decadence that came with the city's new-found wealth. In later years, daring citizens even spoke out against the emperors, reminding them that Rome was once free.

The original rostrum was a raised platform, 10 feet high and 75 feet long, decorated with statues, columns, and the prows of ships (*rostra*). Picture the backdrop these speakers would have had—a mountain of marble buildings piling up on Capitol Hill. The impressive Temple of Saturn (eight remaining columns) stood to the left. And in imperial times, these voices of democracy would have been dwarfed by images of the emperor like the huge Arch of Septimius Severus (A.D. 203). The tall Column of Phocas (over your left shoulder), one of the last great monuments erected in the Forum, was originally topped by a bronze statue.

● *Julius Caesar built the large Basilica of Julia, on the opposite side of the square from the Curia. Walk clockwise (left) around the guardrail to the opposite side of the Rostrum. Turn to face the ...*

Basilica Julia

A *basilica* was a Roman hall of justice. In a society as legal-minded as modern America, you needed a lot of lawyers and a big place to put them. Citizens came here to work out matters like inheritances and building permits, or to sue somebody. When they got bored, they played games like jacks or marbles on the steps—you can see the circles scratched into the marble floors.

Notice the layout. It was a long, rectangular building. The brick stumps all in a row were originally piers, forming one long, central hall, flanked by two side aisles. Medieval Christian churches adopted this *basilica* floor plan.

● *Looking east (in the direction of the Colosseum) you'll see the three tall Corinthian columns of the Temple of Castor and Pollux. Walk around the left side of this temple to the three remaining columns of a small, white circular temple.*

The Temple of Vesta

This was Rome's most sacred spot. Rome considered itself one big family, and this temple represented a circular hut like the kind Rome's first families lived in. Inside, a fire burned, just as in a Roman home. As long as the sacred flame burned, Rome would stand. The flame was tended by priestesses known as Vestal Virgins.

● *Around the back of the Temple of Vesta, you'll find two rectangular brick pools. These stood in the courtyard of …*

The House of the Vestal Virgins

The Vestal Virgins lived in a two-story building surrounding a central courtyard with these two pools at one end. Rows of statues to the left and right marked the long sides of the building. This place was the model—both architecturally and sexually—for medieval convents and monasteries.

The six Vestal Virgins, chosen from noble families before the age of 10, served a 30-year term. Honored and revered by the Romans, they even had their own box opposite the emperor in the Colosseum.

As the name implies, they were virgins, having taken a vow of chastity. If she served her term faithfully—abstaining for 30 years—she was given a huge dowry, a statue in her honor (like the ones at left), and allowed to marry (life begins at 40?). But if they found any Virgin who wasn't, she was strapped to a funeral car, paraded through the streets of the Forum, taken to a crypt, given a loaf of bread and a lamp … and buried alive. Many women suffered the latter fate.

House of the Vestal Virgins. *This place was the model—both architecturally and sexually—for monasteries and convents throughout the Middle Ages.*

● *Return to the Via Sacra. Pause at the well-preserved Temple of Antoninus and Faustina with its 50-foot Corinthian columns. Now head uphill, up the Via Sacra, in the direction of the Colosseum.*

Via Sacra

The "Sacred Way" was Rome's Main Street, the oldest in the city and site of the grandest and holiest parades. It ran east-west from the Arch of Titus on the east end to the Arch of Septimius Severus on the west, then jogging left, up to the Temple of Saturn (the eight large columns at the foot of Capitol Hill). Religious processions by torchlight passed along here. And when conquering generals returned to Rome they paraded their booty for all Rome to see. Many of the large basalt stones under your feet were walked on by Caesar Augustus 2,000 years ago.

● *As you head up the Via Sacra you'll see three enormous arches off to the left. Follow the lane to the left and find shade near a brick pillar or under an arch.*

Basilica Maxentiu3s

Big arches, huh? But look at the stub of brick sticking up from them. Extend that across the open field. The three arches are only side niches in this grand hall of justice. They were matched by a similar set along the Via Sacra side. Between them ran the central hall spanned by a roof 120 feet high, or about 50 feet higher than the side arches you see. The hall itself was a football field long, lavishly furnished with colorful inlaid marble, fountains, and statues and filled with strolling Romans. At the far (west) end stood an enormous statue of the emperor Constantine on a throne.

This building was larger than Basilica Julia but had the same general shape—a rectangular building with a long central hall flanked by two side halls.

Rome Falls

This peak of Roman grandeur is a good place to talk about the Fall of Rome. Again, Rome lasted a thousand years—500 years growing, 200 years at its peak, and 300 years of gradual decay. The Fall had many causes. Christians blame it on moral decay. Marxists blame it on a shallow economy based on spoils of war. (Ronald Reagan blamed it on Marxists.) Whatever the reasons, the far-flung Empire could no longer

Basilica Maxentius *(interior—existing rubble in dark). A Roman hall of justice, 100 yards long. The three standing arches were only the side aisles of this enormous structure, supporting a central roof that towered much higher.*

keep its grip on conquered lands and pulled back. Barbarian tribes from Germany and Asia attacked the Italian peninsula and even looted Rome itself in A.D. 410, leveling many of the buildings in the Forum. In 476, the last emperor checked out, switched off the lights, and Europe plunged into centuries of ignorance, poverty, and weak government—the Dark Ages.

But Rome lived on in the Catholic Church, the state religion of Rome's last generations. Emperors became popes (both called themselves Pontifex Maximus), senators became bishops, orators became priests, and basilicas became churches. Christian worship services required a larger meeting hall than Roman temples provided, so they used the spacious Roman basilica (hall of justice) as the model for their churches. Cathedrals from France to Spain to England, from Romanesque to Gothic to Renaissance all have the same basic floor plan as a Roman basilica. And remember that the goal for the greatest church of all, St. Peter's, was to "put the dome of the Pantheon atop the Basilica Maxentius." The glory of Rome never quite died.

● *Return to the Via Sacra and stop at the triumphal arch on the left and the drinking fountain on the right. There's a view of the Colosseum through the arch.*

Arch of Titus (Arco di Tito)

Conquest and booty fueled Rome's expansion. Conquering generals brought the spoils of war back for homecoming parades. They built these arches to march under and to commemorate their victories.

Looking back over the Forum (standing on the steps next to the arch), picture a triumphal procession heading down the Via Sacra. The street would be lined with citizens waving branches and carrying torches. First would come porters, carrying chests full of booty. Then a parade of exotic animals from the conquered lands—elephants, giraffes, hippopotamuses—for the crowd to "ooh" and "ahh" at. Then the prisoners in chains, with the captive king on a wheeled platform so the people could jeer and spit at him. Finally, the conquering hero would drive down in his four-horse chariot, with rose petals strewn in his path. The whole procession would go the length of the Forum to the Temple of Saturn where they'd place the booty in Rome's coffers, then up to the top of Capitol Hill to the Temple of Jupiter (not visible today) to dedicate the victory to the King of the Gods.

The Arch of Titus celebrated the Roman victory over the province of Judea (Israel) in A.D. 70. The Romans had a reputation as benevolent conquerors, tolerating the local customs and rulers. All they required was allegiance to the Empire, shown by worshiping the current emperor as a god. No problem for most conquered people who already had half a dozen gods on their prayer lists. But the Israelites' god was jealous, and refused to let his people worship the emperor. Israel revolted, but after a short but bitter war, the Romans defeated the rebels, took Jerusalem, and sacked their temple.

The propaganda value of Roman art is clear on the inside of this arch where a relief shows the emperor Titus in a chariot being crowned by the Goddess Victory (though they both look like they've been through the wars as modern pollution takes its toll). The other side shows the sacking of the temple—soldiers carrying the Jewish candelabrum and other plunder. The two (unfinished) plaques on poles were to have listed the conquered cities.

The brutal crushing of this rebellion (and one 60 years later) devastated the nation of Israel. With no temple as a center for their faith, they were scattered throughout the world (the Diaspora). There was no Jewish political entity again for 2,000 years, until after World War II when modern Israel was created.

● *It costs 12,000 L to visit the Palatine Hill and museum. If you opt to visit, buy your ticket and follow the Via Sacra as it curves up toward Palatine Hill.*

Palatine Hill and Circus Maximus (Optional)

The Palatine Hill was the birthplace of Rome and the site of the luxurious palaces of the emperors (*palatine* gives us our word "palace"). The ruined palaces are hardly luxurious today, looking similar to the ruins of the Palace of Caligula at the foot of the hill overlooking the

Forum. The Palatine Museum offers a chronological display of archaeological finds, frescoes, and sculptures illustrating the history of the hill that Roman emperors called home. There is also an impressive stadium for private games and races (on the left side of the hill) and a view of the Circus Maximus from atop the hill, a 10-minute hike.

● *The Palatine Hill/Circus Maximus view is optional. If you're wilting you can exit the Forum the way you came in. The Circus Maximus is on the far side of the Palatine Hill. Hike uphill from the Arch of Titus. At the summit, bear either left or right around the modern-looking building to the railings overlooking the Circus.*

Circus Maximus

If the gladiator show at the Colosseum was sold out, you could always get a seat at the Circus Max. Like an early version of today's Demolition Derby, Ben Hur and his fellow charioteers once raced recklessly around this oblong course.

This was a huge race course. Chariots circled around the cigar-shaped mound in the center. Bleachers (now grassy banks) originally surrounded the track. The track was 400 yards long, while the whole stadium measured 650 by 220 yards, seating—get this—300,000 people. The wooden bleachers once collapsed during a race, killing 13,000.

Races consisted of seven laps (about a mile altogether). In such a small space collisions and overturned chariots were very common. The charioteers were usually poor low-borns who used this dangerous sport to get rich and famous. Many succeeded.

The public was crazy about it. There were 12 races a day, 240 days a year. Four teams dominated competition—Reds, Whites, Blues, and Greens—and every citizen was fanatically devoted to one of them. Obviously, the emperors had the best seats in the house from their palaces on the hill. They occasionally had the circus floor carpeted with designs in colored powders for their pleasure.

The spectacles continued into the Christian era (until 549) despite church disapproval.

● *Exit the Forum by the way you came in (not at the Colosseum end). Head left (west) on the walkway that borders the Forum. Watch for 12-year-old thieves and their mothers. After 100 yards, take your first left.*

Enjoy the view of the Forum from the railing at the huge Arch of Septimus Severus. Until modern times the history of Rome and its remains were no big deal. The Forum lay buried to the height we're at now. Only

In any crowd, it's wise to be on the lookout for pickpockets.

a few tips of columns interrupted what for centuries was called "the cow field." One evening 200 years ago, Edward (Rise and Decline) Gibbon stood here. He heard the song of Christian monks praying among pagan ruins and pondered the cyclical history of civilizations …

Now turn about-face and view the Capitol Hill. Ahead of you is a staircase to the top. To the right of that is a church with an iron fence, labeled "MAMERTINUM." Let's drop in.

Capitol Hill

Mamertine Prison

Tip the monk (1,000 L will do), pass through the turnstile, and descend into the 2,500-year-old cistern. There came a time when Rome needed prisons more than extra water, and this former cistern became the Mamertine Prison, noted for its famous inmates. Inside, on the wall near the entryway you'll see lists of the most important prisoners and how they died. Secular criminals are listed on the left, Christian ones on the right. *Suppliziato* means quartered, *strangolati* is strangled, *morto di fame* is starvation … Saints Peter and Paul are said to have done time here.

The floor of the prison has a hole with a grate over it. Long before pilgrims added the more convenient stairs this was the standard entryway. Walk down the stairs past a supposed miraculous image of Peter's face when a guard pushed him into the wall. Downstairs you'll see the column that Peter was chained to. It's said that in this room a miraculous fountain sprung up so Peter could baptize other prisoners. The upside-down cross commemorates Peter's upside-down crucifixion.

● *Escape this prison and climb the long hot stairs past the guy who'll give you a deal on more slides and postcards of Rome than you could ever use and on up until you find a drinking fountain. Block the spout with your finger and a cool jet of refreshing water will knock your glasses off. Continue up to the large square on the hilltop.*

On the left-hand corner at the summit is the statue of the symbol of Rome—Romulus and Remus being suckled by the she-wolf. These were the mythological founders of Rome who, according to legend …

CAPITOL HILL

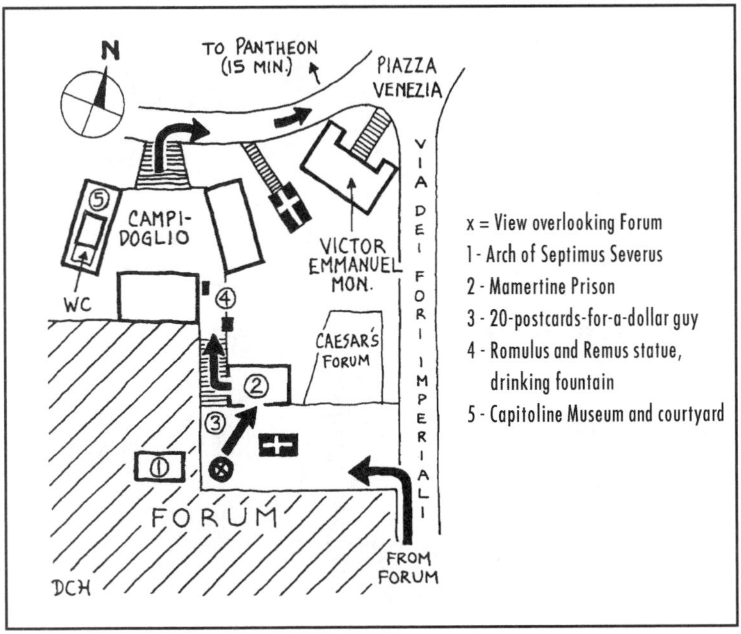

N

TO PANTHEON
(15 MIN.)
PIAZZA
VENEZIA

CAMPI-
DOGLIO

VICTOR
EMMANUEL
MON.

WC

CAESAR'S
FORUM

FORUM

DCH

FROM
FORUM

V I A   D E I   F O R I   I M P E R I A L I

x = View overlooking Forum
1 - Arch of Septimus Severus
2 - Mamertine Prison
3 - 20-postcards-for-a-dollar guy
4 - Romulus and Remus statue,
    drinking fountain
5 - Capitoline Museum and courtyard

OK, I know it's hot—let's skip the legend. This hilltop has been sacred to Romans ever since 500 B.C. when an Etruscan Temple of Jupiter stood here.

● *Enter the square and head for the stairs at the far end. Go down a few stairs, turn around, and come back up, entering the square the way its designer, Michelangelo, wanted you to …*

Michelangelo's Renaissance Piazza del Campidoglio

In spite of the awkward shape of the square, Michelangelo masterfully created a wonderfully harmonious space (the façades, grand stairway, and pavement design are his). Notice how the columns of the buildings ignore the fact that there are two stories, uniting the upper and lower halves and making the square a bit more intimate. The building with the fountain houses the offices and official residence of Rome's mayor. The other two are classical museums.

The Capitoline Museum (right) has many ancient statues, including a gallery of emperors' busts. Here you'll find the original Etruscan *Capitoline Wolf*, the famous *Boy with a Thorn in His Foot*, and a seductive statue of the demonic Emperor Commodus dressed as Hercules.

Its entertaining courtyard is littered with chunks of a giant statue of Constantine. How creative can you be with your camera? (A WC and fine bookshop are in the museum lobby. They sell a cool wall map of ancient Rome.) The entry to this building lists local marriages and it's not uncommon to see newlyweds here in cummerbunds of bliss.

● *Now descend the stairs for good and pause at the bottom.*

The Modern World

Look down the street to your left at the building which incorporates an ancient Roman colonnade into its walls. Then backtrack to the right and look up the long stairway that rises to the early Christian church high above you. There's no need to climb those stairs.

Follow the sidewalk to the right along the immense white Victor Emmanuel II monument. As you go, look down at and ponder on the forgotten parts of ancient Rome that lie quietly under the entire city. Leave the ancient world for a minute and walk to the front of the monument for a look at Italy's guarded Tomb of the Unknown Soldier and the eternal flame. Turn around to see the busy Piazza Venezia. The balcony of the palace on the right is where Mussolini whipped his fans into a fascist fury. The long Via del Corso stretching away from you is Rome's grand boulevard. Much of it is closed to traffic each early evening for the daily *passagiata* ritual—"cruising" without cars.

● *From the far end of Piazza Venezia (opposite the V.E. monument) walk left down Via del Plebiscito. At the first square (Largo Argentina) turn right and you'll walk straight three blocks to the Pantheon. Face the Pantheon from the obelisk fountain in front.*

The Pantheon

Exterior

It doesn't look like much from here, but this is perhaps the most influential building in art history. Its dome was the model for the Florence cathedral dome which launched the Renaissance and for

Michelangelo's dome of St. Peter's which capped it all off. Even Washington, D.C.'s Capitol was inspired by this dome.

The Pantheon was a Roman temple dedicated to all (*pan*) the gods (*theos*). First built in 27 B.C., it was completely rebuilt around A.D. 120 by the Emperor Hadrian. In a gesture of modesty admirable in anyone but astounding in a Roman emperor, Hadrian left his own name off of it, putting the name of the original builder on the front—"M. Agrippa."

● *Pass between the enormous one-piece granite columns and through the enormous original bronze door. Stand awestruck for a moment, then take a seat on the bench to your right.*

Interior

The dome, the largest made until modern times, is set on a circular base. The mathematical perfection of this dome-on-a-base design is a testament to Roman engineering. The dome is as high as it is wide—142 feet. (Imagine a basketball set inside a wastebasket so that it just touches bottom.)

The dome is made from concrete that gets lighter and thinner as it reaches the top. The walls at the base are 20 feet thick made from heavy travertine concrete, while near the top they're only five feet thick made of a light volcanic rock. Both Brunelleschi and Michelangelo studied this dome before building their own (in Florence and in the Vatican). Remember, St. Peter's Cathedral is really only "the dome of the Pantheon on top of the Basilica Maxentius."

The *oculus*, or eye-in-the-sky, at the top, the building's only light source, is almost 30 feet across. The 1,800-year-old floor has holes in it and slants towards the edges to let the rainwater drain. The marble floor is largely restored though the designs are close to the originals.

In ancient times, this was a one-stop-shopping temple where you could worship any of the gods whose statues decorated the niches. If you needed a favor, you might buy a live animal outside in the square, then have the priests sacrifice it on the altar placed in the center. The fumes would rise up through the *oculus* to heaven, where the gods could smell it and—if the odor was pleasing unto them—grant you a blessing.

This is Rome's best-preserved ancient building. What you see is what Hadrian, Constantine, Augustine, Charlemagne, Michelangelo, Dean Martin, and every other visitor to Rome has seen for the last 2,000 years. The barbarians passed it by when they sacked Rome. Early in the Middle Ages it became a Christian church (from "all the gods" to "all the martyrs") saving it from architectural cannibalism and ensuring its upkeep through the Dark Ages. The only major destruction came in the 17th century when the pope stole the bronze plating and melted it down to build the huge bronze canopy over the altar at St. Peter's. About the only new things in the interior are the decorative statues and the tombs of famous people like the artist Raphael (to the left of the main altar, in the glass case) and modern Italy's first king, Victor Emmanuel II (to the right).

The Pantheon is the only continuously used ancient building in Rome. When you leave you'll notice how the rest of the city has risen on 20 centuries of rubble.

The Pantheon also contains the world's greatest Roman column. There it is spanning the entire 142 feet from heaven to earth—the pillar of light from the *oculus*.

19 St. Peter's Cathedral

St. Peter's is the greatest church in Christendom. It represents the power and splendor of Rome's 2,000-year domination of the Western world. Built on the memory and grave of the first pope, St. Peter, this is where the grandeur of ancient Rome became the grandeur of Christianity.

BASILICA DI SAN PIETRO, VATICAN

Hours: Daily 7:00–19:00 May–September, 7:00–18:00 October–April; Mass daily at 9:00, 10:00, 11:00, 12:00, and 17:00, lift to the dome opens at 8:30 and closes one hour before the church closes. Best time to visit is early or late. Strictly enforced dress code—no shorts or bare shoulders.

Cost: Free

Tour length: One hour, plus another hour if you climb the dome, 300 feet.

Getting there: Subway to "Ottaviano," then 15-minute walk south on Via Ottaviano. Several city buses go right to St. Peter's Square (#64 is convenient but filled with pickpockets). Taxis are reasonable.

Information: There's a guide booth just inside front door. Tourist office on left side of square is excellent (free Vatican and church map). This office (open 8:30–18:30) conducts special insider tours for 18,000 L of the Vatican Gardens, offering the only way to see the gardens until shuttle bus service (between St. Peter's and the Vatican Museum) resumes in about 2000—book tours at least one day ahead in person or by fax at 06-6988-5100 (not by phone). Free, 90-minute English "Pilgrim Service" church tours usually leave at 10:00 and 12:30. Tel. 06-6988-4466. WCs to right and left (near tourist office) of church and on the roof. Drinking fountains at obelisk and near WCs. Post office next to tourist office on left of square (Vatican post is more reliable than Italian).

Cloakroom: Free, usually mandatory bag check is outside at right of entrance.

Starring: Michelangelo, Bernini, Bramante, St. Peter, a heavenly host, and, occasionally, the pope.

Old St. Peter's

● *Find a shady spot where you like the view under the columns around St. Peter's circular "square." Sit—if the pigeons left you a clean spot.*

Nearly 2,000 years ago this area was the site of Nero's Circus, a huge Roman chariot racecourse. The obelisk you see in the middle of the square was the centerpiece of the course. The Romans had no marching bands, so for halftime entertainment they killed Christians. This persecuted minority was forced to fight wild animals and gladiators, or they were simply crucified. Some were tarred up, tied to posts, and burned—human torches to light up the evening races.

One of those killed here, around A.D. 65, was Peter, Jesus' right-hand man who had come to Rome to spread the message of love. Peter was crucified on an upside-down cross at his own request because he felt unworthy to die as his master had. His remains were buried in a nearby cemetery where, for 250 years, they were quietly and secretly revered.

When Christianity was finally legalized in 313, the Christian emperor Constantine built a church on the site of the martyrdom of this first "pope," or bishop of Rome, from whom all later popes claimed their authority as head of the church. "Old St. Peter's" lasted 1,200 years (A.D. 324–1500).

By the time of the Renaissance, Old St. Peter's was falling apart and was considered unfit to be the center of the Western church. The new larger church we see today was begun in 1506, and actually built around the old one. As it was completed 120 years later, after many changes of plans, Old St. Peter's was dismantled and carried out the doors of the new one.

● *Ideally you should head out to the obelisk to view the square and read this. But let me guess—it's 95 degrees, right? Okay, stay in the shade of these stone sequoias awhile longer and read on.*

St. Peter's Square

St. Peter's Square with its ring of columns symbolizes the arms of the church reaching out to its people. It was designed by the Baroque architect Bernini, who also did much of the work we'll see inside. Numbers first—284 columns, 50 feet high, in stern Doric style. Topping them are Bernini's 140 favorite saints, 10 feet tall. The "square" itself is elliptical, 200 by 150 yards.

The obelisk in the center is 80 feet of solid granite weighing over 300 tons. Think for a second of how much history this monument has seen. Erected originally in Egypt over 2,000 years ago, it witnessed the fall of the pharoahs to the Greeks and then to the Romans. It was then

ST. PETER'S SQUARE

ST. PETER's CHURCH

BRAMANTE +
MICHELANGELO
GREEK
CROSS →
PLAN

(DOME)

N

MADERNO'S
ADDITION →

WC

1 - Obelisk

2 - Pope's apartments (top story, right)

3 - Sistine Chapel

4 - "Centro del Colonnato" plaque

5 - Post Office, Tourist Info, and bookstore

6 - Swiss Guard at Vatican City entrance

7 - Holy trinkets

③

⑥ ⑦

⑤

②

FOUNTAINS

① ④

VATICAN WALL

VIA DI PTA. ANGELICA →

TO SUBWAY
"OTTAVIANO" (15 MIN.)

↓
VATICAN MUSEUM (15 MIN.)

VIA DEL
CONCILIAZIONE

moved to Imperial Rome were it stood impassively watching the slaughter of Christians at the racecourse. Today it watches over the church, a reminder that each civilization builds on the previous ones. The puny cross on top only serves to remind us that much of our Christian culture is but a thin veneer over our pagan origins.

● *Now venture out across the burning desert to the obelisk which always provides a narrow sliver of shade.*

Face the church, then turn about-face and say *"Grazie, Benito."* I don't make a habit of going around thanking Fascist dictators, but

Benito Mussolini did at least one good thing with his power. This broad boulevard he built in the 1930s finally let people see the dome of St. Peter's that the façade had hidden for centuries. From here at the obelisk, Michelangelo's magnificent dome can only peek its top over the bulky Baroque front entrance. You have to back up into Mussolini's boulevard to truly appreciate Michelangelo's original vision.

The building at two o'clock to the right (as you face the church) rising up behind Bernini's colonnade is where the pope lives. The last window on the right of the top floor is his bedroom. The window to the left of that is his study, where he appears occasionally to greet the masses. If you come to the square at night as a Poping Tom, you might see the light on—the pope burns much midnight oil.

On more formal occasions (which you may have seen on TV) the pope appears on the balcony in the center of the church's façade, under the triangular pediment.

The Sistine Chapel is just to the right of the façade. The tiny chimney at the peak of its brown stone triangular roof (with the long antenna) is where the famous smoke signals announce the election of each new pope. If the smoke is black, a 75 percent majority hasn't been reached. White smoke means a new pope has been selected.

Walk to the right, five pavement plaques from the obelisk, to one marked "Centro del Colonnato." From here all of Bernini's columns on the right side line up. The curved Baroque square still pays its respects to Renaissance mathematical symmetry.

● *Climb the gradually sloping stairs past crowd barriers and the huge statues of St. Mark with his two-edged sword and St. Peter with his bushy hair and keys.*

Stop by the Vatican City entrance on the left side of the church. Guarding this border crossing into Vatican City—a separate country—are the mercenary guards from Switzerland. You have to wonder if they really know how to use those pikes. Their colorful uniforms are said to have been designed by Michelangelo, though he was not known for his sense of humor.

The Vatican is a country, tiny but powerful. It's a remnant of feudal Italy when there were countless king- and duke-doms. At one time the Vatican actually controlled a good chunk of Italy, and its territory was the last step in the unification of Italy just over a hundred years ago. Today the Vatican has its own stamps, radio station, a tiny train station, a heliport, a few bits of territory (actually, other churches) scattered in and around Rome, and more guards dressed to kill.

● *Enter the atrium (entrance hall) of the church. You'll pass by the dress-code enforcers and a gaggle of ticked-off guys in shorts.*

The Basilica

The Atrium

The atrium is itself bigger than most churches. Facing us are the five famous bronze doors—each a work of art. Each symbolic door leads into the main church. The central door, made from the melted-down bronze of the original door of Old St. Peter's, is only opened on special occasions.

The far right entrance is the Holy Door, opened only during Holy Years. On Christmas Eve every 25 years the pope knocks three times with a silver hammer and the door is opened. At the end of the year, he bricks it up again (as you'll see inside) with a ceremonial trowel to await another 24 years. On the door, note Jesus' shiny knees, polished by pious pilgrims who touch them for a blessing.

The other doors are modern, reminding us that amid all this tradition the Catholic Church has changed enormously even within our lifetimes. One has a portrait of a kneeling pope, John XXIII, who presided over the landmark "Vatican II" council in the early 1960s. This meeting of church leaders brought the medieval church into the modern age, making old doctrines—like the use of Latin in the Mass—"relevant" to the 20th century.

● *Now for one of Europe's great wow experiences. Enter the church. Look around and gape for a while. But don't gape at Michelangelo's famous* Pietà *(on the right). That's this tour's finale. I'll wait for you at the round maroon pavement stone between the entrance and exit doors.*

The Church

While ancient Rome fell, its grandeur survived. Roman basilicas became churches, senators became bishops, and the Pontifex Maximus … remained the Pontifex Maximus. This church is appropriately huge.

Size before beauty: The golden window at the far end is two football fields away. The dove in the window above the altar has the wingspan of a 747 (okay, maybe not quite, but it is big). The church covers six acres—if planted with wheat it could feed a small city. The babies at the base of the pillars along the main hall (the nave) are adult size. The lettering in the gold band along the top of the pillars is six feet high. Really. The church has a capacity of 95,000 worshippers standing (that's over 2,000 tour groups).

ST. PETER'S BASILICA

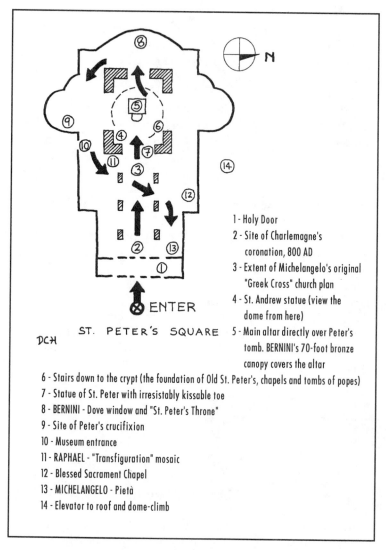

ST. PETER'S SQUARE

DCH

1 - Holy Door

2 - Site of Charlemagne's coronation, 800 AD

3 - Extent of Michelangelo's original "Greek Cross" church plan

4 - St. Andrew statue (view the dome from here)

5 - Main altar directly over Peter's tomb. BERNINI's 70-foot bronze canopy covers the altar

6 - Stairs down to the crypt (the foundation of Old St. Peter's, chapels and tombs of popes)

7 - Statue of St. Peter with irresistably kissable toe

8 - BERNINI - Dove window and "St. Peter's Throne"

9 - Site of Peter's crucifixion

10 - Museum entrance

11 - RAPHAEL - "Transfiguration" mosaic

12 - Blessed Sacrament Chapel

13 - MICHELANGELO - Pietà

14 - Elevator to roof and dome-climb

The church is huge and it feels huge, but everything is actually designed to make it seem smaller than it really is. Its Baroque architects went to great lengths to give it a surprisingly intimate and homey atmosphere despite the overwhelming size and decoration. For example, the statue of St. Theresa at the bottom of the first pillar on the

right is 15 feet tall. The statue above her near the top looks the same size but is actually six feet taller, giving the impression that it's not as far away as it really is. Similarly, the fancy bronze canopy over the altar at the far end is as tall as a seven-story building. That makes the great height of the dome seem smaller.

Looking down the nave we get a sense of the grandeur of ancient Rome that was carried on by the Catholic Church. The floor plan is based on the ancient Roman basilica, or law court building, with a central aisle (nave) flanked by two side aisles.

The goal of this unprecedented building project was to "put the dome of the Pantheon on top of the Roman Forum's Basilica Maxentius." If you've seen these two Roman structures you have an idea of this mega-vision. In fact, many of the stones used to build St. Peter's were scavenged from the ruined basilicas of the ancient Roman Forum.

On the floor near the central doorway is a round slab of porphyry stone in the maroon color of ancient Roman officials. This is the spot where, on Christmas night, A.D. 800, the French King Charlemagne was crowned "Holy Roman Emperor." Even in the Dark Ages, when Rome was virtually abandonded and people reported that the city "had more thieves and wolves than decent people," its imperial legacy made it a fitting place to symbolically establish a briefly united Europe.

You're surrounded by marble, gold, stucco, mosaics, columns of stone, and pillars of light. This is Baroque, the decorative style intended to overwhelm and impress the masses with the authority of the church. St. Peter's was very expensive to build and decorate. The popes financed it by selling "indulgences," or papal pardons. The rich could literally buy forgiveness from the church. This kind of corruption inspired an obscure German monk named Martin Luther to rebel and start the Protestant Reformation. The Baroque interior by Bernini was part of the church's "Counter"-Reformation, a time when the church aggressively defended itself and art became a powerful propaganda tool. Here we see a glorious golden vision of heaven available to everyone—if they remained a good Catholic.

● *Now, walk straight up the center of the nave toward the altar.*

"Michelangelo's Church" — The Greek Cross

The plaques on the floor show where other, smaller churches of the world would end if they were placed inside St. Peter's: St. Paul's Cathedral in London (Londinense), the Florence Cathedral, and so on.

You'll also walk over circular golden grates. Stop at the second one (at the third pillar from the entrance). Look back at the entrance and realize that if Michelangelo had had his way, this whole long section of the church wouldn't exist. The nave was extended after his death.

Michelangelo was 72 years old when the pope persuaded him to take over the church project and cap it with a dome. He agreed on three conditions: (1) that he receive no payment; (2) that he have a thousand workers at his disposal in order to finish it in his lifetime; and (3) that he could put the dome over a "Greek Cross" floor plan. Of these three conditions, the Pope was more than happy to meet the first one. But Michelangelo died (18 years later) before the project was completed, and later architects changed the original design. They extended the Greek cross into a Latin cross plan.

The Greek cross plan (+) called for a central dome topping four equal arms. In Renaissance times this symmetrical arrangement symbolized perfection—the orderliness of the created world and the goodness of man (who was created in God's image). But Michelangelo was a Renaissance Man in Counter-Reformation times. The church, struggling against Protestants and its own corruption, opted for a plan designed to impress the world with its grandeur—the Latin cross of the Crucifixion with its extended nave to accommodate the grand religious spectacles of the Baroque period.

● *Continue toward the altar, entering Michelangelo's Church. Park yourself in front of the statue of St. Andrew to the left of the altar, the guy holding an X-shaped cross. Like Andrew, gaze up into the dome. Gasp if you must—never stifle a gasp.*

The Dome

The dome soars higher than a football field on end, 390 feet to the top of the lantern. It glows with light from its windows, the blue and gold mosaics creating a cool, solemn atmosphere. In this majestic vision of heaven we see (above the windows) Jesus, Mary, and a ring of saints, more rings of angels above them, and way up in the ozone, God the Father (a blur of blue and red, without binoculars).

Listen to the hum of visitors echoing through St. Peter's. Churches are an early form of biofeedback where we can become aware of ourselves, our own human sounds, and can reflect on our place in the cosmos. Half animal, half angel, stretched between heaven and earth, born to live only a short while, a bubble of foam on a great cresting wave of humanity.

Peter

The base of the dome is ringed with a banner telling us in letters six feet tall why this church is the most important in Catholicism. According to Catholics, Peter was selected by Jesus to head the church. The banner in Latin quotes from the Bible where

Jesus says to him, "You are Peter (*Tu es Petrus* ...) and upon this rock I will build my church" (Matthew 16:18). Peter was the first bishop of Rome, and his authority has supposedly passed in an unbroken chain to each succeeding bishop of Rome—that is, the 250-odd popes that followed.

Under the dome, under the bronze canopy, under the altar, some 20 feet under the marble floor rest the bones of St. Peter, the "rock" upon which this particular church was built. Go to the railing and look down into the small lighted niche eight feet below the altar with a box containing bishops' shawls—a symbol of how Peter's authority spread to the other churches. Peter's tomb is several feet below this box.

Are they really the bones of Jesus' apostle? According to a papal pronouncement: definitely maybe. The traditional site of his tomb was sealed up when Old St. Peter's was built on it in A.D. 326 and remained sealed until 1940 when it was opened for archaeological study. Bones were found, dated from the first century, of a robust man who died in old age, whose body was wrapped in expensive cloth. Various inscriptions and graffiti in the tomb indicate that second and third century visitors thought this was Peter's tomb. Does that mean it's really Peter? Who am I to disagree with the pope? Definitely maybe.

If you line up the cross on the altar with the dove in the window you'll notice that the niche below the cross is a foot-and-a-half off-center left with the rest of the church. Why? Because Michelangelo designed the church around the traditional location of the tomb, not the actual location discovered by modern archaeology.

● *You can go down to the crypt and the foundations of Old St. Peter's, containing tombs of Popes and memorial chapels. The staircase is to your right. It's free, but the visit takes you back outside the church, a 15-minute detour ending up at a water fountain, a WC, a wacky-sometimes-tacky religious souvenir store, and the elevator to the dome.*

To the right of the staircase, in the nave, is a bronze statue of Peter under a canopy. This is one of a handful of pieces of art that was in the earlier church. In one hand he holds the keys, the symbol of the authority given him by Christ, while with the other he blesses us. He's wearing the toga of a Roman senator. It may be that the original statue was of a senator and the bushy head and keys were added later to make it Peter. His big right toe has been worn smooth by the lips of pilgrims. Stand in line and kiss it, or, if

you're worried about hoof and mouth disease, touch your hand to your lips, then rub the toe. This is simply an act of reverence with no legend attached, though you can make one up if you like.

The Main Altar

The main altar beneath the dome is used only when the pope himself says Mass. He often conducts the Sunday morning service when he's in town, a sight worth seeing. I must admit, though, it's a little strange being frisked at the door for weapons at the holiest place in Christendom.

The white marble slab of the altar would be lost in this enormous church if it weren't for Bernini's seven-story bronze canopy which "extends" the altar upward and reduces the perceived distance between floor and ceiling. Bernini, who designed the Baroque interior, gave a surprising unity to an amazing variety of pillars, windows, statues, chapels, and aisles. The canopy is his crowning touch. The Baroque-looking corkscrew columns are actually copies of ancient columns from Old St. Peter's. The bronze used was stolen and melted down from the ancient Pantheon.

On the marble base of the columns you see three bees on a shield, the symbol of the Barberini family who commissioned the work and ordered the raid on the Pantheon. As the saying went, "What the Barbarians didn't do, the Barberini did."

Starting from the column to the left of the altar, walk clockwise around the canopy. Notice the female faces on the marble bases, about eye level above the bees. Someone in the Barberini

family was pregnant during the making of the canopy, so Bernini put the various stages of childbirth on the bases. Continue clockwise to the last base to see how it came out.

● *Walk into the apse (it's the area with the golden dove window) and take a seat.*

The Apse

Bernini also did the dove window over the smaller front altar which is used for everyday services. The Holy Spirit in the form of a six foot dove shines light on the faithful as sunlight pours through the alabaster windows, turning into artificial rays of gold and reflecting off swirling gold clouds, angels, and winged babies. This is the epitome of Baroque—a highly decorative, glorious, mixed-media work designed to overwhelm the viewer.

Beneath the dove is the centerpiece of this structure, the so-called "Throne of Peter," an oak chair built in medieval times for a Holy Roman emperor and subsequently encrusted with tradition and encased in bronze by Bernini as a symbol of papal authority. Statues of four early church fathers support the chair, a symbol of how bishops should support the pope in troubled times— times like the Counter-Reformation. Bernini's Baroque was great propaganda for the power of the Catholic Church.

This is a good place to remember that this is a church, not a museum. In the apse, Mass is said daily at 5:00 p.m. for pilgrims and Roman citizens alike. (You're welcome to take communion during any Mass.) Wooden confessional booths are available for Catholics to tell their sins to a listening ear and receive forgiveness and peace of mind. The faithful renew their faith and the faithless gain inspiration. Sit here, look at the light streaming through the windows, turn and gaze up into the dome, and quietly contemplate your god.

Or ...

Contemplate this: the mystery of empty space. The bench you're sitting on and the marble at your feet, solid as they may seem, consist overwhelmingly of open space—99.9999 percent open space. The atoms that form these "solid" benches are themselves mostly open space. If the nucleus of your average atom were as large as the period at the end of this sentence, its electrons would be specks of dust orbiting around it ...at the top of Michelangelo's dome. Empty space. Perhaps matter is only an aberration in an empty universe.

● *Like wow. Poke around the south transept, the arm to the left of the bronze canopy (as you approach from the entrance). Look at the Bernini doorway with the gold skeleton smothered in jasper poured like maple syrup. Bizarre Baroque.*

Now look left to the far end with the painting of St. Peter crucified upside down.

Left Transept

The painting is at the exact spot (according to tradition) where Peter was killed 1,900 years ago.

The Romans were actually quite tolerant of other religions. All they required of their conquered peoples was allegiance to the empire by worshiping the emperor as a god. For most religions this was no problem, but monotheistic Christians were children of a jealous God who would not allow worship of any others. They refused to worship the emperor and valiantly stuck by their faith even when burned alive, crucified, or thrown to the lions. Their bravery, optimism in suffering, and message of love struck a chord among slaves and members of the lower classes. The religion started by a poor carpenter grew despite occasional "pogroms" by fanatical emperors. In three short centuries, Christianity went from a small Jewish sect in Jerusalem to the official religion of the world's greatest empire.

If you like old jewels and papal robes, St. Peter's Museum (Museo—Tesoro) is just past the transept on your right. It displays the treasures and splendors of Roman Christianity, a marked contrast to the poverty of early Christians.

Opposite the entrance to the museum is a large painting. This "painting" is no painting at all. It's a mosaic, like all but one of the pictures in St. Peter's, since smoke and humidity would damage real paintings. This is made with thousands of colored chips the size of your little fingernail. The Vatican's renowned mosaic studio boasts that it builds these "paintings" with 5,000 shades of color to choose from.

Around the corner on the right (heading back towards the central nave), pause at the copy of Raphael's huge painting *The Transfiguration*, especially if you won't be seeing the original in the Vatican Museum.

● *Cross the nave to the other side of the church, then head back towards the entrance. You're welcome to step into the Blessed Sacrament Chapel, an oasis of peace reserved for prayer and meditation inside metal-work gates.*

Continue toward the entrance of the church. In the corner, behind bullet-proof glass is ...

The *Pietà*

Michelangelo was 24 years old when he completed this *Pietà*. A pietà (pron: pee-ay-TAH) is a work showing Mary with the dead body of Christ taken from the cross. Here, Mary cradles her crucified son in her lap.

Michelangelo, with his total mastery of the real world, captures the sadness of the moment. Christ's lifeless right arm drooping down lets us know how heavy this corpse is. His smooth skin is accented by the rough folds of Mary's robe. Mary tilts her head downward, looking at her dead son with sad tenderness. Her left hand is upturned as if asking, "How could they do this to you?"

Michelangelo didn't think of sculpting as creating a figure, but as simply freeing the God-made figure from the prison of marble around it. He'd attack a project like this with an inspired passion, chipping away to reveal what God put inside.

Realistic as this work is, its true power lies in the subtle "unreal" features. Look how small and childlike Christ is compared with the massive Mary. Unnoticed at first, this accentuates the subconscious impression of Mary enfolding Jesus in her maternal love. Notice how young Mary is. She's the mother of a 33-year-old man, but here she's portrayed as a teenage girl. Michelangelo did it to show how Mary was the eternally youthful "handmaiden" of the Lord, always serving Him even at this moment of supreme sacrifice. She accepts God's will, even if it means giving up her own son.

The statue is a solid pyramid of maternal tenderness. Yet within this, Christ's body tilts diagonally down to the right and Mary's hem flows with it. Subconsciously we feel the weight of this dead God sliding from her lap to the ground.

On Christmas morning, 1972, a madman with a hammer entered St. Peter's and began hacking away at the *Pietà*. The damage was repaired, but that's why there's the shield of bulletproof glass.

This is Michelangelo's only signed work. The story goes that he overheard some people praising his finished *Pietà*, but attributing it to a second-rate sculptor from a lesser city. He was so enraged he grabbed his chisel and chipped "Michelangelo Buonarotti of Florence did this" in the ribbon running down Mary's chest.

On your right is the inside of the Holy Door, mortared up until it will next be opened, on Christmas Eve, 1999. If there's a prayer inside you, maybe ask that when it's opened for Holy Year 2000, St. Peter's will no longer need security checks or bulletproof glass.

● *Back outside, follow signs (left) to "Cupola."*

Up to the Dome

A good way to finish a visit to St. Peter's is to go up to the dome for a view of Rome. Take the elevator to the roof with a commanding view of St. Peter's Square, the statues on the colonnade, Rome across the Tiber in front of you, and the dome itself—almost terrifying in its nearness—looming behind you.

If you're energetic, climb up the dome itself for the best view of Rome anywhere. The staircase actually winds between the outer shell and the inner one. It's a long, sweaty, stuffy, claustrophobic 10-minute climb, but worth it. The view from the summit is great, the fresh air even better. Find the big white Victor Emmanuel Monument with the two statues on top and the Pantheon with its large light shallow dome. The large rectangular building to the left of the obelisk is the Vatican Museum, stuffed with art. Survey the Vatican grounds with its mini-train system and lush gardens. The climb back down is much faster and easier—in these stairways, people circulate better than air.

(The dome opens daily at 8:00 and closes at 18:00 April–September and at 17:00 October–March. Allow one hour for the full trip up and down, a half hour to go only to the roof and gallery.)

Even if you don't hike to the summit, from the elevator everyone goes up a few steps to the gallery ringing the interior of the dome. From here you look down inside the church. Notice the dusty top of Bernini's seven-story-tall canopy far below, study the mosaics up close … and those six-foot letters! It's worth the elevator ride for this view alone, to look down into the church and on the tiny pilgrims buzzing like electrons around the nucleus of Catholicism.

20 The Vatican Museum

The glories of the ancient world displayed in a lavish papal palace, decorated by the likes of Michelangelo and Raphael ... the Museo Vaticano (pron: mew-ZAY-oh vah-tee-KAHN-oh). Unfortunately, many tourists see the Vatican Museum as an obstacle between them and its grand finale, the Sistine Chapel. True, this huge, confusing, and crowded mega-museum can be a jungle, but with this book as your vine, you should swing through with ease, enjoying the highlights and getting to the Sistine just before you collapse. On the way, we'll enjoy some of the less appreciated but equally important sections of this warehouse of Western civilization.

MUSEO VATICANO

Hours: From April to mid-June and in September and October, open Monday–Friday 8:45–16:30, Saturday 8:45–13:45, closed Sunday except last Sunday of the month (when it's free and open 8:45–13:45). Rest of the year open Monday–Saturday 8:45–13:45. Closed 13 religious holidays, including Corpus Christi and St. Peter and Paul Day (June 29), and Assumption Day (August 15). Some individual rooms close at odd hours, especially after 13:00. A lighted board at the ground level entrance lists closures. The rooms we'll see are generally open. Modest dress (no short shorts) is appropriate, and often required, to visit the museum. It's generally hot and crowded. Saturday, Sunday, and Monday are the worst; late afternoons are best. Last entrance is 30 minutes before closing, Sistine closes 30 minutes early.

Cost: 18,000 L, free on last Sunday of each month.

Tour length: Until you expire, or 2.5 hours, whichever comes first.

Getting there: Subway to "Ottaviano" and a 15-minute walk. It's a 15-minute walk from St. Peter's Square. Taxis are reasonable (hop in and say "mew-ZAY-oh vah-tee-KAHN-oh").

Information: Information booth on ground floor at entry (English spoken). The museum has signs to four color-coded, self-guided tours (A—the Sistine blitz, C—a good tour, D—everything). If you veer from our tour you'll find pretty good English explanations. You can (but I wouldn't) rent cassette tours of the Raphael Rooms and Sistine just before the Raphael Rooms. Post office, writing room, exchange bank, and bookshop are next to the ticket booth. Tel. 06-6988-3333.

Cuisine art: There's a great produce market three blocks directly in front of the entrance.

Starring: Michelangelo, Raphael, Laocoön, the Greek masters, and their Roman copyists.

THE POPE'S COLLECTION

● *Leave Italy by entering the doors. Climb the impressive, modern double-spiral staircase or take the lift. At the top are the ticket windows.*

Find a quiet spot to read ahead—try the writing tables in the lobby post office. Or buy your ticket, pass through the entry, then pull off into the courtyard immediately to your left or the courtyard near the cafeteria.

With the fall of Rome, the Catholic (or "universal") Church became the great preserver of civilization, collecting artifacts from cultures dead and dying. Renaissance popes (15th and 16th centuries) collected most of what we'll see. Those lusty priests-as-Roman-emperors loved the ancient world. They built these palaces and decorated them with classical statues and Renaissance paintings. They combined the classical and Christian worlds, finding the divine in the creations of man.

We'll concentrate on classical sculpture and Renaissance painting. But along the way (and there's a lot of along-the-way in this place), we'll stop to leaf through a few yellowed pages from the 5,000-year-

VATICAN MUSEUM—OVERVIEW

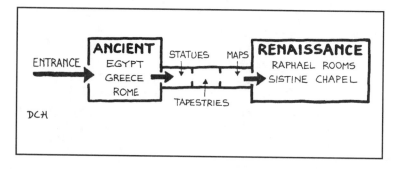

old scrapbook of mankind. The museum's one-way-only policy makes it difficult to get lost, so directions will be kept to a minimum.

This heavyweight museum is shaped like a barbell—two buildings connected by a long hall. The building you're now in contains the ancient world, the one at the far end (near St. Peter's) is the Renaissance (including the Sistine Chapel). The halls there and back are a mix of old and new.

We're headed to see three of the greatest Greek sculptures, but we have to pass through the Egyptian collection first. Move quickly—don't burn out before the Sistine Chapel at the end—but by pausing to look at some of the things along the way, you'll see how each civilization borrows from and builds on the previous one.

● *Follow the crowds down the corridor to the left of the cafeteria courtyard, turn left up the stairs, then right into the Egyptian Rooms. Don't stop until you find your mummy.*

Egypt (3000–1000 B.C.)

Egyptian art was for religion, not decoration. A statue or painting preserved the likeness of someone, giving him a form of eternal life. Most of the art was for tombs, where they put the mummies. Notice that the art is only realistic enough to get the job done. You can recognize that it's a man, a bird, or whatever, but these are stiff, two-dimensional, schematic figures … functional rather than beautiful.

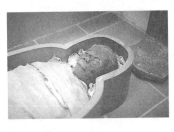

Mummies

In the second room, a large glass case contains the mummy of a woman from about 1000 B.C. The Egyptians tried to cheat death by preserving their corpses. In the next life, the spirit was homeless without its body. They'd mummify the body, place it in a wooden coffin and, often, put that coffin inside a larger one made of stone.

To mummify a body: disembowel it (store the organs in canopic jars, displayed nearby), fill the body cavities with pitch or other substances, and dry the body with natron, a natural form of sodium carbonate. Wrap it head to toe with fine linen strips and place in a coffin.

Notice what the deceased "packed" for the journey to eternity, painted inside the coffins. The insides of the coffin were decorated with magical spells to protect the body from evil and to act as crib notes for the confused soul in the nether world.

ANCIENT WORLD—EGYPT, GREECE, ROME

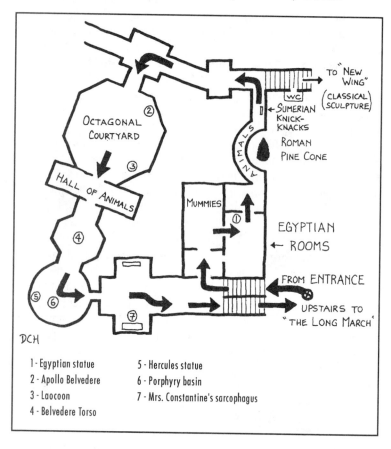

TO "NEW WING"
(CLASSICAL SCULPTURE)

OCTAGONAL COURTYARD

② ③

HALL OF ANIMALS

④

⑤ ⑥

⑦

WC
←SUMERIAN KNICK-KNACKS
ROMAN PINE CONE

ANIMALS

MUMMIES
①

EGYPTIAN
← ROOMS

FROM ENTRANCE

UPSTAIRS TO "THE LONG MARCH"

DCH

1 - Egyptian statue
2 - Apollo Belvedere
3 - Laocoon
4 - Belvedere Torso

5 - Hercules statue
6 - Porphyry basin
7 - Mrs. Constantine's sarcophagus

Egyptian Statues

Remember these statues as you look at later, more realistic Greek sculpture. Stiff and unnatural, they step out awkwardly with arms straight down at their sides. Each was made according to an established set of porportions. Little changed over the centuries. These had a function and they worked. In Egyptian belief, a statue like this could be a place of refuge for the wandering soul of a dead man.

● *Continuing on through several rooms, you'll turn left down a curving corridor overrun with animals.*

Various Egyptian Gods as Animals

Before technology made humans top dog on earth, it was easier to appreciate our fellow creatures. The Egyptians saw the superiority of animals, and worshiped them as incarnations of the gods. Wander through a pet store of Egyptian animal gods. The lioness portrays the fierce goddess Sekhmet, the clever baboon is the god of wisdom, Thot, and Horus has a falcon's head.

● *Continue through three more rooms, pausing at the glass case in the third room, containing brown clay tablets.*

Sumerian Writing

Even before Egypt, civilizations flourished in the Middle East. The Sumerian culture in Mesopotamia (modern Iraq) invented writing around 3000 B.C. You can see the clay tablets with this cuneiform (wedge-shaped) script. Also see the ingenious cylinder seals with which they made impressions in soft clay to seal documents and mark property.

● *Pass through the next small room of Assyrian bas reliefs and go left. But for an* optional *detour—I'll wait for you here—tumble down the stairs (WC nearby) into a gallery lined with 976 portrait busts. Then turn right into the …*

New Wing (Braccio Nuovo) of Classical Statues

A Greek and Roman statue hall of fame, including busts of all your favorite gods and emperors. The Romans may not have been great artists in general, but one area they excelled in was portrait busts. The Roman religion required realistic portrait busts of the emperor, who was worshiped as a god, and the family patriarch, who was revered as the preserver of tradition. Look into their eyes and try to see the flesh-and-blood man behind the noble pose.

● *Return up the stairs (catching the view of Rome out the window to your right), then left into the octagonal courtyard. There are benches in the middle.*

Sculpture —
Greece and Rome (500 B.C.–A.D. 500)

This palace wouldn't be here, this sculpture wouldn't be here, and you'd be spending your vacation in South Dakota at Reptile Gardens if it weren't for a few thousand Greeks in a small city about 450 years before Christ. Athens set the tone for the rest of the West. Democracy, theater, economics, literature, and art all got their start there during a 50-year period. Greek culture was then appropriated by Rome and revived again 1,500 years later during the Renaissance. The Renaissance popes built and decorated these palaces, recreating the glory of the classical world.

Apollo Belvedere

The Greeks loved balance. A well-balanced man was both a thinker and an athlete, a poet and a warrior. In their art they also wanted balance. The *Apollo Belvedere* is possibly the best example in the world. Apollo, the god of the sun and also music, is hunting. He has spotted his prey and is about to go after it with his (missing) bow and arrows.

Compare this with the stiff Egyptian statues we saw. Here, the great Greek sculptor Praxiteles has fully captured the beauty of the human form. The anatomy is perfect, the pose is natural. Instead of standing at attention, face forward with his arms at his sides, Apollo is on the move, stepping forward slightly with his weight on one leg.

Though this is an action shot, the overall mood is of balance and serenity. Apollo eyes his target, but hasn't attacked yet. He's moving, but not out of control. He's also a balance between a real person and an ideal god. And the smoothness of his muscles is balanced by the rough folds of his cloak.

During the Renaissance, when this Roman copy of the original Greek work was discovered, it was considered the most perfect work of art in the world. The handsome face, eternal youth, and the body that seems to float a half-inch off the pedestal made it an object of wonder and almost worship. Apollo's grace was something superhuman, divine, and godlike, even for devout Christians.

● *In the neighboring niche to the left, a bearded old Roman river god is lounging in the shade. This is a pose that inspired Michelangelo's Adam in the Sistine Chapel (coming soon). While there are a few fancy bathtubs in this courtyard, most of the carved boxes you see in this museum are sarcophagi—Roman coffins and relic-holders, carved with the deceased's epitaph in picture form.*

● *See how we've come full circle in this building—the Egyptian Rooms are ahead on your left. We now start the Long March toward the Sistine Chapel and Raphael Rooms.*

Go up the stairs one flight (don't look back—there's a world-class Etruscan collection) and prepare to enter the long, long hall lined with statues.

The Long March — Sculpture, Tapestries, Maps, and Views

Remember, this building was originally a series of papal palaces. They loved beautiful things, and as heirs of Imperial Rome, they felt they deserved such luxury. This quarter-mile walk gives you a sense of the scale that Renaissance popes built on. The palaces and art represent both the peak and the decline of the Catholic Church in Europe. It was extravagant spending like this that inspired Martin Luther to rebel, starting the Protestant Reformation.

Gallery of the Candelabra— Classical Sculpture

This statue gallery is named for the large Roman candlesticks that separate the "rooms." In the second room, stop at the statue *Diana the Huntress* on the left. Here, the virgin goddess goes hunting. Roman hunters would pray to statues like this to get divine help in their hunt for food.

THE LONG MARCH

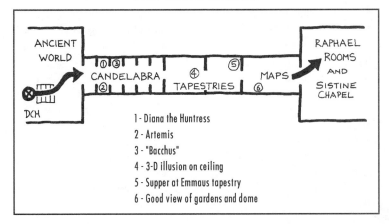

ANCIENT WORLD

DCH

CANDELABRA

TAPESTRIES

MAPS

RAPHAEL ROOMS AND SISTINE CHAPEL

1 - Diana the Huntress
2 - Artemis
3 - "Bacchus"
4 - 3-D illusion on ceiling
5 - Supper at Emmaus tapestry
6 - Good view of gardens and dome

Farmers might pray to another version of the same goddess, *Artemis*, on the opposite wall. This billion-boobed beauty stood for fertility. "Boobs or bulls' balls?" That's the question historians debate. Some say that bulls were sacrificed and castrated, with the testicles draped over the statues as symbols of fertility.

● *Shuffle along to the* Bacchus *on the left with a baby on his shoulders.*

Fig Leaves

Why do the statues have fig leaves? Like *Bacchus*, many of these statues originally looked much different than they do now. First off, they were painted, usually in gaudy colors. *Bacchus* may have had brown hair, rosy cheeks, and purple grapes. Even the *Apollo Belvedere*, whose cool grey tones we now admire as "classic Greek austerity," may have had a hot pink cloak or some such. Also, many statues had glass eyes like the little *Bacchus* here.

And the fig leaves? Those came from 1550–1800 when the church decided that certain parts of the human anatomy were obscene. (Why they didn't pick the feet, which are universally ugly, I'll never know.) Or perhaps the church leaders associated these full-frontal statues with the outbreak of Renaissance humanism that reduced their power in Europe. Whatever, they reacted by covering classical crotches with plaster fig leaves, the same leaves Adam and Eve had used when the concept of "privates" was invented.

Note: The leaves could be removed at any time if the museum officials were so motivated. There are suggestion boxes around the museum. Whenever I see a fig leaf, I get the urge to picket. We could start an organized campaign …

● *Cover your eyes in case they forgot a fig leaf or two and continue to the tapestries.*

Tapestries

Along the left wall are tapestries designed by Raphael and his workshop and made in Brussels. They show scenes from the life of Christ, starting with the *Slaughter of the Innocents* before his birth.

Check out the beautiful sculpted reliefs on the ceiling, especially the panel near the end of the first tapestry room showing a centurion ordering Eskimo Pies from a vendor. Admire the workmanship of this relief, then realize that it's not a relief at all—it's painted on a flat surface!

Illusions like this were proof that painters had mastered realism. In the tapestry *The Supper at Emmaus* at the end the second tapestry room, watch how the head of the table follows you as you walk past.

Map Gallery

This gallery still feels like a pope's palace, with the ornate decoration and the view of the Vatican gardens. Look out the third or fourth window on your right. The Vatican is a separate state, formed in 1929. It has its own radio station, as you see from the tower on the hill. What you see here is pretty much all there is—these gardens, the palaces you're in, and St. Peter's. If you lean out and look left you'll see the dome of St. Peter's the way Michelangelo would have liked you to see it—without the bulky Baroque façade.

The ceiling here is pure papal splendor. The maps are decorations from the 16th century. You can plan the next leg of your trip with the two maps of Italy at the far end of the hall— "New Italy" and "Old Italy"—both with a smoking Mt. Vesuvius next to Napoli/ Neapolis/Naples. There's an interesting old map of Venice on the right as you exit.

● *Take a breather in the next small tapestry hall before turning left into the crowded Raphael Rooms.*

Renaissance Art
Raphael Rooms — Papal Wallpaper

We've seen art from the ancient world; now we'll see its rebirth in the Renaissance. We're about to enter the main palaces built by the great Renaissance popes. This is where they lived, worked, and worshiped. They wanted these rooms to reflect the grandeur of their position. They hired the best artists—mostly from Florence—to paint the walls and ceilings. The decorations combine classical and Christian values.

We'll see a suite of several rooms painted by Raphael and then the Sistine Chapel by Michelangelo.

● *Turn left, and pass through two rooms.*

The first room has a huge non-Raphael painting on the wall of Sobieski liberating Vienna from the Muslim Turks in 1683, finally tipping the tide in favor of a Christian Europe. See the Muslim tents on the left and the spires of Christian Vienna on the right.

The second room's paintings celebrate the doctrine of the Immaculate Conception, establishing that Mary herself was conceived free from original sin. This medieval idea wasn't actually made dogma until a century ago. Modern popes have had to defend this and other doctrines against the onslaught of the modern world, which questions "superstitions," the divinity of Jesus, and the infallibility of the pope.

● *Next, you'll pass along an outside ramp overlooking a courtyard (is that the pope's car?), finally ending up in the first of the Raphael Rooms—the Constantine Room.*

Constantine Room

Only one of these scenes from the life of Constantine was personally designed by Raphael (roff-eye-ELL), but the room is fascinating anyway.

The frescoes celebrate the passing of the baton from one culture to the next. Remember, Rome was a pagan empire persecuting a fanatic cult from the East—Christianity.

....

RAPHAEL ROOMS

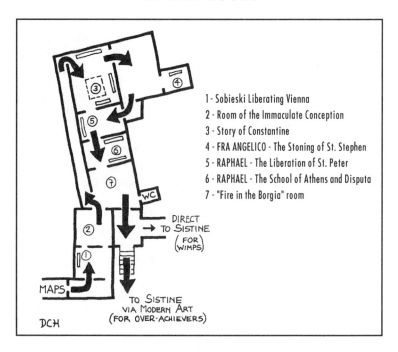

1 - Sobieski Liberating Vienna
2 - Room of the Immaculate Conception
3 - Story of Constantine
4 - FRA ANGELICO - The Stoning of St. Stephen
5 - RAPHAEL - The Liberation of St. Peter
6 - RAPHAEL - The School of Athens and Disputa
7 - "Fire in the Borgia" room

WC

DIRECT TO SISTINE (FOR WIMPS)

MAPS

TO SISTINE VIA MODERN ART (FOR OVER-ACHIEVERS)

DCH

Then, on the night of October 27, A.D. 312 (left wall), as Constantine was preparing his troops for a *coup d'état*, he saw something strange. A cross appeared in the sky with the words, "You will conquer in this sign."

Next day (front wall), his troops raged victoriously into battle with the Christian cross atop their Roman eagle banners. There's

Constantine in the center, slashing through the enemy, with God's warrior angels riding shotgun overhead.

Constantine was supposedly baptized a Christian (right wall). As emperor, he legalized Christianity and worked hand in hand with the pope (window wall). Rome soon became a Christian empire that would dominate Europe. Even after the government fell, Rome's glory lived on through the Dark Ages in the pomp, pageantry, and learning of the Catholic Church.

Look at the ceiling painting. A classical statue falls and crumbles before the overpowering force of the cross. Whoa! Christianity triumphs over pagan Rome. (This was painted, I believe, by Raphael's colleague, Salvadoro Dalio.)

● *In the next room, there's a small chapel in the far corner. Check out the fresco there on the left wall, upper part.*

The Stoning of St. Stephen

Raphael wasn't the only famous painter to work here. Italy's greatest painters preceded him. Two generations earlier, the Florentine monk Fra Angelico decorated part of this tiny room. In this scene the early Christian martyr is stoned during a heavenly vision. The apostle Paul, who started out as a harsh critic of Christianity, stands to the side holding the cloaks of the executioners.

● *Return to the main room and enjoy one of the rarest of rare artifacts, a bench.*

Raphael

Raphael was only 25 when Pope Julius II invited him to paint the walls of his private apartments. Julius was so impressed by Raphael's talent that he had the work of earlier masters scraped off and gave Raphael free rein to paint what he wanted.

Raphael lived a charmed life. He painted masterpieces effortlessly. He was handsome and sophisticated, and soon became Julius' favorite. In a different decade, he might have been thrown out of the Church as a great sinner, but his love affairs and devil-may-care personality seemed to epitomize the optimistic pagan spirit of the Renaissance. His works are graceful, but never lightweight or frilly—they're strong, balanced, and harmonious in the best Renaissance tradition. When he died young in 1520, the High Renaissance died with him.

● *Continue through the next small hallway. In the following room, block the sunlight with your hand to see ...*

The Liberation of St. Peter

Peter, Jesus' right-hand man, was thrown into prison in Jerusalem for his beliefs. In the middle of the night, an angel appeared and rescued him from the sleeping guards (Acts 12). The chains miraculously fell away (and were later brought to the St. Peter in Chains church in Rome) and the angel led him to safety (right) while the guards took hell from their captain (left). This little "play" is neatly divided into three separate acts that make a balanced composition.

Raphael makes the miraculous event even more dramatic with the use of three kinds of light illuminating the dark cell—half-moonlight, the captain's torch, and the radiant angel. Raphael's mastery of realism, rich colors, and sense of drama made him understandably famous.

● *Enter the next room ...*

The School of Athens

In both style and subject matter, this fresco sums up the spirit of the Renaissance, which was not only the rebirth of classical art, it was a rebirth of learning, of discovery, of the optimistic spirit that man is a rational creature. Raphael pays respect to the great thinkers and scientists of ancient Greece gathered together at one time in a mythical school setting.

In the center are Plato and Aristotle, the two greatest. Plato points up, indicating his philosophy that mathematics and pure ideas are the source of truth ("right brain" thinking?) while Aristotle points down, showing his preference for scientific study of the material world (left brain). There's their master, Socrates, midway to the left, ticking off

arguments on his fingers. And in the foreground at right, Euclid bends over a slate to demonstrate a geometrical formula.

This isn't just a celebration of classical learning, but a chance to show that Renaissance thinkers were as good as the ancients. The bearded figure of Plato is none other than Leonardo da Vinci, whom Raphael worshiped. That's Raphael himself among the greats, next to last on the far right, with the black beret, looking out at us. And the "school" building is actually a Renaissance setting taken from early designs for St. Peter's.

The balanced style is also the epitome of Renaissance. Raphael has created a spacious three-dimensional setting of Renaissance architecture and peopled it with figures balanced evenly, left and right. Look at the tops of the columns that support the arches. If you laid a ruler over them and extended the line that recedes into the arch, it would run right to dead center of the picture. Similarly, the floor tiles in the foreground all point to dead center. All the lines of sight draw our attention to Plato and Aristotle, and to the small arch over their heads—a halo over these two secular saints in the divine pursuit of knowledge.

Raphael painted this room while Michelangelo was at work down the hall in the Sistine Chapel. Raphael popped in on the sly to see the master at work. He was astonished. Raphael's early work had always been graceful, pretty, and delicate (like the *Apollo Belvedere*). When he saw Michelangelo's powerful figures and dramatic scenes, he began to beef up his work to a more heroic level. As he was finishing up *The School of Athens*, perhaps his greatest work, he tipped his brush to the master by painting Michelangelo into the scene—the brooding, melancholy figure in front leaning on a block of marble.

The Disputa

As if to underline the new attitude that pre-Christian philosophy and church thinking could co-exist, Raphael painted *The Disputa* facing the *School of Athens*. Here we see Christ and the saints in heaven overseeing a discussion of the Eucharist (the communion wafer) by mortals below. The classical-looking woman in blue looks out and points in as if to say there's the School of Athens, but here's the School of Heaven. Balance and symmetry reign, from the angel trios in the upper corners to the books littering the floor.

In Catholic terms, the communion wafer miraculously becomes the body of Christ when it's eaten, bringing a little bit of heaven into the material world. Raphael's painting also connects heaven and earth, with descending circles: Jesus in a halo, down to the dove of the Holy Spirit in a circle, which enters the communion wafer in its holder. The composition drives the point home. By the way, these rooms were the papal library, so themes featuring learning, knowledge, and debate were appropriate.

The last Raphael Room (called the "Fire in the Borgia" Room) shows work done mostly by Raphael's students, who were influenced by the muscularity and dramatic, sculptural poses of Michelangelo.

● *Get ready. It's decision time. From here there are two ways to get to the Sistine Chapel. One is definitely the better way, so pay attention.*

Leaving the final Raphael Room and passing through two small rooms, you'll soon see two arrows—one pointing left to the Sistine (Cappella Sistina) and one pointing right to the Sistine. Go right. Meet you on a bench at the bottom of the stairs.

The advantage of this route (which really isn't much longer) is that you can sit down in peace and quiet to read ahead before entering the hectic Sistine Chapel. Also, you get to stroll through the impressive Modern Religious Art collection on the way to the Sistine, a few minutes' walk away. Sit, relax, and read about the Sistine Chapel here.

The Sistine Chapel

The Sistine Chapel contains Michelangelo's ceiling and his huge *Last Judgment*, painted two decades later on the wall over the altar. For now, let's concentrate on the ceiling.

Not only is the Sistine the personal chapel of the pope, this is where new popes are elected. When Julius II asked Michelangelo to take on this important project, he said, "No, *grazie*."

Michelangelo insisted he was a sculptor, not a painter. The Sistine ceiling was a vast undertaking and he didn't want to do a half-vast job. But the pope pleaded, bribed, and threatened until Michelangelo finally consented on the condition he be able to do it all his own way.

Julius had asked for only 12 Apostles along the sides of the ceiling, but Michelangelo had a grander vision. The next four years (1508–1512) were spent lying on his back on scaffolding six stories up covering the entire ceiling with frescoes of scenes from the Old Testament. With frescoes, painting on wet plaster, if you don't get it right the first time, you have to scrape the whole thing off, replaster it, and start over. In sheer physical terms, it's an astonishing achievement: 600 square yards with every inch done by his own hand. (Raphael only designed most of his rooms, letting assistants do the grunt work.) If you've ever struggled with a ceiling light fixture or worked underneath a car for even five minutes, you know how heavy your arms get. The physical effort, the paint dripping in his eyes, the creative drain, and the mental stress from a pushy pope combined to almost kill him.

But when it was finished and revealed to the public, it simply blew 'em away. Like the *Laocoön* statue discovered six years earlier, it was unlike anything seen before. It both caps the Renaissance and turns it in a new direction. In perfect Renaissance spirit, it mixes Old Testament prophets with classical and classical-looking figures. But the style is more dramatic, shocking, and emotional than the balanced Renaissance works before it. This is a very personal work—the Gospel according to Michelangelo—but its themes and subject matter are universal. Almost without exception, art critics concede that the Sistine ceiling is the single greatest work of art by any one human being.

The Sistine Ceiling — Understanding What You're Standing Under

The ceiling shows the history of the world before the birth of Jesus. We see God creating the world, creating man and woman, destroying the earth by flood, and so on. Along the sides we see the Old Testament prophets and pagan Greek prophetesses that foretold the coming of Christ. Dividing these scenes and figures is a painted architectural framework (a 3-D illusion) decorated with nude figures with symbolic meaning.

The key is to see these three simple divisions underneath the tangle of bodies:

(1) The central spine of rectangular panels with nine scenes from Genesis.

(2) The two rows of panels on either side with prophets.

(3) The triangles in between the prophets showing the ancestors of Christ.

● *Ready? Signs will direct you through the Modern Art section to the Sistine. Enter the Chapel and grab a seat at the screen (if possible) two-thirds of the way back. Face the altar and get oriented.*

There's the *Last Judgment* on the big wall behind the altar. Now look

THE SISTINE CEILING—UNDERSTANDING WHAT YOU'RE STANDING UNDER

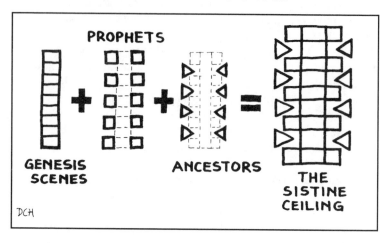

up to the ceiling and find:

(1) The central spine of Genesis scenes.

(2) The prophets along the sides of this spine.

(3) The ancestors in the triangles.

The *Creation of Adam* is near the very center of the ceiling.

The Creation of Adam

God and Man are equal in this Renaissance version of creation. Adam, newly formed in the image of God, lounges dreamily in perfect naked innocence. God, with his entourage, swoops in, in a swirl of activity. Their reaching hands are the center of this work. Adam's is limp and passive, God's is strong and forceful, His finger twitching upward with energy. Here is the very moment of creation, as God passes the spark of life to man, the crowning work of His creation.

This is the spirit of the Renaissance. God is not a terrifying giant reaching down to puny and helpless man from way on high. Here they are on an equal plane, co-creators, divided only by the diagonal patch of sky. God's billowing robe and the patch of green upon which Adam is lying balance each other. They are like two pieces of a jigsaw puzzle, or two long-separated continents, or like the yin and yang

THE SISTINE CEILING

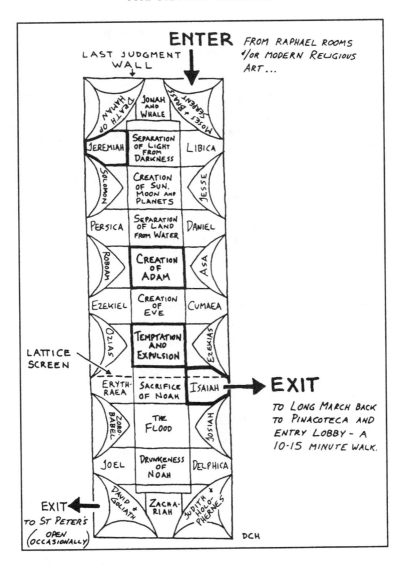

symbols finally coming together, uniting, complementing each other, creating wholeness. God and man work together as equals in the divine process of creation.

● *This celebration of man permeates the ceiling. Notice the Adonises-come-to-life on the pedestals that divide the central panels. And then came woman. Two panels away from* The Creation of Adam, *towards the rear of the chapel, you'll find* ...

The Garden of Eden: Temptation and Expulsion

In one panel we see two scenes from the Garden of Eden. On the left is the leafy garden of paradise where Adam and Eve lie around blissfully. But the devil comes along—a serpent with a woman's torso— and winds around the forbidden Tree of Knowledge. The temptation to gain new knowledge is too great for these Renaissance people. They eat the forbidden fruit.

At right, the sword-wielding angel drives them from Paradise into the barren plains. They're grieving, but they're far from helpless. Adam's body is thick and sturdy, and we know they'll survive in the cruel world. Adam firmly gestures to the angel, like he's saying, "All right, already! We're going!"

The Nine Scenes from Genesis

Take some time with these Genesis scenes to understand the story the ceiling tells. They run in sequence, starting at the front:

(1) God, in purple, divides the light from darkness.

(2) God creates the sun (burning orange) and the moon (pale white, to the right). Oops, I guess there's another moon.

(3) God bursts towards us to separate the land and water.

(4) The Creation of Adam.

(5) God creates Eve, who springs out of Adam's side.

(6) The Garden of Eden: Temptation and Expulsion.

(7) Noah kills a ram and stokes the altar-fires to make a sacrifice to God.

(8) The great Flood, sent by God, destroys the wicked, who desperately head for higher ground. In the distance, the Ark carries Noah's family to safety.

(9) Noah's sons come across Noah drunk. (Perhaps Michelangelo chose to end it with this scene as a reminder that even the best of men are fallible.)

Prophets

By 1510 Michelangelo had finished the first half of the ceiling, the end farthest from the *Last Judgment* wall. When they took the scaffolding down and could finally see what he'd been working on for two years, everyone was awestruck ... except Michelangelo. As powerful as his figures are, from the floor they didn't look dramatic enough for Michelangelo. For the other half he pulled out all the stops.

Compare the many small figures in the Noah scenes with, say, Adam and God at the other end. Or compare an early prophet with a later one. Isaiah ("Esaias," find him on the map) is shown in a pose like a Roman senator. He is a stately, sturdy, balanced, composed Renaissance Man. Now look at Jeremiah in the corner by the *Last Judgment*. This prophet, who witnessed the destruction of Israel, is a dark, brooding figure. He slumps his chin in his hand and ponders the fate of his people. The difference between the small, dignified Isaiah and the large, dramatic Jeremiah is like the difference between *Apollo Belvedere* and the *Laocoön*. This sort of emotional power was a new element in Renaissance painting.

The Cleaning Project

The ceiling and the *Last Judgment* have been cleaned—a 12-year project, finished in 1994, that removed centuries of dirt and soot from candles, oil lamps, and the annual Papal Barbecue (just kidding), plus animal glues used to preserve the works.

The project was controversial. The bright, bright colors that emerged upset those who grew up with the Sistine's darker tones. Critics charge that the cleaners were also removing shading deliberately put on by Michelangelo. The colors are a bit shocking, forcing many art experts to re-evaluate Michelangelo's style.

● The Last Judgment *is best viewed from the screen where, hopefully, you've found a spot on the bench.*

The Last Judgment

When Michelangelo was asked to paint the altar wall 23 years later (1535), the mood of Europe— and of Michelangelo—was completely different. The Protestant Reformation had forced the Catholic Church to clamp down on free thought. The Renaissance spirit of optimism was fading. Michelangelo, himself, had begun to question the innate goodness of mankind.

THE LAST JUDGMENT

1 - Christ with Mary at his side
2 - Trumpeting Angels
3 - The dead come out of their graves, the righteous ascend
4 - One of the damned
5 - Charon in his boat
6 - The demon/critic of nudity
7 - St. Bartholomew with flayed skin containing Michelangelo's self-portrait

It's Judgment Day and Christ—the powerful figure in the center, raising his arm to strike down the wicked—has come to find out who's naughty and nice. Beneath him, a band of angels blows its trumpets Dizzy Gillespie–style to wake the dead. The dead at lower left leave their graves and prepare to be judged. The righteous, on Christ's right hand (the left side of the picture), ascend to the glories of Heaven. The wicked on the other side are hurled down to Hell where demons wait to torture them. Charon, from the underworld of Greek mythology, waits below to ferry the souls of the damned to Hell.

It's a grim picture. No one, but no one, is smiling. Even many of the righteous being resurrected (lower left) are either skeletons or cadavers with ghastly skin. The angels have to play tug-of-war with subterranean monsters to drag them from their graves.

Over in Hell, the wicked are tortured by gleeful demons. One of the damned (to the right of the trumpeting angels) has an utterly lost expression, as if saying, "How could I have been so stupid!" Two demons grab him around the ankles to pull him down to the bowels of Hell, condemned to an eternity of constipation.

But it's the terrifying figure of Christ who dominates this scene. As He raises His arm to smite the wicked, He sends a ripple of fear through everyone, and they recoil. Even the saints that surround Him—even Mary beneath His arm (whose interceding days are clearly over)—shrink back in terror. His expression is completely closed, and He turns his head, refusing to even listen to the whining alibis of the damned. Look at Christ's bicep. If this muscular figure looks familiar to you, it's because you've seen it before—the *Belvedere Torso*.

When *The Last Judgment* was unveiled to the public in 1544, again, it caused a sensation. The pope is said to have dropped to his knees and cried, "Lord, charge me not with my sins when thou shalt come on the Day of Judgment." And it changed the course of art. The complex composition with more than 300 figures swirling around the figure of Christ was far beyond traditional Renaissance balance. The twisted figures shown from every angle imaginable challenged other painters to try and top this master of creating the illusion of 3-D. And the sheer terror and drama of the scene was a striking contrast to the placid optimism of, say, Raphael's *School of Athens*. Michelangelo had Baroque-en all the rules of the Renaissance, signaling a new era of art.

Originally, the figures in *The Last Judgment* were naked. In the Renaissance, the naked human body was seen as an expression of God's glorious creative powers. But even as Michelangelo was painting it, he got murmurs of discontent from the church authorities. He rebelled by painting his chief critic into the scene—in Hell. He's the demon in the bottom right corner wrapped in a serpent.

But after Michelangelo's death, there was no defense. The prudish church authorities enforced the new Vatican penal code, hiring an artist to paint wisps of decency over their privates. In Mary's case, she got a whole new wardrobe. (The artist who did it—known to history as "The Tailor"—got in one lick for his beloved Michelangelo. Out of the countless figures who were covered up, the only one that was left buck naked was ... the critic in the corner.)

Now move up close. In fact, move up close to the prude to see what "covers" his privates. Sweet revenge. Study the details of the lower part of the painting from right to left. Charon, with Dr. Spock ears and a Dali moustache, paddles the damned in a boat full of human turbulence. Look more closely at the J-Day band. Are they reading music or is it the Judgment Day tally? Before the cleaning, these details were lost in murk.

The Last Judgment marks the end of Renaissance optimism. Think back on The Creation of Adam, with its innocence and exaltation of man. There he was the equal of a fatherly God. Here, man cowers in fear and unworthiness before a terrifying, wrathful deity. Michelangelo himself must have questioned his own innate good-

ness. Look at St. Bartholomew, the bald bearded guy at Christ's left foot (our right). In the flayed skin he's holding is a barely recognizable face— the twisted self-portrait of a self-questioning Michelangelo.

● *Exiting the Sistine you'll soon find yourself facing the Long March back to the museum's entrance. You're one floor down from the long corridor you walked to get here.*

(The Sistine–St. Peter's shortcut: From the back of the chapel there's a tour group exit that shortcuts you directly to St. Peter's Basilica. If you're going there next and a group is leaving, you can slip out with them and save a lot of travel time. Occasionally a guard can be sweet-talked into opening the door for an individual. If you do this you'll miss the Pinacoteca.)

The Long March Back

Along this corridor you'll see some of the wealth amassed by the popes, mostly gifts from royalty. Find your hometown on the map of the world from 1529 (in a glass case near an astrological globe)—look in the land called "Terra Incognita." The elaborately decorated library that branches off to the right contains rare manuscripts.

● *Exiting the corridor, turn left. At the courtyard with a great view of the dome, follow signs to the …*

Pinacoteca (Painting Gallery)

How would you like to be Lou Gehrig—always batting behind Babe Ruth? That's the Pinacoteca's lot in life, following the Sistine & Co. But after the Vatican's artistic feast, this little collection of paintings is a delicious 15-minute after-dinner mint.

See this gallery of paintings as you'd view a time-lapse blossoming of a flower, walking through the evolution of painting from medieval to Baroque with just four stops.

● *Enter and stroll up to Room IV.*

Melozzo Da Forli — Musician Angels

Salvaged from a condemned church, this playful series of frescoes shows the delicate grace and nobility of Italy during the time known fondly as the *quattrocentro* (1400s). Notice the detail and the classical purity given these religious figures.

● *Walk on to the end room (Room VIII) where they've turned on the dark to let Raphael's* Transfiguration *shine. Take a seat.*

PINACOTECA—PAINTING GALLERY

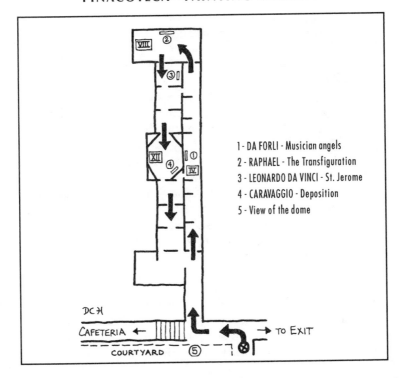

1 - DA FORLI - Musician angels
2 - RAPHAEL - The Transfiguration
3 - LEONARDO DA VINCI - St. Jerome
4 - CARAVAGGIO - Deposition
5 - View of the dome

DC H

CAFETERIA ←

→ TO EXIT

COURTYARD

Raphael — The Transfiguration

Raphael's *Transfiguration* shows Christ on a mountaintop visited in a vision by the prophets Moses and Elijah. Peter, James, and John cower in awe under Jesus, "transfigured before them, his face shining as the sun, his raiment white as light." (As described by the Evangelist Matthew—taking notes in the painting's lower left.)

The nine remaining Apostles try in vain to heal a boy possessed by demons. Jesus is gone, but "Lady Faith" in the center exhorts them to carry on.

Raphael died in 1520, leaving this final work to be finished by his pupils. The last thing Raphael painted was the beatific face of the ecstatic Jesus, perhaps the most beautiful Christ in existence.

● *Heading back down the parallel corridor, stop in Room IX at the brown unfinished work by Leonardo.*

Leonardo da Vinci — St. Jerome (c. 1482)

This unfinished work gives us a glimpse behind the scenes at Leonardo's technique. Even in the brown undercoating we see the psychological power of Leonardo's genius. The intense penitence and painful ecstasy of the saint comes through loud and clear in the anguished body on the rocks and in Jerome's ecstatic eyes, which see divine forgiveness. Leonardo wrote that a good painter must paint two things: "man and the movements of his spirit." (The patchwork you see is because Jerome's head was cut out and used as the seat of a stool in a shoemaker's shop.)

● *Roll on through the sappy sweetness of the Mannerist rooms into the shocking ultra-realistic world of Caravaggio, Room XII.*

Caravaggio — Deposition

Caravaggio was the first painter to intentionally shock his viewers. By exaggerating the light/dark contrasts, shining a brutal third-degree-interrogator-type light on his subjects, and using low-life models in sacred scenes, he takes a huge leap away from the Raphael-pretty past

and into the "expressive realism" of the modern world.

A tangle of grief looms out of the darkness as Christ's heavy, dead body nearly pulls the whole group with him from the cross into the tomb.

● *Walk through the rest of the gallery's canvas history of art, enjoy one last view of the Vatican grounds and Michelangelo's dome, then follow the grand spiral staircase down. Go in peace.*

MADRID

The Prado

*M*adrid proudly shows off the remains of its once vast and powerful empire: the greatest collection of paintings in Europe. Filled with masterpieces by Velázquez, El Greco, Goya, and Bosch, the Prado brilliantly chronicles the rise and fall of Spain, its rich Catholic heritage, and its bloody wars.

21 The Prado

The Prado (pron: PRAH-doh) is the greatest painting museum in the world. If you like art and you plan to be in Europe, a trip to Madrid is a must. In its glory days, the Spanish Empire was Europe's greatest, filling its coffers with gold from the New World and art from the Old. While there are some 3,000 paintings in the collection, we'll be selective, focusing on just the top 1,500 or so.

MUSEO DEL PRADO

Hours: Tuesday–Saturday 9:00–19:00; Sunday and holidays 9:00–14:00; closed Monday.

Cost: 500 ptas, free on Saturday after 14:30 and all day Sunday (and any time if you're over 65).

Tour length: Three hours (not including *Guernica*)

Getting there: Fifteen-minute walk from Puerta del Sol; bus nos. 9, 10, 19, 27, 34, 45; subway to "Banco de España" or "Atocha" and 15-minute walk; cheap taxis (say "moo-SAY-oh del PRAH-doh").

Information: Good small pamphlets on Flemish, Goya, and Velázquez on racks in appropriate rooms. Museum tel. 91-330-2800.

Misc.: Good, reasonable cafeteria in basement at south end. The royal gardens are just south, and the huge, pleasant Retiro park is three blocks east. Most crowded Tuesday and Sunday and all mornings.

Starring: Bosch, Goya, Titian, Velázquez, Dürer, El Greco.

NEW WORLD GOLD — OLD WORLD ART

Heaven and earth have always existed side by side in Spain—religion and war, Grand Inquisitors and cruel conquistadors, spirituality and sensuality, holiness and horniness. The Prado has a surprisingly worldly collection of paintings for a country in which the medieval Inquisition lasted up until modern times. But it's just this rich combination

THE PRADO—OVERVIEW

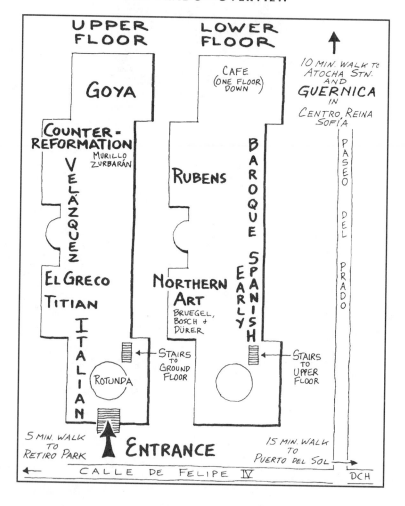

of worldly beauty and heavenly mysticism that is so typically Spanish.

Gold from newly discovered America bought the sparkling treasures of the Prado. Spain, the most powerful nation in Europe in the 1500s, was growing rich on her New World possessions just about the time of the world's greatest cultural heyday, the Renaissance.

The collection's strengths reflect the tastes of Spain's cultured kings from 1500 to 1800: (1) Italian Renaissance art (especially the lush and sensual Venetian art which was the rage of Europe); (2) Northern art from what was the Spanish Netherlands; and (3) their own Spanish court painters. This tour will concentrate on these three areas, with a special look at some individual artists who are especially well-represented—Velázquez, Goya, Titian, Rubens, El Greco, and Bosch.

● *Enter the Prado at the north end, upper floor (the "Puerta de Goya"). Orient yourself from the rotunda.*

From the rotunda, look through the huge doorway marked "Escuela Espanola," down the long gallery. The Prado runs north-south. Rooms branch off to the left (east of this long hall). The layout is similar on the floor below.

We'll start with Italian Renaissance art on this floor. Then head downstairs to Northern Renaissance art. Then back upstairs for Spanish art.

● *Enter Room 4, the door to the left marked "Escuela Italiana" (Italian School), and belly up to the Annunciation altarpiece on your right.*

Italian Renaissance (1400–1600)

Modern Western civilization began in the prosperous Renaissance cities of Italy during the years 1400 to 1600. Florence, Rome, and Venice led the way out of the Gothic Middle Ages, building on the forgotten knowledge of ancient Rome and Greece. So it's fitting that we start our tour here.

Unlike the heaven-centered medieval artists, Renaissance artists gloried in the natural world and the human body. They painted things

as realistically as possible. For the Italians, "realistic" meant "three-dimensional," and they set out to learn how to capture the 3-D world on a 2-D canvas.

Fra Angélico —
The Annunciation (La Anunciación)

Fra Angelico was a mix of the passing Middle Ages and the coming Renaissance. He was a

ITALIAN RENAISSANCE

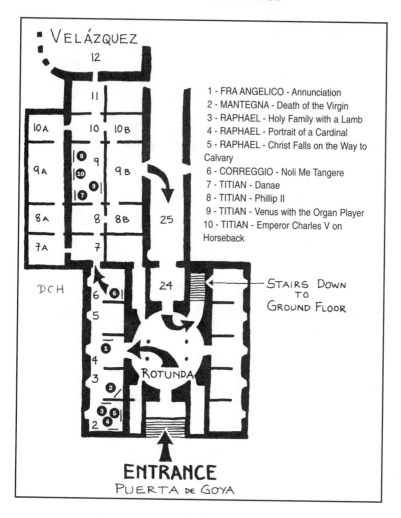

monk of great piety (his nickname means "Angelic Brother") who combined medieval religious sentiment with new Renaissance techniques. This is more like two separate paintings in one: (1) on the left, the medieval-style story of Adam and Eve in the Garden of Eden and (2) on the right (under the porch), the Renaissance-style scene of the angel telling Mary she'll give birth to the Messiah.

The Fall (on the left side) expresses a characteristic medieval idea—

man is sinfully weak and undeserving of the pleasures of Paradise. Adam and Eve, scrawny and two-dimensional, seem to float in an unrealistic space above the foliage. Eve folds her hands nervously, scrunching down, waiting for her punishment from an angry God. The style is also medieval, with detailed flowers, a labor of love by a caring monk who was also a miniaturist. Another medieval element is the series of storytelling scenes below illustrating events in the life of Mary for the illiterate faithful.

The Annunciation scene on the right is early Renaissance. The porch makes a 3-D setting. Then Fra Angelico fills it with two massive, almost sculptural bodies. The message of the scene is upbeat and humanistic, as the Angel tells Mary she'll give birth to a Savior who'll redeem sinful man from the Fall. (Is it good news to Mary? She doesn't look too thrilled.)

Still, the painting is flat by modern standards, and the study in depth perspective is crude. Aren't the receding bars of the porch's ceiling a bit off? And Mary's hands just aren't right—like when you have to wash the dishes with two left-hand rubber gloves. But it's a lot better (and more 3-D) than its medieval neighbors here.

Above all, notice the serene atmosphere of the painting. There are no harsh shadows or strong light sources. Everything is bathed in a pristine, glowing, holy light. The only movement is the shaft of light shooting down from the hands of God, bringing redemption from the Fall, connecting the two halves of the painting and fusing medieval piety with Renaissance humanism.

● *Face the windows, then turn left around the partition into the next small alcove (Room 3).*

Mantegna —
Death of the Virgin (El Transito de la Virgen)

The true pioneer of Renaissance 3-D was Andrea Mantegna (pron: mon-TAYN-ya). He creates a spacious setting, then peoples it with sculptural figures.

The dying mother of Christ is surrounded by statue-like apostles with plates on their heads and pots in their hands. The architectural setting is heroic and spacious. Follow the lines in the floor tiles and side columns. They converge toward the window, then seem to continue on to the far horizon in the lines of the bridge. This creates a subconscious feeling of almost infinite spaciousness, bringing a serenity to an otherwise tragic death scene. You can imagine Mary's soul leaving her body and floating easily out the window, disappearing into the infinite distance.

• *Turning the corner into Room 2, your eye will go immediately to some large Raphael canvases. Let them overwhelm you, then turn about-face and refocus your eyes on the tiny Holy Family with a Lamb. The sheer difference in size and scope of these works gives you a sense of Raphael's vision.*

Raphael — Holy Family with a Lamb (Sagrada Familia del Cordero)

Raphael reproduced reality perfectly on a canvas, but also gave it harmony, geometry, and heroism that made it somehow more real than reality. Combining idealized beauty with down to-earth realism, he was the ultimate Renaissance painter.

Raphael (pron: roff-eye-ELL) was only 21 when he painted this. He learned Leonardo da Vinci's technique of *sfumato*, spreading a kind of hazy glow around the figures (this is the technique that gives the *Mona Lisa* her vague, mysterious smile). He also used Leonardo's trademark pyramid composition—the three figures form a pyramid, with Joseph's head at the peak.

Raphael — Portrait of a Cardinal (Cardenal Desconocido)

Compare the idealized beauty of *Holy Family* with the stark realism of this portrait. This isn't an idealized version of an ideal man, but a living, breathing—in this case almost sneering—man. Raphael captures not just his face, but his personality—the type of man who could become a cardinal at such a young age in the Renaissance Vatican's priest-eat-priest jungle of holy ambition. He's cold, intelligent, detached, and somewhat cynical—a gritty portrayal of a gritty man.

Raphael — Christ Falls on the Way to Calvary (Caída en el Camino del Calvario)

Raphael puts it all together—the idealized grace of the *Holy Family* and the realism of *Portrait of a Cardinal*. Look at the detail on the muscular legs of the guy in yellow (at left) and the arms of Simon, who has come to help Jesus carry his cross. Then contrast that with the idealized beauty of the mourning women. When this painting was bought in 1661, it was the costliest in existence.

Raphael has added drama to the work by splitting the canvas into two contrasting halves. Below the slanting line made by the crossbar is a scene of swirling passion—the sorrow of Christ and the women, the tangle of crowded bodies. Above it is open space and indifference—the bored soldiers and onlookers and the bleak hill in the background where Jesus is headed to be crucified.

● *Backtrack to Fra Angélico's* Annunciation, *then continue past it to Room 6.*

Correggio — *Nole Me Tangere (Don't Touch Me)*

Raphael could paint idealized beauty, but this is simply the most beautiful painting in captivity. That's it. Period. If it were any sweeter you could get diabetes just looking at it.

It's Easter morning and Jesus has just come back to life. One of his followers, Mary Magdalene, has run into him in the garden near the tomb. She is amazed and excited and reaches toward him. "Don't touch me!" (*Nole me tangere*) says Jesus (though he spoke neither English nor Latin), and points up to Heaven.

The colors accentuate the emotion of the scene. Blazing like a flame against the cool landscape of blue and green, Mary Magdalene—the ex-prostitute in a fiery yellow dress and yellow hair—is hot to touch the cool Christ with his blue cloak and pale, radiant skin. The composition also accentuates the action. The painting's energy runs in a diagonal line up the rippling Mary, through Christ and his upstretched arm to heaven, where he will soon go.

Titian (c. 1490–1576)

Look around. What do you see? Flesh. Naked bodies in various poses; bright, lush, colorful scenes. Many scenes have "pagan" themes, but even the religious works are racier than anything we saw from the Florentine and Roman Renaissance.

Venice in 1500 was the richest city in Europe, the middleman in the lucrative trade between Europe and the Orient. Wealthy, cosmopolitan, and free, Venetians loved life's finer things—rich silks, beautiful people, jewels, banquets, music, wine, and impressive buildings—and Venetian painters enjoyed painting them in bright colors.

The chief Venetian was Titian (they rhyme). Titian (Tiziano in Spain) was possibly the most famous painter of his day—more famous than Raphael, Leonardo, and even Michelangelo. His reputation reached Spain, and he became the favorite portraitist for two kings, who bought many of his works.

Titian — *Danae*

In Greek mythology, Zeus, the king of the gods, was always zooming to earth in the form of some creature or other to fool around with some mortal woman. Here, he descends as a shower of gold to consort with the willing Danae. You can almost see the human form of Zeus within the cloud. Danae is rapt, opening her legs to receive him, while her servant tries to catch the heavenly spurt with a towel.

This is one of the world's finest and most famous nudes. Danae's rich, luminous flesh on the left of the canvas is set off by the dark servant at right and the threatening sky above. The white sheets beneath her make her glow even more.

But this is more than a classic nude—it's a Renaissance Miss August. How could Spain's ultra-conservative Catholic kings have tolerated such a downright pagan and erotic painting?

Titian — *Phillip II (Felipe II)*

The mystery is heightened when we look at the man who bought this and many other paintings of nudes, King Phillip II. Phillip deserved his reputation as a repressed prude—pale, suspicious, lonely, a cold fish; the sort of man who would build the severe and tomb-like Escorial Palace. Freud would have had a field day with such a complex man who could be so sternly religious and yet have such sensual tastes. Here, he is looking as pious and ascetic as a man can while wearing that outfit.

Titian — *Venus with the Organ Player (Venus El Amor y La Música)*

A musician turns around to leer at a naked woman while keeping both hands at work on his organ. This was another painting that aroused Phillip's interest. The message must have appealed to him—the conflict between sacred, artistic pursuits as symbolized by music, and worldly, sensual pursuits as embodied in the naked lady.

Titian emphasized these two opposites with color—"cool" colors on the left, hot crimson and flesh on the right. The center of the painting is where these two color schemes meet, so even though the figures lean and the poplar trees in the background are off-center, the painting is balanced and harmonious in the Renaissance tradition.

A century after Phillip's reign, his beloved nudes were taken down from the Escorial and Royal Palace and hidden away as unfit to be seen. For more than a century these great Titians were banned.

Titian — *Emperor Charles V on Horseback* (*El Emperador Carlos V en la Batalla de Muhlberg*)

Are you glad to be here? If so, then tip your book to that guy on horseback, the father of the Prado's collection.

In the 1500s, Charles was the most powerful man in the world. He was not merely King Charles of Spain, but Holy Roman Emperor with possessions stretching from Spain to Austria, from Holland to Italy, from South America to Burgundy. He was defender of the Catholic Church against infidel Turks, French kings, and in this picture, rebellious Protestants.

Here, Titian shows him in the classic equestrian pose of a Roman conqueror. His power is accentuated by his control over his rearing horse and the lance with its optimistic tilt.

Once Charles met Titian and saw what he could do, he never wanted anyone else to paint him. And the story goes that, while sitting for a portrait one day, this greatest ruler in the world actually stooped over to pick up a brush Titian dropped.

We've seen painting move from Gothic two-dimensionality to Renaissance realism and balance. The next style—Baroque—took Renaissance realism to unrealistic heights. But before we get tangled in the steaming jungle of Baroque, let's take a refreshing break in the cooler climes of the Northern countries. Their down-to-earth realism is a delightful contrast to the idealized beauty of the Italian school.

● *The Northern art is downstairs. Return to the rotunda and take the staircase to the ground floor. Start down the long gallery, then take your first left, into Room 57B. We'll start in Room 58.*

NORTHERN ART

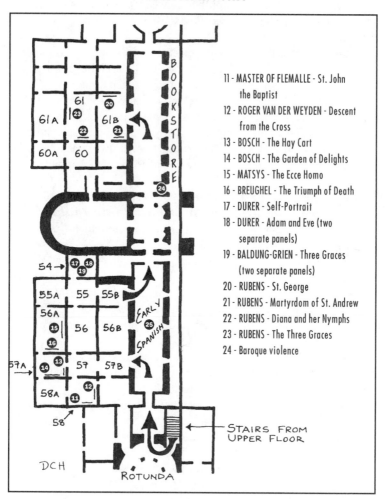

11 - MASTER OF FLEMALLE - St. John the Baptist

12 - ROGER VAN DER WEYDEN - Descent from the Cross

13 - BOSCH - The Hay Cart

14 - BOSCH - The Garden of Delights

15 - MATSYS - The Ecce Homo

16 - BREUGHEL - The Triumph of Death

17 - DURER - Self-Portrait

18 - DURER - Adam and Eve (two separate panels)

19 - BALDUNG-GRIEN - Three Graces (two separate panels)

20 - RUBENS - St. George

21 - RUBENS - Martyrdom of St. Andrew

22 - RUBENS - Diana and her Nymphs

23 - RUBENS - The Three Graces

24 - Baroque violence

Northern Art

Master of Flemalle (Robert Campin) — *St. John the Baptist*

The Northern Renaissance was less a rebirth of classical ideas than an improvement on medieval painting. Remember the detailed flowers in Fra Angelico's *Annunciation*? That sort of attention to detail is the first thing we notice in Northern art. Here, not only are the wood, the glass, and the cloth done with loving care, but look at the curved mirror in the middle—the whole scene is reflected backwards in perfect detail!

Roger Van Der Weyden — Descent From the Cross (El Descendimiento)

In this powerful and sober *Descent*, again, it's the detail that first draws our attention—notice the robe of Joseph of Arimathea holding Christ's feet. And look at the veins in Joseph's forehead!

This is a human look at a traditional scene. Each of the faces is a different study in grief. Joseph's expression seems to be asking, "Why do the good always die young?" Look how Mary has swooned in the same S-curve as Jesus' body—the death of her son has dealt her a near-fatal blow as well. But the overwhelming tone of the scene is one of serenity. These are people of Northern piety who know and accept that Jesus must die.

Along with Titian's nudes, this was one of Phillip II's favorite paintings—quite a contrast! Yet this *Descent* and Titian's *Danae* both have the power to send us into ecstasy. Hmm.

● *Exit the real world and enter into the Garden of Delights, Room 57A.*

Bosch (c. 1450–1516)

The work of Hieronymous Bosch can be summed up in one word—wow! It's difficult to be any more articulate because his unique vision lends itself to so many different interpretations.

Bosch (rhymes with "Gosh!") was born, lived, and died in a small town in Holland—that's about all we know of him, his life being as mysterious as his work. He was much admired by his contemporaries, who understood his symbolism better than we.

Here are some possible interpretations of Bosch's work—he was: (1) crazy; (2) commenting on the decadence of his day; (3) celebrating the variety of life and human behavior; (4) painting with glue in a badly ventilated room. Or perhaps it's a combination of these.

Bosch — The Hay Cart (El Carro de Heno)

Before unraveling the tangle of the cryptic triptych *The Garden of Delights,* let's get warmed up on a "simpler" three-paneled work. Its message is that the pleasures of life are transitory, so we'd better avoid them or we'll wind up in hell.

CENTER PANEL: An old Flemish proverb goes, "Life is a cart of hay from which everyone takes what they can." The whole spectrum of greedy, grabby humanity is here: rich and poor, monks and peasants, scrambling for their share of worldly goods. Even the pope and the Holy Roman emperor (with the sword) chase the cart on horseback. In the very center is a man with a knife at another man's throat, getting his share by force. Two lovers on top of the cart are oblivious to the commotion but are surrounded by symbols of hate (the owl) and lust (the jug). The cart itself is drawn by Satan's demons.

With everyone fighting for his piece of the pie, it's easy to overlook the central figure—Christ above in heaven, watching unnoticed. Is He blessing them or throwing up His hands?

Bosch describes the world's pleasures in the center panel, then puts them in the eternal perspective. The left panel tells us where this crazy world of temptation came from, while the right panel reminds us where it leads.

LEFT: The story of Creation and the Garden of Eden can be "read" from top to bottom. At the top, God has sprayed D-Con and rousted Satan's vermin from heaven, setting them loose on earth. Then God creates Eve from Adam's rib, Eve gets tempted by a (female) serpent, and finally, they're driven from Paradise. It was this first sin that brought evil into the world.

RIGHT: Here's the whole point of Bosch's sermon—worldly pleasures lead to hell. Animal-like demons symbolizing various vices torture those who succumbed to the temptation of hay cart planet Earth.

Bosch —
The Garden of Delights (El Jardin de las Delicias)
With this traditional Christian interpretation in mind, let's turn to the overwhelming *Garden*. To make it less so, I'd suggest "framing off" one-foot squares to peruse at your leisure.

The *Garden* was interpreted like the *Hay Cart*; that is, the pleasures of the world are transitory, so you'd better watch out or you'll wind up in hell.

In the central panel, men on horseback ride round and round, searching for but never reaching the elusive Fountain of Youth. Lower

down and to the left are two lovers in a bubble, illustrating that "pleasure is as fragile as glass" and will soon disappear. Just to their right is a big mussel shell, a symbol of the female sex, swallowing up a man. My favorite is the kneeling figure in front of the orange pavilion in the foreground—talk about "saying it with flowers!"

One of the differences between *The Hay Cart* and *The Garden of Delights* is Columbus. Discoveries of new plants and animals in America gave Bosch a whole new continent of sinful pleasures to paint—some real, some imaginary. In the left panel, check out the cactus tree in the Garden of Eden and the bizarre two-legged dog near the giraffe.

Bosch was certainly a Christian, but there's speculation he was a heretical Christian painting forbidden rites of a free-wheeling cult called Adamites. The Adamites were medieval nudists who believed the body was good (as it was when God made Adam) and that sex was healthy. They supposedly held secret orgies. So, in the central panel we see Adamites at play, frolicking two-by-two and two-by-three and so on in the meadows, as innocent as Adam and Eve in the garden. Whether or not Bosch approved, you must admit that some of the folks in this Garden are having a delightful time.

This "Adamist" interpretation makes a lot of sense in the left panel. Here, the main scene, virtually nonexistent in the Bible, is the fundamental story of the Adamites—the marriage (sexual union) of Adam and Eve. God himself is performing the ceremony, wrapping them in the glowing warmth of His aura.

The right panel is hell, a burning, post-holocaust wasteland of perverse creatures and meaningless rituals where sinners are tortured by half-human demons. In this hell, poetic justice reigns supreme, with every sinner getting his just desserts—a glutton is eaten and re-eaten eternally, while a musician is crucified on a musical instrument for neglecting his church duties. Other symbols are less obvious. Two big ears pierced with a knife blade mow down all in the way. A pink bagpipe symbolizes the male and female sex organs (call Freud for details). In the center, hell is literally frozen over. At lower right a pig dressed as a nun tries to seduce a man. And in the center of this wonderful nightmare is a creature with a broken eggshell body, tree trunk legs, a witch's cap, and the face of Bosch himself staring out at us.

● *This room is crawling with Bosches. Take some time to look around. Don't miss the illustrated table, the nun who looks like a haystack, and the guy with the Tin Man's funnel doing brain surgery on Andy Rooney. When you're done, let's meet in Room 56A.*

Northern Renaissance (1500–1600)

The sunny optimism of the Italian Renaissance didn't quite penetrate the cold Northern lands. Italian humanists saw people as almost like Greek gods—strong, handsome, and noble—capable of standing on their own without the help of anyone, including God and the Catholic Church.

On the other hand, when you divorce people from what's holy, life on earth can seem pretty pointless. Northern artists concentrated on the folly of humankind (think of Bosch's puny humans) cast adrift in a chaotic world.

Matsys — Ecce Homo (Cristo Presentado al Pueblo)

The mob—a menagerie of goony faces—is railing on the prisoner Christ before his execution. Christ seems quite fed up with it all. The painting is especially effective because of our perspective. We're looking up at Christ on the balcony—we've become part of the hooting mob.

Brueghel — The Triumph of Death (El Triunfo de la Muerte)

The brief flowering of the Renaissance couldn't last. The optimism and humanism of the Renaissance met the brutal reality of war and lost. In the 16th century, the openness of the Renaissance fueled the Reformation, the bitter break between the Catholic Church and the "Protest"-ants. The resulting wars involved almost every nation of Europe (remember Charles V, who led the Catholics). The Northern countries were the hardest hit—in Germany alone, a third of the population died. The battles were especially brutal, with atrocities on both sides—the predictable result when politicians and generals claim God is on their side.

Pieter Brueghel (pron: BROY-gull) the Elder lived in these violent times, witnessing the futility of this first "world war." In violent times the message turns simple and morbid—no one can escape death.

The canvas is one big chaotic, non-symmetrical, confusing battle scene. Death in the form of skeletons (led by the one on horseback with a scythe) attacks a crowd of people, herding them into a tunnel-like building (prescient of a Nazi death camp). Elsewhere, other skeletons dole out the inevitable fate of all flesh. No one is spared. Not the jester (lower right, crawling under the table), not churchmen, not the emperor himself (at lower left, whose gold is also plundered), not even the poor man (upper right) kneeling, praying for mercy with a cross in his hands.

We can imagine these scenes being played out in real life on the battlefields of Europe, leaving countries as wasted as the barren countryside in the background. In the end, after a hundred bloody years of war, a truce (in 1648) divided countries into Catholic or Protestant (divisions that survive today), and Europe began to learn the lesson of tolerance—to exist we must coexist.

● *Continue to Room 54.*

Dürer — *Self-Portrait (Auto-retrato)*

Before looking into the eyes of 26-year-old Albrecht Dürer, look first at his clothes and hairdo—they tell half the story of this remarkable personal statement. It's the look of a mod/hip/fab/rad young guy, a man of the world. The meticulous detail-work (Dürer was also an engraver) is the equivalent of preening before a mirror. Dürer (pron: DEWR-er), recently returned from Italy, wanted to impress his bumpkin fellow Germans with all that he had learned.

But Dürer wasn't simply vain. Renaissance Italy treated its artists like princes, not workmen. Dürer learned not only to paint like a great artist, but to act like one as well.

Now look into his eyes, or rather, look up at his eyes, since Dürer composed the painting so that he is literally looking down on us. We see an intelligent, bold, and somewhat arrogant man, confident of his abilities. The strong arms and hands reinforce this confidence.

This is possibly the first true self-portrait. Sure, other artists used themselves as models and put their likeness in scenes (like Bosch in hell), but it was a whole new thing to paint your own portrait to proudly show your personality to the world. Dürer painted probably ten of them in his life—each showing a different aspect of this complex man.

Dürer put his mark on every painting and engraving. Note the pyramid-shaped "A.D." (D inside the A) on the windowsill.

Dürer — *Adam and Eve* (two separate panels)

These are the first full-size nudes in Northern European art. It took the boldness of someone like Dürer to bring Italian fleshiness to the more modest Germans.

The title is *Adam and Eve,* but of course that's just an excuse to paint two nudes in the classical style. Or maybe we should say to "sculpt" two nudes, because they are more like Greek statues on pedestals than paintings. Dürer emphasized this by taking the one scene (Eve is giving the apple—notice how their hair is blown by the same wind) and splitting it into two canvases—each "statue" has its own niche.

Compared with Bosch's smooth-limbed, naked little *homunculi,* Dürer's *Adam and Eve* are three-dimensional and solid, with anatomically correct muscles. They're a bold humanistic proclamation that the body is good, man is good, the things of the world are good.

● *Now, look backwards, both literally and figuratively, at the two panels on the opposite wall that face* Adam and Eve.

Hans Baldung-Grien — *The Three Graces*

Painted about the same time as Dürer's works, these, too, have a classical touch—the Graces were goddesses of joy in Greek mythology—but what a different message! While Dürer portrayed the Renaissance glory of man, the Three Graces are a gloomy medieval reminder that all flesh is mortal and we're all on the same moving sidewalk to the junk pile.

In the left panel are the Three Graces in youth—beautiful, happy, in a playful green grove with the sun shining, and surrounded by angelic babies. But with grim Northern realism, the right panel shows what happens to all flesh (especially that of humanists!). The Three Graces become the three stages of sagging decay—middle age, old age, and death. Death holds an hourglass of that devouring army of ants, Time.

● *Return to the main gallery and turn left, heading toward the far (south) end of the museum. Near the bookstore, you'll see a bull raping a woman, a man preparing to hack a baby in two, and Hercules riding four white horses up to heaven. Welcome to Baroque.*

Rubens' work is in Rooms 61 and 61B just off the main gallery. But first, take a seat in the long gallery (Room 75) and soak in Baroque.

Rubens and Baroque (1600s)

You're surrounded by Baroque. Large canvases, bright colors, rippling bodies, plenty of flesh, violent scenes. This room contains more rapes per square foot than any gallery in the world.

Baroque art overwhelms. It play on our emotions, titillates our senses, and carries us away. Baroque was made to order for the Catholic Church and absolute monarchs who used it as propaganda to combat the dual threats of Protestantism and democracy. They impressed the common masses with beautiful palaces and glorious churches, showing their strength and authority.

Peter Paul Rubens of Flanders (Belgium) was the favorite of Catholic rulers. He painted the loves, wars, and religion of Catholic kings. His huge canvases were in great demand, and Rubens—like Titian before him—became rich and famous, a cultured, likable man of the world, who was even entrusted with diplomatic missions by his employers.

● *Enter the first Rubens Room (61B) through the door midway down the gallery.*

Rubens — *St. George Slaying the Dragon (San Jorge y El Dragón)*

This was a popular subject for Catholic kings involved in the wars of the Counter-Reformation. Like the legendary early Christian warrior who killed a dragon to save a princess, these kings saw themselves as righteous warriors saving the holy Church from the dragon of Protestantism.

In this typically Baroque tangle of bodies, we see the exciting moment just as George, who has already speared the dragon, is about to apply the *coup de bludgeon* with his sword. The limp princess has a lamb, the symbol of Christ and His church.

Baroque art often looks confusing, but it's almost always anchored in Renaissance-style balance. This painting has an X-like composition, the rearing horse slanting one way and George slanting the other. Above where the X intersects are the two stars of the scene, George with his rippling plumed helmet and the horse, with its rippling mane.

Speaking of X-like compositions, check out the *Martyrdom of St. Andrew* on an X-cruciating cross. All around these rooms are Rubens paintings of religious subjects. Glance at the series of smaller paintings with titles championing the Catholic cause—*Triumph of the Church*, *Triumph of the True Catholic*, and so on.

Rubens — *Diana and Her Nymphs Discovered by a Satyr (Ninfas y Satiros)*

A left-to-right rippling wave of figures creates a thrilling chase scene. Four horny satyrs (half-man, half-beast—though why mythical creatures like this never have their human half at the bottom, I'll never know) have crashed a party of woodland nymphos who flee from left to right. Only the Greek goddess Diana, queen of the hunt, stands with her spear to try to stem the tide of flailing limbs.

All the elements of a typical Rubens work are here—action, emotion, sensuality, violence, bright colors, fleshy bodies, and rippling clothes and hair with the wind machine on high.

Another typical feature is that it wasn't all painted by Rubens. Rubens was in such demand that he couldn't fill all the orders himself. In his home/studio/factory in Antwerp, he put assistants to work with the backgrounds and trivial details of his huge works, then, before shipping a canvas out the doors, Rubens would bring the work to life with a few final strokes.

Rubens — *The Three Graces (Las Tres Gracias)*

Have a seat and gaze at the pure beauty of Rubens' *Three Graces*. These ample, sensual bodies—like all his women—with glowing skin, rhythmic limbs, and grace and delicacy against a pleasant background show Rubens at his best. This particular painting was for his own private collection. His young second wife was the model for the Grace at left. She shows up fairly regularly in Rubens' paintings. Remember that in later, more prudish years, many of Rubens' nudes, like Titian's, were wrapped in brown paper and locked in the closet.

● *Break time? The cafeteria is not far away, in the basement at the south end of the museum.*

Most of the Spanish art is upstairs on the upper floor, but let's start here on the ground floor in the long Spanish Primitives gallery (Rooms 48–49) back near the rotunda.

Spanish Art

The final section we'll look at is Spanish painting, the Prado's forte. The three big names—El Greco, Velázquez, and Goya—are well represented, but we'll glance at a few others as well.

Spanish religious devotion and fanaticism are legendary. Look around. In this whole room of medieval Spanish art, is there even one

SPANISH ART

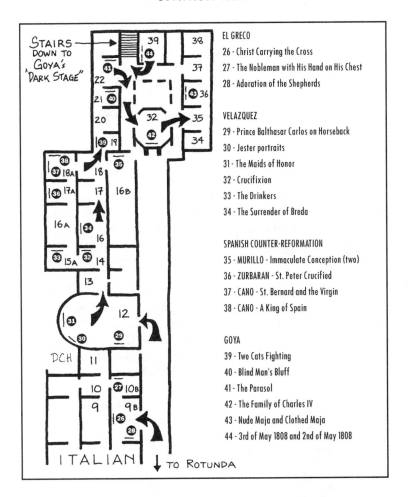

STAIRS DOWN TO GOYA'S "DARK STAGE"

EL GRECO
26 - Christ Carrying the Cross
27 - The Nobleman with His Hand on His Chest
28 - Adoration of the Shepherds

VELAZQUEZ
29 - Prince Balthasar Carlos on Horseback
30 - Jester portraits
31 - The Maids of Honor
32 - Crucifixion
33 - The Drinkers
34 - The Surrender of Breda

SPANISH COUNTER-REFORMATION
35 - MURILLO - Immaculate Conception (two)
36 - ZURBARAN - St. Peter Crucified
37 - CANO - St. Bernard and the Virgin
38 - CANO - A King of Spain

GOYA
39 - Two Cats Fighting
40 - Blind Man's Bluff
41 - The Parasol
42 - The Family of Charles IV
43 - Nude Maja and Clothed Maja
44 - 3rd of May 1808 and 2nd of May 1808

ITALIAN   ↓ TO ROTUNDA

DCH

painting that isn't of saints or Bible stories? I found one once. It showed heretics being punished by the Inquisition during an auto-da-fé—a combination revival meeting and barbecue (coals provided, B.Y.O. sinner). An estimated 2,000 enemies of God were burned alive during the reign of one notorious Grand Inquisitor.

One reason for Spanish fanaticism is that they had to literally fight for their religion. Moslems from North Africa (the Moors) controlled much of the peninsula for most of the Middle Ages (711–1492) making Christians a second-class and sometimes persecuted minority. It took centuries of fierce warfare to finally drive the Moors out. Spain couldn't officially call herself a Christian nation until the same year Columbus sailed for America. The iron-strong Spanish faith was forged in the fires of those wars.

Later, in the Counter-Reformation (16th century), when the Catholic Church shored up its defenses against the threat of the Protestant Reformation, Spain's militant religion was rallied against the Protestant "infidels." Much of the Spanish art we'll see was affected by the struggles between Catholics and Protestants, art designed to inspire the common people to have faith in the Catholic Church.

● *Head upstairs. From the rotunda, start down the long gallery, then take your first left, into the El Greco Rooms 9B and 10B.*

El Greco (c. 1540–1614)

The first great Spanish painter was Greek. El Greco (Spanish for "the Greek") was born in Greece, trained in Venice, then settled in Toledo, Spain. The combination of these three cultures, plus his own unique personality, produced a highly individual style. His paintings are Byzantine icons drenched in Venetian color and fused in the fires of Spanish mysticism.

Phillip II, the ascetic king with sensual tastes who bought so many Titians, didn't like El Greco's bizarre style (perhaps because the figures—thin and haunting—reminded him of himself). So El Greco left the Spanish court at El Escorial and moved south to Toledo, where he was accepted. He married and spent the rest of his life there. If you like El Greco, make the 90-minute trip to Toledo.

El Greco — *Christ Carrying the Cross (Cristo Abrazado a la Cruz)*

Even as the blood runs down his neck and he trudges toward his death, Christ accepts his fate in a trance of religious ecstasy. Notice how the crossbar points upward. Jesus, clasping the cross lovingly to him, sights along it like a navigational instrument to his destination—Heaven.

However, it's the upturned eyes that are the soul of this painting. (Someone has suggested it be titled "The Eyes of Jesus.") They are close to tears with humility and sparkle with joyful acceptance. (Warning: Do not get too close to this painting. Otherwise you'll see that the holy magic in the eyes is only a simple streak of white paint.)

El Greco — *The Nobleman with His Hand on His Chest (El Caballero de la Mano al Pecho)*

For all the mysticism of his paintings, we should remember that El Greco was not a mystic, but a well-traveled, learned, sophisticated, down-to-earth man. Despite his distorted paintings, with their elongated bodies and bright unreal colors (which he may have learned during his training with Titian in Venice), he could paint realistically.

This is an exceptionally realistic and probing portrait. The sitter was an elegant and somewhat arrogant gentleman, who was obviously trying to make an impression. The sword probably indicates the portrait was done to celebrate his becoming a knight.

El Greco reveals the man's personality, again, in the expressive eyes and in the hand across the chest. Notice how the middle two fingers touch—El Greco's trademark way of expressing elegance. Look for it in other works.

The signature is on the right in faint Greek letters—"Domenicos Theotocopoulos," El Greco's real name.

El Greco — *The Adoration of the Shepherds (La Adoración de los Pastores)*

El Greco painted this for his own burial chapel in Toledo, where it hung until the 1950s. It combines all of his trademark techniques into a powerful vision.

The shepherds, with elongated bodies and expressive hands, are stretched upward, flickering like flames toward heaven, lit from within by a spiritual fire. Christ is the light source, shining out of the darkness, giving a sheen to the surrounding colors. These shepherds will never be able to buy suits off the rack.

Notice El Greco's typical two-tiered composition—earth below, heaven above. Over the Christ Child is a swirling canopy of clouds and angels. Heaven and earth seem to intermingle, and the earthly figures look as though they're about to be sucked up through a funnel into the vault of heaven. There is little depth to the picture—all the figures are virtually the same distance from us—so our eyes have nowhere to go but up and down, up and down, linking heaven and earth, God and humankind.

● *Continue down the main gallery, turning left into the large lozenge-shaped Velázquez Room 12 and adjoining Rooms 13–15.*

Velázquez (1599–1660)

For 35 years, Diego Velázquez (pron: vel-LOSS-kes) was the king of Spain's court painters. Look around the room. While El Greco and other Spanish artists painted crucifixions, saints, and madonnas, Velázquez painted what his boss, the king, told him to—mostly portraits.

Unlike the wandering, independent El Greco, Velázquez was definitely a career man. Born in Seville, apprenticed early on, he marries the master's daughter, moves to Madrid, impresses the king with his skill, and works his way up the ladder at the king's court—valet to the king, director of new buildings, director of festivities, and so on. He becomes the king's friend and art teacher and, eventually, is knighted.

What's amazing in this tale of ambition is that, as a painter, Velázquez never compromised. He was the photojournalist of his time, chronicling court events for posterity.

Velázquez — *Prince Balthasar Carlos on Horseback (El Príncipe Baltasar Carlos)*

As court painter, this was exactly the kind of portrait Velázquez was called on to produce—the prince, age five, looking like the masterful heir to the throne. But the charm of the painting is the contrast between the pose—the traditional equestrian pose of a powerful Roman conqueror—with the fact that this "conqueror" is only a cute, tiny tyke in a pink and gold suit. The seriousness on the prince's face adds the crowning touch. We can see why Velázquez was such a court favorite.

While pleasing his king, Velázquez was also starting a revolution in art. Stand back and look at the prince's costume—remarkably detailed, right? Now move up closer—all that "remarkable detail" is nothing but messy splotches of pink and gold paint! In the past, artists painted details meticulously. But Velázquez learned how just a few dabs of colors on a canvas blend in the eye when seen at a distance to give the appearance of great detail. Two centuries later this technique would eventually be taken to its extreme by the Impressionists.

Velázquez — *Jester Portraits (Bufones)*

In royal courts, dwarfs were given the job of entertaining the nobles. But some also had a more important task—social satire. They alone

were given free rein to say anything they wanted about the king, however biting, nasty, or—worst of all—true. Consequently, these dwarfs were often the wittiest and most intelligent people at court, and Velázquez, who must have known them as colleagues, painted them with great dignity.

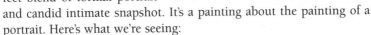
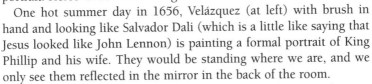

Velázquez — *The Maids of Honor (Las Meninas)*

Velázquez has made the perfect blend of formal portrait and candid intimate snapshot. It's a painting about the painting of a portrait. Here's what we're seeing:

One hot summer day in 1656, Velázquez (at left) with brush in hand and looking like Salvador Dali (which is a little like saying that Jesus looked like John Lennon) is painting a formal portrait of King Phillip and his wife. They would be standing where we are, and we only see them reflected in the mirror in the back of the room.

Their daughter, the Infanta Margarita (the main figure in the center), has come to watch her parents being painted. With her are her two attendants (*meninas*, or girls), one of whom is kneeling, offering her a cool glass of water. Also in the picture is the young court jester (far right) poking impishly at the family dog. A female dwarf looks on, as do others in the background. Also, at that very moment, a member of court is passing by the doorway in the distance on his way upstairs, and he, too, looks in on the progress of the portrait.

Velázquez was smart enough to know that the really interesting portrait wasn't the king and queen, but the action behind the scenes. We're sucked right in by the naturalness of the scene and because the characters are looking right at us. This is true Spanish history, and Velázquez the journalist (who is shown wearing the red cross of knighthood, painted on after his death—possibly by Phillip IV himself) has told us more about this royal family than have volumes of history books.

The scene is lit by the window at right. Using gradations of light, Velázquez has split the room into five receding planes: (1) the king and queen, standing where we are; (2) the main figures, lit by the window;

(3) the darker middle distance figures (including Velázquez); (4) the black wall; and (5) the lit doorway. We are drawn into the painting, living and breathing with its characters, free to walk behind them, around them, and among them. This is art come to life.

Velázquez — *Crucifixion*

King Phillip IV was having an affair. He got caught and, being a good Christian king, was overcome with remorse. He commissioned this work to atone for his adulterous ways. (That's Phillip, pious and kneeling, to the left of the Crucifixion.)

Velázquez's *Crucifixion* must have matched the repentant mood of his king (and friend). You can often tell the tone of a crucifixion by the tilt of Christ's head. Here, it's hanging down, accepting His punishment, humble and repentant.

Meditating on this Christ would truly be an act of agonizing penance. We see him straight from the front, no holds barred. Every detail is laid out for us, even down to the knots in the wood of the crossbar. And the dripping blood! We feel how long Jesus has been hanging there by how long it must have taken for that blood to drip ever so slowly down.

Velázquez — *The Drinkers (Los Borrachos)*

Velázquez's objective eye even turns Greek gods into everyday folk. Here the Greek god of wine crowns a drinker for his deeds of debauchery. Bacchus is as finely painted as anything Titian or Rubens ever did, but what a difference in scenes! The real focus isn't the otherworldly Bacchus but his fellow, human merry-makers.

This isn't a painting, it's a Polaroid snapshot in a blue-collar bar. Look how natural the guy is next to Bacchus, grinning at us over the bowl of wine he's offering us—and the guy next to him, clambering to get into the picture and mugging for the camera! Velázquez was the master at making a carefully composed scene look spontaneous.

Velázquez —
The Surrender of Breda
(La Rendición de Breda)

Here's another piece of artistic journal-ism, the Spanish victory over the Dutch after a long siege of Breda, a strongly for-tified city. The scene has become famous as a model of fair play. The defeated Dutch general is offering the keys to the city to the victorious Spaniards. As he begins to kneel in humility, the Spanish conqueror restrains him—the war is over and there's no need to rub salt in the wounds. The optimistic calm-after-the-battle mood is enhanced by the great open space highlighted by the 25 lances (the painting is often called "The Lances") silhouetted against the sky.

● *From the cool objectivity of Velázquez, enter the heat and passion of Spain's religious art of the Counter-Reformation, in Rooms 16B–18.*

Counter-Reformation Art — Fighting Back With Brushes (1600s)

Europe was torn in two by the Protestant Reformation. For 100 years, Catholics and Protestants bashed Bibles in what has been called the first "world war." The Catholic Church also waged a propagan-da campaign (the Counter-Reformation) to bolster the faith of the confused, weary masses. Art was part of that campaign. Pretty pictures brought abstract doctrines to the level of the common man.

Murillo — The Immaculate Conception (La Immaculada)

For centuries, the No. 1 deity in the Christian "pantheon" was the goddess Mary. This paint-ing is a religious treatise, explaining a Catholic doctrine that many found difficult to comprehend—the Immaculate Conception of Mary. Since all humans are stained by the orig-inal sin of Adam (so the doctrine went), didn't that mean Jesus was as well, since His mother was human? Not so, said the Catholics. Mary, by a special act of God, was conceived and born without taint of original sin.

The Spanish have always loved the Virgin. She's practically a cult figure. Common people pray directly to her for help in troubled times. Murillo (pron: mur-REE-oh) used this fanatic devotion to Mary to teach the dull theological concept of Immaculate Conception. He painted a beautiful, floating, and Ivory-Soap-pure woman—the most "immaculate" virgin imaginable—radiating youth and wholesome goodness.

Zurbarán — St. Peter Crucified Appearing to Peter Nolasco

After Murillo's sweet beauty, Zurbarán is like a bitter jolt of *café solo*.

In Spain, miracles are real. When legends tell of a saint who was beheaded but didn't die, that isn't an allegory on eternal life to the Spanish—they picture a real man walking around with his head under his arm.

So, when Zurbarán paints a mystical vision, he gives it to us in photographic realism. Bam, there's the Apostle Peter crucified upside down right in front of us. Nolasco looks as shocked as we are at the reality of the vision. This is "People's Art" of the Counter-Reformation, religious art for the masses. (Zurbarán has the sort of literal-minded religion that makes people wonder things like—"When the Rapture comes, what if I'm sitting on the toilet?")

Cano — St. Bernard and the Virgin

Here's another heavenly vision brought right down to earth. St. Bernard is literally enjoying the "milk of paradise," a vision he had of being suckled on the heavenly teat of Mary. When God's word was portrayed in this realistic way, the common folk lapped it up.

Cano — A King of Spain (Un Rey de España)

By 1600, Spain had peaked as Europe's great power. The quick wealth from the Americas began to dry up, the Spanish fleet was defeated by the British, and France emerged as a European power. Spain's influence sank.

I like to think of Cano's *A King of Spain* as a picture of the country at the moment it passed its peak. This unknown king in mythical dress, slumped unhappily on his throne, with a globe of the world in his hands, waves his sword, bored. There's nothing left to conquer. His look says, "I've got the whole world. Now what?"

● *Enter the Early Goya Rooms, 19–23.*

Goya (1746–1828)

Goya's *Two Cats Fighting* (*Gatos Riñendo*) represents the two warring halves of a human soul, the dark and light sides, anger and fear locked in immortal combat, fighting for dominance of a man's life. We're entering the Age of Romanticism.

Francisco de Goya, a true individual in both his life and his painting style, is hard to pigeonhole—his personality and talents were so varied. We'll see several different facets of this rough-cut man—cheery apprentice painter, loyal court painter, political rebel, scandalmaker, disillusioned genius. His work runs the gamut, from pretty Rococo to political rabble-rousing to Romantic nightmares.

For convenience, let's divide Goya's life into three stages: the Court Painter, Political Rebel, and Dark Stage.

Goya: Court Painter, Early Years, Light and Playful

Born in a small town, Goya, unlike Velázquez, was a far cry from a precocious painter destined for success. In his youth he dabbled as a matador, kicking around Spain before finally landing a job in the Royal Tapestry. The canvases in these rooms were designs made into tapestries bound for the walls of nobles' palaces.

Browse through these rooms and watch lords and ladies of the 1700s with nothing better to do than play—toasting each other at a picnic, dancing with castanets, flying kites, playing paddleball, listening to a blind guitarist, walking on stilts, or playing Blind Man's Bluff.

Notice—how do I say this?—how BAD the drawing is in some of these canvases, especially the early ones. However, in the few short years he worked in the tapestry department, Goya the inexperienced apprentice slowly developed into a good, if not great, draftsman. *The Parasol* (*El Quitasol*) was one of his first really good paintings, with a simple composition and subtle shadings of light. Goya worked steadily for the court for 25 years, dutifully cranking out portraits before finally becoming First Court Painter at age 53.

● *Exiting the "tapestry" rooms, turn right and walk down the hall, entering the octagonal (or something-agonal) Room 32 to the left. Here you'll find portraits of Goya's employers, the Royal Family of Spain.*

Goya — The Family of Charles IV (La Familia de Carlos IV)

They're decked out in all their finest, wearing every medal, jewel, and ribbon they could find for this impressive group portrait. Goya has captured all the splendor of the court in 1800—but with a brutal twist of reality. For underneath all the royal finery, he captured the inner personality—or lack thereof—of these shallow monarchs.

This isn't so much a royal portrait as it is a stiff family photo of Ma and Pa Kettle in their Sunday best. The look in their eyes seems to say "I can't wait to get this monkey-suit off." (I always picture Goya deliberately taking his own sweet time making them stand and smile for hours on end.)

Goya, the budding political liberal, shows his disgust for the shallow king and his family. King Charles, with his ridiculous hairdo and silly smile, is portrayed for what he was—a vacuous, good-natured fool, a henpecked husband controlled by a domineering queen. She, the true center of the composition, is proud and defiant. She was vain about the supposed beauty of her long, swan-like neck, and here she stretches to display every centimeter of it. The other adults, with their bland faces, are bug-eyed with stupidity. Catch the crone looking out at us bird-like, fourth from left.

As a tribute to Velázquez' *Maids of Honor,* Goya painted himself painting the scene at far left. But here Goya stands back in the shadows looking with disdain on the group. Only the children escape Goya's critical eye, painted with the sympathy he always showed to those lower on the social ladder.

● *Look around the room at other portraits, equally judgmental of the king, queen, and prince, then cross the hall into Room 36.*

GOYA: POLITICAL REBEL
Goya — *Nude Maja (La Maja Desnuda)* and *Clothed Maja (La Maja Vestida)*

Goya remained at court because of his talent, not his political beliefs—or his morals. Rumor flew that he was fooling around with the beautiful, intelligent, and vivacious Duchess of Alba. Even more scandalous was a painting, supposedly of the Duchess in a less-than-devoutly-Catholic pose.

A *maja* was a hip working-class girl. Many of Goya's early tapestries show royalty dressed in the garb of these colorful commoners. Here the Duchess has undressed as one.

The Nude Maja was a real shocker. Spanish kings enjoyed the sensual nudes of Titian and Rubens, but it was unheard of for a pious Spaniard to actually paint one. Goya incurred the wrath of the

Inquisition, the Catholic court system that tried heretics and sinners.

Tour guides explain that the painting caused such a stir that Goya dashed off another version with her clothes on. The quick brushwork is sloppier, perhaps because Goya was in a hurry, or because he was anxious to invent Impressionism. The two paintings may have been displayed in a double frame—the nude could be covered by sliding the clothed *maja* over it to hide it from Inquisitive minds that wanted to know.

Artistically, the nude is less a portrait than an idealized nude in the tradition (and reclining pose) of Titian's *Venus and the Organ Player*. The pale body is highlighted by the cool green sheets, à la Titian, as well. Both paintings were locked away in obscurity, along with the Titians and Rubenses, until 1901.

● *Down the hall, in Room 39, you'll find …*

Goya — *Third of May, 1808* and *Second of May, 1808*

Goya became a political radical, a believer in democracy in a world of kings. During his time, the American and French Revolutions put the fear of God in the medieval minds of Europe's aristocracy. In retaliation, members of the aristocracy were determined to stamp out any trace of political liberalism.

Goya admired the French leader Napoleon, who fought for the democratic ideals of the French Revolution against the kings of Europe. But then Napoleon invaded Spain (1808), and Goya saw war firsthand. What he saw was not a heroic war liberating the Spaniards from the feudal yoke, but an oppressive, brutal, senseless war in which common Spaniards were the first to die.

The *Second of May, 1808* and *Third of May, 1808* show two bloody days of the war. On the second, the common citizens of Madrid rebelled against the French invaders. With sticks, stones, and kitchen knives, they rallied in the Puerta del Sol in protest. The French sent in their fearsome Egyptian mercenary troops to quell the riot. Goya captures the hysterical tangle of bodies as the Egyptians wade through the dense crowd hacking away at the overmatched *Madrilenos* who have nowhere to run.

The next day the French began reprisals. They took suspected rebels to a nearby hill and began mercilessly executing them. The *Third of May, 1808* is supposedly a tribute to those brave Spaniards who rebelled against the French, but it's far from heroic. In fact, it's anti-heroic, showing us the irrationality of war—an assembly line of death, with each victim toppling into a crumpled heap. They plea for mercy and get none. Those awaiting death bury their faces in their hands, unable to look at their falling companions. The central victim in luminous white spreads his arms Christ-like and asks, "Why are you doing this to us?"

Goya goes beyond sympathy for the victims. In this war, even the executioners are pawns in the game, only following orders without understanding why. The colorless firing squad, with guns perfectly level and feet perfectly in step, is a faceless machine of murder, cutting people down with all the compassion of a lawnmower. They bury their faces in their guns as though they, too, are unable to look their victims in the eye. This war is horrible, and what's worse, the horror is pointless.

The violence is painted with equally violent techniques. There's a strong prison-yard floodlight thrown on the main victim, focusing all our attention on his look of puzzled horror. The distorted features, the puddle of blood, the twisting bodies, the thick brushwork—all are features of the Romantic style that emphasized emotion over beauty. It all adds up to a vivid portrayal of the brutality and ultimate senselessness of war. Like the victims, we ask, "How can one human being do this to another?"

Goya was disillusioned by the invasion led by his hero Napoleon. Added to this he began to go deaf. His wife died. To top it off, he was exiled as a political radical. Goya retreated from court life to his own private, quiet—and dark—world.

● *To get to the Black Paintings, exit back into the hallway, turn right, silently flagellate yourself, then turn right again winding down the stairs. At the foot of the stairs continue straight, then take the first right into Room 67.*

GOYA'S DARK STAGE
In 1819, Goya—deaf, widowed, and exiled—moved into a villa and began decorating it with his own oil paintings. The works were painted right on the walls of rooms in the villa, later transferred here.

You immediately see why these are the Black, or Dark, Paintings—both in color and mood. They're nightmarish scenes, scary and surreal, the inner visions of an embittered man smeared onto the walls as though finger-painted in blood.

Goya — *The Witches' Sabbath (Aquellare)*
Dark forces convened continually in Goya's dining room. This dark coven of crones swirls in a frenzy of black magic around a dark, Satanic goat in monk's clothes who presides, priest-like, over the

GOYA—DARK STAGE

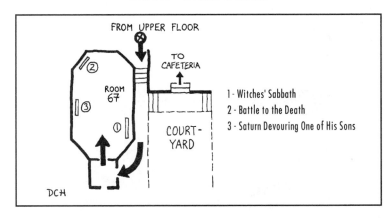

FROM UPPER FLOOR

TO CAFETERIA

ROOM 67

1 - Witches' Sabbath
2 - Battle to the Death
3 - Saturn Devouring One of His Sons

COURT-YARD

DCH

obscene rituals. The main witch, seated in front of the goat, is the very image of wild-eyed adoration, lust, and fear. (Notice the one noble lady sitting just to the right of center with her hands folded primly in her lap—"I thought this was a Tupperware party ... ")

Goya — Battle to the Death (Duelo a Garrotazos)

Two giants buried up to their knees, face to face, flail at each other with clubs. Neither can move, neither can run, neither dares rest or the other will finish him off. It's a standoff between superpowers caught in a never-ending cycle of war. Can a truce be reached? It looks bleak.

The Black Paintings foreshadow 20th-century Surrealism with their dream images, and Expressionism with their thick smeared style and cynical outlook. Are these really by the same artist who did the frilly *Blind Man's Bluff* in the tapestry room?

Goya — Saturn Devouring One of His Sons (Saturno Devorando a un Hijo)

Fearful that his sons would overthrow him as king of the gods, the Roman god Saturn ate them. Saturn was also known as Cronus, or Time, and this may be an allegory of how Time devours us all. Goya was a dying man in a dying, feudal world. The destructiveness of time is shown in all its horror by a man unafraid of the darker side.

Guernica

● *Probably the single most impressive piece of art in Spain is Picasso's* Guernica *in the Centro Arte de Reina Sofia, Madrid's slick new modern art*

museum located three long blocks south of the Prado across the street from the Atocha train station (open 10:00–21:00, Sunday 10:00–14:30, closed Tuesday, tel. 91-467-5062).

Picasso's monumental canvas *Guernica* is not only a piece of art but a piece of history. It's one of Europe's must-see sights, so leave time for it.

Guernica is the product of the right artist in the right place at the right time. Pablo Picasso, a Spaniard, was in Paris in 1937, preparing an exhibition of paintings for its world's fair. Meanwhile, a bloody civil war was being fought in his own country. The legally elected democratic government was being challenged by traditionalist right-wing forces under Francisco Franco. Franco would eventually win and rule the country with an iron fist for three decades.

Guernica was a small town in northern Spain of no strategic importance, but it became the target of the world's first saturation-bombing raid. Franco gave permission to his Fascist ally, Hitler, to use the town as a guinea pig to try out Germany's new air force. The raid leveled the town, causing destruction that was unheard of at the time—though by 1944 it would be commonplace.

News of the bombing reached Picasso in Paris. He scrapped earlier plans and immediately set to work on the Guernica mural for the Spanish pavilion. It was finished in a matter of weeks. Thousands of people attended the fair, and the Guernica mural had a profound impact on those who saw it. They witnessed the horror of modern technology of war, the vain struggle of the Spanish Republicans, and the cold indifference of the Nazi war machine. It was a prophetic vision of the world war to come.

Picasso shows Guernica in the aftermath of the bombing. It's as if he'd picked up the shattered shards and pasted them onto a canvas. It looks like a jumble of overlapping shades on first sight, but looking closer, we can see each piece of this broken city. The figures are twisted, but recognizable. Let's sort the main ones out.

On the left is a bull. In typical Cubist fashion, we see the head from two angles at once. The body extends to the left, ending with a tail like a wisp of smoke. Beneath the bull is a modern pietà—a grieving mother with her dead child.

The central figure is a horse with a twisted head and a sword piercing its newsprint body. The horse's rider has fallen, dismembered, at the horse's feet. We see his severed head and severed arm with a broken sword.

On the right, a woman runs screaming. Above her, another pokes her head out a window shining a shaft of light on the horse and the woman below. To the far right another figure cries with grief inside a building.

This is a gruesome and, despite the modern "abstract" style, remarkably realistic portrayal of the bombing's destruction. But Picasso has suggested a symbolic interpretation that raised the work to the universal level, a commentary on all wars.

Picasso himself said that the central horse, with the spear in its back, symbolizes humanity succumbing to brute force. The bull represents brutality, standing triumphant over the mourning mother and child.

The Guernica raid was a completely senseless and pointless act of brute force without any military purpose. In fact, the entire Spanish Civil War was an exercise in brutality. As one side captured a town, it might systematically round up every man, old and young—including priests—line them up and shoot them in revenge for atrocities by the other side. The bare bulb at the top of the canvas shines an interrogator's third-degree light on all this ugliness.

Near the bull is a crying dove, the symbol of peace in defeat. The rider's broken sword could be the futility of trying to fight brutality with brutality.

This is a scary work. The drab, concrete-colored grey tones create a depressing, almost nauseating mood. We are like the terrified woman at right, trying to run from it all. But her leg is too thick, dragging her down, like trying to run from something in a nightmare. The figure thrusting her head out of the window with a lamp in her hand is humanity itself, coming out of its shell, seeing for the first time the harsh horror of modern war.

22 *Modern Art*

If you don't "get" modern art, you're on the right track. It's meant to disorient and disrupt your normal outlook, to make you see things in a new way. Find your own meaning. You are a co-creator with the artist and a co-author of this chapter.

You'll bump into modern art museums throughout your travels: Paris' Picasso Museum (the Pompidou Center's collection will re-open in 2000), Amsterdam's Stedelijk Museum, Venice's Peggy Guggenheim Collection, and Madrid's Centro Arte de Reina Sofia (includes Picasso's *Guernica*, described at the end of chapter 21). Regardless of

the museum, the same artists are usually represented: Picasso, Kandinsky, Mondrian, Klee, Dali, and so on. This chapter is a guide to modern art, the artists, and their principles rather than a look at specific pieces of art in specific museums.

THE DEATH OF REALITY

Why doesn't modern art look like the real world? That's the thing that many people don't like about it. Its also exactly what modern art is all about, so let's keep asking the question as we go.

The most obvious response is—hey, if you want reality, get a camera. And if you want a beautiful object, buy it at the mall. Machines have taken over artists' traditional duties, freeing them to be irrelevant.

But beyond that—what is reality? Our century has been plagued by that question like no other. Our common-sense view of the world is attacked daily on all fronts. Modern art reflects the turbulent, anything-goes "reality" of our end-of-the-millennium world.

A.D. 1900

A new century dawns. War is a thing of the past. Science and technology would soon wipe out poverty and disease. The knowledge that began budding in the Renaissance was about to reach full flower. Rational Man was poised at a new era of peace and prosperity …

Right.

Even before this cozy Victorian dream was shattered by world wars, the ground was starting to shift. Darwin stripped off man's robe of culture and found a naked ape beneath. Nietzsche murdered God. Freud washed ashore on the beach of a vast new continent inside each of us. Einstein made every truth merely "relative." Even the fundamental building blocks of the universe—atoms—were behaving erratically.

Technology arrived, but instead of bringing the promised paradise, it brought noise, pollution, and ugliness. Worst of all, fast-paced modern life was turning people into robots, leading lives that were empty, programmed, and sterile.

Progress was killing them, rationality was approaching a dead-end, and artists, who were particularly sensitive to the trends, were troubled. They looked for an alternative. They weren't just exploring new art techniques. Like Matisse, they were looking for a whole new approach to life.

Matisse

Bam. We know we're not in Kansas anymore. Matisse's colorful "wallpaper" works are a far cry from realistic paintings. Most do have a recognizable subject, but the figures are simplified (almost childlike) and distorted, and the colors are unnatural. Also, Matisse obviously didn't try very hard to create the illusion of distance and 3-D that was so important to the Renaissance Italians.

Traditionally, the canvas was like a window that you looked "through" to see a slice of the real world stretching off into the distance. If you try to look "through" a Matisse canvas, you won't get very far. Instead, try looking "at" it, as if it were wallpaper. *Voilà!* What was a crudely drawn scene now becomes a sophisticated and decorative pattern of colors and shapes.

More Fauves

Matisse was one of the Fauves, or "wild beasts," who tried to inject a bit of the jungle into bored French society. Their style was intentionally crude, with bright, clashing colors. The mask-like faces came from African art and voodoo dolls.

The Fauves were to art what Louis Armstrong was to music and Josephine Baker's topless "Savage Dance" was to dance—an attempt to reconnect rational man with his primitive roots.

Let's let the Fauves ferry us from familiar waters into the rapids of the modern world.

The Fauves are still painting the real world, but the subject matter is starting to get lost in the blur of paints (think of Monet's gauzy water lilies and cathedrals). Soon, artists will drop the subject altogether, finding beauty in the colors and shapes themselves—Abstract Art.

The Fauves use the bright colors of van Gogh, the primitive figures of Gauguin, and the colorful designs of Japanese prints. And like the Impressionists, they use "messy" globs of paint that only blend together at a distance.

The Artist as Shaman

Science toppled us from our place at the pinnacle of the universe. Technology stripped the world bare of mystery. Something was missing. Artists tried to rekindle a sense of wonder in life. They saw art as a way to express some of the—how do I say it?—the holiness? mystery? magic? that had been lost. With traditional Christianity losing ground, artists looked to the arts for their religion.

They found inspiration in the "primitive" peoples of Africa, the South Seas, and Asia, whose art reflected a whole different outlook, a voodoo world inhabited by spirits and demons.

The modern artist became the industrial world's shaman—wild and holy, living different from "normal" people—entering a trance and connecting with the hidden world, then "channeling" it to us through art.

The result? Modern art that looked primitive: simple figures, mask-like faces with geometric features, and "flat," two-dimensional scenes.

Artists adopting a more primitive attitude makes some sense, but why return to crude techniques that don't portray the real world? Let's return to that Reality Thing.

3-D — A Western Obsession?

Which is closer—a bear cub at your feet or the mama bear a hundred yards away who's charging at you? If you're painting that scene

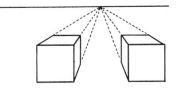

and want it to reflect your actual experience, you'd make mama huge, terrifying, and very close.

Renaissance technique emphasized the 3-D element, rather than the emotion, placing the closest thing prominently in the foreground, center, with the background objects smaller and fainter.

In art from other cultures, however, the "main" figure doesn't always stand out so clearly. It's enmeshed in the web of its surroundings, so we see it in its context, as part of the big picture, not isolated. Primitive art is less visual, but more visceral and emotional, coming from lower down the brain stem. When the full moon stirs your blood, it's so "close" you could hit it with a rock.

CUBISM — *Reality Shattered* (Picasso, Braque, Leger)

I throw a rock at a statue made of glass, shatter it, pick up the pieces, and glue them onto a canvas. I'm a Cubist.

Braque and Picasso

Braque sees the world through a kaleidoscope of brown and grey. His subjects are somewhat recognizable (with the help of the titles), but they're broken into geometric shards—let's call them "cubes," though there are many different shapes—then pieced back together.

The shards often overlap. A single shard might contain both an arm and the room in the background, both painted the same color. The foreground and background are woven together, so that the subject dissolves into a pattern.

Cubism gives us several different sides of the subject at once. For example, to paint a woman's head, Picasso might show us a front view and a side profile together. The result is a face with both eyes on the same side of the nose.

Okay, it's all very interesting, but what's the point?

On the one hand, they were simply asking the age-old question—how to paint a 3-D world on a 2-D canvas. The Cubist "solution" is a kind of Mercator map projection, where the round world is sliced up like an orange peel and laid flat.

But there's more to Cubism. They recognized that real life is never as orderly as a Raphael painting, where the most important object is right up front center, and the less important thing is in the faint distance.

In fact, our attention darts from one thing to the next—from the woman's eyes to her profile to the wall behind her to the guitar in her lap to a memory from childhood and back. It's up to our brains to piece together the flickering snapshots it receives. Cubism simply paints this jumble of sense-data in its raw, random form.

Picasso and Braque were shattering old concepts of "3-D space" in art at the same time that science was doing the same. Einstein told us there was actually a fourth dimension—time. We experience this dimension when we, say, take 15 seconds to walk around a 3-D object. Picasso saves us the trouble by showing several views at once, translating that fourth dimension into something we can see on a canvas.

Pablo Picasso (1881–1973)

Okay, so the Cubists were as smart as Einstein. But why couldn't they draw a picture to save their lives?

Picasso was one modern artist who really could draw and draw well. But he wasn't content to crank out paintings that look great with a sofa underneath. He constantly explored and adapted his style to new trends, becoming the most famous painter of our century.

Born in Spain, Picasso moved to Paris as a young man. At first, he felt out of place and lonely, and he painted his fellow loners—thin beggars and haunted outcasts. The dark colors and melancholy mood make this his "Blue" period.

Then he met Georges Braque, and these two modern-day shamans locked themselves into a Paris studio together. They worked on each other's paintings—it's hard to tell whose is whose without the titles. They shared meals, ideas, and girlfriends.

Soon Picasso began to use more color rather than just brown and grey cubes. Eventually (1917–1925), he used curved shapes to build the subject, rather than the straight-line shards of early Cubism.

Picasso married and had children. Works from this period (the 1920s) are more realistic, with full-bodied (and big-nosed) women and children, where he tries to capture the solidity, serenity, and volume of classical statues.

As his relationships with women deteriorated, he vented his sexual demons by twisting the female body into grotesque balloon-animal shapes (1925–1931).

All through his life, Picasso was exploring new materials. He made collages, tried his hand at "statues" out of wood, wire, or whatever, and even made statues out of everyday household objects. These "multi-media" works, so revolutionary at the time, have become stock-in-trade today.

Leger

Fernand Leger's style has been called "Tubism"—breaking the world down into cylinder shapes rather than cubes. (He supposedly got his inspiration during World War I from the gleaming barrel of a cannon.) Leger captures the feel of the encroaching Age of Machines, with all the world looking like an internal combustion engine.

Abstract vs. Representational

The art most of us know is "representational," that is, it represents or depicts the world we see—a chair, a woman with a guitar, and so on. "Abstract" art plays with patterns of lines, shapes, and colors. Another way to put it: with representational art you look "through" the canvas like a window. With abstract you look "at" it.

Most modern art—like Cubism—is a combination of representational and abstract art. You may find yourself facing a canvas of squiggles and blobs, asking, "Is that a man's face? Or just squiggles and blobs?"

ABSTRACT ART —
Painting the Hidden Reality

Abstract art tries to express a feeling or idea through colors and shapes alone. Madison Avenue ad-men are fully aware that red gets us excited, blue calms us, jagged lines suggest turmoil, and arches make you want a cheeseburger. Abstract art uses the same effects of color and line to show things that can't be shown with a picture.

What things? Well, the world of emotions. The world of sounds, smells, taste, and touch—things which, while not exactly hidden, are at least non-visual. Certain abstract concepts like "justice," "beauty," and "2 + 2 = 4" can't be seen, but they're real. And finally, there's the world that's been lost in our secular age—the world of holiness, magic, the feeling of being connected to other people, the world of spirits and demons and angels. All these things may be just as real— and certainly as powerful—as the tables, chairs, nudes, and landscapes of realistic painting. But, being unseen, the best way to show them is using abstract designs.

Kandinsky

The bright colors, bent lines, and lack of symmetry tell us that Kandinsky's world was passionate, emotional, and intense. He gives

us a slice of raw sense-data before it's been tamed and digested rationally.

Traditionally, the artist helped us find some order out of life's chaos. But in a programmed, regimented, climate-controlled environment where so much is sorted out for us, an artist has to rediscover wildness. I don't think he could have done that as well by using recognizable figures.

Notice that Kandinsky uses titles like Improvisation and Composition. Kandinsky was inspired by music, an art form that's also "abstract" though it still packs a punch. Like a jazz musician improvising a new pattern of notes from a set scale, Kandinsky plays with new patterns of related colors, looking for just the right combination that makes us yell, "Go man, go!"

Using line and color, Kandinsky translates the unseen reality into a new medium … like lightning crackling over the radio.

Mondrian

While reality in the raw may be chaotic, humans long for order. We find symmetry attractive (maybe because our own bodies are roughly symmetrical) and geometric shapes restful, even worthy of meditation.

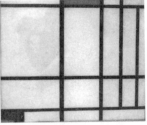

Mondrian's T-square style boils painting down to its basic building blocks—

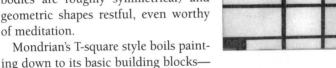

black lines, white canvas, and the three primary colors. He then arranges them into orderly patterns.

When you come right down to it, that's all painting ever has been, even with Leonardo or Raphael. If you've ever seen a schematic drawing of, say, the *Mona Lisa*, you'll know that it's less about a woman than about the triangles and rectangles that she's composed of.

(Are Mondrian's shapes based on anything in the real world? Well, he started out painting realistic landscapes of the orderly fields in his native Holland. Hmm.)

Mondrian appeals to our most basic instinct for order, the instinct that has driven art from earliest times, from the Egyptian pyramids to Stonehenge circles to Greek columns to Roman arches to Renaissance symmetry to the American Indian medicine "wheel."

Brancusi

Imagine how a Neanderthal might feel stumbling across one of Brancusi's curved, shiny statues gleaming in an open field. Think of the sense of wonder, that such a smooth, orderly, confident, geometric form could have emerged out of a rough rock, a tree stump, or crude metal. Even for us, the very simplicity strikes us on a primitive level, deep in our collective unconscious, taking us back to a time when sculpture was the ritual circumcision of stones.

Brancusi reduces things to their essence. A bird is shown as a single stylized wing—the one feature that sets it apart from other animals. What Brancusi leaves out, we fill in from memory, with all the associations and emotions that go with it.

Klee

Paul Klee's small and playful canvases are deceptively simple.

Klee thought certain shapes were so basic they could be read like universal symbols—think of our modern international traffic symbols. Klee thought a wavy line, for example, would always suggest the idea of motion, and a stick-figure would always mean a human. (By the way, Klee's fellow Swiss, the psychologist Carl Jung, also spoke of universal symbols found in dreams and stories—all part of our "collective unconscious.")

But which shapes are truly universal? Klee looked to the art of children, who express themselves more honestly, without censoring themselves or cluttering it up with learned symbols. His art has a childlike playfulness, fantasy and simple figures painted in an uninhibited frame of mind.

Klee also turned to nature. The same forces that cause the wave to draw a line of foam on the beach, can cause the artist to draw a line of paint on the canvas. The result is a universal shape. The true artist doesn't paint Nature, he becomes Nature.

Representational Art

Not every modern artist turned away from the real world. But camera-eye realism was obsolete. Artists purposely distorted their subjects for effect, to let us see it with fresh eyes.

In a sense, every painting has two "subjects:" (1) the subject itself (a chair, a nude, a landscape), and (2) the mood or message it conveys. Modern artists are free to distort #1 to enhance #2.

If a painting looks distorted to us, it may be because we're looking through the artist's glasses. The French writer Proust once said: "Only through art can we get outside ourselves and know another's view of the universe."

World War I — The Death of Values

A soldier—shivering in a trench, ankle-deep in mud, waiting to be ordered "over the top," to run through barbed wire, over fallen comrades, and into a hail of machine-gun fire, only to capture a few hundred yards of meaningless territory that would be lost the next day—was not thinking about art.

World War I left 9 million dead. (Many times, France lost more men in a single day than America lost in all of Vietnam.) The war also killed the optimism and faith in humankind that had guided Europe since the Renaissance. Now, rationality just meant scheming, technology meant more efficient machines of death, and morality meant giving your life for an empty cause.

Expressionism — Grosz, Kirchner, Beckmann, Kokoschka

Cynicism and decadence settled over post-war Europe. Artists "expressed" their disgust by showing a distorted reality that emphasized the ugly. Using the lurid colors and simplified figures of the Fauves, they slapped paint on in thick brushstrokes. Expressionism was a new kind of Primitivism—depicting a barbaric, hard-edged, dog-eat-dog world that had lost its bearings. The people have a haunted look in their eyes, the fixed stare of corpses and of those who must bury them.

Dada

When they could grieve no longer, they turned from crying to its giddy twin, laughter. The war killed Renaissance civilization, and all old values became a joke, including artistic ones. The Dada movement, choosing a purposely childish name, made art that was appropriately absurd: a moustache on the *Mona Lisa*, a shovel hung on the wall with a serious title, or Duchamp's modern version of a Renaissance "fountain"—a urinal.

It was a dig at all the pompous pre-war artistic theories based on the noble intellect of Rational Women and Men. While the experts ranted on, Dadaists sat in the back of the class and made cultural fart noises.

Hey, I love this stuff. My mind says its sophomoric, but my heart belongs to Dada.

Chagall

Marc Chagall views the world with the wide-eyed wonder of a country boy. Lovers are weightless with bliss. Animals smile and wink at us. Musicians, poets, peasants, and dreamers ignore gravity, tumbling in slow-motion circles high above the rooftops. The colors are deep, dark, and earthy—a pool of mystery that suggests that if we could plunge in we'd find still more treasures.

Chagall's very personal style fuses many influences. He was raised in a small Russian village, which may explain his "naive" outlook and fiddler-on-the-roof motifs. He paints recognizable things, but they're more like universal symbols (remember Klee?) than specific, real-life objects. Since his upbringing was Orthodox Jewish, Chagall learned early the power of "graven images."

Stylistically, he "builds" his figures like a Cubist and scatters them in a jumble of images that often overlap. The way he puts powerful images side by side without explaining their connection is something that would later be called Surrealism.

Chagall's otherworldy style was a natural for religious works, and his murals and stained glass, with both Jewish and Christian motifs, decorate buildings around the world (for example, the ceiling of Paris' Garnier Opera House).

Rouault

Georges Rouault's father made stained-glass windows. Enough said?

The paintings have the same thick, glowing colors, heavy black outlines, simple subjects, and (mostly) religious themes. The style is Expressionist, but the mood is medieval, solemn, and melancholy. Rouault captures the tragic spirit of those people—clowns, prostitutes, and sons of God—who have been made outcasts by society.

Surrealism

Surrealism is a version of connect-the-dots with no numbers. The artist scatters seemingly unrelated images on the canvas, leaving it to us to trace the connections among them. When it does come together, the synergy of unrelated things can be pretty startling. But even if the juxtaposed images don't ultimately connect, the artist has achieved one thing—he's made you think, rerouting your thoughts through new neural paths as you try vainly to relate unrelated things. As with Dada and so much other modern art, if you don't "get" it ... you got it.

Many a Surrealist canvas is a "landscape" of the artist's inner world, painted in a stream-of-consciousness frame of mind where nothing is censored. Dreams are a big inspiration. Freud said that the bizarre images of dreams were not just silly fantasies, but actually reveal our deepest urges, uncensored by the waking mind.

In dreams, sometimes one object can be two things at once. "I dreamt that you walked in with a cat ... no, wait, maybe you were the cat ... no ...."

Surrealists take opposites like these and combine them, as in a dream shoes become feet, Greek statues wear sunglasses, and black ants act as musical notes.

Dali

Salvador Dali could draw exceptionally well. He painted "unreal" scenes with photographic realism, making us believe they could really happen. Seeing familiar objects in an unfamiliar setting— like a grand piano adorned with disembodied heads of Lenin—creates an air of mys-

tery, the feeling that anything can happen. A new arpeggio. That feeling is both liberating and unsettling. Dali's images—crucifixes, political and religious figures, and naked bodies—usually pack an emotional punch. Take one mixed bag of reality, jumble in a blender, and serve on a canvas—Surrealism.

Abstract with a Twist of Surrealism — Miró, Calder, Arp

Abstract artists revealed their subconscious using color and shapes alone—kind of like Rorschach inkblots in reverse.

The thin-line scrawl of Joan Miró's work is like the doodling of a three-year-old. You'll recognize crudely drawn birds, stars, animals, and strange cell-like creatures with whiskers ("Biological Cubism"). Miró, like Klee, was trying to express the most basic of human emotions using the most basic of techniques.

Alexander Calder's mobiles hang like Mirós in the sky, waiting for a gust of wind to bring them to life.

And talk about a primal image! Jean Arp uses amoeba-like shapes to make vaguely recognizable things—*Female Dancer, Peasant's Head, Head, Moustache and Bottle.*

Post–World War II Patterns and Textures

We enjoy lines and colors, but let's add a new element—texture. Many works have very thick paint where you can see the brushstroke clearly. Some have substances besides paint applied to the canvas, like Dubuffet's brown, earthy rectangles of real dirt and organic wastes. The artist might puncture the canvas so we notice the fabric. Increasingly, art becomes more multi-media, and we need to pay attention to the materials themselves. Think of the canvas as a tray, serving up a delightful array of different substances with interesting colors, patterns, shapes, and textures.

Giacometti

Giacometti's skinny statues have the emaciated, haunted, and faceless look of concentration camp survivors. Their simplicity is "Primitive," but these aren't stately, sturdy Easter Island heads. People are weak in the face of technology and the winds of history.

Abstract Expressionism — Pollock, Newman, Rothko, Rauschenberg

America emerged from World War II as the globe's superpower. With Europe in ruins, New York replaced Paris as the art capital. The trend was toward bigger canvases, abstract designs, and experimentation with new materials and techniques.

We can get a handle on "Abstract Expressionism," since we have already seen both "Abstract" and

"Expressionism"—it's a way to "express" strong emotions using color and form alone.

Jackson Pollock

"Jack the Dripper" attacks convention with a can of paint, dripping and splashing a dense web onto the canvas. Picture Pollock in his studio, leaping about, flinging paint in a moment of enlightenment. Of course, the artist loses some control this way—over the paint flying in mid-air and over himself in an ecstatic trance. Painting becomes a whole-body activity, a "dance" between the artist and the elements.

The act of creating is what's important, not the final product. The canvas is only a record of that moment of ecstasy.

Big, Empty Canvases

All those big, empty canvases with just a few lines or colors—what reality are they trying to show?

In the modern world, we find ourselves insignificant specks in a vast and indifferent universe. Each of us must confront that universe and decide how we're going to make our mark on it. The Existentialist artist confronts the huge, blank canvas in the same way. Like wow.

Another influence on artists was the simplicity of Japanese landscape painting. A Zen master studies and meditates for years to achieve the state of mind where he can draw one pure line. These canvases, again, are only a record of that state of enlightenment. (What is the sound of one brush painting?)

On more familiar ground, post-war painters were following in the footsteps of artists like Mondrian, Klee, and Kandinsky—whose work they must have considered "busy."

Pop Art

Pop Art is created from the "pop"-ular objects of our everyday throw-away society—a soup can, a car fender, mannequins, tacky plastic statues, movie icons, advertising posters. Take something out of Sears and hang it in a museum, and you have to think about it in a whole different way.

Is this art? Are these mass-produced objects beautiful? Or crap? If not art, why do we work so hard to acquire them? Pop Art, like Dada, makes us question our society's values.

Andy Warhol concentrated on another mass-produced phenomenon—celebrities. He took publicity photos of famous people and repeated them. The repetition—like the constant bombardment we get from repeated images on TV—cheapens even the most beautiful things.

Design

Hey, if you can't handle modern art, sit on it. The applied arts (chairs, tables, lamps, and vases) are as much a part of the art world as the fine ones. (Some say the first art object was the pot.) This is one area where artists can embrace new technology and mass production.

Contemporary Collections

The modern world is history. Picasso and his ilk are now gathering dust and boring art students everywhere. Let's enter the postmodern world as seen through the eyes of current artists.

You'll see very few traditional canvases. Artists have traded paintbrushes for blowtorches, exploring new materials and new media. (Miró said he was out to "murder" painting.) Mixed-media work is the norm, combining painting, sculpture, photography, welding, film/slides/video, lighting, and sound systems.

One of the "new" materials is using ready-made objects ("found art"), especially the mass-produced, throwaway things we saw in Pop Art and Dada. Artists raid the dumpster, recycling junk into the building-blocks for a larger "assemblage."

Modern artists critique (or "deconstruct") society by examining things that are so familiar that we take them for granted. They'll take an object loaded with meaning (a crucifix, for example), remove it from its familiar circumstances (in a church) and put it in a new setting (in a jar of urine, to cite one notorious art project). If we now see that object in a different way, it's a reminder that we have beliefs so fundamental that we may never have questioned them.

Installations

In some museums, an entire room is given to an artist to prepare as he or she chooses. It's like an art funhouse, where we walk in without quite knowing what to expect. (In the back of my mind I'm always thinking, "Is this safe?") The artist has our complete attention, and we enter without any preconceptions, maybe even with something like the sense of wonder that "primitives" are supposed to have. The artist, using the latest technology, engages all our senses, controlling the lights, sounds, and sometimes even smells. Exploring, we become active participants rather than passive observers.

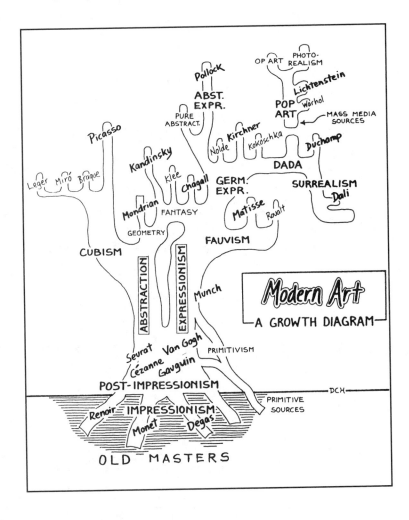

Interaction

Some art exhibits require your participation, whether it's pushing a button to get the contraption going or just walking around the room or touching something. In some cases, the viewer does art, not just stares at it. If art is really meant to change us, it has to move us, literally.

Many artists who in another day and age would have been painting canvases are turning to the performing arts—music, dance, theater, and performance art, which is a kind of mixed-media of live performance. These too have become more interactive, dropping the illusion of a performance and encouraging audience participation.

A New Enlightenment Through Travel

Thomas Jefferson said, "Travel makes you wiser but less happy." "Less happy" is a good thing. It's the growing pains of a broadening perspective. After viewing our culture from a coffeehouse in Vienna or a village in Tuscany, I've found truths that didn't match those I always assumed were "self-evident" and "God-given." And flying home gives me a healthy dose of culture shock in reverse. You know how I love Europe. But I haven't told you about my most prized souvenir—a new way of thinking.

The "land of the free" has a powerful religion—materialism. Its sophisticated priesthood (business, media, military, and political leaders) worships unsustainable growth. Contentment and simplicity are sins. Mellow is yellow. Evil is anything steering you away from being a good producer/consumer.

Yes, greater wealth could be wonderful. But for whom? The gap between rich and poor—both within our society and among humankind in general—is growing. Regulatory, tax, and spending policies in the United States since 1982 have caused the greatest trickle-up of wealth in our nation's history. And globally, the richest 358 people now own as much as the poorest 45 percent of humanity put together. Designer fortifications protect the wealthy in much of the world. In the United States two kinds of communities are the rage: "gated communities" and prisons. The victims are the politically meek—those who don't or can't vote: the young, the poor, the environment, and the future. More and more Americans have lost hope. And when "freedom" grows at hope's expense, your children will ponder their blessings behind deadbolts.

Whoa! What happened to me? The young Republican traveled. I saw countries less wealthy than ours (but with bigger governments) where everyone had a home, enough food, and healthcare. And, like the early astronauts, I saw a planet with no boundaries—a single, tender organism painted with the faces of 6 billion equally precious people. I unpack my rucksack marveling at how politically active American Christians can believe that we're all children of God—while fighting aid for the hungry and homeless.

A new Enlightenment is needed. Just as the French "Enlightenment" led us into the modern age of science and democracy, this new Enlightenment will teach us the necessity of sustainable affluence, peaceful co-existence with other economic models, controlling nature by obeying her, and measuring prosperity by something more human than material consumption.

I hope your travels will give you a fun and relaxing vacation or adventure. I also hope they'll make you an active patriot of our planet and a voice for people in our country who will never see their names on a plane ticket.

Rick Steves

ABOUT YOUR AUTHORS

RICK STEVES (1955–2018)
Rick gained fame and notoriety as a guru of alternative European travel. From 1980 to 1998 he published the Back Door travel newsletter, wrote and hosted the *Travels in Europe with Rick Steves* public television series, organized and led "Back Door" tours of Europe, and wrote 21 travel books. His classic guidebook *Rick Steves' Europe Through the Back Door* started a cult of people who insisted on washing their socks in sinks, taking showers "down the hall," and packing very, very light, even when not traveling.

GENE OPENSHAW (1956–)
Gene is both an author and composer. After graduating from Stanford University, he promptly put his degree to work by writing joke books and performing stand-up comedy. He has written an opera entitled *Matter.* Seriously.

Guidebooks *that* really *guide*

City•Smart™ Guidebooks
Pick one for your favorite city: *Albuquerque, Anchorage, Austin, Calgary, Charlotte, Chicago, Cincinnati, Cleveland, Denver, Indianapolis, Kansas City, Memphis, Milwaukee, Minneapolis/St. Paul, Nashville, Pittsburgh, Portland, Richmond, Salt Lake City, San Antonio, San Francisco, St. Louis, Tampa/St. Petersburg, Tucson.*
US $12.95 to 15.95

Retirement & Relocation Guidebooks
The World's Top Retirement Havens, Live Well in Honduras, Live Well in Ireland, Live Well in Mexico.
US $15.95 to $16.95

Travel•Smart® Guidebooks
Trip planners with select recommendations to *Alaska, American Southwest, Arizona, Carolinas, Colorado, Deep South, Eastern Canada, Florida, Florida Gulf Coast, Hawaii, Illinois/Indiana, Kentucky/Tennessee, Maryland/Delaware, Michigan, Minnesota/Wisconsin, Montana/Wyoming/Idaho, New England, New Mexico, New York State, Northern California, Ohio, Pacific Northwest, Pennsylvania/New Jersey, South Florida and the Keys, Southern California, Texas, Utah, Virginias, Western Canada.* US $14.95 to $17.95

Rick Steves' Guides
See *Europe Through the Back Door* and take along guides to *France, Belgium & the Netherlands; Germany, Austria & Switzerland; Great Britain & Ireland; Italy; Scandinavia; Spain & Portugal; London; Paris;* or *Best of Europe.* US $12.95 to $21.95

Adventures in Nature
Plan your next adventure in *Alaska, Belize, Caribbean, Costa Rica, Guatemala, Hawaii, Honduras, Mexico.*
US $17.95 to $18.95

Into the Heart of Jerusalem
A traveler's guide to visits, celebrations, and sojourns.
US $17.95

The People's Guide to Mexico
This is so much more than a guidebook—it's a trip to Mexico in and of itself, complete with the flavor of the country and its sights, sounds, and people. US $22.95

JOHN MUIR PUBLICATIONS
A DIVISION OF AVALON TRAVEL PUBLISHING
5855 Beaudry Street, Emeryville, CA 94608

Please check our web site at www.travelmatters.com for current prices and editions, or see your local bookseller.

Cater Your Interests
on Your Next Vacation

**The 100 Best Small Art Towns in America
3rd edition**
Discover Creative Communities, Fresh Air, and
Affordable Living
U.S. $16.95

Healing Centers & Retreats
Healthy Getaways for Every Body and Budget
U.S. $16.95

Cross-Country Ski Vacations, 2nd edition
A Guide to the Best Resorts, Lodges, and
Groomed Trails in North America
U.S. $15.95

Gene Kilgore's Ranch Vacations, 5th edition
The Complete Guide to Guest and Resort, Fly-
Fishing, and Cross-Country Skiing Ranches
U.S. $22.95

Yoga Vacations
A Guide to International Yoga Retreats
U.S. $16.95

Watch It Made in the U.S.A., 2nd edition
A Visitor's Guide to the Companies That Make
Your Favorite Products
U.S. $17.95

The Way of the Traveler
Making Every Trip a Journey of Self-Discovery
U.S. $12.95

Kidding Around®
Guides for kids 6 to 10 years old about what to
do, where to go, and how to have fun in *Atlanta,
Austin, Boston, Chicago, Cleveland, Denver,
Indianapolis, Kansas City, Miami, Milwaukee,
Minneapolis/St. Paul, Nashville, Portland,
San Francisco, Seattle, Washington D.C.*
U.S. $7.95

 **JOHN MUIR PUBLICATIONS
A DIVISION OF AVALON PUBLISHING
5855 Beaudry Street, Emeryville, CA 94608**

Available at your favorite bookstore.